X.media.publishing

Springer
*Berlin*
*Heidelberg*
*New York*
*Hong Kong*
*London*
*Milan*
*Paris*
*Tokyo*

Ralf Steinmetz   Klara Nahrstedt

# Multimedia Systems

With 172 Figures

Springer

Ralf Steinmetz
Technische Universität Darmstadt
KOM
Merckstr. 25
64238 Darmstadt, Germany
ralf.steinmetz@kom.tu-darmstadt.de

Klara Nahrstedt
University of Illinois
Department of Computer Science
1304 West Springfield Avenue
Urbana, IL 61801
klara@cs.uiuc.edu

ISSN 1612-1449
ISBN 3-540-40867-3 Springer-Verlag Berlin Heidelberg New York

Library of Congress Cataloging-in-Publication-Data applied for

Bibliographic information published by Die Deutsche Bibliothek
Die Deutsche Bibliothek lists this publication in the Deutsche
Nationalbibliografie; detailed bibliographic data is available in the
Internet at <http://dnb.ddb.de>.

Springer-Verlag is a part of Springer Science+Business Media
springeronline.com

© Springer-Verlag Berlin Heidelberg 2004
Printed in Germany

Cover design: KünkelLopka, Heidelberg
Typesetting: Camera-ready by the authors
Printed on acid-free paper     33/3142GF – 5 4 3 2 1 0

# Preface

**M**ultimedia Applications and Systems are an increasingly common part of our everyday lives—emerging mobile terminals which can display pictures and video data, DVD players in the home, downloadable games, streaming in the Internet, radio stations on the World Wide Web—are just a few examples. These applications and systems are becoming an integral part of our heterogeneous computing and communication environment. Over the last decade, we have experienced an explosive growth of multimedia computing, communication, and applications (World Wide Web, conferencing, digital entertainment, etc.) which provide not just text and images but also video, audio, and other continuous media. In the future, all computers and networks will contain multimedia devices. They will also require appropriate processing and communication support to provide seamless and ubiquitous services and protocols for the relevant multimedia applications.

This book is one of three closely related volumes which aim to cover the whole area of multimedia technology and its applications: The first volume (*Ralf Steinmetz, Klara Nahrstedt, "Multimedia Fundamentals Volume 1: Media Coding and Content Processing", Prentice-Hall, 2002*) deals mainly with the fundamentals of media per se, and covers media-specific considerations such as individual media characteristics, media processing, and optical storage, content analysis, and processing. It includes coding, compression, and a detailed discussion of optical storage. The third volume (*Ralf Steinmetz, Klara Nahrstedt, "Multimedia Applications", Springer-Verlag 2004*) discusses multimedia database and document issues, programming of multimedia applications, multimedia security, human-computer interfaces, multimedia learning, design and different types of applications. Taken together, our three books are intended to be the standard reference books on "multimedia fundamentals".

Do the individual volumes contain sufficient information which readers might need to make the most out of reading this book?

The present volume can be read (and understood) without detailed knowledge of media coding and content processing. However, a basic grasp of the notion of compression would certainly be very useful. Furthermore, it is of crucial importance that the readers have an introductory background in the areas of operating systems and networking systems.

In this book, we emphasize multimedia systems and networking to provide fundamental understanding what are the underlying concepts, mechanisms and frameworks that multimedia applications stand on. Chapter 2 on quality of service provides the basic definitions and concepts (1) to explain quality differentiation and quality-aware resource management, and (2) to present one of the most fundamental building blocks of multimedia systems. Chapter 3 on multimedia operating systems touches upon fundamentals in processor soft-real-time scheduling, based on earliest deadline first and rate-monotonic scheduling policies, as well as in memory and device management. Chapter 4 continues the discussion of multimedia operating systems and presents media servers, one of the most researched domains in multimedia operating systems. Topics range from multimedia file structure, file placement, overall storage organization, to disk management, disk scheduling, and caching policies. Chapter 5 describes basic concepts for multimedia transmission at the physical and Medium Access Control layers, presenting past and existing networking technologies (e.g., Gigabit Ethernet, ATM) that embed appropriate algorithms, protocols and services for multimedia communication. Chapter 6 on multimedia communication is the core chapter for multimedia-enabled protocols executing at the network IP and transport layers. The readers will find discussion on existing protocols, that have been modified to assist in multimedia communication such as the TCP protocol, as well as on new protocols such as IPv6 and RTP protocols. Chapter 7 continues the discussion of multimedia-enabling concepts in the protocol stack and presents group communication services and protocols at the session layer. Chapter 8 is the glue of the whole book because it describes the synchronization concepts and mechanisms across the whole multimedia system architecture. It ties together synchronization mechanisms at the operating system and network levels with synchronization mechanisms at the application and user levels to deliver the overall goal of a multimedia system—the best perceptual quality of multimedia data to the user.

Overall, the book covers a wide scope of multimedia system and networking concepts, due to its intended purpose of serving as a reference, or as an introductory book in an undergraduate multimedia systems class. It evolved from the third edition of our book on multimedia technology, published in German in 2000 [Ste00]. (Figures from this book have been reused with the permission of Springer-Verlag). However, several sections of the English text depart from the corresponding material in the German edition. The present volume can be used by computer professionals who are interested in multimedia systems, or by instructors as a textbook for introductory multimedia courses in computer science and related disciplines.

To help instructors use this book, additional material is available on our Web site: `http://www.kom.tu-darmstadt.de/mm-book/`. Please enter `mm_book` and `mm_docs` for user name and password, respectively.

Many people have helped us to prepare this book: R. Ackermann, M. Bräuer, D. Dimitriu, J. Dittmann, A. El Saddik, M. Farber, S. Fischer, J. Geißler, N. Georganas, C. Griwodz, T. Hollmer, T. Kamps, T. Kunkelmann, J. Liang, A. Mauthe, A. Meissner, K. Reichenberger, J. Schmitt, K. Schork-Jakobi, C. Seeberg, A. Steinacker, N. Streitz, P. Tandler, H. Thimm, D. Tietze, M. Wessner, L. Wolf. Thank you!

However, we would especially like to thank Ivica Rimac for his outstanding dedication to this project.

Last but not least, we would like to thank our families for their support, love, and patience.

*Ralf Steinmetz*
Darmstadt, Germany
www.kom.tu-darmstadt.de

*Klara Nahrstedt*
Urbana, IL, USA
cairo.cs.uiuc.edu

# Contents

# Introduction

**M**ultimedia is probably one of the most overused terms of the 90s (for example, see [Sch97]). The field is at the crossroads of several major industries: computing, telecommunications, publishing, consumer audio-video electronics, and television/movie/broadcasting. Multimedia not only brings new industrial players to the game, but adds a new dimension to the potential market. For example, while computer networking was essentially targeting a professional market, multimedia embraces both the commercial and the consumer segments. Thus, the telecommunications market involved is not only that of professional or industrial networks—such as medium- or high-speed leased circuits or corporate data networks—but also includes standard telephony or low-speed ISDN. Similarly, not only the segment of professional audio-video is concerned, but also the consumer audio-video market, and the associated TV, movie, and broadcasting sectors.

As a result, it is no surprise when discussing and establishing multimedia as a discipline to find difficulties in avoiding fuzziness in scope, multiplicity of definitions, and non-stabilized terminology. When most people refer to multimedia, they generally mean the combination of two or more continuous media, that is, media that have to be played during some well-defined time interval, usually with some user interaction. In practice, the two media are normally audio and video, that is, sound plus moving pictures.

One of the first and best known institutes that studied multimedia was the Massachusetts Institute of Technology (MIT) Media Lab in Boston, Massachusetts. MIT has been conducting research work in a wide variety of innovative applications, including personalized newspapers, life-sized holograms, or telephones that chat with callers

[Bra87]. Today, many universities, large-scale research institutes, and industrial organizations work on multimedia projects.

From the user's perspective, "multimedia" means that information can be represented in the form of audio signals or moving pictures. For example, movement sequences in sports events [Per97] or an ornithological lexicon can be illustrated much better with multimedia compared to text and still images only, because it can represent the topics in a more natural way.

Integrating all of these media in a computer allows the use of existing computing power to represent information interactively. Then this data can be transmitted over computer networks. The results have implications in the areas of information distribution and cooperative work. Multimedia enables a wide range of new applications, many of which are still in the experimental phase. Think for a moment that the World Wide Web (WWW) took its current form only at the beginning of the 90s. On the other hand, social implications inherent in global communication should not be overlooked. When analyzing such a broad field as multimedia from a scientific angle, it is difficult to avoid reflections on the effects of these new technologies on society as a whole. However, the sociological implications of multimedia are not the subject of this book. We are essentially interested in the technical aspects of multimedia.

## 1.1   Interdisciplinary Aspects of Multimedia

If we look at applications and technologies, there is a strong interest in existing multimedia systems and their constant enhancement. The process of change that takes place in the background in various industrial sectors should not be underestimated:

- The telecommunications industry used to be interested primarily in telephony. Today, telephone networks evolve increasingly into digital networks that are very similar to computer networks. Switching systems used to be made up of mechanical rotary switches. Today, they are computers. Conventional telephones have been evolving into computers, or they even exist as pure software in the form of "IP telephony."

- The consumer electronics industry—with its "brown ware"—contributed considerably to bringing down the price of video technology that is used in computers. Optical storage technology, for example, emerged from the success of CD players. Today, many manufacturers produce CD drives for computers and hi-fi equipment or television sets and computer screens.

- The TV and radio broadcasting sector has been a pioneer in professional audio-video technology. Professional systems for digital cutting of TV movies are commercially available today. Some of these systems are simple standard computers equipped with special add-on boards. Broadcasters now transmit their information over cables so it is only natural that they will continue to become information vendors over computer networks in the future.

• Most publishing companies offer publications in electronic form. In addition, many are closely related to movie companies. These two industries have become increasingly active as vendors of multimedia information.

This short list shows that various industries merge to form interdisciplinary vendors of multimedia information.

Many hardware and software components in computers have to be properly modified, expanded, or replaced to support multimedia applications. Considering that the performance of processors increases constantly, storage media have sufficient capacities, and communication systems offer increasingly better quality, the overall functionality shifts more and more from hardware to software. From a technical viewpoint, the time restrictions in data processing imposed on all components represent one of the most important challenges. Real-time systems are expected to work within well-defined time limits to form fault-tolerant systems, while conventional data processing attempts to do its job as fast as possible.

For multimedia applications, fault tolerance and speed are the most critical aspects because they use both conventional media and audio-video media. The conventional data (e.g., control information, metadata) must be delivered in a reliable fashion in order to assist audio-video data. The data of both media classes needs to get from the source to the destination as fast as possible, i.e., within a well-defined time limit. However, in contrast to real-time systems and conventional data processing, the elements of a multimedia application are not independent from one another. In other words, they must be integrated and synchronized. This means that in addition to being an integrated system, composed of various components from both data types, there has to be some form of synchronization between these media.

Our goal is to present the multimedia application and systems from an integrated and global perspective. However, as outlined above, multimedia applications and systems include many areas, hence we have decided to split the content about multimedia system fundamentals into three books. The first book deals with media coding and content processing (*Ralf Steinmetz, Klara Nahrstedt, "Media Coding and Content Processing", Prentice Hall 2002*). The second book describes media processing and communication (*Ralf Steinmetz, Klara Nahrstedt, "Multimedia Systems", Springer Verlag 2004*). The third book presents topics such as multimedia documents, security, and various applications (*Ralf Steinmetz, Klara Nahrstedt, "Multimedia Applications and Security", Springer Verlag 2004*).

## 1.2   Contents of This Book

This book is on *Multimedia Systems*, dealing with media processing and communication, and presenting fundamentals in multimedia operating systems and networking. The primary objective is to provide a comprehensive panorama of multimedia processing and communication technologies, and their integration. Understanding of the close relationship among the wide range of disciplines and components that make up a multimedia system is a key design principle towards successful building of a multimedia system and their applications.

The book is structured as a *reference book*, so that it allows fast familiarization with all issues concerned. However, it can be also used in educational process as an introductory book for an undergraduate multimedia systems class in computer science and related disciplines. It is important to stress that the readers will enjoy the book more and it will be helpful to them if they would have solid introductory background on concepts in media coding as well as in general purpose operating systems and networking.

## 1.3   Organization of This Book

As mentioned above, this book as an integral part of a comprehensive overview and practical view on multimedia technologies. Figure 1-1 shows the global view of the most important multimedia fields spanning across the three volumes. The overall organization attempts to explain the largest dependencies between the components involved in terms of space and time. We distinguish between:

- *Basics*: One of the most important aspects is a media-specific consideration, in addition to the computer architecture for multimedia systems.
- *Systems*: This group of multimedia fields relates system areas such as processing, storage, and communication, and their relevant interfaces.
- *Services*: The multimedia fields such as content analysis, document handling, security and others represent important multimedia functions that rely and are implemented on the basis of system components.
- *Applications*: The group of multimedia fields such as design, learning and user interfaces studies the type and design of applications and the interface between users and multimedia applications and systems.

In this book, we present the basics of multimedia processing and communication in the *system* and *services* multimedia fields (see Figure 1-1), concentrating on quality of service, soft-real-time scheduling, media servers, multimedia-enabling network technologies and communication protocols, and their overall integration through appropriate synchronization mechanisms.

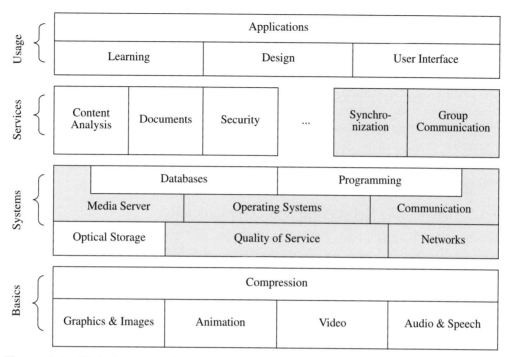

**Figure 1-1**  Global presentation of most important fields, as discussed in this book.

The book covers four major areas: (1) basic concepts in *quality of service* which present fundamentals for further investigation of system and service components in operating system and networks, (2) algorithms, policies and frameworks in *multimedia operating systems* to schedule and store multimedia data, (3) services and protocols in *multimedia networks and communication* to transmit multimedia streams, and (4) *synchronization* of media streams and various system and service components to achieve the best end-to-end perceptual quality for the user.

## 1.3.1  Quality of Service

The information on quality of service will cover basic concepts and definitions of qualities in different layers of multimedia systems, and various operations to manipulate quality parameters such as negotiation of quality parameters, routing of information according to quality requirements, and quality translation and transformation operations. Once quality of service concept is introduced, it allows us to talk about service differentiation in multimedia systems and networks via a quality-aware resource management. We will describe resource management concepts such as admission control., resource reservation, rate control and resource adaptation to prepare the reader for further multimedia operating system and networking concepts.

### 1.3.2   Multimedia Operating Systems

Multimedia support in operating systems is one of the crucial prerequisites for a successful multimedia system. At the processor level, this book investigates soft-real-time scheduling concepts and algorithms, including earliest deadline scheduling, processor-level reservation, task admission control, and various experimental scheduling systems. The multimedia support in OS is also examined with respect to memory and buffer management approaches, caching policies and device management. Extensive discussion is dedicated to media servers ranging from multimedia file structure and file management to disk scheduling, data placement, and overall storage management.

### 1.3.3   Multimedia Networking and Communication

Discussion on multimedia networking covers the protocol stack starting with multimedia-enabling concepts at the physical and MAC layers, continuing with fundamental services and protocols at the network and transport layer, and closing with extensive analysis of group communication at the session layer.

The multimedia-enabling concepts at the lower networking layers are presented via past or existing networking technologies. For example, analysis of the token concept in Token Ring and FDDI network technologies allows us to discuss the end-to-end delay control. On the other hand, the ATM technology allows us to present network level QoS parameters, service class concept, and connection-oriented networks with differentiated support of end-to-end QoS.

This book analyzes existing Internet network and transport protocols for their multimedia suitability and presents new services and protocols for multimedia transmission support. Examples of improved protocols are multimedia-enabled versions of the TCP protocol and rate-control/error control augmented versions of the UDP protocol. Examples of new protocols include IPv6 and RTP (Real-Time Transport Protocol).

The group communication at the session layer introduces important concepts such as conference control, session management, session control, and experimental systems that provide group communications such as MBone.

### 1.3.4   Synchronization

The synchronization area represents the glue of multimedia systems, integrating all system components in a meaningful and successful framework. We revisit various low level per-medium synchronization mechanisms that exist at the operating system and network level such as scheduling, and traffic shaping to stress their importance in the overall synchronization scheme. However, the main emphasize is on higher level synchronization mechanisms among different media, clear specification of user level synchronization requirements such as lip synchronization, and pointer synchronization.

Major part of our discussion also includes synchronization specification and important case studies to illustrate the importance and integrating aspect of synchronization.

## 1.4 Further Reading About Multimedia

Several fields discussed in this book are covered by specialized books, conference papers and journals. There are several edited books, that present a collection of multimedia processing and communication papers (e.g., [PC00], [JZ02]), and multimedia networking books with narrower scope (e.g., [RT98a]).

There is an extensive literature on all aspects of multimedia systems. Some journals frequently publish multimedia systems and networking research results such as *IEEE Multimedia, IEEE Transactions on Multimedia, ACM/Springer Multimedia Systems Journal*, and *Kluwer Multimedia Tools and Applications Journal*. Many other journals have special issues on this subject such as the *IEEE Journal on Selected Areas on Communication, Elsevier Computer Communication Journal*, and others.

In addition to a large number of system and networking national and international conferences and workshops, that have special tracks or sessions on multimedia system research, there are several international conference focussed on multimedia systems only, in particular: *ACM Multimedia Conference* (the first conference took place in Anaheim, California, August 1993), *IEEE International Conference on Multimedia and Expo* (the first conference was held in May 1994), *SPIE Multimedia Computing and Networking* (MMCN), *ACM Network and Operating System Support for Digital Audio and Video* (NOSSDAV), *IEEE/IFIP International Workshop on Quality of Service* (IWQoS), and *European Workshop on Interactive Distributed Multimedia Systems and Telecommunication Services* (IDMS).

# Quality of Service

**Q**uality of Service and *Resource Management* are basic concepts and central focus in multimedia systems. Data of continuous media needs real-time processing, communication and presentation to delivery their desired media quality to the user. Hence, the overall system, i.e., each computing and communication service component in the end-to-end path must respond to the real-time requirements, and support certain service quality. To provide a corresponding service quality, the system needs necessary system resources, e.g., storage, network bandwidth, and processing bandwidth, to allocate and manage. Today, there exist two major approaches which can be applied either separately or simultaneously:

- The most flexible and simple adjustment of multimedia streams onto a given computing and communication environment can be achieved by *Scaling and Adaptation* of media quality. In this case, the resources interact with the data stream to adapt the resource allocation.
- The second approach considers individual service components and their corresponding resources, needed for multimedia processing and communication, and it *reserves* the required resources before the processing and communication of multimedia streams starts. This concept, called *Resource Reservation*, includes all resources along the end-to-end multimedia stream path. This concept can be also applied to parts of an application, which processes continuous media.

In this chapter we will consider concepts related to Quality of Service and corresponding system resource management to satisfy the heterogeneity of requirements coming from different distributed multimedia applications. These concepts are mapped and executed by operating systems, communication systems, compression methods, and many other components. In the subsequent sections we point out which concepts and in which form they are being used.

## 2.1  Requirements and Constraint

To achieve an acceptance of multimedia systems, these systems must satisfy very heterogeneous requirements under different conditions and constraints of their run-time computing and communication environment. An important requirement is the real-time processing. In this section we will discuss the notion of real-time, as well as real-time requirements and constraints, which influence a successful data stream within its networked multimedia system.

The meaning and the notion of real-time was developed independently of multimedia systems, hence we will first discuss the general concepts around real-time, and then its relevance to multimedia data.

### 2.1.1  The Notion of "Real-Time"

The German National Institute for Standardization, DIN, similar to the American ANSI, defines a *real-time process* in a computer system as follows:

> *A real-time process is a process which delivers the results of the processing in a given time-span.*

A real-time system must satisfy the required timing conditions, and real-time programs for the *deadline-driven processing* of data must be available during the entire run-time of the system. The data may require deadline-driven processing at an *a priori* known point in time, or it may be demanded without any previous knowledge [Ger85]. The system must enforce externally-defined time constraints. Internal dependencies and their related time limits (deadlines) are implicitly considered. External events occur—depending on the application—*deterministically* (at a predetermined instant) or *stochastically* (randomly). The real-time system has the permanent task of receiving information from the environment, occurring spontaneously or in periodic time intervals, and/or delivering it to the environment given certain time constraints.

The main characteristic of real-time systems is the *correctness* of the computation. This correctness does not only apply to errorless computation, but also it depends on the time in which the result is presented [SR89]. Hence, a real-time system can fail not only if massive hardware or software failures occur, but also if the system is unable to execute its critical workload in time [KL91]. Deterministic behavior of the system refers to the adherence of time spans defined in advance for the manipulation of data, i.e., meeting a guaranteed response time. Speed and efficiency are not—as is often mistakenly assumed—the main characteristics of a real-time system. In a petrochemical plant, for example, the result is not only unacceptable when the engine of a vent responds too quickly, but also when it responds with a large delay. Another example is the playback of a video sequence in a multimedia system. The result is only acceptable when the video is presented neither too quickly nor too slowly. Timing and logical dependencies among different related tasks, processed at the same time, also must be considered. These dependencies refer to both internal and external restrictions. In the context of multimedia data streams, this refers to the processing of synchronized audio and video data where the relation between the two media must be considered.

## 2.1.2 Deadlines

A deadline represents the latest acceptable time limit for the presentation of a processing or communication result. It marks the border between normal (correct) and anomalous (failing) behavior. A real-time system has both *hard* and *soft deadlines*.

The term *Soft Deadline* is often used for a deadline which cannot be exactly determined and which failing does not produce an unacceptable result. We understand a soft deadline as a deadline which in some cases is missed and may yet be tolerated (i.e., does not cause a disastrous behavior) as long as (1) *not too many deadlines* are missed and/or (2) the deadlines *are not missed by much*. Such soft deadlines are only reference points with a certain acceptable tolerance. For example, the start and arrival times of planes or trains, where deadlines can vary by about ten minutes, can be considered as soft deadlines.

Whereas soft deadlines may be violated in a controlled manner, *hard deadlines* should never be violated. A hard deadline violation is a system failure. Hard deadlines are determined by the physical characteristics of real-time processes. Failing such a deadline results in costs that can be measured in terms of money (e.g., inefficient use of raw materials in a process control system), or human and environmental terms (e.g., accidents due to untimely control in a nuclear power plant or fly-by-wire avionics systems) [Jef90].

## 2.1.3 Characteristics of Real-Time Systems

The necessity of deterministic and predictable behavior of real-time systems requires processing guarantees for time-critical tasks. Such guarantees cannot be assured for events that occur at random intervals with unknown arrival times, processing requirements or deadlines. Further, all guarantees are valid only under the premise that no processing machine collapses during the run-time of real-time processes. A real-time system is distinguished by the following features (c.f. [SR89]):

• **Predictably fast response** to time-critical events and accurate timing information. For example, in the control system of a nuclear power plant, the response to a malfunction must occur within a well-defined period to avoid a potential disaster.

- **A high degree of schedulability**. Schedulability refers to the degree of resource utilization at which, or below which, the deadline of each time-critical task can be taken into account.
- **Stability under transient overload**. Under system overload, the processing of critical tasks must be ensured. These critical tasks are vital to the basic functionality provided by the system.

Furthermore, real-time systems need to show the following properties to ensure timing guarantees:

- **Multi-tasking:** A real-time application consists of various individual tasks. An appropriate partitioning of these tasks requires an appropriate CPU allocation, which then ensures that the tasks are not blocked due to other system events.
- **Short Interrupt Delays:** Interrupt delay is the time interval between the generation of an electric signal (which shows the wish of a device to preempt the processors) and the execution of the first instruction with the help of the software interrupt handler.
- **Fast Context Switching:** The context switch represents the time interval between the time, when the OS recognizes that a new process/thread (mostly a waiting process/thread in the process queue) needs to run, and the start time of the execution of this new process/thread. This switching activity then includes the correct preemption of the current process/thread (i.e., storing all registers with relevant process information such as program counter of the old process) and starting the new process (i.e., loading all registers with the relevant information of the new process).
- **Control of Memory Management:** A virtual memory operating system, which aims to support real-time programming, must provide a way for the task to lock its code and data into real memory, so that it can guarantee predictable responses to an interrupt.
- **Proper Scheduling:** To ensure that tasks run as the real-time application developer expects, the OS must provide a facility to schedule properly time-constrained tasks.
- **Fine Granularity of Timer Services:** We need timers with fine granularity resolution in the range of millisecond and microseconds.
- **Rich Set of InterTask Communication Mechanisms**: We need a support of time-sensitive IPC mechanisms such as message queues, shared memory, semaphores and event flags.

Management of manufacturing processes and the control of military systems are the main application areas for real-time systems. Such process control systems are responsible for real-time monitoring and control. Real-time systems are also used as command and control systems in fly-by-wire aircraft, automobile anti-lock braking systems and the control of nuclear power plants. New application areas for real-time systems include computer conferencing and multimedia in general, the topic of our work.

### 2.1.4   Real-time Requirements on Multimedia Systems

Audio and video data streams consist of single, periodically changing values of continuous media data, e.g., audio samples or video frames. Each Logical Data Unit (LDU) must be represented by a well-determined deadline. Jitter is only allowed before the final presentation to the user. A piece of music, for example, must be played back at a constant speed. To fulfill the timing requirements of continuous media, the operating system must use real-time scheduling techniques. These techniques must be applied to all system resources involved in the continuous media data processing, i.e., the entire end-to-end data path is involved. The CPU is just one of these resources—all components must be considered including main memory, storage, I/O devices and networks.

The real-time requirements of traditional real-time scheduling techniques (used for command and control systems in application areas such as factory automation or aircraft piloting) have also a high demand for security and fault-tolerance. However, the requirements derived from these demands somehow counteract real-time scheduling efforts applied to continuous media. Multimedia systems, which are not used in traditional real-time scenarios, have different (in fact more favorable) real-time requirements:

- The **fault tolerance** requirements of multimedia systems are usually less strict than those of traditional real-time systems. A short time failure of a continuous media system will not directly lead to a destruction of technical equipment or constitute a threat to human life. Note that this is a general statement which can have exceptions and does not always apply. For example, if a multimedia system assists in remote surgery, then the video and audio delivered to the remote surgeon for decision making have stringent delay and correctness requirements.
- For many multimedia system applications, **missing a deadline** is not a severe failure, although it should be avoided. An occasional error may even go unnoticed. For example, if an uncompressed video frame (or parts of it) is not available on time, then it can simply be omitted. The viewer will hardly notice this omission, assuming it does not happen for a contiguous sequence of frames. Audio requirements are more stringent than video requirements because the human ear is more sensitive to audio gabs than the human eye is to presentation jitters of video media.
- A sequence of digital continuous media data is the result of **periodically sampling** a sound or image signal. Hence, in processing the data units of such a data sequence, all time-critical operations are periodic. Schedulability considerations for periodic tasks are much easier than for sporadic ones [Mok84].

• The **bandwidth demand** of continuous media is not always that stringent; it must not be a priori fixed, but it may be eventually lowered. As some compression algorithms are capable of using different compression ratios—leading to different qualities—the required bandwidth can be negotiated. If not enough bandwidth is available for full quality, the application may also accept reduced quality (instead of no service at all). The quality may also be adjusted dynamically to the available bandwidth, for example, by changing encoding parameters. This is known as scalable video.

In a traditional real-time system, timing requirements result from the physical characteristics of the technical process to be controlled, i.e., they are provided externally. Some multimedia applications must meet external requirements too. For example, let us consider a distributed music rehearsal as a futuristic example: music played by one musician on an instrument connected to his/her workstation must be made available to all other members of the orchestra within a few milliseconds, otherwise the underlying knowledge of a global unique time is disturbed. On the other hand, if human users are involved just at the input or only at the output of continuous media streams, the delay bounds are more flexible. For example, let us consider the playback of a video from a remote disk (Video on Demand). The actual transmission delay of a single video frame to be transferred from the disk to the monitor is not important. What is important is the interarrival time of the video frames at the playback side. It means the frames must arrive in a regular fashion. The user will then notice only a difference in a start-up delay when the first video frame arrives (i.e., for the first video frame to be displayed).

### 2.1.5   Service and Protocol Requirements

The user/applications, utilizing Networked Multimedia Systems (NMS)[1], put various requirements on their services and protocols. The requirements span from (1) time-sensitive requests, (2) high data throughput, (3) service guarantees, (4) high or partial reliability requests with timing constraints, to (5) cost-based fairness decisions:

• **Time-sensitive requirements** are important because the audio/video communication needs to be bounded by deadlines or even defined within a time interval. This requirement then implies that end-to-end jitter must be bounded, synchronization skews among dependent streams must be bounded, or end-to-end delay for conversational applications must be bounded.

• **High data throughput requirements** come from the video representation of images and its stream-like behavior. This behavior can represent a long-lived requirement in case of applications such as video on demand or video

---

[1] When referring to Networked Multimedia Systems, we include requirements for both OS and networks.

conferencing. Even in compressed form, audio-visual streams demand high throughput from a workstation or a network.

- **Service guarantees requirements** mean that processing and communication services must provide guarantees during the whole time the audio-visual media are processed and communicated within applications. This means that the time-sensitive requirements and the high-throughput might be provided and sustained over a long period of time which is very different from previous data applications. Furthermore, difficulties are caused by different shapes of the network traffic produced by heterogeneous multimedia applications. The applications require that the NMS accommodates the bursty shape of the audio-visual streams and provides in addition to CBR (constant bit rate) traffic guarantees, also VBR (variable bit rate) traffic service provision.

- **High or partial reliability requirements** with timing constraints represent an important request on the multimedia system because traditional systems until now supported either unreliable or highly reliable processing and communication without any timing constraints. However, various multimedia applications require mostly at least a partial reliability to provide a good service quality and some high-quality video applications require high reliability with timing constraints.

- **Cost-based fairness requirements** are triggered by the request for quality and resources allocated to provide timing and throughput service guarantees. The applications may request that if they pay the corresponding resource cost for its requested quality, then the quality of the audio-visual streams should be delivered to the applications. This means that the fairness principle to let every application process and communicate through FIFO queues will not apply here because in this case the timing requirements of the audio-visual streams could be violated. However, some fairness should be enforced during the sharing of resources between time-sensitive and time-insensitive applications, so that the processing and communication of discrete data does not starve.

## 2.1.6  Processing and Communication Constraints

Due to the layered communication architectures, processing and communication services and protocols have also several constraints. These constraints need to be carefully considered when we want to match user/application requirements onto the system and communication platforms. The constraints include (1) *limitations to data movement*, (2) *segmentation and reassembly* of Protocol Data Units (PDU)s, (3) *error-recovery* mechanisms, and others.

The **data movement constraint** relates to protocols which move a lot of data through the layered communication architecture. However, this movement involves copying which is very expensive and has become a bottleneck. Therefore, new mechanisms for buffer management must be found.

The layered communication architecture considers different PDU sizes at different layers, therefore **segmentation and reassembly** operations on PDUs must occur. These operations must be done fast and efficiently.

Some parts of protocols may use **error-recovery mechanisms** via retransmission which imposes constraints on the buffer space for queues at the expense of larger end-to-end delays. These constraints must be considered when requesting the granularity of end-to-end timing guarantees.

## 2.2   Quality of Service Concepts

The user/application requirements on multimedia systems need to be mapped into services which then make the effort to satisfy the requirements. Due to the heterogeneity of requirements, services in multimedia systems must be parameterized. Parameterization of requirements as well as underlying services allows for flexibility and customization of services. The result is the "*quality-controllable services*" which then allow to classify and differentiate system and communication services. The parameterization of services and classification of services according to quality requirements also easy the application development efforts because each application does not result in implementing of a new set of services for each quality requirement.

Parameterization of services was defined first in ISO (International Standard organization) standards through the notion of Quality of Service (QoS). The ISO standard defined QoS as a concept for specifying how "*good*" the offered networking services are. Hereby, we will agree on the following understanding of the QoS notion:

*Quality of Service indicates the defined and controlling behavior of a service expressed through quantitative measurable parameter(s)* [Sch01].

The QoS concept was further developed, and several new QoS considerations emerged such as layering of QoS, QoS specification languages and programming, QoS management, relation between QoS and resource management, and others as discussed in the remaining sections of this chapter.

### 2.2.1   Quality Layering

Traditional QoS (ISO standard) was defined for the network layer of the communication system. Further enhancement of the QoS concept was achieved through inducing QoS into transport services. For networked multimedia systems the QoS concept must be further extended because many services besides network and transport services contribute to end-to-end quality behavior. Therefore, we assume throughout this section that a networked multimedia system and QoS models comply with a layered architecture, for example, as shown in Figure 2-1.

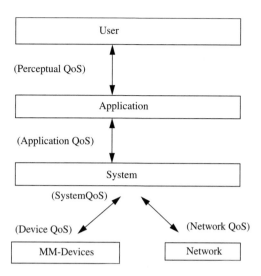

**Figure 2-1**  Example of a QoS layered model for networked multimedia systems.

The QoS Model differentiates among users, application, system (including communication and operating system services), and individual device components. Note that individual layers can have sublayers and with them connected QoS parameters if necessary. However, as the requirements and constraints analysis above suggests, too many layers in a communication architecture may impose a large performance overhead, hence low end-to-end quality and violation of user/application requirements on multimedia processing and communication. In case of a human user it is important to consider specification of perceptual QoS [ZKSS03] as it is also discussed in the Chapter on Synchronization.

### 2.2.2  Service Objects

Services are performed on different objects, for example, media sources, connections and Virtual Circuits (VC). Hence, the QoS parameterization reflects these service objects.

In *ISO standards*, the QoS description is meant to be for services processing transport and network *connections* (e.g., connection setup delay bound). In *Tenet* protocol suite, representing real-time protocols for multimedia delivery [FV90], transport and network services operate over *real-time channels* of a packet switched network, and the quality parameters describe allowed packet jitter over a real-time channel or end-to-end delay of a packet, sent over a real-time channel. In *Lancaster's Multimedia Enhanced Transport System (METS)*, a QoS parameter specification is given for a *media call, transport connection*, and *VC objects* []. In *Resource Reservation Protocol*

(RSVP), part of the Internet Integrated Services, a *flow* specification is given for parameterization and control of the packet scheduling mechanism in routers and hosts [ZDE+93]. At higher layers in communication systems, the service objects such as *media* [NS95] or *streams* [SE93] may be labeled with quality of service parameters.

In operating systems, which are an integral part in provision of the end-to-end quality guarantees, the service objects are *tasks* [LRM96, CN97b] or *memory chunks* [KN97a] and they are characterized with quality parameters such as deadline, processing time, memory size, access pattern, to control the CPU bandwidth allocation and pinned memory bandwidth availability.

In middleware systems, service objects such as *distributed objects, invocation methods, CORBA objects, software components* [ZLSB98], [BZS97], WNGX01] are being labeled by quality parameters to control distributed services in timely fashion during their configuration, distribution, mapping and processing phases.

### 2.2.3   QoS Specification

The set of chosen parameters for the particular service determines what will be measured as the QoS. Most of the current QoS parameters differ from the parameters described in ISO because of the heterogeneity of applications, media types, networks and end-systems. The traditional ISO network layer QoS parameters included QoS parameters such as the *throughput, delay, error rate, secrecy and cost.* Figure 2-2 shows the relationship among the QoS parameters throughput, delay and error rate.

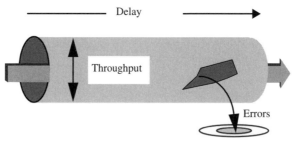

**Figure 2-2**   Relationship among QoS parameters.

The transport layer QoS parameters included *connection establishment delay, connection establishment failure, throughput, transit delay, residual error rate, transfer failure probability, connection release delay, connection release failure probability, protection, priority, and resilience.* These parameters were further expanded according to the layered model and led to many different quality specifications and algorithms to distinguish multimedia quality [dACDP03]. We give here one possible set of QoS parameters for each layer.

The **perceptual QoS** parameters need to allow for description of two major requirements: (1) description of *perceptive qualities* such as media quality (e.g., excellent, good, or bad quality), windows size (e.g., big, small), response time (e.g., interactive, batch), security (e.g., high, low), and (2) description of *pricing choices*, i.e., users should be able to specify the range of price they are willing to pay for the desired service [JN01] Interesting examples of user-level perceptual QoS specifications can be found in the INDEX project [AV98], and QoSTalk project [Gu00].

**Application QoS** parameters describe requirements for application services in terms of (1) *media quality,* including media characteristics (e.g., frame rate, frame resolution), and their transmission characteristics (e.g., end-to-end delay, jitter); (2) *media relations*, specifying relations among media (e.g., media transformation, inter and intra frame synchronization skews); and (3) *adaptation rules* (e.g., actions if network bandwidth is scare) [NS95] [KN97b].

Application-level QoS specifications take different approaches to be represented. Possible approaches are: (a) *script-based* approach, where QoS is added to script languages such as Tcl (e.g., QoS scripts written in SafeTcl [RB00]), (b) *parameter-based* approach, where QoS parameters are represented via data structures, i.e., application-tion developers define data structures to express and declare qualitative and quantitative parameters (e.g., OMEGA QoS Broker from University of Pennsylvania [Nah95] and QoS-A from Lancaster [Cam96]), (c) *process-oriented* approach, where communicating end-ports, represented by processes, are associated with QoS (e.g., QuAL from Columbia [Flo96]), (d) *control-based logic* approach, where QoS specification describes adaptive policies and flow control to specify QoS changes (e.g., Agilos system from UIUC [LN99]), (e) *aspect-based* approach, where QoS specification is part of the aspect-oriented programming paradigm, i.e., QoS-related tasks are examples of so-called aspects (e.g., QuO framework from BBN [SZK$^+$98]), and (f) *object-oriented* approach, where QoS specification is attached to an object (e.g., QML from HP Labs [FK98]).

**System QoS parameters** describe requirements, placed on communication and computing services, derived from application QoS. They may be specified in terms of quantitative and qualitative criteria. *Quantitative criteria* represent concrete measures such as bit per second, number of errors, task processing time, task period. The QoS parameters include then throughput, delay, response time, data rate, data corruption at the system level, task and buffer specifications [NS96] KN97b]. *Qualitative criteria* specify the expected functions needed for provision of QoS such as interstream synchronization, ordered data delivery, error-recovery mechanisms, scheduling mechanisms and others. The expected functions are then associated with specific parameters. For example, the interstream synchronization function is associated with an acceptable synchronization skew within the particular data stream [SE93]. Qualitative criteria can be used by the coordination control to invoke proper services for particular applications. Examples of system-level QoS specifications can be found in RSL (Resource Specification Language) from Globus project [KF98], SPDF (Simple Prerequisite Description Format) from UIUC [Kon00], and parameter-based description of QoS in the DSRT system [Chu99].

**Network QoS parameters** describe requirements, placed on low level network services. They may be specified in terms of (1) *network load,* describing the ongoing network traffic and characterized through average/minimal interarrival time on the network connection, burstiness, packet/cell size and service time in the node for a connection's packet/cell [FV90] and (2) *network performance*, describing network service guarantees. Performance might be expressed through a source to destination delay bound for a packet, or packet loss rate, or others [FV90]. Generally, network performance QoS parameters such as latency, bandwidth, or delay jitter are bounded, and the network QoS specification, represented through the *traffic envelope,* will carry the bounds as the contract parameters for network services. For example, network services, depending on a traffic model (arrival of connections), need to perform within the traffic envelope with parameters such as average and peak data rate or burst length. Hence, calculated traffic parameters are dependent on network QoS and specified in the traffic envelope as a traffic contract [Ber01] [Arm00].

**Device QoS parameters** typically specify timing and throughput demands for media data units given by audio/video devices such as audio speakers or video capture boards.

As a concrete and simple example of a layered QoS model, we will discuss application and system QoS parameters for MPEG compressed video streams [KN97b] as shown in Table 2-1. Note that the application QoS is quite complex to express the source coding and to capture the compression algorithm behavior. In Table 2-1 we provide also the symbol description of QoS parameters because later on we will use this example to illustrate QoS translation and other relations in the overall QoS management.

| QoS Type | Requirement Class | QoS Parameters | Symbol |
|---|---|---|---|
| Application-QoS | Processing Requirements | Sample Size | $M_A$ |
| | | Sample Size for I,P,B Frame | $M_A^I, M_A^P, M_A^B$ |
| | | Sample Rate | $R_A$ |
| | | Number of Frames per GOP | G |
| | | Compression Pattern | $G_I, G_P, G_B$ |
| | | Original Size of GOP | $M_G$ |
| | | Processing Size of GOP | $M'_G$ |
| | Communication Requirements | End-to-end Delay | $E_A$ |
| | | Synchronization Skew | $Sync_A$ |
| System-QoS | CPU Requirements | Processing Time | C |
| | | Period Time | P |
| | | CPU Utilization | U |
| | Memory Requirements | Memory Space | $Mem_{req}$ |
| | Communication Requirements | Packet Size | $M_N$ |
| | | Packet Rate | $R_N$ |
| | | Bandwidth | B |
| | | End-to-end Delay | $E_N$ |

**Table 2-1**   Application and system QoS parameters for MPEG video streams.

Note that the classification of the QoS specification as described above happens due to our layered QoS model (see Figure 2-1). However, there is also another angle which needs to be considered when specifying QoS parameters: Individual quality parameters at each level need to be classified into *input QoS ($QoS^{in}$)* and *output QoS ($QoS^{out}$)* parameters. This classification is crucial because the resulting output quality of service very much depends on the input quality of data into the service. It means that if the input data quality is poor, then even if the service has plenty of resources available for its processing and communication the output quality of the service may be poor. For example, if a display service receives only 10 frames per second from the video digitizer as the input QoS of the video stream, we can not display 30 different frames per second as the output QoS frame rate (we could display 30 frames per second if the display service has enough CPU resource, but only every 3rd frame would be different). The relation between the input QoS and output QoS might be defined through a *service curve* [Cru97] or a *reward profile* [LNH+97]. This relation then allows for decisions how to reach output quality starting from the input quality.

## 2.2.4  QoS Parameter Values and Service Classes

The specification of QoS parameter values determines the type of service, called *service class*. There are at least three service classes: *guaranteed, predictive* and *best effort services*. This service class classification determines at least two important factors: (1) *reliability* of the offered QoS, and (2) *utilization* of resources. Figure 2-3 shows the reliability and utilization of resources for guaranteed and best effort classes.

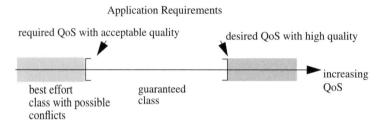

**Figure 2-3**  Reliability and utilization of resources for guaranteed and best effort classes.

**Guaranteed services** provide QoS guarantees, as specified through QoS parameter values (bounds) either in deterministic or statistical representation. The *deterministic QoS* parameters can be represented by positive real numbers at certain time, which means that

$$QoS; T \rightarrow R$$

where $T$ is a time domain representing the lifetime of a service during which QoS should hold and $R$ is the domain of positive real numbers representing the QoS parameter value. The overall QoS deterministic bounds can be specified by

- a *single value* (e.g., average value, contractual value, threshold value, target value);
- a *pair of values* $[QoS_{min}, QoS_{max}]$ (e.g., minimum and average values, lowest and target values) which can represent an interval of values with lower bound as the minimum value and upper bound as the maximum value.

$$QoS_{min} \leq QoS(t) \leq QoS_{max}$$

For example, ATM network allows to specify a pair of values of bandwidth requirement (B) for the VBR service class as shown below.

$$B_{min} \leq B(t) \leq B_{max}$$

The pair value specification also divides the QoS range into *acceptable quality* regions *[QoS$_{min}$, QoS$_{max}$]*, and *unacceptable quality* regions *QoS(t) < QoS$_{min}$* as shown in Figure 2-4.

- a *triple of values* can be also used to specify the overall QoS. For example, we can use best value *QoS$_{max}$*, average value *QoS$_{ave}$*, and worst value *QoS$_{min}$*.

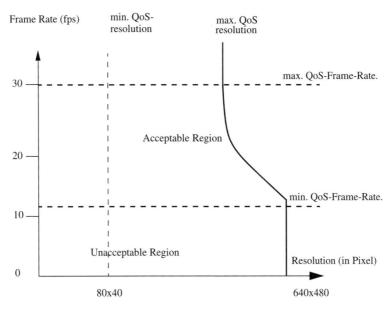

**Figure 2-4**    Range representation of QoS parameters (example for video data).

Guaranteed services may also deal with *statistical bounds* of QoS parameters [FV90], such as statistical bound on packet error rate, bandwidth or others. For example, the requirement for bandwidth parameter value may be represented as probability *P(B >* *B$_{min}$) = p* (i.e., probability that bandwidth *B* will be larger than the low bound *B$_{min}$* is *p*, where *p* is close to 1.

A **predictable service** (historical service) is based on past network behavior, hence the QoS parameter bounds are estimates of the past behavior which the service tries to match [CSZ92]. For example, if predicted network bandwidth *B$^p$* was calculated as an average of the bandwidth which the service provided in the past, i.e.,

$$B^p = \frac{1}{n} \times \sum_i B_i$$

where *i=1,...n, B$_i$* is a past history value, then the predictable service class could promise to provide bandwidth *B* up to B$^p$. In this example, the history values taken into account are from the start of the communication. One could also predict QoS parameter values based on a recent history. For example, if $L$ is the length of the sliding bandwidth history window, then

$$B^p = \frac{1}{L} \times \sum_{i=n-L}^{n} B_i$$

**Best effort services** are services based on either no guarantees or partial guarantees. There is either no specification of QoS parameters required or a non-binding bound in deterministic or statistical forms is given. Most of the current computing and communication services are best effort services.

Multimedia services require guaranteed service class or at least a predictive service class, hence in our further discussion about QoS guarantees we will concentrate on these classes of service.

Note that various systems may provide different service classification:

- IETF standard committee introduced *Internet integrated service model* [BCS94] which supports in addition to the traditional best effort Internet service also *real-time services* (guaranteed service class) and *controlled load link sharing* service.
- ATM Forum standard committee considers four service classes: *Constant Bit Rate (CBR), Variable Bit Rate (VBR), Available Bit Rate (ABR),* and *Unspecified Bit Rate (UBR)* service classes. The VBR class is further refined supporting *real-time VBR* traffic class and *non-real-time VBR* traffic class.

## 2.2.5   Quality-Aware Service Model

Based on the above discussion of QoS parameterization, we can now refine the *service model* which is aware of its QoS and aims to deliver QoS guarantees. We will first define a single autonomous service and then a composite service which aims to deliver end-to-end QoS guarantees[GN02].

An *autonomous single service* consists of a set of functions and it accepts input data with a QoS level $QoS^{in}$ and it generates output data with a QoS level $QoS^{out}$, both of which are vectors of QoS parameter values $QoS^{in} = [q_1^{in}, q_2^{in},..., q_n^{in}]$, and $QoS^{out} = [q_1^{out},..., q_n^{out}]$. In order for the autonomous service to process input data of quality $QoS^{in}$ and generate output data of quality $QoS^{out}$, a specific amount of resources $R$ is required, where $R$ is a vector of different resource requirements $R = [r_1, r_2,..., r_m]$ (e.g., CPU, memory, bandwidth).

Multimedia services consist of a set of services. Hence, a distributed multimedia service represents a *composite service* which is constructed through a sequence of autonomous services performing independent operations, such as transformations, synchronization, filtering, on the data stream passing through them. Services can be connected into a directed acyclic graph (DAG), which is called the *service graph*. The quality-aware composite service is correct if the inter-service "*satisfaction*" relation is valid. It means that if an autonomous service $K$ is connected to an autonomous service $M$, then the output QoS of $K$ ($QoS^{out}_K$) must "match" the input QoS requirement of service $M$ ($QoS^{in}_M$). More formally, $QoS^{out}_K$ "satisfies" $QoS^{in}_M$ if and only if

$$\forall i, 1 \leq i \leq Dim(QoS^{in}_M), \exists j, (1 \leq j \leq Dim(QoS^{out}_K))$$

$$q_{Kj}^{out} = q_{Mi}^{in}, q_{Mi}^{in} \, singlevalue$$

$$q_{Kj}^{out} \subseteq q_{Mi}^{in}, q_{Mi}^{in} \, rangevalue$$

where $Dim(QoS_K)$ represents the dimension of the vector $QoS_K$. The single value QoS parameters include deterministic value such as frame resolution, or end-to-end delay bound. QoS parameters with range values are given through a pair of values as discussed above and can represent, for example a range of frame rates a video can be played at.

## 2.3 Resources

When discussing provision of QoS, one must consider resources because the resource availability determines the actual output QoS which the network, OS or application services deliver.

A **resource** is a system entity required by tasks for manipulating data. Each resource has a set of distinguished characteristics and they can be classified as follows:

- We differentiate between *active* and *passive* resources. An active resource is a resource which provides a service. Examples of active resources are the processor unit or the network adapter for protocol processing. A passive resource brings space required by active resources. Examples of passive resources are main memory, frequency range or file system.

- A resource can be used by a process at a certain time point *exclusively*, or several processes can *share* a resource. Active resources can be mostly used exclusively, where passive resources are usually shared.

- A resource which exists as a single entity in the computer system is called a *single resource*. If we have multiple entities of a resource in the computer system, we refer to the resource as a *multiple resource*. An example of a single resource is a video card in a PC. An example of a multiple resource is a parallel processor machine with multiple processors at work.

Each resource needs a certain capacity for accomplishment of a task. This capacity can be a processor bandwidth, a network bandwidth, or a memory space. For real-time processes, major interest is on the timely division of a resource capacity, i.e., not only *how much* resource a process can get but also *when* a process can get the requested resource.

Figure 2-5 shows the most important resources of two end-systems communicating with each other over a router. The process management falls into the category of an exclusive, active, single resource; the file system over an optical storage with CD-ROM/XA format is a passive, shared resource.

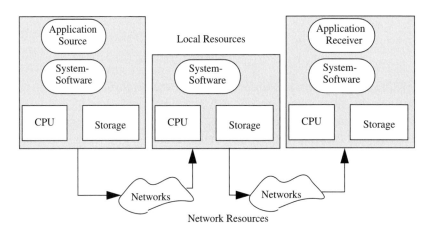

**Figure 2-5**   Interaction among resources.

## 2.3.1   Resource Management

Multimedia systems with their intergrated audio and video processes reach often their capacity limits despite the usage of data compression and utilization of newest computing and communication technologies. Current multimedia systems require therefore their own resource management; here the availability of resource reservation may provide an advantage for quality provision in these systems. The development phases with respect to available capacity and upcoming requirements are shown in Figure 2-6 [ATW+90].

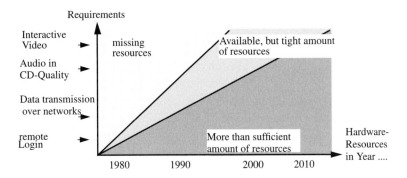

**Figure 2-6**   The "Window of Resources" matched towards current state-of-the-art.

With the help of CD-DA-Quality (Compact Disc Digital Audio—see chapter on optical storage), the highest requirements on audio quality can be satisfied. In the area of video technology, the requirement on the network bandwidth will strongly increase with the deployment of the digital TV. Therefore, a redundancy of resource capacity is not expected in the near future.

In a multimedia system, to achieve end-to-end timing QoS guarantees for multimedia data delivery, all hardware and software system components along the data path should adhere to time guarantees, although the actual requirements will depend on the type of media and the nature of the application supported [SM92a]. For example, a video image should not be presented late because the communication system has been busy with a transaction from a database management system. It means that in any realistic scenario we will encounter several multimedia applications which make a use of shared resources, hence we need to put in place algorithms to allow us to deal with these scenarios in a high quality manner. It is important to stress that a slight modification of traditional applications will not solve the integration problem of delivering QoS for shared multiple applications.

To solve the problem of delivering QoS for an integrated distributed multimedia system, where several applications compete for system resources, we need to consider a careful *resource allocation* and a *system resource management* that employes adequate scheduling algorithms.

Resource management in distributed multimedia systems covers several computers, including their connecting communication networks. It has to allocate resources to the data transfer process between sources and sinks. For instance, a CD-ROM/XA device must be allocated exclusively, each CPU on the data path must provide 20% of its capacity, the network must allocate a certain amount of its bandwidth and the graphic processor must be reserved up to 50% for such a process. The required throughput and a certain delay need to be guaranteed.

The resource management performs operations during two major phases of a distributed multimedia system: (1) *establishment phase* and (2) *runtime phase*. During the establishment phase, the resource management ensures that a new "multimedia connection" will have sufficient resources allocated and it does not violate performance guarantees, already provided to existing connections. During the runtime phase, the resource management ensures appropriate scheduling of resources as well as adaptation in resource allocation in case some conflicts arise.

In the following subsections we discuss general requirements on resource management, as well as provide a generic resource model and relationship between resources and QoS.

### 2.3.2   Requirements on Resource Management

Requirements of multimedia applications and data streams must be served by service components of a multimedia system. The resource management maps these requirements onto the respective capacity. Hence, transmission and processing requirements of local and distributed multimedia applications can be specified according to the following characteristics:

- *Throughput* can be determined from the needed data rate and the data unit size, transmitted over a connection.

- *Delay* needs to be distinguished between the local and the global end-to-end delay:

  - *Local delay* at a resource represents the time interval from the time a process is ready for processing until the time a process finished its processing. The local delay must be less than the period of processing because after that a new data unit arrives and is ready for processing.

  - *End-to-end delay* is measured as the total delay for a data unit to be transmitted from the source to its destination. For example, in a video telephony application it is important to keep the end-to-end delay below 200 ms between the camera source and the video window screen as a destination.

- *Jitter* determines the maximum allowed variance in the arrival of data at the destination.

- *Reliability* maps to the error handling algorithms. The error handling may consist of error detection only if data losses can be accepted, or it can also include error correction algorithms. However, error correction may include retransmission methods which can cause delays in time-sensitive data delivery. In case of this type of data delivery, the error handling should deploy forward error correction or other pro-active error correction algorithms.

### 2.3.3 Model for Continuous Streams

To present more precisely QoS parameters and the multimedia stream characteristics at the system level, often a *continuous media model* is considered. Here we present the model of *Linear Bounded Arrival Processes (LBAP)* as described in [And93]. In this model a distributed system is decomposed into a chain of resources traversed by the message on their end-to-end path. Examples of such resources are single active devices such as CPU or multiple resources such as network cards on routers along the path.

The data stream consists of LDUs. In this context, we call them *messages,* and use an abbreviation in equations as 'Msg'. We assume that the data stream itself is characterized as strictly periodic, irregular with a definite *maximum message size.* Various data streams are independent of each other. If a possible variance in the message rate exists, then we need to also define the *maximum rate.* The variance of the data rate results in an accumulation of messages, called *burst,* where the maximum range is defined by the maximum allowed number of messages. In the LBAP model, a burst of messages consists of messages that arrive ahead of schedule.

In summary, LBAP model is a message arrival process at a resource defined by three parameters: (1) *Maximum message size M*, measured in bytes per message (bytes/Msg), (2) *Maximum message rate R,* measured in messages per second (Msg/s), and (3) *Maximum burstiness B* measured in messages (Msg).

### 2.3.3.1 Example

The LBAP model and the corresponding three parameters are discussed in terms of a specific example. Let us consider two workstations, interconnected via LAN. A CD player is attached to one workstation and a single channel audio data are transferred from the CD player over the network to the other workstation's speaker. The audio signal is sampled with the frequency of 44.1 KHz and each sample is coded with 16 bits. This characteristics yields then the resulting data rate of:

$$R_{byte} = 44100 \text{ Hz} \times \frac{16 \text{ bit}}{8 \text{ bit}/byte} = 88200 \text{ byte}/s$$

The samples on a CD are assembled into frames (these are the blocks of a CD disk). These frames are the audio messages to be transmitted, and 75 messages per second can be transmitted according to the CD format standard. Therefore, we encounter a maximum message size of:

$$M = \frac{88200 \text{ byte}/s}{(75 Msg)/s} = (1176 byte)/(Msg)$$

Up to 12000 bytes are assembled into one packet and transmitted over LAN. In a packet size of 12000 bytes we will never encounter more messages than:

$$\frac{12000 \text{ byte}}{1176 \text{ byte}/Msg} \geq 10 \text{ Msg} = B$$

It obviously follows that:

M = 1176 bytes/Msg

R = 75 Msg/s

B = 10 Msg

### 2.3.3.2    Burst

In the following calculation we assume that because of lower adjacent data rate, a burst never exceeds the maximum data rate. Hence, bursts do not succeed one another. During the time interval of length $t$, the maximum number of messages arriving at a resource must not exceed:

$$\overline{M} \; = \; B + R \times t$$

For example, if we assume t = 1 s, then

$$\overline{M} \; = \; 10 \text{ Msg} + 75 \text{ Msg}/s \times 1 \text{ s} \; = \; 85 \text{ Msg}$$

The introduction of burstiness $B$ allows for short time violations of the rate constraint. This way, programs and devices that generate bursts of messages can be modeled. Bursts are generated, e.g., when data is transferred from disks in a bulk transfer mode, or when messages are assembled into larger packets.

### 2.3.3.3    Maximum Average Data Rate

The maximum average data rate of the LBAP can be calculated as follows:

$$R \; = \; M \times R$$

For example:

$$R \; = \; 1176 \text{ byte}/Msg \times 75 \text{ Msg}/s \; = \; 88200 \text{ byte}/s$$

### 2.3.3.4    Maximum Buffer Size

Messages are processed according to their rate. Messages which arrive "ahead of schedule" must be queued. Under the assumption that the waiting and processing times of a message are smaller than the period of the data stream, we can calculate the *maximal buffer space S* as follows:

$$S \; = \; M \times (B + 1 \text{ Msg})$$

For example:

$$S \; = \; 1176 \text{ byte}/Msg \times 11 \text{ Msg} \; = \; 12936 \text{ byte}$$

### 2.3.3.5    Logical Backlog

The function *b(m)* represents the *logical backlog* of messages. This is the number of messages which have already arrived "ahead of schedule" at the arrival of message *m*. Let $a_i$ be the actual arrival time of message $m_i$:

$$0 \le i \le n$$

Then *b(m)* is defined as follows:

$b(m_0) = 0$ Msg

$b(m_i) = \max\ (0$ Msg, $b(m_{i-1}) - (a_i - a_{i-1})R + 1$ Msg)

For example:

Let $a_{i-1} = 1.00$ s, $a_i = 1.013$ s, $b(m_{i-1}) = 4$ Msg, then

$b(m_i) = \max\ (0, 4$Msg $- (1.013$s $- 1.00$s$) \times 75$ Msg/s $+ 1$Msg) $= 4$Msg

### 2.3.3.6    Logical Arrival Time

The *logical arrival time* defines the earliest time a message $m_i$ can arrive at a resource when all messages arrive according to their rate. The logical arrival time of a message can then be defined as

$$l(m_i) \;=\; a(m_i) + \frac{b(m_i)}{R}$$

For example,

$l(m_i) = 1.013$ s $+ 4$ Msg/75Msg/s $= 1.06$ s

Alternatively, we can calculate the logical arrive time as follows:

$$l(m_0) \;=\; a_0$$

$$l(m_i) \;=\; max\!\left(a_i,\, l(m_{i-1}) + \frac{1}{R}\right)$$

For example, let $l(m_{i-1}) = 1.05\overline{3}$ s

$$l(m_i)= \; max\!\left(1.01\overline{3} \text{ s},\, 1.05\overline{3} \text{ s} + \frac{1 \text{ Msg}}{75 \text{ Msg}/(s)}\right) \;=\; 1.0\overline{6} \text{ s}$$

### 2.3.3.7    Guaranteed Logical Delay

The *guaranteed logical delay* of a message *m* denotes the maximum time between the logical arrival time of a "schedule" and its latest valid completion time. It results from the processing time of the messages and the competition for resources among different sessions, i.e., the waiting time of the message. If a message arrives "ahead of schedule", the actual delay is the sum of the logical delay and the time by which it arrives too early. It is then larger than the guaranteed logical delay. It can also be smaller than the logical delay when it is completed "ahead of schedule". The deadline $d(m)$ is derived from the delay for the processing of a message $m$ at a resource. The deadline is the sum of the logical arrival time and its logical delay.

### 2.3.3.8    Workahead Messages

If a message arrives "ahead of schedule" and the resource is in an idle state, the message can be processed immediately. The message is then called the *workahead message* and the process is called the *workahead process*. A maximum workahead time $A$ can be specified (e.g., from the application) for each process. This results in a maximum workahead limit $W$:

$$W = A \times R$$

For example: if $A = 0.04$ s , then

$$W = 0.04 \text{ s} \times 75 \text{ Msg}/s = 3 \text{ Msg}$$

If a message is processed "ahead of schedule", the logical backlog is greater than the actual backlog. A message is *critical* if its logical arrival time has passed. Throughout the rest of the chapter, as well as throughout the chapters on operating systems and networks, we assume LBAP model and apply it to the arrival processes at each resource. The resource ensures that the arrival process at the output interface obeys the LBAP parameters (maximum message size, maximum rate and maximum burst).

Relationship between QoS and Resources

The requested output QoS parameters are dependent on the input quality, the resource capacity allocated to services (processes) as discussed above, and on the scheduling algorithms managing the shared resources for the distributed multimedia system.

According to the requested output QoS parameters, we can determine how much resources are required to achieve it. For example, the requested end-to-end delay parameter determines the behavior of transmission services along the path between media source and sink with respect to *packet scheduling* (bandwidth allocation), *queueing* (buffer allocation) and *task scheduling* (CPU allocation).

The above described relation between QoS and resources can be expressed in the form of different mappings, service curves, and profiles. The relation between QoS and resources is established in two phases:

1. *Establishment Phase* (Setup) and

2. *Runtime Phase* (Enforcement)

**Figure 2-7**  Establishment phase.

**Establishment Phase**  As shown in Figure 2-7, resources are reserved (planned) and allocated during the connection setup according to the QoS specification. This means that during the establishment, an application client requests a resource allocation by specifying its requirements through an application QoS specification. This QoS specification is then translated[2] by a QoS translator entity (e.g., QoS compiler, QoS broker [Nah95] [WNGX01]) into the system QoS specification and their required resources.The required resources represent then the reservation request to the resource management. The resource management checks the resource utilization and decides if the reservation request can be served. If the reservation can be granted along the end-to-end path, a QoS contract is provided to the application/user. If reservation cannot be granted, the request is rejected.

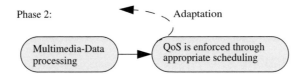

**Figure 2-8**  Runtime phase.

**Runtime Phase**  As shown in Figure 2-8, resources must be provided according to QoS specifications during the lifetime of an application. This means, that once the resource reservation and allocation are performed during the establishment phase, the QoS enforcement must occur during the runtime phase. The resource allocation must be enforced through mechanisms such as traffic shaping and appropriate scheduling mechanisms. If any changes in resource allocation occur, an adaptation needs to be in place to adjust the data transfer if necessary.

---

[2] Note that the translation step includes various algorithms and protocols as the process is distributed. This step may include services such as service discovery, service component loading, negotiation among services, consistency checking of QoS parameters between two consecutive services in the service graph, admission control, etc. We will discuss some of the services in the next section in more detail.

## 2.4    Establishment Phase

Before any data transfer with QoS guarantees can occur, several preparation steps need to be taken. We need to deploy several QoS management and resource management services during the establishment phase of a multimedia connection.

1. The application or the user define required application or perceptual QoS parameters.

2. QoS parameters must be distributed within the same peer level and negotiated among service components, representing a composite service according to the service graph. Note that this step may also include service discovery and service deployment before any QoS negotiation can occur [Xu01] [XNW02].

3. QoS parameters and corresponding services must be translated and negotiated between different layers if their semantics or representation are different.

4. Requested QoS parameters of individual services must be mapped to requested underlying resources.

5. Requested resources must be admitted, reserved, allocated and coordinated along the path between the source(s) and destination(s) [HSS02a] [SHKS02] [HSS02b].

6. QoS network services are typically not free. During or prior to the establishment phase prices and tariffs have to be exchanged [HDKS01] and accounting has to be initiated [BDH+03].

In the following subsections we will discuss individual services needed during the establishment phase.

### 2.4.1    QoS Negotiation

If we assume that a user of a multimedia application service specifies its perceptual or application QoS requirements, then these parameters must be distributed to individual peer services as well as to corresponding service components of the resource management. The distribution of QoS parameters requires (a) *negotiation* of QoS parameters among single peer services if the requested multimedia service is a composite service and the location of single services is known, (b) *discovery* (routing) of single services if they are required for the composite service, but the location is not known, (c) *consistency checking* of QoS parameters between peer services to match QoS, (d) *translation* of QoS parameters if different representations of QoS occur among different peer services or different layer services, and (e) *negotiation* among services at different layers. In this subsection we will discuss the negotiation process which includes the steps (a), (c) and (d) of the distribution process. We assume that the location of single services is known to the negotiation process as well as the negotiated QoS parameters are semantically consistent, i.e., the output QoS parameters of one service are semantically the same as the input QoS parameters of the consecutive service (e.g., if the service $K$ has output parameters frame rate and error rate, then the consecutive service *M*, following service *K*, has the input parameters frame rate and error rate as well).

To characterize an actual negotiation, we need to specify parties who participate in the negotiation and protocols how the parties negotiate. There are at least two parties to any QoS negotiation. We will consider two negotiation relations: (1) *peer-to-peer negotiation* and (2) *layer-to-layer negotiation*. Peer-to-peer negotiation happens between two or more peer services of a composite service, for example as an application-to-application negotiation. Layer-to-layer negotiation happens between two or more services which reside in different layers. An example of a layer-to-layer negotiation can be application-to-system negotiation or user-to-application negotiation. Figure 2-9 shows the two different negotiation relations.

The purpose of negotiation is to establish common QoS parameter values among services users (peers) and between service users and service providers (underlying layers), so that consistency is established and the output QoS of one service satisfies the input QoS of the consecutive service as discussed in Chapter 2.2.5. We present negotiation of QoS parameters where the QoS parameter values are specified with single or pair of deterministic bounds (minimum value $QoS_{min}$ and average value $QoS_{ave}$).

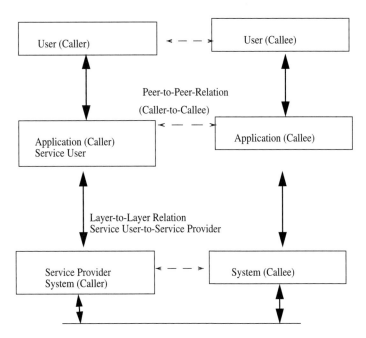

**Figure 2-9**   Negotiation concept: involved parties and relations.

Note that in some systems when user cannot specify QoS parameters immediately, negotiation protocols may apply *probing service* [NHK96a] to learn what kind of bounds the system can provide at all, and then they use the learned QoS values to start real negotiation. *Probing service* allows to send a probe message, which does not have any QoS specification, through the measured system. The probe gets processed by the system, and the monitoring service captures its resource requirements which may be translated back to QoS requirements. The probe returns to the sender with suggested (estimated) QoS requirements which can be used in the negotiation and reservation process.

There are several negotiation protocols among peers and the service provider(s):

1. **Bilateral Peer-to-Peer Negotiation:** This type of negotiation takes place between two peers, and the service provider is not allowed to modify the QoS value, proposed by the service user. Only the receiving service user (callee) can modify the requested QoS value $(QoS_{ave}^{req})$ and suggest a lower bound $(QoS_{ave}^{confirm} < QoS_{ave}^{req})$, which should be in the acceptable range of the application as shown in Figure 2-10.

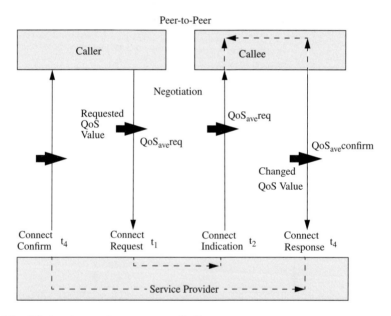

**Figure 2-10**   Bilateral peer-to-peer negotiation.

2. **Bilateral Layer-to-Layer Negotiation**: This type of negotiation takes place only between the service user and provider. This negotiation covers two possible communications (1) *negotiation between local service users* and *providers* (e.g., negotiation between application and OS services), and (2) *negotiation between host*

*sender and the network* (e.g., negotiation between host sender and the network provider when the sender wants to broadcast multimedia streams).

3. **Unilateral Negotiation:** In this negotiation the service provider as well as the called service users are not allowed to change QoS parameters proposed by the calling user. This negotiation is reduced to "take it or leave it" approach [DBB+93]. Further, this negotiation allows the case in which the receiver may take the proposed QoS and, although it may not have the capacity to accommodate the QoS parameters, it can modify the host receiver and participate with lower quality in the communication. A similar case occurs in TV broadcasting. The color TV broadcasts the signal uniformly to every user, but users with black and white TVs can still watch the TV program, i.e., the control and adjustment of quality is done at the receiver device.

4. **Hybrid Negotiation:** In the case of broadcast or multicast communication, every participating host-receiver may have different capabilities from the host-sender, but it still wants to participate in the communication (e.g., conference). Hence, between the host-sender and network, the QoS parameter values can be negotiated using bilateral layer-to-layer negotiation and between the network and host-receiver, unilateral negotiation occurs as described above.

5. **Triangular Negotiation for Information Exchange:** In this type of negotiation, the calling user requests the average value of a QoS parameter value ($QoS_{ave}^{req}$). This value can be changed by the service provider ($QoS_{ave}^{sp}$) or the callee ($QoS_{ave}^{ca}$) along the path through an indication and response primitive before presenting the final value ($QoS_{ave}^{confirm}$) in the confirm primitive to the caller. The changed values should satisfied the following relation

$$QoS_{ave}^{confirm} < QoS_{ave}^{ca} < QoS_{ave}^{sp} < QoS_{ave}^{req}.$$

At the end of the negotiation, all parties have the same QoS value.

6. **Triangular Negotiation for a Bounded Target:** This is the same type of negotiation as the previous one, only the values of a QoS parameter are represented through two bounds (a) *target bound* ($QoS_{target}$) and (b) *lowest acceptable quality* ($QoS_{min}$). The goal is to negotiate target value

$$QoS_{target} = QoS_{ave}^{confirm} \geq QoS_{min}.$$

$QoS_{target}$, i.e., the service provider is not allowed to change the value of the $QoS_{min}$ (if the service provider cannot provide at least the minimal quality, then the negotiation request should be rejected). However, the service provider is free to modify the target value satisfying relation

$$QoS_{min} \leq (QoS_{ave}^{sp} = QoS_{target}) \leq QoS_{ave}^{req}.$$

The callee will make the final decision about $QoS_{target}$ satisfying relation

$$QoS_{min} \leq (QoS_{target} = QoS_{ave}^{\ confirm}) \leq QoS_{ave}^{\ sp}$$

The selected value will be returned to the caller by the confirm primitive,

7. **Triangular Negotiation for Contractual Value:** In this case, the QoS parameters are specified through a minimum requested value $QoS_{min}^{\ req}$ and a bound of strengthening $(QoS_{bound} > QoS_{min}^{\ req})$. The goal of this negotiation is to agree on one contractual value $QoS_{contract}$, which satisfies relation below.

$$QoS_{min}^{\ req} \leq (QoS_{contract} = QoS_{min}^{\ confirm}) \leq QoS_{bound}$$

The service provider can modify $QoS_{min}^{\ req}$ towards the value $QoS_{bound}$. The callee makes the final decision and reports the final QoS contract with the response and confirm primitive to the caller. The contractual value can be also applied to the maximum QoS parameter value or other threshold values which the service user wants to achieve as a contract value [DBB+93]. Figure 2-11 shows the behavior.

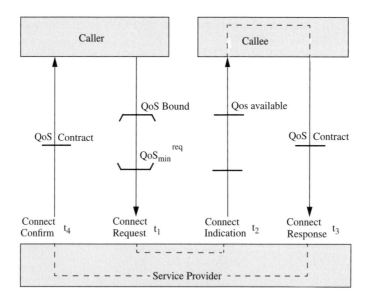

**Figure 2-11**   Triangular negotiation with contractual value.

In all of the negotiations, we need to invoke consistency checking to check for satisfaction relation (see Chapter 2.2.5) between the output QoS of one service and input QoS of consecutive service. For example, in the bilateral peer-to-peer negotiation the considered input $QoS_{ave}^{req}$ on the callee side is actually the output $QoS_{ave}^{req}$ at the caller side, it means

$$QoS^{req(out)}_{ave(caller)} = QoS^{req(in)}_{ave(callee)}$$

Note that inside the caller or callee or network service provider the QoS parameter values may change as the negotiation protocols show, but at the boundary between two services (two service peers or service provider and service user) the QoS parameters need to match.

There exist already several multimedia call establishment protocols which have negotiations built in. The call establishment protocols include several levels of negotiation. The negotiation can be done at the network level, at the system level, at the application level or between the levels in a cross-layer design. We present some protocol examples which have the concept of negotiation in them.

The *ST-II protocol* is a network protocol which provides end-to-end guaranteed services across the Internet network [WH94]. The parameters related to throughput are negotiated with a triangular negotiation for a bounded target. Delay-related parameters do not go through negotiation. The calling user specifies the maximum transit delay in the connect request. During the establishment of the connection, each ST agent, participating in the stream, will have to estimate the average transit delay and the average variance of this delay (delay jitter) that it will provide for this stream. The provider presents in the connect indication primitive the total estimated average delay and the average jitter. The called user decides if the (expected) average delay and jitter are sufficient before accepting the connection. The parameters related to error control are not negotiated.

The *ATM Signaling Protocol (UNI 3.0)* includes the bilateral peer-to-peer negotiation for the CBR (Constant Bit Rate) traffic parameter peak cell rate (PCR) as well as the triangular negotiation for bounded target which is applied to the real-time VBR (Variable Bit Rate) traffic. In this ATM class, the minimum bandwidth, called sustainable cell rate (SCR), is requested and the PCR is negotiable. CBR and VBR traffic allow also negotiation for delay guarantees such as the cell delay and its variation [Ken97].

Other network establishment protocols such *RCAP* (Real-time Channel Administration Protocol [BM91], *RSVP* (Resource Reservation Protocol) [ZDE+93] [Gro00b] [KSS01] [RGKS00] and others use triangular negotiation for different network QoS parameter values such as bandwidth or end-to-end delay [Ber01].

At the session and application level of the communication, various establishment protocols became part of the QoS management. Examples of negotiation protocols exist in the *QoS broker* entity that uses a bilateral peer-to-peer negotiation at the application level, and triangular negotiation with the underlying ATM transport subsystem [NS96]. Another example is the *RTCP* protocol which is a control and negotiation protocol to the multimedia transport protocol, called *RTP* (for more details see the Chapter on Networking).

### 2.4.2  QoS Translation

It is widely accepted that different multimedia service components may require different QoS parameters. For example, the mean packet loss rate, known from the packet network, has no meaning as a QoS parameter to a video capture device. Likewise, video frame quality is of little use to a link layer service provider, but the frame quality in terms of number of pixels is an important QoS value to a video capture card to initialize its frame buffer.

We distinguish between user, application, system and network layers with their different QoS parameters as it was discussed in Chapter 2.2.1. However, there exist other systems that may have even more or less "layers" or there may be a hierarchy of layers where some QoS values are inherited and others are specific to certain service components. In general, it should be possible to derive required QoS parameter values and resources at lower system and network levels from user or application QoS requirements. This derivation, known as QoS *translation,* may require 'additional knowledge', stored together with the specific component. The additional knowledge might be a rule or a preference specified by the user or application if the translation mappings are ambiguous. Overall, translation is an additional service for peer-to-peer or layer-to-layer communication. In general, translations are known and used in layered systems for functions, such as naming, for long time. For example, in file systems the high-level user file name is translated into file identifier and block number, where the file physically starts.

In our layered distributed multimedia systems, we will concentrate on translation between QoS requirements in individual layers. Note that peer-to-peer translation may be also necessary if output QoS of one service semantically does not match the input QoS of the following service, it means semantic consistency is violated. In this case transcoders and other transformers need to be inserted between two services to accomplish semantic consistency. For example, if a source produces an MPEG stream, but the receiver can display only video in a bitmap format, then a transcoder from MPEG to bitmap format is needed to establish semantic consistency [Gu00].

Due to the layering, as shown in Figure 2-1, the split of parameters requires translation functions as follows:

- **User-Application QoS Translation**: The service which may implement the translation between a human user and application QoS parameters is called the *tuning service*. A tuning service provides a user with a graphical user interface (GUI) for input of perceptual QoS, and it delivers the requested application QoS. The tuning service presents video and/or audio clips, which will run at the requested perceptual quality (HIGH, MEDIUM, LOW). The tuning services then internally maps the perceptual quality to application QoS with its set of parameters such as frame rate, frame resolution and others. The tuning service can also use sliders, meters and other animated GUI elements to easy the input of perceptual QoS parameters. If the GUI shows both perceptual and application QoS, then it is important to guarantee corresponding translation between those parameters. For example, if a user views a video clip and its corresponding video frame rate, then it is important to show the correct frame rate value. In this case, the user can also use a slider to adjust the perceptual quality by changing the frame rate which will immediately show in the playback of the viewed video clip. Several current multimedia systems offer perceptual QoS specification and their corresponding GUIs for translation [Gu00] [AV98].

• **Application-System QoS Translation**: This type of translation maps application QoS requirements into system QoS parameters. For example, this translation may lead to the mapping from "high quality" synchronization user requirement to a synchronization skew QoS parameters for interstream synchronization (in milliseconds), or from video frame size, expressed in terms of frame height, width and pixel resolution, to transport packet size. It is important to stress that not all translations can be analytically expressed. In many cases the mapping between application and system QoS parameters requires probing service, usage of benchmarks, off-line derived performance curves or profiles [CN99] [Gu00] [LN99]. We will present some examples of analytical translations between application QoS and communication, CPU and memory QoS parameters shown in Table 2-2. The semantics of the individual symbols is given in Table 2-1. The translation relations show examples of mappings between application protocol data units (APDU) sizes $M_A$ and their corresponding transport PDU (TPDU) sizes $M_N$, their rates $R_A$, $R_N$ and bandwidth dependencies $B$, as well as processing times $C_A^F$, $C_A^G$ for MPEG video applications and their dependencies on scheduling decisions (frame-based versus group-based scheduling). Note that the translation from the communication QoS to application QoS parameters after the negotiation response from the remote site can be *ambiguous*. It means that if the service provider changes the bandwidth allocation from $B$ to $B'$, then we can change either the frame rate $R_A'$ or the frame size $M_A'$ as the result of a bandwidth change. To solve the ambiguity, the translation service will need an additional information from the application or user to decide which translation to take.The following example illustrates some of the translation relations in Table 2-2. Let us assume the application frame size $M_A$ characteristics of 320x240 pixels and pixel resolution of 8 bits per pixel. Let us assume the application frame rate $R_A$ of 10 frames per second. If we assume that $M_N$ = 4 KBytes, then the requested bandwidth $B$ is 622,592 bits per second and the requested packet rate $R_N$ = 19 packets per second.

The following example illustrates some of the translation relations in Table 2-2. Let us assume the application frame size $M_A$ characteristics of 320x240 pixels and pixel resolution of 8 bits per pixel. Let us assume the application frame rate $R_A$ of 10 frames per second. If we assume that $M_N = 4$ KBytes, then the requested bandwidth $B$ is 622,592 bits per second and the requested packet rate $R_N = 19$ packets per second.

| Relation | Affects | Affected By | Additional Notes |
|---|---|---|---|
| $\lceil (M_A)/(M_N) \rceil > 1$ | Fragment and $C_A$ | Size of $M_A$, $M_N$ | |
| $R_N = \lceil (M_A)/(M_N) \rceil \times R_A$ | Traffic Shaping | $M_A$, $R_A$ | |
| $B = R_N \times M_N$ | B | $R_N$, $M_N$ | After computation of $R_N$ |
| $E_N = \dfrac{(E - (C_A^S + C_A^R))}{A\lceil (M_A)/(M_N) \rceil}$ | $E_N$ | $E_A, C_A^S, C_A^R,$ $\lceil (M_A)/(M_N) \rceil$ | |
| $R'_N = (B')/(M_N)$ | $R_N'$ | $B' < B$ | After negotiation response |
| $M'_A = \lfloor (R'_N)/(R'_A) \rfloor \times M_N$ | $M_A'$ | $B'$ | $R_A$ is fixed |
| $R'_A = (R'_N)/\lceil (M_A)/(M_N) \rceil$ | $R_A'$ | $B'$ | $M_A$ is fixed |
| $max(C)_A^F = max(C(M_A^I), C(M_A^P), C(M_A^B))$ | $C_A^F$ | $C(M_A)$ and $M_A$ for I-,P-,B-Frames | Results from frame-based schedule |
| $C_A^G = C(M_G)$ | $C_A^G$ | $C(M_G) = G_I \times C\left(M_G^I\right) + G_P \times C(M_G^P) + G_B \times C(M_G^B)$ | Results from GOP-based schedule |
| $Mem = k \times M_A$ | Memory | | |

**Table 2-2**   Translation between application and system QoS.

- **System - Network QoS Translation:** This translation maps the system QoS (e.g., transport packet end-to-end delay) into the underlying network QoS parameters (e.g., in ATM the end-to-end delay of cells) and vice versa. The translations between system and network QoS are similar to the translation between APDU and TPDU messages as shown in Table 2-2.

An important property of the translation service is that is be *bidirectional* translation [NS95]. This can cause problems as we have already discussed during the application-system QoS translation because an ambiguity in translation can occur. Additional knowledge in form of rules may help. For example, if bandwidth must be relaxed, then it can influence the spatial quality of image or the temporal resolution of video. Rules, such as (1) reduce frame size until we encounter 112 pixels in the horizontal direction, (2) reduce the frame rate until we have only 5 frames per second, or (3) ensure that no further reduction is possible and close the connection, will allow to resolve the ambiguity.

The reversed translation results in *media scaling*. In general, media scaling methods perform different degrees of media quality degradation if resources are not available. Dynamic QoS changes (translation, negotiation, renegotiation) are used in conjunction with scaling techniques [TTCM92]. We discuss scaling in more detail in the next section.

This subsection discussed QoS translations, performed during the establishment phase, which are performed when a user or application enter their desired QoS parameters, and the multimedia session as well as corresponding connection setup needs to be executed. However, several of these QoS translations can be also performed during the application development time before the multimedia application is being used. Here, the QoS translations become part of the *QoS compilation* process [NWX00] and can assist in preparation of multimedia applications with respect to their QoS awareness. Meta-level compilers such as the QoS compiler from UIUC [WNGX01] are able to provide profiles and configuration templates for distributed multimedia applications which then allow to shorten the setup time, even optimize the resource utilization along the end-to-end path, and speed up the overall establishment process of an application.

## 2.4.3   QoS Scaling

Scaling means to subsample a data stream and only present a fraction of its original content. In general, scaling can be done either at the source or at the receiver. Scaling methods, used in multimedia systems, can be classified as follows [DHH+93]:

- **Transparent scaling methods** can be applied independently from the upper protocol and application layers. This means that the transport system scales the media down. Transparent scaling is usually achieved by dropping mechanisms where insignificant parts of the multimedia stream will be dropped. The insignificant parts can be determined (1) by the multimedia processing and the resulting structure (e.g., in MPEG video compression processing, the video ends up with three different types of frames of different significance) or (2) by the multimedia content and its corresponding context information resulting in content-aware scaling [TC01] and context-aware processing. The insignificant portions need to be identifiable by the transport system. For example, in case of MPEG video, the compressed data stream consists of basic layer (I frames), and enhancement layers (P and B frames) which can be labeled with different priority bits. In case of shortage in resource availability, enhancement layers should be dropped first to scale down the resource utilization and resolve resource contention. This kind of property can be expressed with the degradation QoS parameter D (see Table 2-1). For example, in case of MPEG video frames [KN97b], which use GOP-based scheduling, we may have to scale the processing time for a GOP as follows:

$$C_G = C(M'_G) = C(M_G \times D)$$

where $D$ is the degradation ratio.

- **Non-transparent scaling** methods require an interaction of the transport system with the upper layers. This kind of scaling implies a modification of the media stream before it is presented to the transport layer. Non-transparent scaling typically requires modification of some parameters in the coding algorithms, or even recording of a stream that was previously encoded in a different format. For example, if a video stream will scale down to the change of its frame resolution, then this change must be done at the video encoding side and not in the transport subsystem level. The reason is that this level does not have any internal semantic information about the PDU payload nor services to process the internal payload information.

In a multimedia system, scaling can be applied to both audio and video data:

- **Audio**: Transparent scaling is difficult because presenting a fraction of the original data is easily noticed by the listener. Dropping a channel of a stereo stream is an example. Hence, non-transparent scaling should be used for audio streams. For example, a change of the sampling rate or sample bit resolution (audio sample quantization) at the audio encoding source achieves an audio scaling.
- **Video:** The applicability of a specific scaling method depends strongly on the underlying compression technique. There are several domains to which scaling can be applied:

  a. *Temporal scaling* reduces the resolution of the video stream in the time domain. This means that the number of video frames transmitted within a time interval decreases. Temporal scaling is best suited for video streams in which individual frames are self-contained and can be accessed independently. An example is the motion JPEG (MJPEG) encoded video where individual I frames are self-contained and can be accessed independently. Hence, we can drop different frames within the stream if the frame rate needs to be reduced.

b. *Spatial scaling* reduces the number of pixels of each image in a video stream. For spatial scaling, hierarchical arrangement is ideal because it has the advantage that the compressed video is immediately available in various resolutions. Several MJPEG video compression cards provide this capability and allow the multimedia system to serve video clients with different resolutions.

c. *Frequency scaling* reduces the number of DCT coefficients applied to the compression of an image.

d. *Amplitude scaling* reduces the color depth for each image pixel. This can be achieved by introducing a coarser quantization of the DCT coefficients, hence requiring a control of the scaling algorithm over the compression procedure.

e. *Color space scaling* reduces the number of entries in the color space. One way to realize color space scaling is to switch from color to gray scale presentation.

A combination of these scaling methods is possible. In the case of non-transparent scaling, frequency, amplitude and color space scaling are applied at the source during the encoding of the video. Transparent scaling may use temporal scaling or spatial scaling. This type of scaling can be applied at the source or at the destination.

### 2.4.4   QoS Routing

The next generation of multimedia systems and networks will need to provide QoS routing capabilities during the establishment phase or during the runtime phase (for adaptation purposes) to discover a path (route) that meets QoS requirements, such as throughput, end-to-end delay, loss rate and others, between two or more users [CN98c]. At this point we discuss network path discovery (routing) along the end-to-end route, assuming each network node has corresponding routing services. The routing problems can be divided into two major classes: *unicast routing* and *multicast routing*. The two classes of routing problems are closely related. The multicast routing can be viewed as a generalization of the unicast routing in many cases.

### 2.4.4.1   Unicast QoS Routing

The unicast routing problem is defined as follows: given a source node $s$, a destination node $t$, a set of QoS constraints $C$ and possibly an optimization goal, we aim to find the best feasible path from $s$ to $t$, which satisfies $C$.

For some QoS metrics such as residual bandwidth and residual buffer space, the state of the path is determined by the *state of the bottleneck link*. For these QoS metrics, two basic routing problems can be defined. One is called the *link-optimization routing problem*, such as the bandwidth-optimization routing which aims to find a path that has the largest bandwidth on the bottleneck link. Such a path is called the widest path. Another problem is the *link-constrained routing problem* such as the bandwidth-constrained routing, which aims to find a path whose bottleneck bandwidth is above a required value. These routing problems can be solved by a slightly modified Dijkstra's algorithm [Dij59] or Bellman-Ford algorithm [Bel57].

For other QoS metrics such as delay, jitter and cost (additive QoS metrics), the state of a path is determined by the *combined state over all links*. Two basic routing problems can be defined for this type of QoS metrics. One is called the *path-optimization routing problem* such as the least-cost routing, which aims to find a path whose total cost is minimized. The other problem is called the *path-constrained routing problem* such as the delay-constrained routing, which aims to find a path whose delay is bounded by a required value. Both problems can be directly solved by Dijkstra's or Bellman-Ford algorithms.

Many composite routing problems can be derived from the above four basic problems. For example, the bandwidth-constrained least delay routing problem belongs to the link-constrained path-optimization routing problem class. It is to find the least delay path that has the required bandwidth. This problem can be solved by a shortest path algorithm on the graph, where the links violating the bandwidth constraint have been removed. There are four other problem classes that are solvable in polynomial time by a modified shortest path algorithm: *link-constrained link-optimization* routing, *multi-link-constrained* routing, l*ink-constrained path-constrained* routing, and *path-constrained link-optimization* routing.

There are two NP complete problem classes: *path-constrained path-optimization* routing (PCPO) and *multi-path constrained* routing (MPC). An example of PCPO is the delay-constrained least-cost routing, which aims to find the least-cost path with bounded delay. An example of MPC is the itter constrained routing, which wants to find a path with both bounded delay and bounded jitter. For the above problems to be NP-complete, there are two assumptions: (1) QoS metrics are independent, and (2) they are allowed to be real numbers or unbounded integer numbers. If all metrics except one take bounded integer values, then the problems are solvable in polynomial time by running extended Dijkstra's or Bellman-Ford algorithms [CN98b]. If all metrics are dependent on a common metric, then the problems may also be solvable in polynomial time. For example, worst-case delay and jitter are functions of bandwidth in networks using Weighted Fair Queueing scheduling.

### 2.4.4.2    Multicast QoS Routing

The multicast routing problem is defined as follows: given a source node $s$, a set $R$ of destination nodes, a set of constraints $C$ and possibly an optimization goal, we aim to find the best feasible tree covering $s$ and all nodes in $R$, which satisfies $C$.

The multicast routing algorithms can be similarly partitioned as discussed in unicast QoS routing, considering basic routing problems and composite routing problems. The difference is that an optimization or a constraint must be applied to the entire tree instead of a single path. For example, the bandwidth-optimization routing problem asks to maximize the bandwidth of the bottleneck link of the tree. The delay-constrained routing finds a tree in which the end-to-end delay from the sender to any destination is bounded by a given value.

There are several well-known multicast routing problems. The *Steiner tree* problem is to find the least-cost tree, where the tree is covering a group of destinations with the minimum total cost over all links. It is also called the *least-cost multicast routing* problem belonging to the tree-optimization routing problem class. The *constrained Steiner tree* problem is to find the least-cost tree with bounded delay, and it is called the *delay-constrained least-cost routing* problem, belonging to the tree-constrained tree-optimization routing problem class. Finding either a Steiner tree or a constrained Steiner tree is NP complete [SRV97b]. The delay-jitter-constrained multicast problem belongs to the multi-tree-constrained routing problem class. It is also NP-complete under the assumptions that (1) the metrics under the constraints are independent, and (2) they are allowed to take real numbers or unbounded integer numbers. However, this problem (or any other multi-tree-constrained routing problem) is solvable in polynomial time if all metrics except one take bounded integer values. If all metrics are dependent on a common metric, then the problem may also be solvable in polynomial time.

### 2.4.4.3    Relation of QoS Routing and Other QoS/Resource Management Services

**QoS Routing versus Best-effort Routing**    The QoS routing is different from the traditional best-effort routing. The former is normally connection-oriented with resource reservation to provide the guaranteed services. The latter can be either connection-oriented or connectionless with a dynamic performance subject to the current availability of shared resources. Meeting the QoS requirement of each individual connection and reducing the call-blocking rate are important for the QoS routing service, while the fairness, overall throughput and average response time are the essential issues for the traditional routing.

**QoS Routing and Resource Reservation**    QoS routing and resource reservation [ZDE+93] are two important, closely related components. In order to provide the guaranteed services, the required resources (e.g., CPU time, buffer, bandwidth) must be reserved when a QoS connection is established. Hence, the data transmission of the connection will not be affected by the traffic dynamics of other connections sharing the common links. Before the reservation can be done, a path with the best chance to satisfy the resource requirement must be selected. That is the job of routing. While routing is decoupled from resource reservation in most existing schemes, some solutions combine routing and resource reservation in a single multi-path message pass from the source to the destination [CS97].

**QoS Routing and Admission Control**   The task of admission control is to determine whether a connection request should be accepted or rejected as discussed in the next section. Once a request is accepted, the required resources must be guaranteed. The admission control is often considered as a by-products of QoS routing and resource reservation. If the resource reservation is successfully done along the route(s) selected by the routing algorithm, the connection request is accepted; otherwise, the request is rejected.

**QoS Routing and QoS Negotiation**   A QoS routing algorithm may fail to find a feasible path for a new connection, either because there does not exist a feasible path, or because the searching space of a heuristic approach does not cover any existing feasible path. When this happens, the system can either reject the connection or negotiate with the application for a looser QoS constraint. The QoS routing can assist the negotiation by finding the best available path and returning the QoS bounds supported. If the negotiation is successful according to the provided bounds, the best available path can be used immediately.

### 2.4.4.4   QoS Routing Strategies

Routing involves two basic tasks: (1) *collecting the state information* and keeping it up-to-date, and (2) *searching the state information* for a feasible path. In order to find an optimal path which satisfies the constraints, the state information about the intermediate links between the source and destination(s) must be known. The search of feasible paths greatly depends on how the state information is collected and where the information is stored. There are three routing strategies, *source routing, distributed routing* and *hierarchical routing*. They are classified according to the way how the state information is maintained and how the search of feasible paths is carried out.

In the **source routing**, each node maintains the complete global state, including the network topology and the state information of every link. Based on the global state, a feasible path is locally computed at the source node. A control message is then sent out along the selected path to inform the intermediate nodes of their precedent and successive nodes. A *link state protocol* is used to update the global state at every node. This strategy avoids the dealing with the distributed computing problems such as distributed state snapshot, deadlock detection and distributed termination problem. It guarantees loop-free routes. Many source routing algorithms are conceptually simple and easy to implement, evaluate, debug and upgrade. In addition, it is much easier to design centralized heuristics for some NP-complete problems than to design distributed ones. On the other hand, this strategy has several problems: (1) the global state maintained at every node has to be updated frequently enough to cope with the dynamics of QoS parameters such bandwidth and delay, and it makes the communication overhead excessively high for large scale networks; (2) the link-state algorithm can only provide approximate global state due to the overhead concern and non-negligible propagation delay of state messages. As a consequence, the QoS routing may fail in finding an existing feasible path due to the impression in the global state used; (3) the computation overhead at the source is high. This is especially true in case of multicast routing or when multiple constraints are involved. In summary, source QoS routing has scalability problems. There exist many source routing solutions to the above discussed unicast problems such as the bandwidth-delay-constrained path solution in [WC96], bandwidth-constrained routing solution, delay-constrained routing solution with imprecise network states in [GO97], and solutions to multicast problems such as the constrained Steiner tree solution in [KPP93] and many others.

In the **distributed routing**, the path is computed by a distributed computation. Control messages are exchanged among the nodes and the state information kept at each node is collectively used for the path search. Most distributed routing algorithms need a distance vector protocol to maintain a global state in form of distance vectors at every node. Based on the distance vectors, the routing is done on a hop-by-hop base. The advantage of this strategy is that the path computation is distributed among the intermediate nodes between the source and the destination. Hence, the routing response time can be made shorter and the algorithm is more scalable. Searching multiple paths in parallel for a feasible one is made possible, which increases the chance of success. Most existing distributed routing algorithms (e.g., [SRV97a]) require each node to maintain a global network state (distance vectors), based on which the routing decision is made. Some flooding-based algorithms do not require any global state to be maintained. The routing decision and optimization is done entirely based on local states (e.g., [SC95], [CN98a]). The disadvantage of this strategy, especially when global state sharing is in place, is the same as in case of source routing. The distributed algorithms which do not need any global state tend to send more messages. It is also very difficult to design efficient distributed heuristics for the NP-complete routing problems, especially in multicast case, because there is no detailed topology and link state information available. In addition, if the global states are inconsistent, loops may occur. A loop can be easily detected when the routing message is received by a node for the second time. However, loops generally make the routing fail, because the distance vectors do not provide sufficient information for an alternative path.

In the **hierarchical routing**, nodes are clustered into groups, which are further clustered into higher-level groups recursively, creating a multi-level hierarchy. Each physical node maintains an aggregated global state. This state contains the detailed

state information about the nodes in the same group and the aggregated state information about the other groups. The source routing is used to find a feasible path on which
some nodes are logical nodes representing groups. A control message is then sent along
this path to establish the connection. When the border node of a group, represented by a
logical node, receives the message, it uses the source routing to expend the path through
the group. The advantage of this strategy is scalability. The hierarchical routing has
been long used to cope with the scalability problem of source routing in large networks
(e.g., [BA98]). For example, the PNNI (Private Network-Network Interface) standard
[For96] for routing in ATM networks is also hierarchical.This strategy scales well
because each node only maintains a partial global state where groups of nodes are
aggregated into logical nodes. The size of such an aggregated state is logarithmic in the
size of the complete global state. The well-studied source routing algorithms are
directly used at each hierarchical level to find feasible paths based on the aggregated
state [LN00]. Hence, the hierarchical routing retains many advantages of the source
routing. It has also some advantages of the distributed routing because the routing computation is shared by many nodes. The disadvantage of this strategy is that the network
state, being aggregated, adds additional imprecision and this has a significant negative
impact on QoS routing [GO97].

## 2.4.5  Admission Control

The next step, after every layer inquires or gets its own QoS specification through negotiation, translation and routing, is the *resource admission control*. The admission control service is an important service at every shared resource such as network, CPU, and
buffers along the path between sources and destinations. This service checks resources
for availability. For example, in networks, admission control is a mechanism used to
accept, modify or reject new connections. Note that if the QoS parameter value of a
connection is modified during the admission control, then the admission service
suggests a new lower value $QoS_{target}$ with

$$QoS^{req} \geq QoS_{target} \geq QoS_{min}$$

depending on which negotiation protocol is running.

The admission control checks availability of shared resources using availability
tests in the resource management. The resource availability tests are called *admission
tests*. Based on the results of the admission tests, the corresponding protocol creates
either a "*reserve*" message with admitted or modified QoS values, or "*reject*" message
when $QoS_{min}$ cannot be satisfied. The admitted QoS values may be lower than $QoS^{req}$,
but they must be equal or above $QoS_{min}$ value.

There are at least three types of admission tests which admission control should
perform:

1. **Schedulability test:** This test should be performed over shared resources such as CPU and network. We need CPU schedulability test, packet schedulability test at the entrance to the network and at each network node to delivery timing QoS guarantees.
2. **Spatial test:** This test is needed to ensure a proper buffer allocation and therefore to provide delay and reliability guarantees.
3. **Link bandwidth test:** This test ensures a proper bandwidth allocation and throughput guarantees.

Table 2-3 shows some examples of admission tests for the CPU, buffer and network bandwidth availability [NS96] [KN97b]:

| Admitted Resources | Admission Tests |
|---|---|
| CPU | $$\sum_{i=1}^{n} C_i / P_i \leq 1,$$ where $i$ is the number of tasks |
| Memory | $$\sum_{j=1}^{k} Mem_a^j + Mem_r \leq Mem_g,$$ where $Mem_a^j$ is allocated memory, $Mem_r$ is the requested memory, and $Mem_g$ is the overall available memory |
| Bandwidth | $$\sum_{j} B_a^j + B_r \leq B_g$$ where $B_a^j$ is the allocated bandwidth, $B_r$ is the requested bandwidth, and $B_g$ is the overall available bandwidth |

**Table 2-3**  Examples of admission tests.

The admission tests, as mentioned above, depend on the implementation of control (e.g., rate control) mechanisms in the multimedia processing and communication protocols. Specific admission tests will be also covered in individual chapters on operating systems, networking and communication. At this point, it is important to emphasize that any QoS parameter distribution with its negotiation and resource admission control must be closely related to a *cost* function, expressed in terms of pricing to differentiate between various service classes [VN97]. If no differentiation in terms of pricing exists, users will always request more resources than needed which will decrease the number of users using guaranteed services.

For example, let us assume we have a video-on-demand service running within a community. We can save resources and provide a better response time if we allow a movie to be moved to a server "nearby" respective clients. This can be done more easily if we have prior knowledge of the demand. Hence, a user who "orders" a movie for a certain future time may pay less than another user who chooses a movie and wants access immediately. If the client is not forced to pay, she will always demand the best available QoS. In this case, if immediate access is provided, some clients may end up with a reduction in quality or not use this service due to poor quality as a result of the QoS negotiation. Hence, with the introduction of appropriate pricing, QoS negotiation may well become a real negotiation.

### 2.4.6   Reservation

For the provision of guaranteed QoS in multimedia systems, reservation and proper allocation of resources is desired. Without resource reservation and management in end-systems and routers/switches, transmission of multimedia data leads to lost (dropped or delayed) packets. The reservation and allocation of resources is mostly simplex, it means the resources are reserved only in one direction along the end-to-end path. This also implies that senders are logically distinct from receivers.

Reservation and allocation of resources can be performed in pessimistic or optimistic manner:

- **Pessimistic Approach:** This approach avoids resource conflicts by making reservations for the worst case (e.g., reservation for a task entity with the worst case execution time or highest bandwidth). A MPEG compressed video application can illustrate this approach as follows:

  - Let us consider frame-based scheduling of I, P, and B with processing times $C(M_A^I) > C(M_A^P) > C(M_A^B)$. The pessimistic reservation will allocate $C(M_A^I)$ processing time for each MPEG task, independent of the frame type.
  - In case of bandwidth $B$, the pessimistic reservation requests:

  $$B^{pessimistic} = M_A^I \times R_A$$

  - This might be an over-reservation and leads to under-utilization of resources as there might be only need for:

  $$B^{actuell} = G_I \times M_A^I + G_P \times M_A^P + G_B \times M_A^B$$

- **Optimistic Approach:** This approach reserves resources according to an average workload.

  - In the case of the above mentioned example, CPU is only allocated for the average processing time per frame, i.e.,

  $$C_A^{ave} = (G_I \times C(M_A^I) + G_P \times C(M_A^P) + G_B \times C(M_A^B))/G$$

- This approach may overload resources when unpredictable behavior occurs. QoS parameters are met as far as possible. Resources are highly utilized, though an *overload* situation may result in failure. A *monitoring* function to detect overload should be implemented. This function may related to a function which then preempts processes or other schedulable units according to their importance and deadlines if overrun and overload situations occur.

Both approaches represent points in a continuum because a process requires a resource in a stochastic fashion. They aim either towards $QoS_{max}$ or $QoS_{ave}$ guarantees. Hybrid reservation approaches can aim towards any value between the average and peak values

$$QoS_{ave} \leq QoS \leq QoS_{max}$$

The closer the reservation value assignment is to the peak value, the lower the probability that the process will be denied the use of resources at a certain time. Hence the assignment represents a trade-off between the peak rate multiplexing (pessimistic approach) and the statistical multiplexing (optimistic approach). A method that captures this trade-off quantitatively is given in [PSS02].

Additional reservation mechanisms must be in place to detect and resolve resource conflicts. The resource managers may support data structures and functions for resource reservation as follows:

- **Resource Table:** A resource table, co-located with a resource manager, contains information about the managed resources. The table may include static information like the total resource capacity available (e.g., $CPU^{avail} = CPU^{global} - CPU^{alloc}$), maximum allowable resource capacity (e.g., $CPU^{global}$, which equals to the global CPU bandwidth we want to use for reservations[3]), scheduling algorithm (e.g., Rate Monotonic Scheduling), dynamic information like pointers to connections currently using the resource, and total capacity currently reserved.

- **Reservation Table:** This table provides information about the connections and/or tasks for which portions of the managed resources are currently reserved (e.g., $CPU^{alloc}$). This information includes the contracted QoS guarantees, given to connections, tasks or other schedulable units.

- **Reservation Function:** This function determines the reserved QoS parameter values that can be given to a new connection or task (via admission control), and reserves the corresponding resource capacities via entries in resource and reservation tables.

---

[3] Note that not all resource bandwidth has to be available for reservation and guaranteed services. It is important to leave some resource bandwidth available for best-effort services to avoid starvation of this class of services.

Examples of such reservation structures and functions can be found in many systems, such as the HeiRAT [WH94], QualMan [KN97a] and others.

The reservation and allocation of network resources along the end-to-end path depend on the reservation model, negotiation and reservation protocols, and on the set of resource management functions such as admission, allocation, monitoring and deallocation of individual resources.

### 2.4.6.1    Reservation Model

There are three types of reservation models for the communication architecture of a multimedia system:

1. *Single Sender and Single Receiver* (e.g., RCAP protocol)
2. *Single Sender and Multiple Receivers* (e.g., ST-II protocol)
3. *Multiple Senders and Multiple Receivers* (e.g., RSVP protocol)

The reservation model is also determined by its *reservation direction* and *style* [ZDE+93]. The reservation direction can be *sender-oriented* (e.g., ST-II, RCAP), or *receiver-oriented* (e.g., RSVP). Sender-oriented reservation means that the sender transmits a QoS specification to the destinations. The intermediate routers and switches may adjust the QoS specification according to corresponding negotiation strategies and available resources. The reservation protocol carries the QoS parameters and reserves resource according to admitted QoS parameter values along the -end-to-end path from the sender to the destination. The resulting and confirmed QoS parameter values are then sent back and resources are changed from reserved to allocated along the path from the destination to the sender. Figure 2-12 shows the sender-initiated reservation protocol.

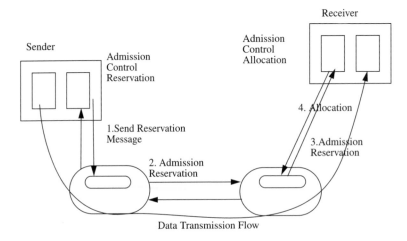

**Figure 2-12**    Sender-initiated reservation.

*Receiver-oriented reservation direction* means that the receiver describes its QoS and resource requirements, sends them to the sender in a reservation message [ZDE⁺93], and reserves resources in the direction from the destination to the sender. It is assumed that a sender has issued a path message before, providing information about itself and its outgoing data. On the way from the sender to the receiver the resources will be allocated. Figure 2-13 shows the receiver-initiated reservation protocol.

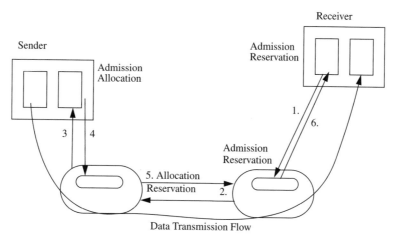

**Figure 2-13**   Receiver-initiated reservation.

The *reservation style* represents a creation of a path reservation and time when senders and receivers perform QoS negotiation and resource reservation. The style for a sender-oriented reservation may be either a *single reservation* or a *multicast reservation*.

The style for receiver-oriented reservation is classified according to *filters*. We will present filters as defined in the *Resource Reservation Protocol (RSVP)* for Internet Integrated Services [ZDE⁺93]:

• **Wildcard Filter style:** A receiver creates a single reservation or a resource pipe along each link and shares it among all senders for the given session. The sender flow is not filtered at all, i.e., all datagrams from any sender are forwarded to the receiver.

• **Fixed Filter style:** Each receiver selects a particular sender whose data packets it wants to receive. Sender traffic is filtered according to a fixed filter for the duration of receiver's reservation.

• **Dynamic Filter style:** Each receiver creates *N* distinct reservations to carry flows from up to *N* different senders. A later dynamic filter reservation from the same receiver may specify the same value of *N* and the same common flow specification, but a different selection of particular senders without a new admission control check. This is known as channel switching which is analogous to program switching in television application. If a receiver, using the dynamic filter style, changes the number $N$ of distinct reservations or the common flow specification, this is treated as a new reservation and it is subject to admission control. In dynamic filter reservation style, the receiver can change how a sender's traffic is filtered over time.

Figure 2-14 shows all three filter styles as defined in RSVP specification. Filters have three important purposes [Par94a]:

1. Filters provide support for *heterogeneity*. Receivers at the end of slow links can still participate in communication by using a filter which will restrict what portion of the flow is passed to it.
2. Dynamic filtering allows receivers to *modify flow properties*. For example, if a receiver is alternately listening to multiple flows, then it can change filters and drop all packets from sender $A$ if it wants to listen and accept all packets from sender $B$.
3. Filters are used to *reduce load* and *improve bandwidth management*.

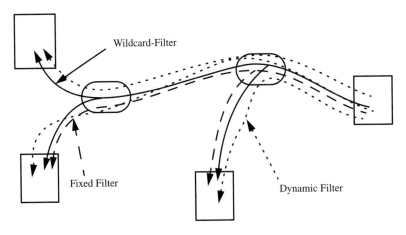

**Figure 2-14**   Filters in receiver-initiated reservation.

The reservation style can be also divided with respect to time when actual resource allocation happens: (1) *immediate reservation* and (2) *advanced reservation*. Immediate reservation means that immediately after a reservation was approved, allocation of resources occurs and immediate usage of resources is expected. Advanced reservation means that reservation is performed for a future time when the resources will be allocated and used [FKL+99]. Advanced reservation service is essential in multi-party multimedia applications. There are two possible approaches to advanced reservation: a *centralized* approach where an advanced reservation server exists to coordinate all future reservations, and a *distributed* approach where each node along the reserved path "remembers" future reservations.

For an example implementation of RSVP the reader is referred to [KSS01] [RGKS00])

### 2.4.6.2    Reservation Protocols

A reservation protocol performs no reservation or allocation of required resource itself, it is only a vehicle to transfer QoS and resource requirements and assist in negotiation of QoS values.Reservation protocols are control protocols embedded in a multimedia call establishment protocol. This protocol implies that every node has QoS and resource management entities which are responsible for sending and receiving control messages, as well as invoking corresponding management functions, such as admission control, QoS translation, QoS routing, and others, needed for establishment of a multimedia session between senders and receivers [Xu01].

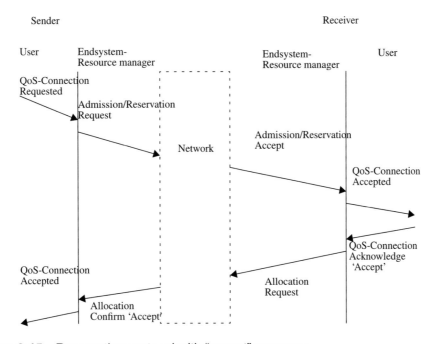

**Figure 2-15**   Reservation protocol with "accept" response.

In general, reservation protocols work as follows: (a) the initiator of the connection (e.g., sender) sends QoS specification in a reservation message (connect request) towards the initiatee. (b) At each router or switch along the path, the reservation protocol passes a new reservation request to the resource manager which may consist of several components (e.g., in RSVP this manager is called the "traffic controller" and it consists of admission control function, packet scheduler and packet classifier). (c) After admission decision the resource manager reserves resources via entry in the reservation table and updates particular service information for QoS provision. (d) On the way back from the initiatee to the initiator an allocation message (connect confirm) enforces the change of the reservation state to allocation state for individual resrouces. Figure 2-15 shows the sender-initiated reservation protocol with the 'accept' confirm message.

After the transmission of media ends, resources must be *de-allocated*. It means CPU, network bandwidth and buffer space must be freed. The deallocation of resources depends on what types of connections were established.

- **Hard Connections:** If a hard connection was established, i.e., each node along the path carries hard state about the connection (e.g., ATM virtual circuits are hard connections), then the tear down process sends a deallocation message, and the deallocation must be done without a disruption of other flows in the network. This tear-down process can be requested by the sender(s) or by the receiver(s). Freeing of resources means that upon receiving the deallocation message resource management updates any resource and reservation tables that carry information about resource allocation for the closed connection.
- **Soft Connections:** If a soft connection was established, i.e., each node along the path carries soft state about a flow and this state expires after certain time-out interval on its own (e.g., RSVP creates soft connections), then the de-allocation of resources happens automatically and no separate tear-down process is necessary. However, it is important to stress that if a connection wants to use resources longer than its soft reservation lasts, then it needs to refresh the reservation state along the path by using refresh messages.

## 2.5   Run-time Phase of Multimedia Call

QoS guarantees must be met in application, system and network levels (see Figure 2-1) to get the acceptance of multimedia systems users. There are several requirements on multimedia systems which must be enforced to provide guarantees during multimedia transmission and processing:

1. time requirements such as delays;
2. space requirements such as systems buffers;
3. device requirements such as frame grabber allocation;
4. bandwidth requirements such as network bandwidth, CPU bandwidth for data transmission
5. reliability requirement.

These requirements can be met if proper QoS and resource management are available at the end-points and networks. However, these five requirements are related to each other in such a way that one parameter may imply choosing another. For example, scheduling delay of a video frame implies bandwidth allocation. We will concentrate in the following section on concepts of QoS enforcement. We will show the concepts on QoS enforcement services for network services and discuss traffic shaping mechanisms, rate control scheduling services for delay, jitter and throughput provision, as well as error control for reliability guarantees. Similar enforcement services apply to computing resources and we discuss them in detail in Chapters on Operating Systems, and Media Servers. Also more information about network-related QoS enforcement services and protocols will be presented in the Chapters on Networking and Communication.

We assume at this point that proper resource reservation and allocation have occurred as described in previous sections of this Chapter.

## 2.5.1  Traffic Shaping

One of important components of QoS enforcement is traffic shaping. In a packet network, that allows resource sharing, admission control and scheduling schemes are not sufficient to provide QoS guarantees. This is due to the fact that users may, inadvertently or otherwise, attempt to exceed rates specified and negotiated during the establishment phase. Therefore, one aims to achieve a rate, which is possibly close to a constant rate as shown in Figure 2-16.

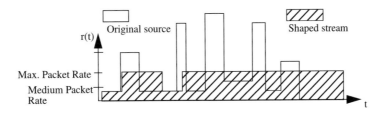

**Figure 2-16**  Shaped traffic rate.

We need traffic shaping at the entry of the network and/or within the network. Traffic shaping provides a set of rules that comply to the flows traffic characteristics. The purpose of traffic shaping is as follows: The resource reservation algorithm needs to *analyze QoS specification,* associated with all connections, utilizing the shared resource in order to determine the service quality that can be offered to individual connections. Since the number of connections, sharing the common network resource, can be very large, it is important that the QoS specification per connection be *simple* for easy management. Unfortunately, traffic generated in multimedia systems is very bursty due to compressed multimedia streams, and often difficult to model and specify. To alleviate the problem, traffic generated by multimedia sources is passed through a *traffic shaper.*

Traffic shaping should allow:

1. a simply way for a connection to *describe its traffic* so that the network knows what kind of traffic to expect. One way to capture a wide range of traffic characteristics is to use *traffic envelope* that includes traffic-related QoS specification;
2. the network to perform an *admission control*; and
3. the network to *monitor connection traffic* and to *police/confirm* that the connection is behaving as it promised [Par94a].

We will examine various shaping schemes which fit different types of traffic. The simplest traffic shaping schemes try to shape all traffic into *isochronous* flows, with regular amounts of data being emitted at regular time intervals between samples as they are sent into the network. We will discuss two such shaping schemes:

• **Leaky Bucket** [Tur86]: In this scheme, each connection has its own leaky bucket. When data is to be sent, the sending host places the connection's packets into a bucket. Packets drain out of the bottom of the bucket and are sent into the network at the rate $R_N$. The rate is enforces by a regulator at the bottom of the bucket. The bucket size, β, limits how much data may build up waiting for the network. If the connection presents more data than the size of bucket allows, the excess data is discarded. In this scheme, the shaped data characteristics measures up to equally spaced packets, each packet being emitted $1/R_N$ units of time after the last one. The effect of the bucket size β is both to bound the amount of delay a packet can incur before getting into the network and to limit the maximum burst size the sender can try to send. Figure 2-17 shows the simple leaky bucket behavior.

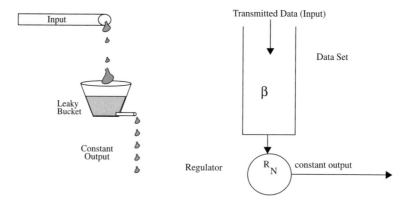

**Figure 2-17**   Simple leaky bucket.

• **(r,T) - Smooth Algorithm** [Gol90]: In an *(r,T)* - smooth traffic system, a connection is permitted to inject no more than *r* data into the network in any *T* bit times, where *T* is a fixed constant through the network.'*r*' varies on a per-connection basis. If the next packet to be sent would cause the connection to use more than $r$ bits in the current frame, then the connection must hold the packet until the next frame starts. If we compare the $(r, T)$ - smooth algorithm with the leaky bucket scheme, then this algorithm, rather than sending one packet of size $M_N$ every $1/R_N$ time units, allows the connection to send $TxM_N/R_N$ bits of data every $T$ bit times. This shaping algorithm is part of the scheduling service discipline, called *stop-and-go*, described in the next subsection. Limitation of this approach is that one cannot send a packet larger than $r$ bits long. Therefore, unless $T$ is very long, the maximum packet size may be very small.

In summary, isochronous shaping schemes are easy to implement, however, the range of behaviors they describe is limited to fixed rate data flows.

Another class of shaping algorithms consists of schemes which integrate *isochronous schemes with priority schemes*. The basic idea is that every packet is tagged with a bit pattern that tells the network how important the packet is to the connection's application. If the network finds itself congested at some point, it discards some or all of the traffic that are marked as less important. For example, ATM network supports a *two-priority scheme* using the CLP bit [Ken97]. This class of shaping schemes has two main problems: (1) the *amount of traffic* that can be guaranteed is rather *low*, typically no more than 50% of the total bandwidth of a link [Par94a]; and (2) *discarding selective packets*, when communication devices use FIFO queues, is *difficult*. The issue is that when the device is overloaded and it needs to discard some low priority packets, it is unable to look inside its FIFO queues. The implication is that such a device employs then a policy to discard the low priority packets as they arrive at the input queue (e.g., CISCO ATM or IP switches use so called *early discard policy*).

In order to support a richer range of traffic characteristics, a class of shaping algorithms was developed which supports *bursty traffic patterns*. We will describe two such algorithms:

- **Token Bucket**: In a token bucket system, $R_N$ is the rate at which tokens are placed in the token bucket. The bucket has the occupancy $\beta$. If the bucket fills up, newly arriving tokens are discarded. When a packet is sent, it is placed in a separate data buffer queue. To transmit the packet, the regulator must remove a number of tokens equal to the packet size from the bucket. Token bucket permits burstiness but bounds it. This scheme guarantees that the burstiness is bounded so that the connection never sends more than $\beta + \tau R_N$ tokens worth of *data in an interval $\tau$ and that the long term transmission rate will not exceed $R_N$*. Limitation of this traffic shaping scheme is that it is difficult to police. At any time the flow is allowed to exceed rate by a number of tokens, hence we need a better policing. Figure 2-18 shows the behavior of the Token Bucket algorithm.

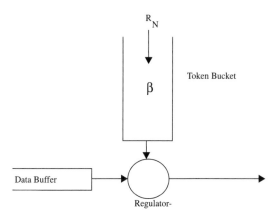

**Figure 2-18**   Token bucket traffic shaping scheme.

  • **Token Bucket with Leaky Bucket Rate Control:** This scheme has a token
    bucket of size β, and data buffer queue sending the data with regulator rate of $R_N$.
    When the regulator lets data through, the data is then placed in a simple leaky
    bucket (also of size β) from which the data is drained at rate $C > R_N$. This scheme
    permits bursty traffic but regulates it so that the maximum transmission rate at any
    time is $C$ and the long-term average has an upper bound of $R_N$.

This class of shaping schemes has more complexity in terms of policing or implementation. Token bucket algorithm has a policing problem when the connection is allowed to
exceed the rate $R_N$ by β tokens because the network tries to police connections by simply measuring their traffic over time interval τ, hence a connection can cheat[4] by sending $β+τR_N$ tokens of data in every interval τ. The token bucket with leaky bucket
requires more complex implementation than token bucket and complex policing.

## 2.5.2   Rate Control

If we assume a multimedia system to be tightly coupled system which as a central process managing all system components, then this central instance can impose a synchronous data handling over all resources; in effect we encounter a fixed imposed data rate.
However, a multimedia system usually comprises loosely coupled end-systems and
proxies which communicate over networks. In such a setup, rates must be imposed.
Here, we make use of all available strategies in the communication environment.
        High-speed networking provides opportunities for multimedia applications to
have stringent performance requirements in terms of throughput, delay, jitter and loss

---

[4] Over the interval of 2τ, the connection would send data equal to $2β+2τR_N$ tokens. However, it is supposed to send at
most $β+2τR_N$.

rate. Conventional packet switching data networks with window-based flow control and FCFS cannot provide services with strict performance guarantees. Hence, for multimedia systems, new *rate-based flow control* and *rate based scheduling* service disciplines are needed [LHJea02]. These control mechanisms are connected with a connection-oriented network architecture which supports resource allocation and admission control policies.

A rate-based service discipline is one that provides a client with a minimum service rate independent of the traffic characteristics of other clients. Such a discipline, operating at a switch, manages the following resources: bandwidth, service time (priority), and buffer space. Together with proper admission policies, such disciplines provide throughput, delay, jitter and loss rate guarantees. Several rate-based scheduling disciplines have been developed [ZK91]:

- **Fair Queueing:** If $N$ channels share an output trunk, then each one should get $1/N$th of the bandwidth. If any channel uses less bandwidth than its share, then this portion is shared among the rest equally. This mechanism can be achieved by the *Bit-by-Bit Round Robin (BR)* service among the channels. The BR discipline serves $N$ queues in the round robin service, sending one bit from each queue that has a packet in it. Clearly, this scheme is not efficient, hence fair queueing emulates BR as follows: each packet is given a *finish number*, which is the round number at which the packet would have received service if the server had been doing BR. The packets are served in the order of the finish number. Channels can be given different fractions of the bandwidth by assigning them weights, where a weight corresponds to the number of bits of service the channel receives per round of BR service.

- **Virtual Clock:** This discipline emulates the *Time Division Multiplexing* (TDM). A virtual transmission time is allocated to each packet. It is the time at which the packet would have been transmitted if the server would actually be doing TDM.

- **Delay Earliest-Due-Date (Delay EDD):** Delay EDD [FV90] is an extension of *EDF scheduling* (Earliest Deadline First), discussed in the Chapter on Operating Systems, where the server negotiates a service contract with each source. The contract states that if a source obeys a peak and average sending rate, then the server provides bounded delay. The key then lies in the assignment of deadlines of packets. The server sets a packet's deadline to the time at which it should be sent, if it had been received according to the contract. This is actually the expected arrival time added to the delay bound at the server. By reserving bandwidth at the peak rate ($B_N^{max}$), delay EDD can assure each channel of a guaranteed delay bound.

- **Jitter Earliest-Due-Date (Jitter EDD):** Jitter EDD extends the Delay EDD to provide jitter bounds. After a packet has been served at each server, it is stamped with the difference between its deadline and its actual finishing time. A regulator at the entrance of the next switch holds the packet for this period before it is made eligible to be scheduled. This provides the minimum and maximum delay guarantees.

- **Stop-and-Go:** This discipline preserves the "smoothness" property of the traffic as it traverses through the network. The main idea is to treat all traffic as frames of fixed length $T$ bits, it means the time is divided into frames. At each frame time, only packets that have arrived at the server in the previous frame time are sent. It can be shown that the delay and jitter are bounded, although the jitter bound does not come for free. The reason is that under Stop-and-Go rules, packets arriving at the start of an incoming frame must be held by full time $T$ before being forwarded. Hence, all packets that would arrive early are instead being delayed. Further, since the delay and jitter bounds are linked to the length of the frame time, improvement of Stop-and-Go can be achieved using multiple frame sizes, which means it may operate with various frame sizes.

- **Hierarchical Round Robin (HRR):** A HRR server has several service levels where each level provides round robin service to a fixed number of slots. Some number of slots at a selected level are allocated to a channel and the server cycles through the slots at each level. The time a server takes to service all slots at each level is called the frame time at the level. The key of HRR is that it gives each level a constant share of the bandwidth. "Higher" levels get more bandwidth than "lower" levels, so the frame time at a higher level is smaller than the frame time at a lower level. Since a server always completes one round through its slots once every frame time, it can provide a maximum delay bound to the channels allocated to that level.

Some other disciplines, suitable for providing guaranteed services, are augmented schemes of fair queueing such as the *Weighted Fair Queueing (WFQ)* [CSZ92]. In WFQ, each packet is stamped with a time stamp as it arrives and it is transmitted in an increasing order of the time stamp. The amount of data to be transmitted is determined by the weight.

Rate-based disciplines are divided depending on the policy they adopt:

- **Work-conserving policy** serves packets at the higher rate as long as it does not affect the performance guarantees of other channels. It means a server is never idle when there is a packet to be sent. Examples of work-conserving disciplines are Delay EDD, Virtual Clock, Fair Queueing.

- **Non-work-conserving policy** does not serve packets at a higher rate under any circumstances, which means that each packet is assigned an *eligibility* time, explicitly or implicitly. Even when the server is idle, if no packets are eligible, none will be transmitted. Examples of non-work-conserving disciplines are Stop-and-Go, HRR and Jitter EDD.

Rate-based service disciplines need to allocate resources per client, hence clients need to specify their traffic using QoS parameters. The traffic specification for Virtual Clock, HRR and Stop-and-Go provides the *transmission rate $R_N$* averaged over an interval. Delay EDD and Jitter EDD have three parameters, *minimum packet inter-arrival time, average packet inter-arrival time* and *interval* over which the average packet inter-arrival time was computed. Fair queueing was described for datagram networks, hence no traffic specification was proposed.

The buffer space requirements for the tree non-work-conserving disciplines are almost constant for each node, traversed by the channel [ZK91]. The buffer space requirement for work-conserving Delay EDD increases linearly for each node along the path. Throughput guarantees are provided by all rate-based services. Delay guarantees are provided only by Delay EDD and all non-conserving services (also by WFQ). Jitter guarantees are provided by Stop-and-Go and Jitter EDD disciplines.

### 2.5.3 Error Control

Multimedia extensions to existing operating systems provide a fast and efficient data transport between sources and destinations located at the same computer. Glitches on video streams may (but should not) occur. Audio should be always conveyed in a reliable way. The solution becomes different if we take into account networks. In the past, several multimedia communication systems have been proposed which usually offer unreliable transport. For example, the UDP/IP protocol was used for experiments to transmit digital audio over the Internet. Other examples were the Tenet protocols such as RMTP (Real-time Message Transport Protocol) and CMTP (Continuous Media Transport Protocols, as well as the current Internet protocol RTP (Real-Time Transport Protocol) which provide unreliable but timely delivery for multimedia communication.

A substantial degree of reliability in multimedia systems is necessary because errors may have negative impact in the following areas:

- **Human Perception:** Loss of digital audio, for example, is detected by a human ear very quickly and results in lower acceptance of the multimedia system. Even in video media if the temporal resolution is too low, users reject the quality of video. Losses impact strongly the inter-stream synchronization and cause out of sync behavior.

- **Decompression Technology:** Many audio and video compression schemes cannot tolerate loss, they are unable to resynchronize themselves after a packet loss or other errors are introduced. For example, the MPEG-1 and many of the MPEG-2 players must receive a full frame with no bit or byte losses if the video data should be decompressed and displayed.

- **Data Integrity:** Data error within a stored material, which is often retrieved, is much more unacceptable than a one-time or non-reproduce-able data error. For example, a color error during a live broadcast is more acceptable than an error within a movie material which is often retrieved and the error repeats itself.

To ensure required reliability and error handling of multimedia systems, end-to-end error control consists of two steps: *error detection and error correction.*

### 2.5.3.1    Error Detection

Reliability should be enforced, although there is some error tolerance in multimedia systems. This works only if the application is able to isolate errors. For example, some wrong colors within a video frame may not matter because they are hardly visible to the human user as they appear for only a short fraction of a second. However, if the frame boundaries are destroyed, there is no way to recover from the error. This means that structural information within a data stream needs to be protected, but not always the content. This also implies that existing error detection mechanisms such as *checksums* and *PDU sequencing* must be extended towards conveying further information. These existing mechanisms allow detection of *data corruption, loss, duplication and misorder* at the lower levels (e.g., packets in transport layer), but at the application PDU level, where the decision should actually be made, if the packet is lost or not, error detection is left out.

Another example for enforcing error detection at a higher layer is *MPEG-2* encoded video. This compression produces three types of frames in the video stream. The most important frame type is the I frame, which contains the structural information of the video stream for a certain time interval. The two other types of video frames (P frame and B frame) follow the I frame with supporting information. Hence, it is important for the multimedia communication system not to lose the I frame (strict reliability requirements on the sequence of I frames), but there is a certain tolerance towards losses of P frames or B frames.

In the transport and lower layers, the error detection mechanisms must be extended too because of the *"lateness" concept.* It means that if a PDU arrives too late at the receiver, this information is useless for an application and should be detected as an error. To identify late data, it is necessary to determine the lifetime of packets and compare their actual arrival time with their latest expected arrival time. The latest expected arrival time can be derived from the traffic model (throughput and rate) associated with a connection. This means that for continuous streams, the expiration time can be calculated from the *PDU rate.* Therefore, only the first PDU has to carry a time stamp. However, this is not an ideal solution because error detection is forced to start with the first PDU, and no interruption of the service is possible. Another approach it to *time stamp* each packet. With a time stamp in every PDU, the error detection can start at any point during the media transmission. This mechanism requires a synchronized system clock at the sender and receiver to allow for an accurate determination of the end-to-end delay. A possible protocol for this kind of synchronization is the *Mill's Network Time Protocol (NTP)* [Mil93].

### 2.5.3.2    Error Correction

The traditional mechanism for reliability provision is *retransmission* (e.g., TCP protocol uses this mechanism), which uses an acknowledgement principle after receiving data, or a window-based flow control. If the acknowledgement is negative, the data is resent by the sender. The traditional reliable transfer strategies are not suitable for multimedia communication because:

1. with explicit acknowledgement the amount of data to be stored at the sender for potential retransmission can become very large (e.g., in case of video data);
2. with the traditional window-based flow control, the sender may be forced to suspend transmission while a continuous flow is required;
3. retransmitted data might be received "too late" to be consumed in real-time;
4. traditional mechanisms also do not scale to multiple target communication, they are not designed for multicasting communication, only for a point-to-point communication,

We will outline some appropriate error correction schemes for multimedia systems:

- **Go-back-N Retransmission:** This method is the most rigid error correction scheme. The mechanism is as follows: if PDU $i$ is lost, the sender will go back to $i$ and restart transmission from $i$. The successive PDUs after $i$ are dropped at the receiver. The lost PDU is recovered only if $i \leq n$ holds, where $n$ is specified at the beginning of transmission. This means it is specified how far back the data should be retransmitted if a packet is lost. This is a simple protocol where no buffering or resequencing of the PDUs at the receiver is necessary. The receiver only sends a negative acknowledgement if PDU $i$ is lost. The problem is that if after that $i$th PDU the packets were transmitted successfully, they are dropped too, which may lead to several implications such as *gap introduction*, and *violation of throughput guarantees*. The retransmission introduces gaps because the receiver has to wait at least $2xE_A$ to get the proper PDU $i$. Also for a multimedia connection where throughput guarantees are provided through rate control, the retransmitted data must be sent either "on top" of the guaranteed throughput or the retransmitted PDU will fall under the rate control. This again leads to a gap in the stream presentation which needs to be handled properly through a mechanism such as freezing the video or turning down the audio stream.
- **Selective Retransmission**: This approach provides a better channel utilization. The receiver sends a negative acknowledgement to the sender if $i \leq n$ PDU $i$ is lost. The sender retransmits only those PDUs which have been reported missing, not the consecutive packets too. The disadvantage of this approach is its complicated implementation. At the receiver, every successfully received PDU must be

stored until all previous PDUs have been received correctly. It had been shown that this resequencing is worthwhile only if the receiver is able to store at least two times the data corresponding to the bandwidth-delay product.

- **Partially Reliable Streams:** This approach introduces a weak concept of reliability. This mechanism limits the number of packets to be retransmitted. Only the last $n$ packets of the stream in a certain time interval will be retransmitted. The value $n$ can be calculated from the timing constraint of the multimedia application, taking into account the reliability of the underlying network. The possible $n$ can be negotiated during the call setup between the sender and receiver.

- **Forward Error Correction (FEC):** In this mechanism, the sender adds additional information to the original data such that the receiver can locate and correct bits or bit sequences. A given FEC mechanism can be specified by its code rate $R$ (code efficiency), which can be computed as $R = S/(S+N)$, where $S$ represents the number of bits to be sent, $N$ represents the number of added check bits. The *redundancy,* introduced by the mechanism, is *(1-R)* and it must be determined by the transport system. The transport system needs two pieces of information, the *error probability* of the network between the sender and receiver, and the *reliability required* from the application. FEC results in a low end-to-end delay and there is no need for exclusive buffering of data before play-out. It also does not require a control channel from the receiver to the sender. The disadvantage of FEC is that it works only for error detection and correction within a packet but not for the complete packet loss. It means FEC cannot guarantee that corrupted or lost packets can always be recovered. Further, FEC increases the demand on throughput significantly. The negative effects of added congestion on a network due to FEC overhead can more than offset the benefits of FEC recovery [Bie93]. FEC may require hardware support at end-systems to encode and decode the redundant information with sufficient speed. FEC is also used in transport protocols for mobile networks and for storing audio data at Compact Disk (CD) devices. There has been and still is an extensive research on multimedia protocols in wireline and wireless networks utilizing FEC (e.g., [WCK03]).

- **Priority Channel Coding***:* Priority channel coding refers to a class of approaches that separates medium into multiple data streams with different priorities. These priorities are then used to tag packets so that during periods of congestion the network is more likely to discard low priority packets which carry less important information for reconstructing the original media stream. This scheme enables multiple priority channels to maintain higher QoS over larger loss ranges than channels using a single priority for all packets. The use of different streams with different priorities requires synchronization at a per-packet granularity to reconstruct the media stream. Examples, where priority channel coding is applicable, are voice packet streams or MPEG-2 encoded video streams. In case of MPEG-2 video stream, I and P frames could be sent at higher priority and B frames could be sent at low priority. Network switches then drop lower priority packets or provide a service degradation during the period of congestion.

- **Slack Automatic Repeat ReQuest (S-ARQ)**: S-ARQ is an error control scheme based on retransmission of lost packets. The packets are subject to jitter, hence the receiver observes gaps which result in interruptions of continuous playback of a media stream. Jitter in packetized media transmission is commonly addressed through a *control time* at the receiver. S-ARQ suggests to artificially delay the first packet at the receiver for a period of the control time to buffer sufficient packets and to provide continuous playback in the presence of jitter timing errors[5]. The slack time of a packet is then defined as the difference between its arrival time at the receiver and its playback time, which is the point in time at which playback of the packet must begin at the receiver to achieve a zero-gap playback schedule for the talk spurt. Due to jitter, a packet may arrive before or after its playback time. In the former case, the packet is placed in a packet receiver queue until it is due for playback. In the latter case, a gap has occurred and the packet is played immediately. For example, in case of voice over LAN networks, the voice data consist of talk spurts and periods of silence. Since talks spurts are generally isolated from each other by relatively long silence periods, voice protocols typically impose the control time on the first packet of each talk spurt. The principle of S-ARQ is to extend the control time at the beginning of a talk spurt and to use it so that the slack time of arriving packets is lengthened [DLW93].

The above error correction schemes for multimedia systems can be partitioned into two classes: *partial retransmission mechanisms* such as Go-back-N, Selective Retransmission, Partial Reliable Streams, S-ARQ, and *preventive mechanisms* such as FEC, Priority Channel Coding. All partial retransmission schemes may introduce the possibility of a discontinuity if we apply them in WAN networks with large end-to-end delays. Hence, preventive scheme should be considered and deployed in multimedia systems.

### 2.5.4 QoS and Resource Monitoring

Resource monitoring is an important part of QoS enforcement in networks as well as at the end-points. Resource monitoring functionality is embedded in the resource managers. For example, in case of network resources, *network management* needs to deploy monitoring capabilities, and MIBs (Management Information Bases) must be extended with QoS parameters. Further, network management may need new functions for QoS supervision and conflict resolution.

---

[5] Note that if a packet gets lost during the delay control time, it can be retransmitted and replaced in the media stream sequence as long as the retransmitted packet arrives before the packet playback deadline.

Monitoring in multimedia systems can add overhead during multimedia transmission, therefore it needs to be done carefully not to cause violation of QoS guarantees. Monitoring should be flexible, i.e., most of the monitoring variables should be optional and be able to be turned on and off [WH94]. There are at least two possible modes to operate resource monitoring: *on-demand mode and pro-active mode*. The former mode means that a service user demands a status report about resources, the latter mode means that the system/network service provider reports regularly and pro-actively the resource status.

*Monitoring at end-systems* includes a supervisor function to continuously observe that the processed QoS parameters do not exceed their negotiated values. For example, a compression component may allow delivery at a peak rate of 6 Mbps over a duration of at most three frame lengths. However, at some point in time the system starts to deliver a continuous bit rate of 10Mbps. The monitoring function will detect this behavior by being called from an exception handler of the rate control component because a buffer overflow occurred at the sender (something which should never happen). The monitoring function should find out that the origin of the exceeded QoS parameter value is an erroneous compressing component. It should be stressed that the design and implementation of such a monitoring function is a non-trivial task and a clearly defined notion of the QoS is a pre-requisite.

### 2.5.5   QoS Renegotiation and Adaptation

In continuous media communication, it is important to support a framework capable of dynamically changing resource capacity during each session. Hence, it is important for multimedia systems to support dynamic change of QoS parameters so that they can be balanced to reach an optimal value for all sessions in a predictable manner.

There are two important factors which must be provided to achieve this goal: *notification of change*, and *adaptation/renegotiation of QoS parameters*. It means that there must be in place a reporting protocol to signal changes in QoS parameter values, there must be available adaptation functions to change and adjust QoS parameter values, and there must exist protocols to distributed and renegotiate the changed values along the end-to-end path between sources and destinations.

There are several reasons why renegotiation and adaptation of QoS parameter values and associated resources occur during a multimedia transmission: (1) changes violating minimum negotiated bound $QoS_{min}$ or modifying the negotiated range, (2) changes within the negotiated range $[QoS_{min}, QoS_{max}]$.

If violation of bounds or modification of ranges occur, the renegotiation of QoS parameters must begin. If fluctuation of QoS parameters within the negotiated range occurs, QoS adaptation must be performed.

### 2.5.5.1   QoS Renegotiation

QoS parameter renegotiation is a process of QoS negotiation during the multimedia transmission when a session is already setup. The renegotiation request can come either from the *user*, who wants to change the quality of service thresholds, from the *host system* due to overload of the workstation (multi-user, multi-process environment) or from the *network* due to overload and congestion. The renegotiation request is sent to the resource management.

- **User Request for Renegotiation:** If the sender requires a change of QoS bounds, this implies change in reservation of multimedia sources, host system resources and network resources. The resource manager must check if local resources are available. Further, the resource reservation and renegotiation protocol must be invoked to check the availability of network resources in case the change of QoS requires a change in network resources. If resources are available, resource reservation and allocation are performed. If the receiver requires changes of QoS for the receiving media, first the resource manager checks the local resources and reserves it, then the sender is notified and the same admission procedure follows as in the case of a sender requiring change in QoS bounds. At the end, the receiver must be notified to change the local resource allocation of necessary. In a broadcast or multicast communication structure, different QoS values may be applied for the same connection to different end-systems using filters.

- **Host System Request for Renegotiation:** This request may come from a QoS-aware operating system [KN97a] in a multi-user environment. In this case, several users are admitted and some of the users are misbehaved users which violate their admitted application requirements. Then, a notification about the QoS degradation must be issued to the application client. The degradation of one's QoS performance may also result in degradation of performance for other users of the end system. The response is either a correction and dispatching misbehaved users and applications to the admitted level, or a renegotiation request for new QoS parameter bounds. If host QoS changes result in the renegotiation of new QoS parameter bounds, then the host resource manager will need to invoke the resource reservation and renegotiation protocol to renegotiate QoS parameters in the network between the sender and receiver.

- **Network Request for Renegotiation:** Overload of the network at some nodes can cause a renegotiation request for QoS change. This request comes as a notification from the resource renegotiation protocol to the host reporting that the reservation and allocation of host resources might change. There are two possibilities: the network can adapt to the overload or the network cannot adapt to the overload situation. In the former case, the network still needs to notify the host because some degradation may occur during the modification of resources (e.g., if the network tears down a connection and establishes a new connection). This actually may interrupt the media flow, so the host must react to this change. In the latter case, the source and application must adapt [VFJF99].

### 2.5.5.2    QoS Adaptation

We describe several mechanisms for QoS adaptation when fluctuation in resource availability is monitored. The adaptation mechanisms implicitly offer partial solutions for cases when the adaptation request comes from the user or the host system.

- **Network Adaptation:** The fixed routing and resource reservation for only lower QoS bounds (e.g., $QoS_{min}$), combined with load fluctuations in the range $[QoS_{min}, QoS_{max}]$, introduce possible problems of network unavailability for $QoS > QoS_{min}$. Thus, a proper balancing of the network load is desirable and necessary to (1) increase network availability, (2) allow network administrators to reclaim resources, and (3) reduce the impact of unscheduled run-time maintenance on clients with guaranteed services. Efficient routing and resource allocation decisions, made for previous clients, which made requests for QoS guarantees, reduce the probability that a new clients's request will be refused by the admission scheme. The more efficient the routing and resource allocation, the more guaranteed connection requests are accepted. One possibility for implementing a load balancing policy is to employ the following mechanisms: *QoS routing*, *performance monitoring* (detecting load changes), *dynamic rerouting* (changing the route) and *load balancing control* (making a decision to re-route a channel) [PZF92]. The QoS routing mechanism implements the routing algorithm, which selects a route in adherence to QoS requirements [MS97, CN97a], as discussed in Chapter 2.4.4. The performance monitoring mechanism monitors the appropriate network performance and reports it to the load balancing control. The dynamic rerouting mechanism is needed to establish the alternative route and to perform a transparent transition from the primary route to the alternative route. The load balancing control mechanism receives information from the performance monitoring mechanism and determines whether load balancing can be attempted using a load balancing algorithm defined by the policy. If load balancing can be attempted, the routing mechanism provides an alternative route and the transition from the primary route to the alternative route is accomplished using the dynamic re-routing mechanism. The adaptive resource scheme in this protocol is the *dynamic rerouting mechanism*. When channel $i$ is to be rerouted, the source tries to establish a new channel that has the same traffic and performance parameters and shares the same source and destination as channel $i$, but takes a different route. The new channel is called the *shadow channel* of channel $i$. After the shadow channel has been established, the source can switch from channel $i$ to the shadow channel and start sending packets on it. After waiting for the maximum end-to-end delay time of channel $i$, the source initiates a tear-down message for channel $i$. If the shadow channel shares part of the route with the old channel, it is desirable to let the two channels share resources. This further implies that the establishment and tear-down procedures are aware of this situation, so that the establishment does not request the new resource and the tear-down procedure does not free the old resource.

- **Source and Application Adaptation:** Another alternative reaction to changes in the network load is to adapt the source rate according to the currently available network resources. This approach requires *feedback* information from the network to the source which results in graceful degradation in the media quality during periods of congestion. For example, in [KMR93], the feedback control mechanism is based on predicting the evolution of the system state over time. The predicted system state is used to compute the target sending rate for each frame of video data. The adaptation policy strives to keep the bottleneck queue size for each connection at a constant level. Each switch monitors the buffer occupancy and service rate per connection. The buffer occupancy information is a count of the number of queued packets for the connection at the instant when the feedback message is sent. The rate information is the number of packets transmitted for the connection in the time interval between two feedback messages. There are two possibilities to implement the feedback transmission mechanism: (1) *per connection state information* is *periodically* appended to a data packet for the corresponding connection. At the destination, this information is extracted and sent back to the source. A switch updates the information fields in a packet only if the local service rate is lower than that reported by a previous switch along the path. (2) a feedback message is sent in a *separate control packet* which is sent back along the path of the connection towards the source.

There is a large body of work on end-system QoS adaptations to support multimedia streaming (e.g., [KR03], [HOV02], [LLZ03]). Other source adaptation schemes (for video traffic) may control the overload as follows:

- **Rate Control using Network Feedback:** In this approach, each source adapts to changes in network conditions caused by an increase or decrease in the number of connections or by sudden changes in the sending rates of existing connections. Changes in the traffic conditions are detected by explicit or implicit feedback from the network. Explicit feedback is in the form of information about the traffic loads or buffer occupancy levels. Implicit feedback information about packet losses and round robin delays is available from acknowledgements.

- **Traffic Shaping at Source:** Another way to control congestion is to smooth out traffic at the source. Typically, most of the burstiness reduction can be obtained by smoothing over an interval of 1-4 frames.

• **Hierarchical Coding:** Hierarchical coding describes algorithms which produce two or more types of packets describing the same block of pixels with different degrees of detail. However, these coders are more complex and use a greater amount of bandwidth to transmit images than single layer coders.

## 2.6  QoS Management Architectures

QoS specification, distribution, enforcement and related resource admission, reservation, allocation and provision services must be embedded in different components of the end-to-end multimedia computing and communication architecture. This means that proper services and protocols, discussed in this chapter, must be provided in the end-to-end architecture of a multimedia system.

Some examples of architectural choices, where QoS and resource management are designed and implemented, include the following:

• The *OSI architecture* provides QoS in the network layer and enhancements in the transport layer. The OSI 95 and later projects consider integrated QoS specification and negotiations in the transport protocols.

• *Lancaster's QoS architecture (QoS-A)* [CCH93] [Cam96] offers a framework to specify and implement the required performance properties of multimedia applications over high-performance networks such as ATM. QoS-A incorporates the notion of flows, service contract and flow management. The Management Enhanced Transport Service (METS) provides the functionality to contract QoS.

• The *Heidelberg Transport System (HeiTS)* [WH94] together with HeiRAT OS support is based on the ST-II network protocol and provides continuous media exchange with QoS guarantees, upcall structures, resource management and real-time mechanisms. HeiTS transfers continuous media data streams from one origin to one or multiple targets via multicast. HeiTS nodes negotiate QoS parameter values by exchanging flow specification to determine the resources required for delay, jitter, throughput and reliability.

• The *UC Berkeley Tenet Protocol Suite* with protocols such as RCAP, RTIP, RMTP, CMTP provides network QoS negotiation, reservation and resource administrations [BM91].

• The *Internet protocol stack*, based on IPv6, provides soft QoS guarantees using soft resource reservations if the RSVP protocol is used [ZDE+93]. Besides Integrated Services framework for support of QoS, also Differentiated Service framework was developed by IETF to support class based QoS requirements. At the session and application level new set of Internet media protocols was developed such as RTP (Real-time Transport Protocol) and its control protocol RTCP (Real-Time Control Protocol) [SCFJ96].

- *UPenn's OMEGA system* [NS96] offers framework for QoS management at the application and transport level. The QoS management entity, QoS Broker, represents the end-to-end control and management protocol and delivers QoS translation between multimedia application and communication subsystems, as well as negotiation and distribution of QoS parameters.

- The *Native Mode ATM Protocol Stack* [KS95], developed in the IDLInet (IIT Delhi Low-cost Integrated Network) testbed, provides extensive network QoS guarantees.

- *UIUC QualMan System* [KN97a] provides QoS-aware resource management architecture at the end-hosts and in integration with ATM QoS provision it delivers application end-to-end QoS guarantees.

- *UIUC 2kQ+ system* [WNGX01] provides a unified QoS management in the middleware level, and introduces an integrated approach of QoS translation, compilation, and reconfiguration of service components for distributed multimedia applications.

- *Lancaster GOPI system* [CC98] [CBD$^+$99] [CM01] [CBM02a] is a middleware framework which aims at the development of generic, configurable and extensible middleware. GOPI offers a generic framework for QoS specification and management and supports high level multimedia oriented programming environment that is backward compatible with the OMG's CORBA. At its lower levels it supports QoS-aware resource management.

- *BBN's QuO Middleware framework* [ZLSB98] [ZSL$^+$01] provides QoS extensions for CORBA messaging services and allows QoS guarantees for message passing and object manipulation services.

There exist many other QoS management frameworks in the networking, middleware/ system and application levels (e.g., [Cam97], [Abd99], [Li00], [SK00], [SDS02a], [LXN02a], [EGPE02]), and we have only enumerated few of them to show a historical perspective of the QoS architectures. It is important to note that QoS management and corresponding architectures started in the network level, and many early QoS architectural solutions were tied to QoS provision in ATM networks and QoS awareness in Internet (e.g., IntServ, IPv6). As the understanding about QoS problems grew, QoS management solutions and corresponding architectures moved towards inclusion of operating systems and applications. Currently, we see a lot of QoS management solutions and proposed QoS architectures in the middleware level, residing between OS/communication subsystem and applications (e.g., [LXN02b], [Pla02], [EGea02], [SDS02b], [CBM02b]). We will discuss results from some of these QoS management frameworks in more detail in the following chapters on Operating Systems and Networks.

## 2.7 Closing Remarks

Provision of end-to-end QoS guarantees is a challenging goal in multimedia systems. It is a challenge due to

- user expectations of multimedia processing and communication in a digital distributed environment which are always compared with the TV quality and radio quality networks;
- large heterogeneity of OS services (e.g., Windows, UNIX, Linux, WindowsCE;) running on different platforms (e.g., SUN workstations, Pentium PCs, handheld devices;
- large heterogeneity of network and transport protocols (e.g., RSVP, IPv6, RTP, RTSP, HTTP, UDP, TCP) running on different networks (e.g., Gigabit Ethernet, 100 Mbps Ethernet, ATM, 802.11 wireless networks, Bluetooth);
- increasing varieties in applications and their requirements; and
- different administrative domains and federated systems with very different policies and security restrictions.

To achieve this goal, above presented QoS and resource management must become an integral part of a distributed multimedia system. Furthermore, all discussed QoS mechanisms in this chapter need to be strongly connected to algorithms which we will present in the Chapters on Operating Systems, Networks and Communication.

# Multimedia Operating Systems

The operating system is the shield of the computer hardware against all software components. It provides a comfortable environment for the execution of programs, and it ensures effective utilization of the computer hardware. The operating system offers various services related to the essential resources of a computer: CPU, main memory, storage and all input and output devices.

For the processing of audio and video, multimedia application demands that humans perceive these media in a natural, error-free way. These continuous media data originate at sources like microphones, cameras and files. From these sources, the data are transferred to destinations like loudspeakers, video windows and files located at the same computer or at a remote station. On the way from source to sink, the digital data are processed by at least some type of move, copy or transmit operation. In this data manipulation process there are always many resources which are under the control of the operating system. The integration of discrete and continuous multimedia data demands additional services from many operating system components.

The major aspect in this context is real-time processing of continuous media data. Process management must take into account the timing requirements imposed by the handling of multimedia data. Appropriate scheduling methods should be applied. In contrast to the traditional real-time operating systems, multimedia operating systems also have to consider tasks without hard timing restrictions under the aspect of fairness as discussed in [PGHA00].

To obey timing requirements, single components are conceived as resources that are reserved prior to execution. This concept of resource reservation has to cover all resources on a data path, i.e., all resources that deal with continuous media. It also may affect parts of the application that process continuous media data. In distributed systems, for example, resource management also comprises network capacity [HVWW94]. The necessary concepts on Quality of Service (QoS) and resource management are presented in the Section on QoS.

The communication and synchronization between single processes must meet the restrictions of real-time requirements and timing relations among different media. The main memory is available as a shared resource to single processes.

In multimedia systems, memory management and corresponding buffer management have to provide access to data with a guaranteed timing delay and efficient data manipulation functions. For instance, physical data copy operations must be avoided due to their negative impact on performance; buffer management operations (such as are known from communication systems) should be used.

Database management is an important component in multimedia systems. However, database management abstracts the details of storing data on secondary media storage. Therefore, database management should rely on file management services provided by the multimedia operating system to access single files and file systems. For example, the incorporation of a CD-ROM XA file system as an integral part of a multimedia file system allows transparent and guaranteed continuous retrieval of audio and video data to any application using the file system; the database system is one of those applications. Various concepts of multimedia file systems are described in the Section on Media Servers.

Since the operating system shields devices from applications programs, it must provide services for device management too. In multimedia systems, the important issue is the integration of audio and video devices in a similar way to any other input/output device. The addressing of a camera can be performed similar to the addressing of a keyboard in the same system, although most current systems do not apply this technique.

An essential aspect of any multimedia operating system is the process management, hence we will mostly concentrate on multimedia scheduling problems. We will provide an overview of hard-real-time as well as soft-real-time scheduling algorithms and the overall scheduling framework for multimedia applications. Besides process management, we will present multimedia-related interprocess communication and synchronization concepts, buffer management for client/server multimedia systems, as well as design of device management. The chapter closes with the presentation of typical system multimedia architectures running on UNIX-like and Windows platforms.

## 3.1  Process Management

Process management deals with the resource *'main processor'*. The capacity of this resource is specified as processor capacity. The process manager maps single processes onto resources according to a specified scheduling policy such that all processes meet their requirements. In most systems, a process under control of the process manager can adopt one of the following states:

- In the *initial state*, no process is assigned to the program. The process is in the *idle state*.
- If a process is waiting for an event, i.e., the process lacks one of the necessary resources for processing, it is in the *blocked state*.
- If all necessary resources are assigned to the process, it is ready to run. The process only needs the processor for the execution of the program. The process is in the *ready state*.
- A process is running as long as the system processor is assigned to it. In this case, the process is in *running state*.

The process manager is the *scheduler*. This entity transfers a process into the ready-to-run state by assigning it a position in the respective queue of the dispatcher, which is the essential part of the operating system kernel. The dispatcher manages the context switch and hence the transition from the ready-to-run to the run state. In most operating systems, the next process to run is chosen according to a priority policy. Between processes with the same priority, the one with the longest ready time is chosen.

Current general-purpose existing operating systems must be considered for multimedia processing and be the basis of continuous media processing on workstations and personal computers. In the next years, there will certainly be no newly developed multimedia operating systems, which will be accepted in the market; therefore, existing multitasking systems must cope with multimedia data handling. The next paragraph provides a brief description of real-time support typically available in such systems.

### 3.1.1 Real-Time Processing Requirements

Continuous media data processing must occur in exactly predetermined—usually periodic—intervals. Operations on these data recur over and over and must be completed at certain deadlines. The real-time process manager determines a schedule for the CPU resource CPU that allows it to make reservations and to give processing guarantees. The problem is to find a feasible scheduler which schedules all time-critical continuous media tasks in a way that each of them can meet its deadlines. This must be guaranteed for all tasks in every period for the whole run-time of the system. In a multimedia system, continuous and discrete media data are processed concurrently.

For scheduling of multimedia tasks, two conflicting goals must be considered:

- An uncritical process should *not suffer from starvation* because time-critical processes are executed. Multimedia applications rely as much on text and graphics as on audio and video. Therefore, not all resources should be occupied by the time-critical processes and their management processes.

- On the other hand, a time-critical process must never be subject to *priority inversion*. The scheduler must ensure that any priority inversion (also between time-critical processes with different priorities) is avoided or reduced as much as possible.

Apart from the overhead caused by the schedulability test and the connection establishment, the costs for the scheduling of every message must be minimized. They are more critical because they occur periodically with every message during the processing of real-time tasks. The overhead generated by the scheduling and operating system is part of the processing time and therefore must be added to the processing time of the real-time tasks. Thus, it is favorable to keep them low. It is particularly difficult to observe the timing behavior of the operating system and its influence on the scheduling and the processing of time-critical data. It can lead to time garbling of application programs. Therefore, operating systems in real-time systems cannot be viewed as detached from the application programs and vice versa.

Real-time requirements of multimedia processes can be partitioned into two groups: (1) *hard-real-time requirements* and (2) *soft-real-time requirements*. Hard-real-time requirements mean that each deadline of a multimedia process must be guaranteed by the process management, and these guarantees are enforced by using concepts known from traditional real-time systems as discussed below. An example of a multimedia process with hard-real-time requirements is a video process within a telesurgery application where each pixel must be seen in precise timely fashion and with high resolution. Soft-real-time requirements mean that most of the deadlines of a multimedia process are guaranteed by the process management, but some deadlines can be violated over the duration of the task without any catastrophic consequences. These guarantees are enforced by using soft-real-time scheduling concepts as will be discussed below. An example of a multimedia process with soft-real-time requirements is a video process within a movie-on-demand application for entertainment purposes.

### 3.1.2  Traditional Real-Time Scheduling

The problem of real-time processing is widely known in computer science [HS89] [ea89] [SG90] [TK91]. Some real-time scheduling methods are employed in operations research. They differ from computer science real-time scheduling because they operate in a static environment, where no adaptation to changes of the workload is necessary [WC87].

The goal of traditional scheduling on time-sharing computers is *optimal throughput, optimal resource utilization and fair queuing*. In contrast, the main goal of real-time tasks is to provide a schedule that allows all, respectively, as many time-critical processes as possible, to be processed in time, according to their deadline. The scheduling algorithm must map tasks onto resources such that all tasks meet their time requirements. Therefore, it must be possible to show, or to prove, that a scheduling algorithm applied to real-time systems fulfills the timing requirements of the task.

There are several attempts to solve real-time scheduling problems. Many of them are just variations of basic algorithms. To find the best solutions for multimedia systems, two basic algorithms are analyzed, *Earliest Deadline First Algorithm and Rate Monotonic Scheduling*, and their advantages and disadvantages are elaborated. In the next section, a system model is introduced, and the relevant expressions are explained.

### 3.1.3   Real-time Scheduling: System Model

All scheduling algorithms to be introduced are based on the following system model for the scheduling of real-time tasks. Their essential components are the resources (as discussed previously), tasks and scheduling goals.

A *task* is a schedulable entity of the system, and it corresponds to the notion of a thread in the previous description. In a hard real-time system, a task is characterized by its *timing constraints*, as well as by its *resource requirements*. In the considered case, only periodic tasks without precedence constraints are discussed, i.e., the processing of two tasks is mutually independent. For multimedia systems, this can be assumed without any major restriction. Synchronized data, for example, can be processed by a single process.

The time constraints of the periodic task $T$ are characterized by the following parameters *(s, e, d, p)* as described in [LM80]:

- *s:* Starting point
- *e*: Processing time of $T$
- *d*: Deadline of $T$
- *p*: Period of $T$
- *r*: Rate of $T\left(r = \dfrac{1}{p}\right)$

whereby $0 \le e \le d \le p$ (see Figure 3-1). The starting point $s$ is the first time when the periodic task requires processing. Afterwards, it requires processing in every period with a processing time of $e$. At $s + (k-1)p$, the task $T$ is ready for $k$-processing. The processing of $T$ in period $k$ must be finished at $s + (k-1)p + d$. For continuous media tasks, it is assumed that the deadline of the period $(k-1)$ is the ready time of period $k$. This is known as the *congestion avoiding* deadlines: the deadline for each message ($d$) coincides with the period of the respective periodic task ($p$).

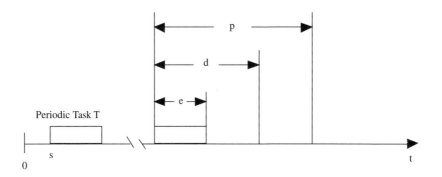

**Figure 3-1**   Characterization of periodic tasks.

Tasks can be *preemptive* or *non-preemptive*. A preemptive task can be interrupted by the request of any task with a higher priority. Processing is continued in the same state later on. A non-preemptive task cannot be interrupted until it voluntarily yields the processor. Any high-priority task must wait until the low-priority task is finished. The high-priority task is then subject to priority inversion. In the following, all tasks processed on the CPU are considered as preemptive unless otherwise stated.

In a real-time system, the scheduling algorithm must determine a schedule for an exclusive, limited resource that is used by different processes concurrently such that all of them can be processed without violating any deadlines. This notion can be extended to a model with multiple resources (e.g., CPU) of the same type. It can also be extended to cover different resources such as memory and bandwidth for communication, i.e., the function of a scheduling algorithm is to determine, for a given task set, whether or not a schedule for executing the tasks on an exclusive bounded resource exists, such that the timing and resource constraints of all tasks are satisfied (planning goal). Further, it must calculate a schedule if one exists. A scheduling algorithm is said to guarantee a newly arrived task if the algorithm can find a schedule where the new task and all previously guaranteed tasks can finish processing to their deadlines in every period over the whole run-time. If a scheduling algorithm guarantees a task, it ensures that the task finishes processing prior to its deadline [CSR88]. To guarantee tasks, it must be possible to check the schedulability of newly arrived tasks.

A major performance metric for a real-time scheduling algorithm is the guarantee ratio. The guarantee ratio is the total number of guaranteed tasks versus the number of tasks which could be processed.

Another performance metric is the processor utilization. This is the amount of processing time used by guaranteed tasks versus the total amount of processing time [LL73]:

$$U = \sum_{i=1}^{n} \frac{e_i}{p_i}$$

### 3.1.4 Soft-Real-Time Scheduling Concepts

Soft-real-time scheduling systems aim to satisfy soft-real-time requirements and their basic concepts of task modeling and scheduling are based on traditional real-time systems and their models as discussed above. However, due to their softer deadline constraints, there are several main differences between *soft-real-time (SRT)* systems and *hard-real-time (HRT)* systems such as (1) SRT systems are designed to run on general-purpose platforms to support multimedia applications, where HRT systems run on special-purpose platforms, (2) SRT systems must consider a richer set of load, for example, coexisting with time-sharing tasks, where HRT systems run HRT tasks only. In summary, the analysis of past existing operating systems shows that a multimedia-aware process management must solve the following problems:

- allow *dynamic co-existence and cooperation* of multiple independently authored real-time applications with varying timing and resource requirements in order to share limited physical resources available to them,
- allow for *co-existence of real-time and non-real-time applications*,
- allow for *scheduling of these different applications* and
- provide *protections between various applications*.

To solve these problems, soft-real-time scheduling frameworks started to become integral parts of process management in multimedia operating system solutions. The soft-real-time scheduling frameworks are currently moving in two basic directions to solve the above problems: (1) *reservation-based systems*, which provide timing guarantees even in overload situations, and (2) *adaptation-based systems*, which provide the best possible timing guarantees, but in case of scarce resources, achieve dynamic re-allocation of resources and deliver graceful degradation for multimedia applications. We will discuss in detail various concepts of the reservation-based systems as well as the adaptation-based systems in the next paragraphs.

### 3.1.4.1 Reservation-based Soft-Real-Time Systems

In order to achieve soft timing guarantees for multimedia applications in any load situation, we need to consider two important functions in the process management:

- *Reservation* of CPU bandwidth with its mechanisms and rules;
- *Scheduling* of CPU bandwidth with its mechanisms and rules;

The CPU management needs, in order to implement these functions, the following important components: (1) a *CPU broker entity*, and (2) a *SRT CPU scheduler/ dispatcher entity*.

The CPU broker provides the following services:

- *Schedulability Test*, which provides the admission control for the CPU scheduling. The schedulability test depends on the scheduling policy which the CPU scheduler uses to choose the next task processing.
- *CPU Reservation Operation,* which reserves CPU bandwidth according to given reservation policies. The granted reservation requests for CPU bandwidth are registered in a *reservation table* (dispatch-table).
- *Quality of Service Calculation*, which computes and prepares scheduling and other performance parameters, needed for the CPU scheduler to satisfy new admitted requests.

The SRT CPU scheduler performs the following services:

- *Scheduling Mechanisms*, which are guided by the scheduling policies.
- *Up-Call Mechanisms for Overrun or Underrun Cases*, which issue events to applications and the CPU broker to request adaptation of resource allocation and/ or renegotiation of new timing guarantees.

Next, we will present reservation concepts for the CPU bandwidth, as well as its mechanisms and policies. The scheduling mechanisms and policies will follow in the next subsection.

The reservation concept is based on the *processor capacity reserve abstraction* [LRM96], which allows the application thread to specify its CPU requirement in terms of its timing guarantees. The application thread specifies to the CPU broker (via an Application Programming Interface (API)) timing quality of service parameters such as the period ($p$) or its CPU utilization in percentage ($U$) within the period. For example, application threads can specify their timing behavior for periodic process in the form of ($p=50ms,\ U=40\%$), which means that the task will require *20 ms* of processing time within the period of *50 ms*. In general, applications can provide their timing behavior in form of time graphs if such exist.

**Reservation Mechanisms**   Using the above API, the application threads send their timing requirements to the CPU broker. The broker performs first the admission control, which is determined by the scheduling policy (see Subsections of Earliest Deadline First and Rate-Monotonic Scheduling Policies). Testing the schedulability determines if the thread can be admitted or not. If the thread is admitted, the process management guarantees its soft timing requirements. Furthermore, the admitted thread is inserted into the waiting queue of other admitted soft-real-time threads (this is done by setting the priority of the thread onto the level of "waiting" priorities). The CPU broker then computes the new schedule, based on the scheduling policy used by the CPU scheduler, and writes it into the dispatch table. If the thread is not admitted, the thread has two options, either it exits and tries later to get admission into the set of soft-real-time processing, or it can execute as a best effort thread with no timing guarantees at all[1]. Note that the CPU bandwidth is partitioned into the bandwidth for soft-real-time threads and bandwidth for best effort threads in order to avoid starvation for the best effort threads. This means that some fixed bandwidth is set aside during the installation process for best effort tasks only. A possible rule of thumb is *70/30*, which means *70%* for soft-real-time tasks and *30%* for best effort tasks. This partitioning is soft in the sense that if some of the CPU bandwidth in the soft-real-time partition is not used, it will be released for best-effort usage.

The *CPU broker process* may be implemented as a background daemon process with superuser status privileges, running at the time sharing dynamic user priority level [CN99] or as a kernel process. It can be started during the system startup as any other system daemon for networks and file systems. The CPU broker wakes up if a new application admission request arrives. The broker must be a superuser process in order to be able to change priorities of admitted threads/processes from user-level priorities to real-time priority range. Note that the CPU broker is not a dispatcher, as it only puts the admitted threads into the "waiting" RT priority range. The reason is that because the CPU broker is responsible for admission control and handling incoming admission requests, the processing time of these requests can vary which would cause violation of deadlines for scheduled tasks. Also the admission control does not have to occur in real-time, therefore the CPU broker runs at a dynamic priority level. So the scheduling of any soft-real-time threads is done by the soft-real-time scheduler and its dispatcher, which are real-time processes. This split of responsibilities between the CPU broker and the CPU scheduler/dispatcher allows the application threads to start as user threads at time-sharing dynamic priority level, and if they are admitted, their priority changes to fixed real-time priority range.

The *reservation table (dispatch table)* is an object in the shared memory which is filled by the CPU broker with the reserved CPU bandwidth values per thread in form of a schedule. The dispatcher reads the entries to find out which thread to dispatch next. The reservation table must be pinned to the memory in order to allow for efficient reading and writing. An example of a reservation table [KN98] for a rate-monotonic scheduling policy is shown in Table 3-1.

---

[1] In best effort case, the multimedia thread may see large jitters resulting either in fast forward or slow motion behaviors.

| Entry Number | Time | Process-PID |
|---|---|---|
| 0 | 0-10 ms | 721 |
| 1 | 10-20 ms | 773 774 775 |
| 2 | 20-30 ms | 721 |
| 3 | 30-40 ms | free |

**Table 3-1**    Example of a reservation table.

The table includes time entries, where each entry is associated with soft-real-time process IDs (PID), that are admitted and considered for soft-real-time scheduling in that time slice. Each time slice can have assigned either one soft-real-time or a group of cooperating processes.

As the Table 3-1 shows, we consider four processes, being scheduled with the rate-monotonic scheduling policy, where the process *PID 721* has the period of *20 ms* and the processing time of *10 ms*, and the cooperative processes *PIDs 773/774/775* have all together the period of *40ms* and processing time of *10ms*. The common time period for all admitted soft-real-time processes is *40ms (GCD(T721,T773,774,775))*. This means that if we have a time slice of size *10 ms*, we will have four time slices in this example, where the first three time slices are assigned, and the forth time slice is free. The free time slice can be used for the best effort time sharing threads/processes. Once the time slice expires, the best effort thread is preempted and soft-real-time thread with *PID 721* is dispatched. The minimal number of free time slots is managed by the CPU broker, depending how big the best effort (time sharing) partition is. The reservation table in Table 3-1 indicates that *25% (10 ms* out of *40ms)* is guaranteed for time sharing threads/processes. The system administrator can change the partition amount depending what load is anticipated. For example, if a system is planned to be heavily loaded with multimedia applications, the best effort partition can be very small, and vice versa.

*Real-time Probing and Real-time Profiling* are important reservation mechanisms to assist multimedia applications in determining thread processing times. If we assume that the CPU scheduling uses its schedulability test, and the reservation allows to guarantee the required processing time, then the application programmer has the problem to determine the processing time e, which is needed for the reservation and scheduling test. In hard-real-time systems, the system designers either do the worst case modeling of their processing times, or run extensive tests and determine by system testing the worst case processing time for each instruction or task. In soft-real-time systems, where multimedia tasks are written to be able to run independently of any platform, the processing time will change on different hardware platforms and over different operating systems. Therefore, it is difficult to hard-code the processing time information into the program. Furthermore, the multimedia tasks and their data content, such as MPEG compressed movies, will yield very different processing times per frame on a PC or workstation. Therefore, the soft-real-time scheduling framework may deploy a probing algorithm to allow the application to estimate an average processing time, needed for the reservation process [NHK96b]. The probing service runs the application thread few iterations of its task without any CPU reservation in a lightly loaded CPU system environment if possible, and the profiling service measures the processing times of the thread. The probing algorithm computes the average processing time from all the measured data points and stores the resulting value for that thread in its quality of service application profile, which is associated with the specific hardware platform. For example, a MpegDecoder.Profile application profile can have the following structure: (*Platform = Ultra1, Resolution= 352x240,e = 40ms*) and (*Platform = SPARC 10, Resolution = 352x240, e = 80ms*). Using the probed value, stored in the profile, an application can then compute required utilization as $U = e/p$, in order to request a reservation.

**Implementation of Reservation Mechanisms**   To enforce the reservation, negotiated by the CPU broker, there exist many possible implementations. Here we will provide one approach. At the end of discussion on process management we will present case studies of various reservation-based schedulers and there, other possible implementations will be described.

The implementation and enforcement of the reservation mechanism is based on *priority mechanisms* within the SRT CPU scheduler/dispatcher [KYO96, CN99]. The SRT CPU scheduler process runs at the highest fixed priority (even higher than the FIFO CPU scheduler of the general purpose OS where the soft-real-time scheduling framework is implemented), so that it is able to preempt any other soft-real-time or non-real-time process/thread. The soft-real-time CPU scheduler wakes up periodically (e.g., every *10 ms*) and checks the reservation table to decide which process needs to be scheduled and dispatched next. The dispatching function of the scheduler relies on a specific priority structure, to do the appropriate context switching and enforce reservation.

| | Priority | Process |
|---|---|---|
| RT- reserved class | highest | Dispatcher |
| | second highest | Running RT-Process |
| | .... | Unused |
| TS-class | each | Each TS-Process |
| RT- waiting class | lowest | Waiting RT-Processes |

**Table 3-2**   Priority scheduling structure.

The priority structure for the soft-real-time scheduling framework is divided into three parts as shown in Table 3-2: (1) the *real-time partition* (RT reserved class) with the fixed real-time priorities, which is used by the soft-real-time CPU scheduler, and the currently running (reserved) process/thread, (2) the *time-sharing partition* (TS class) which is used by the best effort time sharing processes/threads, and (3) the *waiting partition* (RT waiting class with the lowest possible priority in the system) which is used by the waiting soft-real-time processes/threads[2].

The SRT CPU scheduler wakes up periodically and performs *priority switching* when a new reserved process is supposed to be dispatched and the reserved time of the currently running soft-real-time process is over. It means that the CPU scheduler changes the priority of the current running real-time process from the RT reserved class priority to the RT waiting class priority and the next process from the reservation table which should be running next will be switched from the RT waiting class to the RT running class. If no process waits in the RT waiting class, the soft-real-time scheduler goes to sleep and the regular OS CPU scheduler (e.g., the UNIX scheduler) takes over to schedule the time sharing processes/threads. Again once the soft-real-time scheduler wakes up, it preempts the TS tasks and the OS CPU scheduler and checks for next reserved processes to run.

The above implementation of the reservation mechanism has several advantages when compared to other implementations of the processor capacity reserve concept [MT94]:

- Existing OS kernels do not have to be changed as this implementation can be provided in user space if the general purpose OS provides real-time extension capabilities.

- The computational overhead is low.

- This approach allows for implementation and portability flexibility as one can implement various scheduling policies in the soft-real-time scheduler and update the software anytime independent of new OS versions.

The disadvantage of the above implementation is the time granularity at which a user-level SRT scheduler can operate. It is clear that a user-level SRT scheduler will operate at a coarser time granularity than a kernel-level SRT scheduler. For example, in a Solaris environment, a user-level SRT CPU scheduler may operate at the granularity of *10 ms* [CN99], hence if there is a need of a finer granularity scheduling and control of multimedia tasks, other solutions need to be deployed.

---

[2] Note that this is the priority level at which any new admitted thread waits.

**Reservation Policies**  For management and distribution of resource reservations, we need to consider various aspects of reservation policies. There are several considerations that the reservation policy management needs to make [Ven98, KN98, MT94]:

- **Reservation Mode**: There are two types of reservations, the *immediate reservation and the advanced reservation*. In the case of immediate reservation scheme, when the reservation request arrives, it will be immediately served, and the thread will be immediately scheduled if admitted. In case of advanced reservation scheme, the CPU broker needs to keep information about current and future reservation and make the admission control for future scheduled requests. Here, the thread plans to run at some point in the future, and not immediately. This also means that the advanced reservation admission control requires modification when compared to the immediate reservation scheme. The thread needs to specify not only the period and utilization, but also the starting and finishing time point of the task processing to make accurate estimation how many threads can run simultaneously in the future.

- **Quality of Service (QoS) Range and Reservation:** Many QoS parameters are defined within an acceptance range. It means that the QoS values can be specified as the pair of values *($QoS_{min}$, $QoS_{max}$)* or the triple of values *($QoS_{min}$, $QoS_{ave}$, $QoS_{max}$)*. For example, the CPU bandwidth for an MPEG video can have specified minimal processing time of *10ms* and average processing time of *20ms*. Because of the QoS range specification, it is necessary that the reservation policy determines if the thread should be admitted based on its minimal value or its average value or its maximal value. It means that the system may have (1) *minimal reservation policy*, (2) *average reservation policy,* and (3) *maximum reservation policy.*

  - The *minimal reservation policy* yields the admission control based on minimal QoS values, which can lead to large violation of timing guarantees if the multimedia data exhibits large variations. This policy may be useful for multimedia threads where their data has almost constant data size (e.g., Motion JPEG).

  - The *average reservation policy* yields admission control based on average QoS values. This policy may cause some timing violations of the multimedia thread, but as we discuss soft-real-time scheduling frameworks, it is expected that some deadlines will not be met. This policy may be very useful for multimedia tasks with data causing occasional processing variations (e.g., MPEG data with large GOP sequence with most frames being P and B frames).

  - The *maximum reservation policy* yields admission control based on worst case QoS values. This policy will guarantee that all timing deadlines will be met and represents the hard-real-time spectrum. This approach may be used if there are multimedia threads that need strong guarantees.

- **Reservation Ordering:** Reservation policies can assist in determining the ordering of serving reservation requests. There are two types of policies: (1) *First-Come-First-Serve (FCFS) Ordering*, where the reservation requests are served in the order of arrival, and (2) *Priority-based Ordering*, where each reservation request will be marked with a priority according to reservation importance and the CPU broker processes all request according to decreasing priority order. The priority-based reservation allows to differentiate among the requests and partition the requests into general and important requests. However, the priority-based approach has the disadvantage that some general reservation requests may starve. One possibility to remedy this problem is to store the non-satisfied general reservation requests and raise the reservation priority after certain threshold time interval.

- **Reservation Holding Policies:** An important deadlock problem arises in reservation-based soft-real-time systems when multiple CPU resources, or multiple different resources perform reservations. Especially in a distributed system, where one computing node (e.g., source) already reserved CPU and is holding that resource, and another node (destination) runs into problems, such as local deadlock situation over trying to reserve multiple resources (CPU and disk) or other system/network problems, causing no response to the source and no usage of the already holding reservation at the source. In this case we need to have reservation holding policies, it means how long do we hold of reservation which is not used. There exist multiple possibilities:

    - *Time-out Policy,* where the CPU broker sets a timer and the reservation is valid only for a certain period of time. After the time expires, and the reservation is not used (this is in the case of immediate reservation), the reservation expires and is removed from the reservation table. This approach requires that the CPU broker, which frees an existing reservation due to time-out, also informs other brokers along the end-to-end processing and communication path to free the overall end-to-end reservation.

    - *Aging Policy,* where the CPU broker decreases gradually the reservation as the time progresses and the reservation is not used. For example, the CPU broker could start with reserved maximum QoS value, and after certain time-out interval, the QoS value will be degraded to average QoS value, and so on. The last level would be then the degradation to the minimum QoS level before the reservation expires.

    - *Priority-based Policy,* where based on the importance of the reservation some reservations with low priority expire after the time-out interval.

**Extensions of Reservation Concept** Using the above reservation mechanisms and policies we can extend the notion of reservation to soft-real-time processes that support rich timing behaviors and partition the soft-real-time processes/threads into different service classes according to their timing behavior (similarly to the networks as they perform their differentiation of services). At the beginning of the discussion about reservation we have specified that each soft real-time process needs to provide parameters such as the period p and the processing time e to the CPU broker to request a reservation. If we take a closer look at the parameter space, we can partition the soft-real-time tasks into the following CPU Service Classes [CN99, YNK01]:

- **PCPT Class:** If we consider, besides the period $p$, the processing time parameter $e$ as the *peak processing time (PPT)*, then these types of processes/threads represent the *Periodic Constant Processing Time (PCPT)* class of applications. In the PCPT class, the admission control is done with the PPT parameter, hence the system guarantees the worst case processing usage. However, systems that support only the PCPT class are insufficient to handle variable processing time class of applications such as MPEG decoding threads.

- **PVPT Class**: If we consider, besides the period $p$, the processing time $e$ as a pair of the *Sustainable Processing Time (SPT)* and P*eak Processing Time (PPT)*, and a new parameter, called *Burst (BT)*, then these types of applications represent the *Periodic Variable Processing Time (PVPT)* class. In this class, the admission control is done with the SPT parameter, hence the soft-real-time scheduling guarantees only SPT processing usage. The parameters PPT and BT are used in a conformance test that checks if the process behaves according to its reservation contract. It means that as long the process/thread experiences SPT violation and the soft-real-time process runs at PPT level within the specified burst BT, the reservation is preserved and no adaptation is necessary.

- **ACPU Class:** If we consider a class of applications that does not have a fixed period, but it requires guarantee on *Peak Processing Utilization (PPU)* of the processor time, then this type of applications represents the *Aperiodic Constant Processing Utilization (ACPU)* class. Given that ACPU class does not have a period specification, an ACPU process needs a relative deadline at the start of each iteration during its execution.

- **Event Class:** If we consider specification of period $p$ and processing time $e$ as peak processing time that applies only for one period $p$, then this type of applications represent the *Event* class.

To implement the scheduling structure for supporting various CPU service classes, different approaches have been taken [CN99, GGV96]. The case studies at the end of the discussion on process management describe some of the possible implementations.

### 3.1.4.2    Adaptation-based Soft-Real-Time Systems

Adaptation-based soft-real-time systems usually need to adapt and deal with overrun situations in SRT systems to accommodate bursts and overloads. Overruns occur in soft-real-time systems if real-time processes indicate only their minimal or average requirements, however bursts and overload situations occur during their processing. Some SRT systems will aim to adjust and gracefully adapt all real-time processes, some may adjust only the process that experiences overruns and may cause overruns to other processes. However, most of the adaptation-based soft-real-time systems assume adaptive applications which can adjust themselves in overload situations.

Adaptation-based systems can be partitioned into two groups: (1) adaptation systems where *no reservation concept* exists at all, and the adaptation relies mostly on adaptive applications, and (2) adaptation systems with *reservation concept*, but reservation is based on minimum, or average QoS values, hence overruns and violations happen, and the reservation must be adapted and renegotiated.

**Adaptive systems with no reservation**    The first group relies on priority mechanisms where the soft-real-time applications are scheduled with higher priorities than non-real-time threads, and if overload happens, dynamic feedback exists to adaptive applications to allow them to adapt gracefully to the current load. In these systems, the applications also provide explicit time constraints in the form of deadline and processing time, and initial admission happens. However, all real-time tasks run in a RT class at the same time, and share the CPU within this class [NL97}. Hence, if there is an overload situation, or other situation that causes resource fluctuation as new applications come and go, the system adapts by changing resource allocation for all real-time tasks in the RT class, as well as by providing feedback to applications for graceful adaptation. Furthermore, the policy here is that the system should not degrade the performance of a high priority application in the presence of a low priority application. At the end of the discussion on process management we will provide some case studies of such systems and present their specific implementation issues.

**Adaptive reservation systems**    The second group relies on changing reservations for soft-real-time threads when overruns and deadline violations happen[3]. As described above, overruns can happen if minimal or average reservation policies are applied. Also, if overruns repeat many times, it means that the reservation was wrongly estimated, then the reservation needs to be adjusted. The adaptation of reservation can be done either by the system (CPU broker) or by the application.

---

[3] In this adaptation approach, only the reservation of one real-time process, which experiences overruns, is adjusted. Hence, all other well-behaved applications are protected from the overload situation.

- **System-initiated Adaptation** [CN99] can automatically adjust the parameters in the reservation table for RT processes based on the monitored processor usage time. A soft-real-time application can choose from two adaptation strategies:

  - *exponential average strategy*, which is based on the following formula:

  $$X_i = (1 - \alpha) \times X_{i-1} + \alpha \times X_i$$

  where $X$ is the guaranteed processing time and $0 < \alpha < 1$ represents the relative weight between the current $X_i$ value and the previous $X_{i-1}$ in determining the new $X_i$.

  - *statistical strategy* is based on two parameters: frequency of non-conforming overruns $f$ and window size $ws$. It will adjust $X$ to a level where no more than ($f*ws$) number of non-conforming overruns can occur within the $ws$ number of interactions. For example, if ($f = 0.4$, $ws = 5$) and a process has its most recent 5 processing usage history as (*53ms, 50ms, 30ms, 40ms, 55ms*), then the statistical adaptation will adjust $X$ to 50 ms so that only 2 non-conforming overruns (>50ms) occur.

The adaptation strategies can assist in supporting the various CPU service classes.

- **Application-initiated Adaptation** relies on upcalls from the soft-real-time scheduling system to applications threads, where then applications adapt according to their own semantics and issue a new reservation request to the CPU broker for their processing.

**Comparison between Reservation-based and Adaptation-based Soft-Real-time Scheduling Systems**    There are trade-offs between the two approaches. Even within the same approach, different properties can be optimized, hence creating different solutions for multimedia computing environments.

The reservation-based systems provide better handling of timing guarantees of admitted schedulable units under any load conditions, especially if the reservation is based on worst case QoS values. However, the disadvantage such as lower resource utilization, inflexible allocation in case of changes in application behavior, and fairness violation need to be carefully weighted when considering these solutions.

On the other hand, the adaptation-based solutions show high resource utilization and fairness. These solutions show timing guarantees in underload and normal load situations. In case of overloads, it comes to adaptation choices such as dynamic feedback and application adaptation. Therefore, we must also consider seriously the disadvantage of this approach, such as the violation of deadlines in case of overloads and dependency on adaptive capabilities of running applications.

### 3.1.5   Scheduling Policies

SRT systems utilize for multimedia task scheduling mostly the two following scheduling algorithms: the *earliest deadline first algorithm* and the *rate-monotonic algorithm*. In the following paragraphs we will discuss in detail their concepts, extensions and trade-offs.

### 3.1.5.1    Earliest Deadline First Algorithm

The *Earliest Deadline First (EDF)* algorithm is one of the best-known algorithms for real-time processing. At every new ready state, the scheduler selects the task with the earliest deadline among the tasks that are ready and not fully processed. The requested resource is assigned to the selected task. At any arrival of a new task (according to the LBAP model), EDF must be computed immediately leading to a new order, i.e., the running task is preempted and the new task is scheduled according to its deadline. The new task is processed immediately if its deadline is earlier than that of the interrupted task. The processing of the interrupted task is continued according to the EDF algorithm later on. EDF is not only an algorithm for periodic tasks, but also for tasks with arbitrary requests, deadlines and service execution times [Der74]. In this case, no guarantee about the processing of any task can be given.

EDF is an *optimal, dynamic* algorithm, i.e., it produces a valid schedule whenever one exists. A dynamic algorithm schedules every instance of each incoming task according to its specific demands. Tasks of periodic processes must be scheduled in each period again. With n tasks which have arbitrary ready-times and deadlines, the complexity is $\Theta(n^2)$.

For a dynamic algorithm like EDF, the upper bound of the processor utilization is *100%*. Compared with any static priority assignment, EDF is optimal in the sense that if a set of tasks can be scheduled by any static priority assignment it also can be scheduled by EDF. With a priority-driven system scheduler, each task is assigned a priority according to its deadline. The highest priority is assigned to the task with the earliest deadline; the lowest to the one with the furthest. With every arriving task, priorities might have to be adjusted.

Applying EDF to the scheduling of continuous media data on a single processor machine with priority scheduling, process priorities are likely to be rearranged quite often. A priority is assigned to each task ready for processing according to its deadline. Common systems usually provide only a restricted number of priorities. If the computed priority of a new process is not available, the priorities of other processes must be rearranged until the required priority is free. In the worst case, the priorities of all processes must be rearranged. This may cause considerable overhead. The EDF scheduling algorithm itself makes no use of the previously known occurrence of periodic tasks.

EDF is used by different models as a basic algorithm. An extension of EDF is the *Time-Driven Scheduler (TDS)*. Tasks are scheduled according to their deadlines.

Further, the TDS is able to handle overload situations. If an overload situation occurs the scheduler aborts tasks which cannot meet their deadlines anymore. If there is still an overload situation, the scheduler removes tasks which have a low "value density". The value density corresponds to the importance of a task for the system.

In [LLSY91] another *priority-driven EDF* scheduling algorithm is introduced. Here, every task is divided into a mandatory and an optional part. A task is terminated according to the deadline of the mandatory part, even if it is not completed at this time. Tasks are scheduled with respect to the deadline of the mandatory parts. A set of tasks is said to be schedulable if all tasks can meet the deadlines of their mandatory parts. The optional parts are processed if the resource capacity is not fully utilized. Applying this to continuous media data, the method can be used in combination with the encoding of data according to their importance. Take, for example, a single uncompressed picture in a bitmap format. Each pixel of this monochrome picture is coded with 16 bits. The processing of the eight most significant bits is mandatory, whereas the processing of the least-significant bits can be considered optional. With this method, more processes can be scheduled. In an overload situation, the optional parts are aborted. This implementation leads to decreased quality by media scaling. During QoS requirement specification, the tasks were accepted or informed that scaling may occur. In such a case, scaling QoS parameters can be introduced which reflect the respective implementation. Therefore, this approach avoids errors and improves system performance at the expense of media quality.

### 3.1.5.2  Rate Monotonic Algorithm

The *rate monotonic scheduling* principle was introduced by Liu and Layland in 1973 [LL73]. It is an optimal, static, priority-driven algorithm for preemptive, periodic jobs. Optimal in this context means that there is no other static algorithm that is able to schedule a task set which cannot be scheduled by the rate monotonic algorithm. A process is scheduled by a static algorithm at the beginning of the processing. Subsequently, each task is processed with the priority calculated at the beginning. No further scheduling is required. The following five assumptions are necessary prerequisites to apply the rate monotonic algorithm:

1. The requests for all tasks with deadlines are periodic, i.e., have constant intervals between consecutive requests.
2. The processing of a single task must be finished before the next task of the same data stream becomes ready for execution. Deadlines consist of runability constraints only, i.e., each task must be completed before the next request occurs.
3. All tasks are independent. This means that the requests for a certain task do not depend on the initiation or completion of requests for any other task.
4. Run-time for each request of a task is constant. Run-time denotes the maximum time which is required by a processor to execute the task without interruption.

5. Any non-periodic task in the system has no required deadline. Typically, they initiate periodic tasks or are tasks for failure recovery. They usually displace periodic tasks.

Further work has shown that not all of these assumptions are mandatory to employ the rate monotonic algorithm [LSST91] [SKG91]. Static priorities are assigned to tasks, once at the connection set-up phase, according to their request rates. The priority corresponds to the importance of a task relative to other tasks. Tasks with higher request rates will have higher priorities. The task with the shortest period gets the highest priority and the task with the longest period gets the lowest priority.

The rate monotonic algorithm is a simple method to schedule time-critical, periodic tasks on the respective resource. A task will always meet its deadline, if this can be proven to be true for the longest response time. The response time is the time span between the request and the end of processing the task. This time span is maximal when all processes with a higher priority request to be processed at the same time. This case is known as the critical instant (see Figure 3-2). In this figure, the priority of *a* is, according to the rate monotonic algorithm, higher than *b*, and *b* is higher than *c*. The critical time zone is the time interval between the critical instant and the completion of a task.

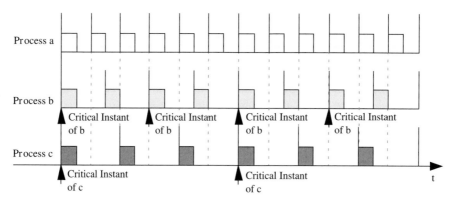

**Figure 3-2**   Example of critical instants.

### 3.1.5.3    EDF and Rate Monotonic: Context switches

Consider an audio and a video stream scheduled according to the rate monotonic algorithm. Let the audio stream have a rate of 1/75 s/sample and the video stream a rate of 1/25 s/frame. The priority assigned to the audio stream is then higher than the priority assigned to the video stream. The arrival of messages from the audio stream will interrupt the processing of the video stream. If it is possible to complete the processing of a video message that requests processing at the critical instant before its deadline, the processing of all video messages to their deadlines is ensured, thus a feasible schedule exists.

If more than one stream is processed concurrently in a system, it is very likely that there might be more context switches with a scheduler using the rate monotonic algorithm than one using EDF. Figure 3-3 shows an example.

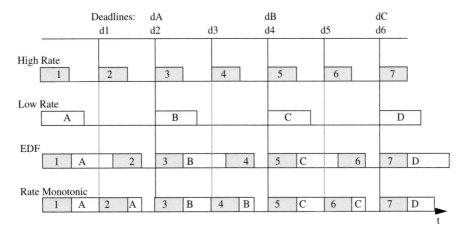

**Figure 3-3**   Rate monotonic versus EDF: context switches in preemptive systems.

### 3.1.5.4    EDF and Rate Monotonic: Processor Utilizations

The processor utilization of the rate monotonic algorithm is upper bounded. It depends on the number of tasks which are scheduled, their processing times and their periods. There are two issues to be considered:

1. The upper bound of the processor utilization, which is determined by the critical instant.

2. For each number $n$ of independent tasks $t(j)$, a constellation can be found, where the maximum possible processor utilization is minimal. The least upper bound of the processor utilization is the minimum of all processor utilizations over all sets of tasks $t(j)$; $j \in (1, \ldots, n)$ that fully utilize the CPU. A task set fully utilizes the CPU, when it is not possible to raise the processing time of one task without violating the schedule.

Following this assumption, [LL73] gives an estimation of the maximal processor utilization, where the processing of each task to its deadline is guaranteed for any constellation. A set of $m$ independent, periodic tasks with fixed priority will always meet its deadline if:

$$U(m) = m \times \left(2^{\frac{1}{m}} - 1\right) \geq \frac{e_1}{p_1} + \ldots + \frac{e_m}{p_m}$$

According to [LS86] and [LL73], for large $m$, the least upper bound of the processor utilization is $U = ln2$. Hence, it is sufficient to check if the processor utilization is less than or equal to the given upper bound to find out if a task set is schedulable or not. Most existing systems check this by simply comparing the processor utilization with the value of $ln2$.

With EDF, a processor utilization of 100% can be achieved because all tasks are scheduled dynamically according to their deadlines. Figure 3-4 shows an example where the CPU can be utilized to 100% with EDF, but where rate monotonic scheduling fails.

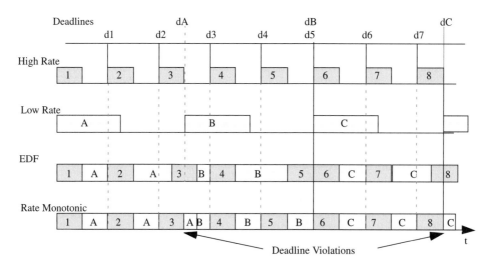

**Figure 3-4**   Rate monotonic versus EDF: process utilization.

The problem of underutilizing the processor is aggregated by the fact that, in most cases, the average task execution time is considerably lower than the worst case execution time. Therefore, scheduling algorithms should be able to handle transient processor overload. The rate monotonic algorithm on average ensures that all deadlines will be met even if the bottleneck utilization is well above 80%. With one deadline postponement, the deadlines on average are met when the utilization is over 90%. [SSL89] mentions an achieved utilization bound for the Nowy's Inertial Navigation System of 88%.

As described above, a static algorithm schedules a process once at the beginning of processing. Single tasks are not explicitly scheduled afterwards. A dynamic algorithm schedules every incoming task according to its specific demands. Since the rate monotonic algorithm is an optimal static algorithm, no other static algorithm can achieve a higher processor utilization.

### 3.1.5.5    Extensions to Rate Monotonic Scheduling

There are several extensions to this algorithm. One of them divides a task into a *mandatory* and an *optional* part. The processing of the mandatory part delivers a result which can be accepted by the user. The optional part only refines the result. The mandatory part is scheduled according to the rate monotonic algorithm. For the scheduling of the optional part, other, different policies are suggested [CL88, CL89, LLN87].

In some systems there are aperiodic tasks next to periodic ones. To meet the requirements of periodic tasks and the response time requirements of aperiodic requests, it must be possible to schedule both aperiodic and periodic tasks. If the aperiodic request is an aperiodic continuous stream (e.g., video images as part of a slide show), we have the possibility to transform it into a periodic stream. Every timed data item can be substituted by n items. The new items have the duration of the minimal life span. The number of streams is increased, but since the life span is decreased, the semantic remains unchanged. The stream is now periodical because every item has the same life span [Her90]. If the stream is not continuous, we can apply a sporadic server to respond to aperiodic requests. The server is provided with a computation budget. This budget is refreshed t units of time after it has been exhausted. Earlier refreshing is also possible. The budget represents the computation time reserved for aperiodic tasks. The server is only allowed to preempt the execution of periodic tasks as long as the computation budget is not exhausted. Afterwards, it can only continue the execution with a background priority. After refreshing the budget, the execution can resume at the server's assigned priority. The sporadic server is especially suitable for events that occur rarely, but must be handled quickly (e.g., a telepointer in a CSCW application) [SG90, Spr90, SSL89].

The rate monotonic algorithm is, for example, applied in real-time systems and real-time operating systems by NASA and the European Space Agency. It is particularly suitable for continuous media data processing because it makes optimal use of their periodicity. Since it is a static algorithm, there is nearly no rearrangement of priorities and hence – in contrast to EDF – no scheduling overhead to determine the next task with the highest priority. Problems emerge with data streams which have no constant processing time per message, as specified in MPEG-2 (e.g., a compressed video stream where one of five pictures is a full picture and all others are updates of a reference picture). The simplest solution is to schedule these tasks according to their maximum data rate. In this case, the processor utilization is decreasing. The idle time of the CPU can be used to process non-time-critical tasks. In multimedia systems, for example, this is the processing of discrete media.

### 3.1.5.6    Other Policies for In-Time Scheduling

Apart from the two methods previously discussed, further scheduling algorithms have been evaluated regarding their suitability for the processing of continuous media data. In the following paragraphs, the most significant approaches are briefly described and the reasons for their non-suitability, compared to EDF and rate-monotonic, are enumerated.

*Least Laxity First (LLF).* The task with the shortest remaining laxity is scheduled first [CW90, LS86]. The laxity is the time between the actual time $t$ and the deadline minus the remaining processing time. The laxity in period $k$ is:

$$l_k = (s + (k-1)p + d) - (t + e)$$

LLF is an *optimal, dynamic* algorithm for *exclusive resources*. Furthermore, it is an optimal algorithm for multiple resources if the ready-times of the real-time tasks are the same. The *laxity* is a function of a deadline, the processing time and the current time. Thereby, the processing time cannot be exactly specified in advance. When calculating the laxity, the worst case is assumed. Therefore, the determination of the laxity is inexact. The laxity of waiting processes dynamically changes over time. During the run-time of a task, another task may get a lower laxity. This task must then preempt the running task. Consequently, tasks can preempt each other several times without dispatching a new task. This may cause numerous context switches. At each scheduling point (when a process becomes ready-to-run or at the end of a time slice), the laxity of each task must be newly determined. This leads to an additional overhead compared with EDF. Since we have only a single resource to schedule, there is no advantage in the employment of LLF compared with EDF. Future multimedia systems might be multi-processor systems; here, LLF might be of advantage.

*Deadline Monotone Algorithm.* If the deadlines of tasks are less than their period ($d_i < p_i$), the prerequisites of the rate monotonic algorithm are violated. In this case, a fixed priority assignment according to the deadlines of the tasks is optimal. A task $T_i$ gets a higher priority than a task $T_j$ if $d_i < d_j$. No effective schedulability test for the deadline monotone algorithm exists. To determine the schedulability of a task set, each task must be checked if it meets its deadline in the worst case. In this case, all tasks require execution to their critical instant [LW82, LSST91]. Tasks with a deadline shorter than their period, for example, arise during the measurements of temperature or pressure in control systems. In multimedia systems, deadlines equal to period lengths can be assumed.

*Shortest Job First (SJF).* The task with the shortest remaining computation time is chosen for execution [CW90, Fre82]. This algorithm guarantees that as many tasks as possible meet their deadlines under an overload situation if all of them have the same deadline. In multimedia systems where the resource management allows overload situations this might be a suitable algorithm.

Apart from the most important real-time scheduling methods discussed above, others might be employed for the processing of continuous media data (an on-line scheduler for tasks with unknown ready-times is introduced by [HL88]; in [HS89], a real-time monitoring system is presented where all necessary data to calculate an optimal schedule are available). In most multimedia systems with preemptive tasks, the rate monotonic algorithm in different variations is employed. So far, no other scheduling technique has been proven to be at least as suitable for multimedia data handling as the EDF and rate monotonic approaches.

### 3.1.5.7 Preemptive versus Non-preemptive Task Scheduling

Real-time tasks can be distinguished into *preemptive* and *non-preemptive* tasks. If a task is *non-preemptive*, it is processed and not interrupted until it is finished or requires further resources. The contrary of non-preemptive tasks are *preemptive tasks*. The processing of a preemptive task is interrupted immediately by a request of any higher-priority task. In most cases where tasks are treated as non-preemptive, the arrival times, processing times and deadlines are arbitrary and unknown to the scheduler until the task actually arrives. The best algorithm is the one which maximizes the number of completed tasks. In this case, it is not possible to provide any processing guarantees or to do resource management.

To guarantee the processing of periodic processes and to get a feasible schedule for a periodic task set, tasks are usually treated as preemptive. One reason is that high preemptability minimizes priority inversion. Another reason is that for some non-preemptive task sets, no feasible schedule can be found; whereas for preemptive scheduling, it is possible.

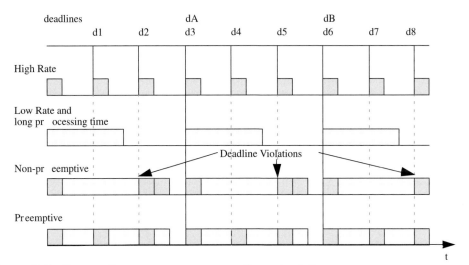

**Figure 3-5**  Preemptive versus non-preemptive scheduling.

Figure 3-5 shows an example where the scheduling of preemptive tasks is possible, but non-preemptive tasks cannot be scheduled.

Liu and Layland [LL73] show that a task set of $m$ periodic, preemptive tasks with processing times $e_i$ and request periods $p_i \forall i \in (1, \ldots, m)$ is schedulable:

- With fixed priority assignment if: $\sum \dfrac{e_i}{p_i} \le \ln 2$

- With deadline driven scheduling if: $\sum \dfrac{e_i}{p_i} \le 1$

Here, the preemptiveness of tasks is a necessary prerequisite to check their schedulability.

The first schedulability test for the scheduling of *non-preemptive tasks* was introduced by Nagarajan and Vogt in [NV92]. Assume, without loss of generality, that task $m$ has highest priority and task 1 the lowest. They prove that a set of $m$ periodic streams with periods $p_i$, deadlines $d_i$, processing times $e_i$ and $d_m \le p_i \forall i \in (1, \ldots, m)$ is schedulable with the non-preemptive fixed priority scheme if:

$$d_m \ge e_m + max_{(1 \le i \le m)} e_i$$

$$d_i \ge e_i + max_{(1 \le j \le m)} e_j + \sum_{j = i+1}^{m} e_j F(d_i - e_j, p_j)$$

where $F(x, y) = ceil\left(\dfrac{x}{y}\right) + 1$

This means that the time between the logical arrival time and the deadline of a task $t_i$ has to be larger or equal to the sum of its processing time $e_i$ and the processing time of any higher-priority task that requires execution during that time interval, plus the longest processing time of all lower- and higher-priority tasks $max_{(1 \le j \le m)} e_j$ that might be serviced at the arrival of task $t_i$ (Figure 3-6).

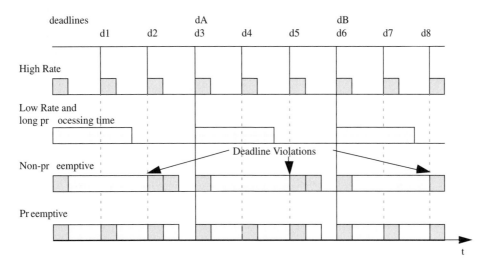

**Figure 3-6**   Deadline requirements for non-preemptive scheduling.

The schedulability test is an extension of Liu's and Layland's. Given $m$ periodic tasks with periods $p_i$ and the same processing time $E$ per message, let $d_i = p_i + E$ be the deadline for task $t_i$. Then, the streams are schedulable:

• With the non-preemptive rate monotonic scheme with:

$$\sum \frac{1}{p_i} \times E \leq \ln 2$$

• With deadline-based scheduling, the same holds with:

$$\sum \frac{1}{p_i} \times E \leq 1$$

Consequently, non-preemptive continuous media tasks can also be scheduled. However, the scheduling of non-preemptive tasks is less favorable because the number of schedulable task sets is smaller compared to preemptive tasks.

### 3.1.6   Prototype Operating Systems: Case Studies

Most multimedia operating systems apply one of the previously discussed methods. In some systems, the scheduler is replaced by a soft-real-time scheduler. Therefore, these systems can be viewed as new operating systems. They are usually not compatible with existing systems and applications. Other systems apply a meta-scheduler based on an existing process manager. Only these systems will have a commercial impact in the short and medium terms because they allow existing applications to run.

**ARTS**   The *Advanced Real Time Technology Operating System* is a real-time operating system for a distributed environment with one real-time process manager. It was developed on SUN3 workstations and connected with a real-time network based on the IEEE.802.5 Token Ring and Ethernet by the Computer Science department of Carnegie Mellon University. To solve the scheduling problems, the *Time-Driven Scheduler (TDS)* with a priority inheritance protocol was adopted. This priority inheritance protocol was used to prevent unbounded priority inversion among communication tasks. Tasks with hard deadlines are scheduled according to the rate monotonic algorithm. The system is also provided with other scheduling methods for experimental reasons [MT90].

**YARTOS**   Yet *Another Real Time Operating System* was developed at the University of North Carolina at Chapel Hill as an operating system kernel to support conferencing applications [JSP91]. An optimal, preemptive algorithm to schedule tasks on a single processor was developed. The scheduling algorithm results from the integration of a synchronization scheme to access shared resources with the EDF algorithm. Here, a task has two notions of deadline, one for the initial acquisition of the processor, and one for the execution of operations on resources. To avoid priority inversion, tasks are provided with separate deadlines for performing operations on shared resources. It is guaranteed that no shared resource is accessed simultaneously by more than one task. Further, a shared resource is not occupied by a single task longer than absolutely necessary.

**Split-level Scheduling**   The *split-level scheduler* was developed within the DASH project at the University of California at Berkeley. Its main goal was to provide a better support for multimedia applications [And93]. The applied scheduling policy is deadline/work ahead scheduling. The LBAP-model is used to describe arrival processes. Critical processes have priority over all other processes and they are scheduled according to the EDF algorithm preemptively. Interactive processes have priority over work ahead processes as long as they do not become critical. The scheduling policy for work ahead processes is unspecified, but may be chosen to minimize context switching. For non-real-time processes, a scheduling strategy like UNIX time-slicing is chosen.

**Three Class Scheduler**   This scheduler was developed as part of a video-on-demand file service at DEC, Littleton. The design of the scheduler is based on a combination of *weighted round-robin* and *rate monotonic scheduling* [RVG+93]. Three classes of schedulable tasks are supported. The isochronous class with the highest priority applies the rate monotonic algorithm, the real-time and the general-purpose classes use the weighted round-robin scheme. A general-purpose task is preemptive and runs with a low priority. The real-time class is suitable for tasks that require guaranteed throughput and bounded delay. The isochronous class supports real-time periodic tasks that require performance guarantees for throughput, bounded latency and low jitter. Real-time and isochronous tasks can only be preempted in "preemption windows".

The scheduler executes tasks from a ready queue in which all isochronous tasks are arranged according to their priority. At the arrival of a task, the scheduler determines whether the currently running task must be preempted. General-purpose tasks are immediately preempted, real-time tasks are preempted in the next preemption window and isochronous tasks are preempted in the next preemption window if their priority is lower than the one of the new task. Whenever the queue is empty, the scheduler alternates between the real-time and general-purpose classes using a weighted round-robin scheme.

**Meta-scheduler**    To support real-time processing of continuous media, a meta-scheduler for the operating systems AIX™ was developed at the European Networking Center of IBM in Heidelberg. Both were based on the LBAP model. According to the rate monotonic algorithm, rates were mapped onto system priorities. The implementation of this scheduler was used to analyze the advantages and disadvantages of a meta-scheduler approach. Several experience showed the limits of this approach. For example, each process in the system was able to run with a priority initially intended for real-time tasks. These processes were not scheduled by the resource manager and therefore violated the calculated schedule. A malicious process could block the whole system by simply running with the highest priority without giving up control.

The management of scheduling algorithms requires exact time measurement. In OS/2, for example, it was not possible to measure the exact time a thread is using the CPU. Any measurement of the processing time includes interrupts. If a process is interrupted by another process, it also includes the time needed for the context switch. The granularity of the OS/2 system timers was insufficient for the processing of real-time tasks. Hence, the rate control was inaccurate because it was determined by the granularity of the system timer.

To achieve full real-time capabilities, the above analysis showed that at least the native scheduler of the operating system must be extended. The operating system should be enhanced by a class of fast, non-preemptive threads and the ability to mask interrupts for a short period of time. Priorities in this thread class should only be assigned to threads that are already registered by the resource manager. This class should be reserved exclusively for selected threads and monitored by a system component with extensive control facilities. Performance enhancement of the scheduler itself, incorporating some mechanisms of real-time scheduling like EDF, would be another solution. The operating system should, in any case, provide a time measurement tool that allows the measurement of pure CPU time and a timer with a finer granularity. This may be achieved through a *timer chip*.

**Hierarchical CPU Scheduler**    The *hierarchical CPU scheduler* [GGV96] is a soft-real-time adaptation-based scheduling framework which supports multimedia application classes with different timing requirements. Goyal, Guo and Vin [GGV96] partitioned the CPU bandwidth into hierarchical classes and organized them into a tree-like structure. The leaves of the tree support different types of scheduling policies such as EDF (earliest deadline first), RM (rate-monotonic) and FIFO (first in first out) to schedule different types of applications. All these schedulers are coordinated and protected from each other by the *Start-time Fair Queueing (SFQ)* scheduler which represents an augmented *Weighted Fair Queueing (WFQ)* algorithm. SFQ is a resource allocation algorithm that can be used for achieving fair CPU partitioning. SFQ's goals are fair allocation of the CPU regardless of variation of server capacity, no *a priori* knowledge about the length of the quantum per thread, and bounded maximum delay and minimum throughput. The disadvantage of this approach is that the implementation is embedded inside of the UNIX kernel, and required a modification of the Sun Solaris Kernel scheduler, hence portability to other systems as well as to new versions of Solaris means an extensive effort. For some applications the fair CPU allocation may also mean a problem in their delivery of timing guarantees. Especially, this problem can arise when the scheduling overhead increases proportionally with the increase of the hierarchical tree depth.

**Processor Capacity Reserve_based Scheduler**  Mercer,  Savage  and  Tokuda [MT94] implemented the abstraction of the *processor capacity reservation* for real-time threads within the Real-time Mach operating system. A follow-up version of this work [LRM96] supports rules for a dynamic quality adjustment. A new thread must provide first its CPU QoS values in the form of period and CPU utilization in percentage during the reservation phase. Once the thread is accepted, it is associated with a "reserve budget" information, including the guaranteed CPU processing time. During the thread processing, the CPU time is charged against the reserve budget. When a new period starts, the reserve budget is replenished. This concept works similar to the token bucket concept in networks. The exact calculation of the system service time is an excellent, but also a very costly feature. It requires non-trivial modifications and computational overhead inside of UNIX kernels in order to support this abstraction.

**Resource Kernels**  Rajkumar and his colleagues [RJMO02] developed a resource management framework, called the *Resource Kernel (RK),* for supporting concurrent activities with different timing constraints. This framework belongs to the reservation-based systems. A resource kernel is a system entity that provides timely, guaranteed and protected access to a system resource. The goals of a resource kernel are to allow an application to specify its timing constraints, to enforce maximum resource usage by applications, to support high utilization of system resources, and to allow an application simultaneous access to different system resources. The RK system consists of a set of resource kernels, where each of them is based on reservation. The reservation approach is based on the processor capacity reserve abstraction. Similarly to the previous schedulers, this resource management system is implemented in the Linux kernel hence carries the trade-offs as discussed above.

**Adaptive Rate-Controlled Scheduler**   Yau and Lam [YL96] implemented the *Adaptive Rate-controlled Scheduler*, which represents a modification of the *Virtual Clock Algorithm*. Each process specifies a reserve-rate and a period for the admission control. During the runtime phase, the reserve-rate is monitored and adjusted either upwards or downwards, to reach equilibrium step-wise between the actual utilization and the reserved rate. This approach is also called the ra*te adaptation approach*. This scheduler belongs to the adaptation-based soft-real-time scheduling frameworks.

**SMART Scheduler**   SMART [NL97] is an adaptive soft-real-time scheduling framework which extended the TS-UNIX scheduler. This scheduler provides soft-real-time guarantees using *dynamic feedback* to applications to allow them to adapt to the current load. The SMART scheduler integrates the real-time and non-real-time computations, and hence influences how the processor is to be shared among applications of the same priority. As the system load changes, SMART adjusts the allocation of resources dynamically, which means that it automatically sheds real-time tasks and regulates their execution rates in the overload state while fully utilizing the resources in the under-loaded conditions. The scheduling algorithm in SMART is based on priorities and weighed fair queueing (WFQ). This scheduler allows SMART to behave as a real-time scheduler when scheduling only real-time requests, as a conventional scheduler when scheduling only conventional requests, and as a hybrid scheduler in case of real-time and non-real-time requests, which ensures that more important tasks obtain their resource requirements. SMART does not have any mechanisms for admission control or reservation, therefore it can not fully enforce any timing guarantees for multimedia tasks in overload scenarios. Similarly, this scheduler is implemented within the Sun Solaris kernel and had the same trade-offs as discussed above.

**BEST Scheduler**   BEST [BB02] is an enhanced best-effort scheduler that combines desirable aspects of multimedia and best effort computing. BEST provides the well-behaved default characteristics of best-effort schedulers while significantly improving support for periodic soft-real-time processes. BEST schedules periodic tasks using *estimated deadlines*. The estimations are based on the dynamically detected periods of processes exhibiting periodic behavior. The scheduler then assigns pseudo-periods to non-periodic processes to allow for good response time. The scheduler is implemented in Linux kernel and it outperforms the Linux scheduler as well as it outperforms real-time schedulers in handling best-effort processes and sometimes even in handling multimedia processes, especially in overload situations.

**Real-Time Upcall Scheduler**   Gopalakkrishnan [Gop96] implemented the Real-Time Upcall (RTU) under the NetBSD UNIX system to support periodic processes. Each RTU includes an event handler which reports to the kernel dispatcher the processing time and period of the process. The kernel dispatcher was modified to use the rate-monotonic scheduling policy for scheduling of RTUs. In order to improve the efficiency and predictability of RTU processing, the kernel dispatcher is not allowed to interrupt the RTU execution, and preempt the RTU in the middle of its processing. This concept is also called as the *non-asynchronous interrupt* or the *delayed interrupt*.

**URsched Scheduler at the User Level**   Kamada, Yuhara and Ono [KYO96] implemented the soft-real-time scheduler at the user level. The *User Level RT Scheduler*, called *URsched*, was implemented under the Sun Solaris 2.4 system, and it is based on the POSIX 4 real-time extension capabilities. This scheduler utilizes the priority switching to let multimedia applications get their required processor resource at required times.

**Dynamic Soft-Real-Time Scheduler**   Chu and Nahrstedt [CN99] developed a reservation-based soft-real-time scheduler, called *Dynamic Soft-Real-Time Scheduler (DSRT)* that runs in the user space on top of various operating systems such as Solaris, Windows and Linux. DSRT is part of the distributed QoS-aware resource management, called *QualMan* [CN97b, KN98], to support timing guarantees for multimedia tasks on general purpose platforms. DSRT consists of a *CPU broker* and a SRT CPU scheduler, where the CPU broker provides admission control and reservation management, and the SRT scheduler provides mechanisms and policies to enforce and adapt reservations for various CPU service classes. The architecture of the SRT scheduler consists of a *top-level scheduler*, which uses a simple credit/debit scheme to schedule three partition schedulers: the *RT scheduler*, the *Overrun scheduler* and the *TS scheduler*. The RT scheduler executes preemptive Earliest Deadline First scheduling policy and utilizes the RT partition of the processor resource. It uses the priority switching concept to serve the reserved runs of soft-real-time processes. The Overrun scheduler manages the overrun partition which is dedicated to serving overruns and bursts from the RT processes. It distinguishes between *conforming overruns* such as the bursts from the PVPT service class that exceed their SPT, but still confirm to their contract, and *non-conforming overruns*. This scheduler maintains three queues: conforming queue, non-conforming queue and permanent non-conforming queue for non-conforming overruns occurring frequently over a long period of time. It uses the multi-level feedback queue scheduling policy among the queues and the round robin scheduling policy within each queue. The TS scheduler is the UNIX TS scheduler and it manages the TS partition to serve TS processes so that traditional TS processes do not starve because of RT processes. The RT and the Overrun schedulers jointly support CPU service classes such as PCPT and PVPT, as well as adaptation of reservations.

## 3.2   Interprocess Communication and Synchronization

In multimedia systems, *interprocess communication* refers to the exchange of different data between processes. This data transfer must be very efficient because continuous media require the transfer of a large amount of data in a given time span. For the exchange of discrete media data, the same mechanisms are used as in traditional operating systems. Data interchange of continuous media is closely related to memory management and is discussed in the respective section.

*Synchronization* guarantees timing requirements between different processes. In the context of multimedia, this is an especially interesting aspect. Different data streams, database entries, document portions, positions, processes, etc., must be synchronized. Thus, synchronization is important for various components of a multimedia system and therefore is not included in this discussion on operating systems, but extensively discussed in a separate Section on Synchronization.

## 3.3 Memory Management

The memory manager assigns physical resource memory to a single process. Virtual memory is mapped onto memory that is actually available. With paging, less frequently used data is swapped between main memory and external storage. Pages are transferred back into the main memory when data on them is required by a process. Note, continuous media data must not be swapped out of the main memory. If a page of virtual memory containing code or data required by a real-time process is not in real memory when it is accessed by the process, a page fault occurs, meaning that the page must be read from disk. Page faults affect the real-time performance very seriously, so they must be avoided. A possible approach is to lock code and/or data into real memory. However, care should be taken when locking code and/or data into real memory. Real memory is a very scarce resource to the system. Committing real memory by pinning (locking) will decrease overall system performance. For example, the typical AIX kernel will not allow more than about 70% of real memory to be committed to pinned pages [IBM91].

The transmission and processing of continuous data streams by several components require very efficient data transfer restricted by time constraints. Memory allocation and release functions provide well-defined access to shared memory areas. In most cases, no real processing of data, but only a data transfer, is necessary. For example, the camera with a digitalization process is the source and the presentation process is the sink. The essential task of the other components is the exchange of continuous media data with relatively high data rates in real-time. Processing involves computing, adding, interpreting and stripping headers. This is well-known in communications. The actual implementation can either be with external devices and dedicated hardware in the computer, or it can be realized with software components.

Early prototypes of multimedia systems incorporated audio and video based on external data paths only. Memory management, in this case, had a switching function only, i.e., to control an external switch. A first step toward integration was the incorporation of the external switch function into the computer. Therefore, some dedicated adapter cards that were able to switch data streams with varying data rates were deployed. A complete integration was achieved with a full digital approach within the computer, i.e., to offer a pure software solution. Data are transmitted between single components in real-time. Copy operations are – as far as possible – reduced to the exchange of pointers and the check of access rights. This requires the access of a shared address space. Data can also be directly transferred between different adapter cards. The transfer of continuous media data takes place in a real-time environment. This exchange is controlled, but not necessarily executed, by the application. The data transfer must be performed by processes running in a real-time environment. The application running in a non-real-time environment generates, manipulates and consumes these data streams at an operating system interface.

### 3.3.1  Reservation Concept for Memory Management

The timely and predictable execution of an application RT process depends on the availability of data which again depends on the availability of memory pages. Therefore, for multimedia applications, a reservation concept may be appropriate which allows RT processes to declare required amount of memory for its processing and the memory management reserves and pins the space for the duration of application execution. To allow this functionality, the memory management needs two functional entities: the memory broker and the memory controller. The memory broker pins a certain size of memory, called global reserve, which it then manages and provides to SRT processes as reserved chunks of memory. The memory size from the global reserve that is already allocated to accepted processes is called accepted storage. The memory size that is still available for new reservation requests is called available storage. Each application sends its memory requirements to the memory broker which performs admission control. The admission control checks the condition

$$requested\ storage \leq available\ storage$$

in order to make sure that the requested reserved memory (*requested storage*) together with already accepted memory (*accepted storage*) does not violate the overall space for the global reserve memory (*global reserve = available storage + accepted storage*). Note that the size of global reserve must be carefully chosen so that there is sufficient space for kernel and TS processes. If we allow too large pinning area for the multimedia memory management to serve soft-real-time processes, then we can cause a frequent swapping of pages for kernel processes and TS processes,. This can again cause unpredictable delays for soft-real-time applications as they need kernel processes as well as may be depend on some TS processes.

If the admission is positive, the broker builds up a *memory reserve* [KN98] according to the application's memory requirement. The memory reserve corresponds to the allocated and pinned amount of space that the application will use during its time-critical run-time. The reserve should include text, data and shared segments of the application. After the successful admission, the memory broker provides a reservation ID (reserve-ID) to the process and creates an entry with information (reserve-ID, accepted storage) in the reservation table. The application uses the reserve-ID during the execution phase and gives it to the memory controller. The memory controller then checks the validity of reserve-ID, and in positive case it allocates/pins shared memory for the application. Furthermore, it gives the key of the shared memory to the application which then attaches the shared memory segment to its own address space. Once the application finishes its execution, it needs to free the pinned space by detaching the shared memory segment from its application space, and sending an event to the memory controller with the key to the shared memory. The memory controller frees the shared memory as well as increases the available storage information for the memory broker.

### 3.3.2  Buffer Management Techniques

Buffers are considered as a spatial representation of time. As discussed above, transmission and processing of cells, packets or frames need to be performed in timely fashion, and buffers play an important role to achieve this goal. Hence, we need to examine techniques for buffer management with respect to multimedia data and their timing constraints. We will consider buffer management techniques that are relevant to local and distributed multimedia applications in this paragraph. The next paragraph examines buffer management techniques and their attributes in client/server systems.

There exist three major techniques for buffer management that multimedia systems consider in their communication and processing components: (1) *data copying*, (2) *offset management*, and (3) *scatter/gather* techniques:

- **Data Copying**: This technique requires that data is physically moved from one memory space to another, hence data is copied from one buffer space to another. This buffer management technique is used between two protocols that reside in different spaces, i.e., one in kernel space and the other one in user space. For example, data copying occurs from the application buffer to the TCP buffer of the TCP protocol stack that resides in the kernel space. The advantage of data copying is that it allows for data protection as different protocols can perform their own operations on data and headers without any sharing and possible errors coming from other protocols. On the other hand, data copying is a very time-expensive operation, especially in multimedia systems. For example, copying large video frames can take substantial amount of time which then can cause violation of end-to-end delay guarantees in live applications such as video conferencing or video phone.

- **Offset Management:** This technique takes into account the memory space that the whole protocol stack requires for data and header information at a single communication end-system node. This approach allocates the overall memory for data and all protocol headers at the application layer, i.e., it considers the data size of an application frame as well as all sizes of headers that other protocols may need to attach for their own protocol processing. For example, if we consider application protocol, transport protocol and network protocol for the video frame processing, the application protocol allocates enough buffer for the application video data as well as headers coming from the application, transport and network protocols. At the sending side, the application protocol fills in the necessary information in its own header space and passes the pointer of the buffer to the transport protocol. The transport protocol fills in the necessary information in its own header space, and passes the whole buffer via pointer to the network protocol. The network protocol fills in the necessary information in its own header space and as the last software protocol, it copies the whole buffer into the network card which then implements the link and physical layer functionality, and sends the frame out onto the network towards the destination. At the receiving side the network layer receives and buffers all information, and passes the buffer pointer to the upper protocols. The advantage of this buffer technique is that it is very time-effective as we do not loose time by copying the data among protocols. The disadvantage of this approach is that the application layer protocol must know additional information about the underlying protocols such as the header sizes which introduces dependencies between protocols and more coordination among the protocols especially during their setup phases. Also there is still some buffer overhead associated with this technique as we allocate spaces in application layer that are not used immediately.

• **Scatter/Gather Technique:** This technique encourages all protocols at a sending communication end system node to share a *scatter/gather table* structure which will carry pointer information to individual buffers inside of protocols. The application layer protocol creates its own buffer where it puts its own Application Protocol Data Unit (APDU), and the header. The pointer to this buffer is then entered into the scatter/gather table. Each consecutive protocol (transport and network protocols) creates its own buffers with its own headers, and enters the pointer information to its header buffers into the scatter/gather table. Hence, all headers and data are scattered memory-wise. The last software protocol then gathers the pointers and copies the buffers in corresponding order onto the network hardware interface. The advantage of this approach is that it is very time-effective as we do not copy any of information until it is ready to leave the end-system, and it allocates only the necessary amount of space, hence the buffer overhead is minimal, consisting only of the additional space for the scatter/gather table. The disadvantage of this approach is that each protocol must know the position information of the scatter/gather, hence there needs to be a sharing mechanism to distribute this information to the protocol components of the end-system protocol stack.

Table 3-3 shows the comparison among the three buffer management techniques.

| | Data Copying | Offset | Scatter/Gather |
|---|---|---|---|
| Memory Band-width | High | Low | Low |
| CPU-Bandwidth | High | Low | Low |
| Memory Usage | Optimal for the individual protocol because exact amount of space will be allocated | High for application protocol because it must allocate space more than it needs | Compromise, segments are sized depending on requirements |
| Protocol Requirements without data copying | Not applicable | No, segmenting cannot be done without copying | Yes |

**Table 3-3**   Comparison of buffer management techniques.

### 3.3.3   Buffer Management for Client/Server Systems

In client/server multimedia systems, such as video on demand, the information flow is directed from the server to the client in a streaming mode. To ensure end-to-end timing requirements, such as low jitter between packets, or bounded end-to-end delay, the movement of data must be carefully considered and designed. Important issues in this consideration are multimedia networking algorithms inside of networks as well as buffer management systems at end-systems residing within transmission protocols. We will discuss various multimedia networking algorithms in the Section on Multimedia Networks. Here, we will concentrate on the end-system buffer management strategies. From the dynamic buffer allocation point of view, buffering strategies can be partitioned into *static* and *dynamic* buffering strategies.

- **Static Buffers:** The static buffering strategy allocates buffers for a distributed multimedia application during the setup phase, and these buffers do not change during the runtime phase.
- **Elastic Buffers:** The dynamic buffering strategy allocates buffers for a distributed multimedia application during the setup phase, but during the runtime phase it changes the allocation according to new application's requirements. Hence, as the traffic changes on the network, or content of an application yields different bandwidth requirements, buffer requirements change and the protocols adapt them.

**Client-Side Buffer Management**   Buffer management techniques play especially important role at the receiver (client) side as it has the responsibility to smooth out any network-caused jitters or other timing violations. We will consider two buffer management strategies [RT98b]: (1) *Minimum Buffering Strategy* (minbuf) and (2) *Maximum Buffering Strategy* (maxbuf).

- **Min-buf Strategy**: This approach aims to minimize buffer requirements by buffering at most one unit of information which may be a frame or other object $O_i$. It means that if $S_{Oi}$ is the size of the object $O_i$ at time $t_i$ in bits, and the object $O_i$ will be delivered from the server at $t_{i-1}$ just after the presentation time $t_{i-1}$ of the object $O_{i-1}$, then the min-buf strategy requires minimum throughput $C_{min}$ from the network:

$$C_{min} \geq \frac{S_{Oi}}{t_i - t_{i-1}}$$

The delivery time of the first information unit is $t_x = S_{Oi}/C_{min}$ seconds before the start of the display.

- **Max-buf Strategy:** This approach aims to deliver on $B_{max}$ bits from the server every $\Gamma$ seconds, where $\Gamma = B_{max}/C$, and $C$ is the throughput offered by the network. For the application, the network should guarantee a minimum throughput $C_{min}$, so that the multimedia objects can be retrieved in time.

$$C_{min} \geq \frac{\left( \sum_{i=1}^{n} S_{Oi} - B_{max} \right)}{StreamDisplayDuration}$$

The summation of $S_{Oi}$ represents the total size of all objects $O_i$, $i=1...n$, that will be presented in the stream.

The above strategies correspond to the case where the system ensures that the production rate of multimedia objects matches consumption rate in each round of continuous media playback. This means that on a round-by-round basis, the data production never lags consumption, and there is never a net decrease in the amount of buffered data, Algorithms having this property are also referred to as *work-ahead-augmentig* or *buffer-conserving*.

However, a buffering strategy could be also developed where the system is not buffer-conserving. It means that such an algorithm allows production to fall behind consumption in one round and compensates for it in a later round. However, this algorithm also requires that we do not introduce starvation. Hence, while buffer conservation is not a necessary condition for preventing starvation, it can be used as a sufficient condition. For example, before initiating a video playback we can prefetch enough data to meet the consumption requirements of the longest possible round and if each round thereafter is buffer conserving, it is clear that starvation is impossible [GVK+02]. This means that to ensure continuous playback at the client side, a sufficient number of blocks must be retrieved for each client during a round to prevent the output device's starvation for the round's entire duration.

To determine the number of blocks, various considerations need to be taken into account such as the consumption rate of each client. Therefore, to minimize the round length, the number of blocks retrieved for each stream during each round should be proportional to the stream's consumption rate [AOG92, RV93].

**Server-Side Buffer Management** A server must also manage buffers to leave sufficient free space for the next reads to be performed. On a per stream basis, the most suitable buffering model is the First-In-First-Out technique [GVK+02]. Using a FIFO, contiguous files, and round-robin scheduling at the media server (for more information, see the Section on Media Servers), the buffer size can approximate the size of the maximum required read. In this case, each stream's FIFO can simply be *topped up* in each round. With a topping-up strategy, the amount read for a stream in each reading period will vary with the amount of free buffer space. If the data are scattered across the disk, variable read amounts might mean that the data to be retrieved is split across two blocks, causing an extra intrafile seek. One solution to this problem is to use *three block-sized buffering strategy*[4]. With three buffers, the only time a whole block cannot be read is when at least two buffers are full, otherwise buffering is sufficient until the next round. Other buffering schemes for media servers are also discussed in the Section on Media Servers (e.g., see the buffering scheme for the Felini media server).

**Implementation Issues** he clients and servers usually deploy multiple buffers. There are buffers to carry (1) *periodic streams*, (2) *non-real-time data*, (3) *requests for scheduling*, (4) *positional metadata buffers* [BPKR97], and others.

- **Buffers for Uncompressed Periodic Streams***:* A set of circular buffers can serve as the prefetching buffers for the data from uncompressed periodic streams, retrieved from the disk at the server side or delivered from the network at the client side. These buffers can be either statically reserved on a per connection basis during the connection setup time, or dynamically allocated during every round of the scheduling scheme. The size of allocated buffers depends on the media type as well as the playback rate as discussed above. For example, the buffer requirement for a video stream is much larger than for an audio stream. Also a video stream playing at 30 frames per second requires larger buffers than a video stream with frame rate of 15 frames per second.

- **Buffers for Compressed Periodic Streams:** The buffers for compressed periodic streams are also circular buffers, but we need to carefully consider the size of a buffer unit and the overall allocation. The reason is that although compression

---

[4] Other solutions with fewer than three buffers are also possible [GH94].

decreases the size of the circular buffers, the size varies with the compression technique. For example, the buffer required for a JPEG encoded stream is significantly larger than its MPEG encoded stream. Another issue, we need to consider, is the varying size of successive frames in the media streams, causing a frame-to-frame variability in buffer requirements. Thus, the static buffer strategy, though simple, requires more memory because the size of the buffer allocated at the connection setup time has to be the maximum expected size of a frame.

- **Buffers for Non-Real-Time Tasks:** A set of buffers needs to be available for storage of non-real-time streams such as still images, and progressive image transmissions. These buffers can use the minbuf strategy or maxbuf strategy with static buffer allocation.

- **Request Buffers:** Servers and clients need request buffers to store control commands for read and write scheduling management. At the server side the request queue controls the disk access and the disk array controller read requests to initiated appropriate transactions to retrieve data from the storage devices. At the client side the request queue controls the network access and the network protocol read requests to initiate event to read data from the network device. The request buffers can be designed as priority queues or FIFO queues depending on the scheduling policy.

- **Positional Metadata Buffers:** The positional metadata represents information about the location of data on the storage devices, or other devices and resources. This data is used by the resource controller to locate the position on the device and read/write data from/to the device. To speed up the access to devices and resources, positional metadata buffers can help in this goal.

Buffers can be allocated and managed by the operating system of the end-system within a disk management component, or within a protocol entity. Also applications may utilize one or more types of buffers for their application processing.

## 3.4   Device Management

Device management and the actual access to a device allows the operating system to integrate all hardware components. The physical device is represented by an abstract device driver. The physical characteristics of devices are hidden. In a conventional system, such devices include a graphics adapter card, disk, keyboard and mouse. In multimedia systems, additional devices like cameras, microphones, speakers and dedicated storage devices for audio and video must be considered. In most existing multimedia systems, such devices are not often integrated by device management and the respective device drivers.

Existing operating system extensions for multimedia usually provide one common system-wide interface for the control and management of data streams and devices. In

Microsoft Windows and OS/2 this interface is known as the Media Control Interface (MCI). The multimedia extensions of Microsoft Windows, for example, provide the following classes of function calls:

- *System commands* are not forwarded to the single device driver (MCI driver); they are served by a central instance. An example of such a command is the query concerning all devices connected to the system (Sysinfo).

- Each device driver must be able to process *compulsory commands.* For instance, the query for specific characteristics (capability info) and the opening of a device (open) are such commands.

- *Basic commands* refer to characteristics that all devices have in common. They can be supported by drivers. If a device driver processes such a command, it must consider all variants and parameters of the command. A data transmission is typically started by the basic command "play".

- *Extended commands* may refer to both device types and special single devices. The "seek" command for the positioning on an audio CD is an example. On the basis of a controllable camera, the required concepts are explained in more detail. A camera has functions to adjust the focal length, focus and position. An abstraction of the functionality provided by the physical camera as an video input device covers the following layers, which relate to different components in a multimedia system:

  - The application has access to a logical camera without knowledge about the specific control functions of the camera. The focal length is adjusted in millimeters. The driver translates a specific "set focal length command" into a sequence of camera hardware control commands and passes them to the control logic. The provision of such an abstract interface and the transformation into hardware-dependent commands is a task of the device management of a multimedia operating system.

  - Different input device classes have similar characteristics. The zoom operation of a camera can be applied in a similar way to the presentation of a still image. The still image could be zoomed. For example, consider an image stored on a Photo-CD with a given resolution. The zoom operation could result in the presentation either of the image with its specified resolution, or of a particular section of the image. This kind of abstraction is part of the programming environment of a multimedia system and not a task of an operating system, although in some cases it is performed by the operating system. The basic commands define several operations supported by different devices. The basic command used for the start of a data transmission between the camera and the video window of an application—called the play command in this context—can be used in a second realization for file transfer—as a kind of copy command.

To complete the description of the camera control, the positioning of the camera is discussed. To change the position of the camera, the application specifies the target coordinates in a polar coordinate system. Yet, a concrete camera control can only execute commands like "move swivel slope head in a specific direction with a defined speed". The direction can be "left" or "right", respectively "up" or "down". Eight different speed levels are given, but it is only possible to change the speed in steps of the maximum two levels. During acceleration, consecutive commands with speed levels 2, 4, 6, 8 must be executed. It is the task of the camera driver to perform the mapping of coordinates into this positioning controlled by time and speed.

To define the required application interface, the selectable control class can be subdivided into four function categories [RSSS90]:

1. *Defined, compulsory and generic*: all operations that must be provided for each device driver, regardless of its specific functionality, belong to this category. This corresponds to the above-mentioned commands of the MCI.

2. *Defined, compulsory and device specific*: all functions and parameters specified in this category must be provided by the device driver. Therefore, there exists a defined interface in the respective operating system. For example, a camera driver must be able to answer an inquiry for an eventual existing auto focus mechanism.

3. *Defined but not compulsory:* for each device type, a set of functions is defined which covers all known possibilities. The functions cannot be provided by all different devices and drivers. In the case of the camera, such functions are, for example, to position and adjust the focal length, because not every camera has these facilities. The interface is defined keeping in mind what is possible and meaningful. If such a function is employed, although it is not supported by the implementation, a well-defined error handling mechanism applies. The application can handle these errors, and therefore it is independent of the connected physical devices.

4. *Not defined and not compulsory:* we must be aware that there will always be unpredictable new devices and special developments. Hence, the operating system provides a fourth category of functions to cover all these calls.

An unambiguous definition of these categories allows easier integration of devices into the programming environment. The multimedia extensions of today's operating systems incorporate device management with a first step of functional distinction toward the above outlined categories.

## 3.5  System Architecture

The employment of continuous media in multimedia systems also imposes additional, new requirements to the system architecture. A typical multimedia application does not require processing of audio and video to be performed by the application itself. Usually, data are obtained from a source (e.g., microphone, camera, disk, network) and are forwarded to a sink (e.g., speaker, display, network). In such a case, the requirements of continuous media data are satisfied best if they take "the shortest possible path" through the system, i.e., to copy data directly from adapter to adapter. The program then merely sets the correct switches for the data flow by connecting sources to sinks. Hence, the application itself never really touches the data as is the case in traditional processing. A problem with direct copying from adapter to adapter is the control and the change of quality of service parameters. In multimedia systems, such an adapter to adapter connection is defined by the capabilities of the two involved adapters and the bus performance. In today's systems, this connection is static. This architecture of low-level data streaming corresponds with proposals for using additional new busses for audio and video transfer within a computer. It also enables a switch-based rather than a bus-based data transfer architecture [Fin91, HM91]. Note, in practice we encounter headers and trailers surrounding continuous media data coming from devices and being delivered to devices. In the case of compressed video data, e.g., MPEG-2, the program stream contains several layers of headers compared with the actual group of pictures to be displayed.

Most of today's multimedia systems must coexist with conventional data processing. They share hardware and software components. For instance, the traditional way of protocol processing is slow and complicated. In high-speed networks, protocol processing is the bottleneck because it cannot provide the necessary throughput. Protocols like VMTP, NETBLT and XTP try to overcome this drawback, but research in this area has shown that throughput in most communication systems is not bounded by protocol mechanisms, but by the way they are implemented [CJRS89]. A time-intensive operation is, for example, physical buffer copying. Since the memory on the adapter is not very large and it may not store all related compressed images, data must be copied at least once from adapter into main memory. Further copying should be avoided. Appropriate buffer management allows operations on data without performing any physical copying. In operating systems like UNIX, the buffer management must be available in both the user and the kernel space. The data need to be stored in shared memory to avoid copying between user and kernel space. For further performance improvement, protocol processing should be done in threads with upcalls, i.e., the protocol processing for an incoming message is done by a single thread. A development to support such a protocol process management is, for example, the x-Kernel.

The architecture of the protocol processing system is just one issue to be considered in the system architecture of multimedia supporting operating systems. Multimedia data should be delivered from the input device (e.g., CD-ROM) to an output device (e.g., a video decompression board) across the fastest possible path. The paradigm of streaming from source to sink is an appropriate way of doing this. Hence, the multimedia application opens devices, establishes a connection between them, starts the data flow and returns to other duties.

As stated above, the most dominant characteristic of multimedia applications is to preserve the temporal requirement at the presentation time. Therefore, multimedia data is handled in a *Real-Time Environment (RTE)*, i.e., its processing is scheduled according to the inherent timing requirements of multimedia data. On a multimedia computer, the RTE will usually coexist with a *Non-Real-Time Environment (NRTE)*. The NRTE deals with all data that have no timing requirements. Figure 3-7 shows the approached architecture.

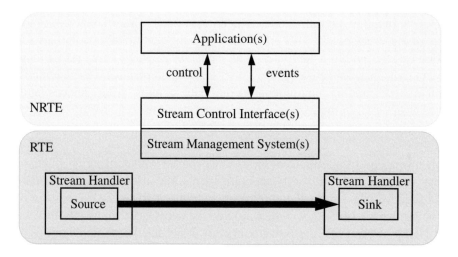

**Figure 3-7**   Real-time and non-real-time environments.

Multimedia I/O devices are, in general, accessed from both environments. Data such as a video frame, for example, is passed from the RTE to the display. The RTE is controlled by related functions in the NRTE. The establishment of communication connections at the start of a stream must not obey timing requirements, but the data processing for established connections is compelled. All control functions are performed in the NRTE. The application usually calls only these control functions and is not involved in active continuous media data handling. Therefore, the multimedia application itself typically runs in the NRTE and is shielded from the RTE. In some scenarios, users may want applications to "process" continuous media data in an application-specific way. In our model, such an application comprises a module running as stream handler in the RTE. The rest of the applications run in the NRTE, using the available stream control interfaces. System programs, such as communication protocol processing and database data transfer programs, make use of this programming in the RTE. Whereas applications like authoring tools and media presentation programs are relieved from the burden of programming in the RTE, they just interface and control the RTE services. Applications determine processing paths which are needed for their data processing, as well as the control devices and paths.

To reduce data copying, buffer management functions are employed in the RTE. This buffer management is located "between" the stream handlers. Stream handlers are entities in the RTE which are in charge of multimedia data. Typical stream handlers are filter and mixing functions, but they are also parts of the communication subsystem described above and can be treated in the same way. Each stream handler has endpoints for input and output through which data units flow. The stream handler consumes data units from one or more input endpoints and generates data units through one or more output endpoints.

Multimedia data usually "enters" the computer through an input device, a source, and "leaves" it through an output device, a sink (where storage can serve as an I/O device in both cases). Sources and sinks are implemented by a device driver. Applications access stream handlers by establishing sessions with them. A session constitutes a virtual stream handler for exclusive use by the application which has created it. Depending on the required QoS of a session, an underlying resource management subsystem multiplexes the capacity of the underlying physical resources among the sessions. To manage the RTE data flow through the stream handlers, control operations are used which belong to the NRTE. These functions make up the stream management system in the multimedia architecture. Operations are provided by all stream handlers (e.g., operations to establish sessions and connect their endpoints) and operations specific to individual stream handlers usually determine the content of a multimedia stream and apply to particular I/O devices.

Some applications which are all in the NRTE have the need to correlate discrete data such as text and graphics with continuous streams, or to post-process multimedia data (e.g., to display the time stamps of a video stream like a VCR). These applications need to obtain segments of multimedia at the stream handler interface. With a grab function, the segments are copied to the application as if stream duplication took place. Due to this operation, the data units lose their temporal properties because they enter the NRTE. Applications that must generate or transform multimedia data keeping real-time characteristics must use a stream handler included in the RTE, which performs the required processing.

The synchronization of streams is a function that is provided by the stream management subsystem. Synchronization is specified on a connection basis and can be expressed using the notions of a clock or logical time systems. It determines points in time at which the processing of data units shall start. For regular streams, the stream rates can be used to relate data units to synchronization points. Sequence numbers can accomplish the same task. Time stamps are a more versatile means for synchronization as they can also be used for non-periodic traffic. Synchronization is often implemented by delaying the execution of a thread or by delaying the receive operation on a buffer exchanged between stream handlers.

Many operating systems already provide extensions to support multimedia applications. In the next paragraphs, three of these multimedia extensions are presented.

### 3.5.1   UNIX-based Systems

In the UNIX operating system, the applications in the user space generally make use of system calls in the NRTE. Either the whole operating system or a part of it is also located in the NRTE and in the kernel space. Extensions to the operating system providing real-time capabilities make up the RTE part of the kernel space (see Figure 3-8).

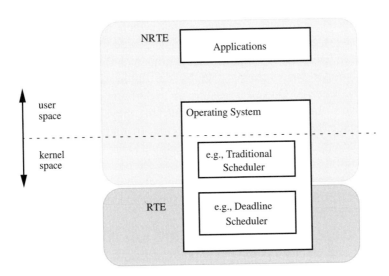

**Figure 3-8**   NRTE and RTE in UNIX systems.

The actual implementation of the RTE varies substantially:

- SUN OS includes real-time static priorities and provides a RTE.
- AIX includes real-time priorities. This feature provides the basis for the RTE in the AIX-based Ultimedia™ server.
- The IRIX operating system on Silicon Graphics Workstations has real-time capabilities, i.e., it includes an RTE.

• Linux OS has partitioning of priority space into static real-time and dynamic priorities, hence allowing RTE. Different implementations of SRT schedulers may use either static real-time or dynamic priority mechanisms.

## 3.5.2 QuickTime

*QuickTime* is a software extension to the Macintosh System. It provides the capability to capture, store, manage, synchronize and display continuous media data. A more detailed description can be found in [DM92]. It introduces digitized video as standard data type into the system, and it allows an easier handling of other continuous media like audio and animation. Standard applications are enhanced by multimedia capabilities. Apple has announced QuickTime to be available for other operating systems like Windows and UNIX as well. An integration of future hardware and software developments is possible.

The standard data type of QuickTime is a movie. All kinds of continuous media data are stored in movie documents. Additionally, time information like the creation and modification date, duration, etc., are also kept in the movie document. With each movie, a poster frame is associated that appears in the dialog box. Other information like current editing selection, spatial characteristics (transformation matrix, clipping region) and a list of one or more tracks are associated with the movie. A track represents a stream of information (audio or video data) that flows in parallel to every other track. With each track, information like creation and modification data, duration, track number, spatial characteristics (transformation matrix, display window, clipping region), a list of related tracks, volume and start time, duration, playback rate and a data reference for each media segment is stored. A media segment is a set of references to audio and video data, including time information (creation, modification, duration), language, display or sound quality, media data type and data pointers. Future releases will have, apart from audio and video tracks, "custom tracks" such as a subtitle track. All tracks can be viewed or heard concurrently. The tracks of a movie are always synchronized. Since movies are documents they cannot only be played (including pausing, stepping through, etc.), but they can also be edited. Operations like cut, copy and paste are possible. Movie documents can be part of other documents. QuickTime is scalable. Hardware components like accelerator or compressor/decompressor cards can be employed.

The QuickTime architecture comprises three major components (see Figure 3-9): the *Movie Toolbox* offers a set of services to the user that allows him/her to incorporate movies into applications. These applications may directly manipulate characteristics of audio and video data of movies. The movie is integrated in the desktop environment. Movie data can be imported and exported with the system clipboard and a movie can be edited within the Movie Toolbox.

The second component, known as the *Image Compression Manager,* provides a common interface for compression and decompression of data, independent of the implementation, to and from hard disk, CD-ROM and floppy. It offers a directory service to select the correct compression component. Different interface levels for different application requirements are available. The compression techniques are a proprietary image compression scheme, a JPEG implementation and a proprietary video compressor for digitized video data (leading to a compression ratio of 8:1, and if temporal redundancies are also removed, to a ratio of 25:1).

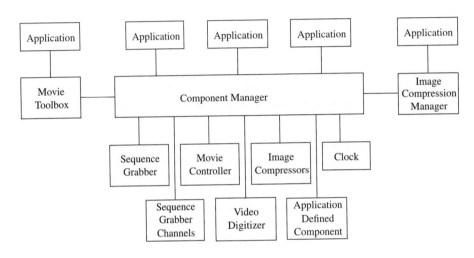

**Figure 3-9**   QuickTime architecture.

An *Animation Compressor* can compress digital data in lossy and lossless (error-free) modes. A graphics compressor is also available. The pixel depth conversion in bits per pixel can be used as a filter to be applied in addition to other compressors.

The *Component Manager* provides a directory service related to the components. It is the interface between the application and various system components. It shields developers from having to deal with the details of interfacing with specific hardware. In the Component Manager, object-oriented concepts (e.g., hierarchical structure, extensible class libraries, inheritance of component functionality, instance-based client/server model) are applied. Thus, applications are independent of implementations, can easily integrate new hardware and software and can adapt to the available resources. The components managed by the Component Manager are the Clock, the Image Compressor and Image Decompressor, the Movie Controller, the Sequence Grabber, Sequence Grabber Channel and the Video Digitizer. Furthermore, application-defined components can be added.

There is a simple resource management scheme applied to the local environment only: in the case of scarce resources, audio is prioritized over video, i.e., audio playback is maintained (if possible) whereas single video frames might be skipped. If an application calls the Movie Toolbox during playback, there are the following possibilities to handle these calls:

- The commonly used mode is a preemptive calling sequence, where the application returns to the system after each update. This might cause jerky movie output.
- With a non-preemptive calling sequence, the application does not return to the system while a movie is played. This counteracts the multitasking capability.
- The high-performance controlled preemptive calling sequence is a compromise, where the application gives up control to the Movie Toolbox for a specified time period (e.g., 50 ms).

As an additional resource management scheme for better performance, it is recommended to turn off the virtual memory while playing QuickTime movies. If it is on, it will cause the sound to skip and it will lower the frame rate during the playback of a movie. However, no RTE exists.

The concept of components in QuickTime allows for easy extension without affecting applications. It attempts to form a hierarchical structure of functionality by components. The movie controller component eases user interface programming. A disadvantage of QuickTime is that there is no clear layering of abstractions for programmers and that the functionality of managers and components sometimes overlaps.

### 3.5.3  Windows Multimedia Extensions

The *Microsoft Windows Multimedia Extensions* (WME) are an enhancement to the Windows programming environment. They provide high-level and low-level services for the development of multimedia applications for application developers, using the extended capabilities of a multimedia personal computer [Win91].

The following services for multimedia applications are provided by the WME:

- A *Media Control Interface* (MCI) for the control of media services. It comprises an extensible string-based and message-based interface for communication with MCI device drivers. The MCI device drivers are designed to support the playing and recording of waveform audio, the playing of MIDI (Musical Instrument Digital Interface) file, the playing of compact disk audio from a CD-ROM disk drive and the control of some video disk players.
- A *Low-level API* (Application Programming Interface) provides access to multimedia-related services like playing and recording audio with waveform and MIDI audio devices. It also supports the handling of input data from joysticks and precise timer services.

- A *multimedia file I/O* service provides buffered and unbuffered file I/O. It also supports the standard IBM/Microsoft Resource Interchange File Format (RIFF) files. These services are extensible with custom I/O procedures that can be shared among applications.
- The most important *device drivers* available for multimedia applications are:
  - An *enhanced high-resolution* video display driver for Video 7 and Paradise VGA cards providing 256 colors, improved performance, and other new features.
  - A *high-resolution VGA* video display driver allowing the use of a custom 16-color palette as well as the standard palette.
  - A *low resolution VGA* video display driver providing 320-by-320 resolution with 256 colors.
  - The *Control Panel Applets* that allow the user to change display drivers, to set up a screen saver, to install multimedia device drivers, to assign wave-form sounds to system alerts, to configure the MIDI Mapper and to calibrate joysticks. A MIDI Mapper supports the MIDI patch service that allows MIDI files to be authored independently of end-user MIDI synthesizer setups.

Figure 3-10 shows the rough architecture of *MS Windows Multimedia Extensions:* MMSYSTEM library provides the Media Control Interface services and low-level multimedia support functions. The communication between the low-level MMSYSTEM functions and multimedia devices, such as waveform, MIDI, joystick and timer, is provided by the multimedia device drivers. The high-level control of media devices is provided by the drivers for the Media Control Interface.

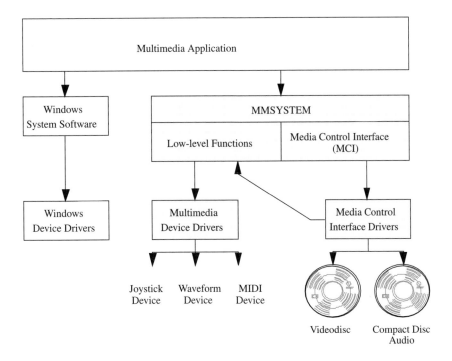

**Figure 3-10** MS Windows Multimedia Extensions architecture.

The main concepts of the architecture of the Multimedia Extensions are *extensibility and device-independence.* They are provided by a translation layer (MMSYSTEM) that isolates applications from device drivers and centralizes device-independent code, run-time linking that allows the MMSYSTEM translation layer to link to the drivers it needs and a well-defined and consistent driver interface that minimizes the development of specialized code and makes the installation and upgrade processes easier.

Current Microsoft Windows platforms provide many advanced technologies, based on underlying multimedia system architectures for media streaming and media processing, to run and display applications rich in multimedia elements such as full-color graphics, video, 3-D animation and surround sound. Some of the technologies are the Microsoft DirectX, Windows Media, Microsoft DirectShow, and others.

### 3.5.4  OS/2 Multimedia Presentation Manager/2

The *Multimedia Presentation Manager/2* (MMPM/2) is part of IBM's Operating System/2 (OS/2). OS/2 is a platform well-suited for multimedia because it supports, e.g., preemptive multitasking, priority scheduling, overlapped I/O and demand-paged virtual memory storage. Figure 3-11 provides an overview of the architecture.

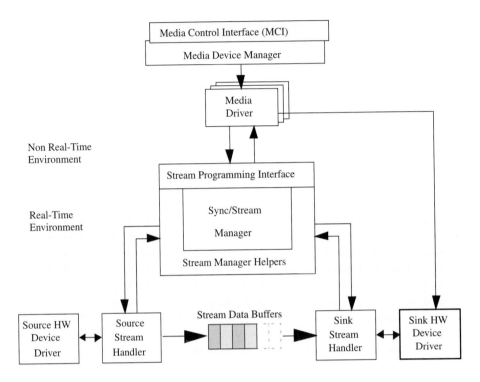

**Figure 3-11**   The architecture of the OS/2 Multimedia Presentation Manager/2.

The *Media Control Interface* (MCI) is a device-independent programming interface that offers commands similar to an entertainment system. The following list comprises a selection of typical MCI-commands:

- "Open", "close", and "status of a device" are provided for all devices.
- For playback and recording device-dependent "play", "record", "resume", "stop", "cue" and "seek" commands exist.
- "Set cue point" allows for synchronization.
- "Get table of contents of a CD-ROM" is an example of a device-specific command.

A logical device in MMPM/2 is a logical representation of the functions available from either a hardware device, a hardware device with software emulation or a software emulation only. The actual implementation is not relevant to an application because the MCI provides this device independence.

Examples of logical devices are an "Amplifier-Mixer Device", similar to a home stereo amplifier-mixer, a "Waveform Audio Device" to record and play digital audio, a sequencer device for MIDI-sounds, a "CD Audio Device" that provides access to audio compact disks (CD-DA), a "CD-XA Device" to support CD-ROM/XA disks and a

"Videodisk Device" to control video disk players which deliver analog video and audio signals.

The multimedia I/O functions enable media drivers and applications to access and manipulate data objects that are stored in memory or on a file system. Storage system I/O processes handle the access to specific storage devices. File format I/O processes manage the access to data stored in file formats like "RIFF Waveform" and "BitMap". They use the services of the storage system I/O processes.

The implementation of data streaming and synchronization is supported by the Stream Programming Interface (SPI). It provides access to the SyncStream Manager that coordinates and manages the data buffers and synchronization data. Pairs of stream handlers implement the transport of data from source to sink.

Ease of use is supported in MMPM/2 on several levels. The installation of programs and setup of devices is supported by unified graphical user interfaces that centralize these functions for easy access. Also, a style guide for applications ensures that there is a common look and feel of applications that correspond to this guide. There is a high degree of flexibility because application developers and device providers can integrate their own logical devices, I/O processes and stream handlers. So, new media devices, data formats, etc. can be integrated in MMPM/2 and can be used by every application using the MCI.

OS/2 with MMPM/2 is a platform that has some basic operating mechanisms to support the processing and presentation of multimedia information as it is needed in multimedia application scenarios. It incorporates an RTE, implemented as a set of device drivers. MMPM/2 is an advanced platform for the development of these multimedia applications, providing the media and stream abstractions.

Finally it should be pointed out that MMPM/2 and WME look very similar and have many concepts in common.

## 3.6  Concluding Remarks

In this chapter we have addressed some of the major issues of operating systems related to multimedia data processing, namely, resource management, scheduling and memory management. This discussion also includes the most relevant existing architectures of such systems.

The concepts employed by current multimedia operating systems have been initially used in real-time systems and were adapted to the requirements of multimedia data. Today's operating systems incorporate these functions either as device drivers or as extensions based on the existing operating system scheduler and memory management. As a next step, an integration of real-time processing and non-real-time processing in the native system kernel can be expected.

Furthermore, current battery-operated mobile devices, ranging from laptops to cellular phones, are becoming important platforms to process multimedia data such as audio, video, and images. Compared to conventional desktop systems, such mobile multimedia systems present both new challenges and new opportunities. New challenges arise because these multimedia-centric devices need to support application QoS and to save the battery energy at the same time. On the other hand, mobile systems also offer new opportunities due to the adaptability of their hardware and software components. There is a large body of work, considering QoS and energy-aware adaptation (a) in the hardware through dynamic voltage scaling (e.g., [WWDS94], [PS01], [LS01], [HSA01]), (b) in the operating system through changes in allocation or changes in scheduling policies in response to application and resource variations (e.g., [BP00], [YN02], [YN03]), and (c) in applications to enable multimedia applications to adjust to their QoS parameters, tradding off quality for resource demands (e.g., [FdLS$^+$01], [MT02]). The development and deployment of energy-aware multimedia operating systems is at the beginning and many new solutions are needed to solve the many challenges and opportunities in order to make energy-efficient mobile multimedia devices ubiquitous.

# Media Server

Media servers are a special variation of file servers with the requirement to deliver their services within a certain time-frame. This basic requirement of media servers can be analyzed at different levels of hardware and software. Consequently, the range of research issues that contribute to media server design is wide. While many research groups deal with multimedia servers as a database issue, this chapter concentrates on multimedia servers' content storage and its distribution. We will not consider the information management aspects of these servers.

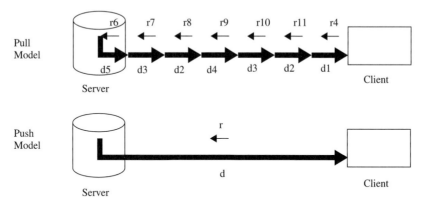

**Figure 4-1**  Pull and push server models.

The design of media servers distinguishes from the applications point of view between access controlled strictly by the client, which requests and receives pieces of content files, and access controlled by the server, where the client tunes into the server and initiates the transfer of data. Figure 4-1 demonstrates the request/response behavior of both approaches.

A media server that uses the client-based access control mode is called the *pull server*, and the server-based access control mode is call the *push server*. Another, frequently used expression for the push server is the term *data pump*, as this characterizes in a simple way its specialization in retrieving data from disk and delivering it to the network efficiently. Pull servers are more appropriate choice for editing multimedia content in a LAN environment, where linear retrieval is frequent but not the rule, pieces of content are rearranged, temporal and spatial cross-connections are introduced. Push servers are the obvious choice for broadcast or multicast distribution of content over wide areas, with no or infrequent user interaction. Applications that are not as clear-cut in their requirements may be solvable with either of the two approaches. Practice and experience with a video server is presented, e.g., in [CLO02b].

Pull and push servers are often considered competing concepts. Media server implementations, however, show that these worlds are not far apart from each other because major parts of a server can be operated in modes that can be used in pull as well as push mode. A recently implemented mixture of these approaches is the definition of play lists, client-defined lists that refer to pieces of content which is stored on the server; these play lists are supposed to be sent to the client in a sequence. Therefore, in the remainder of the chapter, we will consider both concepts as interchangeable.

## 4.1  Architecture

Media servers are responsible for the timely delivery of content to an end-system. To achieve this goal [CLO02a], each component of the media server must conform to the time and space bounds and we need to consider the following areas:

- disk-layout strategies
- disk scheduling
- file systems
- data placement on storage device
- storage and memory management
- CPU scheduling

Figure 4-2 shows the order in which media server components are involved in delivering the content. Some of the tasks that are separated in that figure are historically implemented in a single system component.

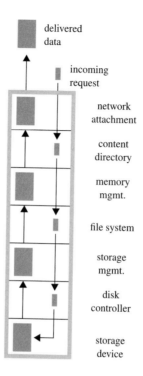

**Figure 4-2** Media server architecture.

The *network attachment* is typically a network adapter or a similar device that connects the media server to the customers. The *content directory* is the entity responsible for verifying whether content is available on the media server and whether the requesting client is allowed to access the data. The *memory management* is a separate entity because although a typical content file of multimedia applications is too large to be kept in the main memory for a long time, the caching of content data in main memory improves the performance considerably for some applications. The *file system* handles all information concerning the organization of the content on the media server. This includes such issues as the assignment of sufficient storage space during the upload phase, probably the transparent segmentation of the content file, the consistency of the data on disk, and the location of the elements of a segmented content file during retrieval operations. The *storage management* is the abstraction of driver implementations that communicate directly with the disk controller. The storage management is concerned with disk scheduling policies and the layout of files. The *disk controller* handles the access to data on the *storage device*. Research on the disk controller level considers the increase of head movement speed, I/O bandwidth [HPG03a], the largest and smallest units that can be read at a time and the granularity of addressing.

Each component of the overall media server architecture must be optimized in a cooperative way for the overall system to work in a desired fashion [PAea03]. The components must cooperate correctly and *scale* even when the system grows and new components are added, removed or replaced. In many cases an extension means that the media server functionality is distributed and spread onto multiple heterogeneous components. This means that it may become necessary to replicate parts of the data to access it in a timely manner from all components of the distributed system. The distributed nature of the media server architecture yields therefore the Griwodz architecture [TF95], shown in Figure 4-3.

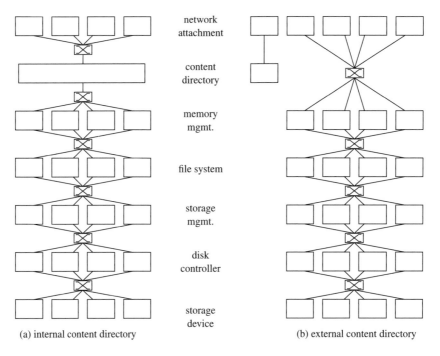

Figure 4-3 indicates the following component labels: network attachment, content directory, memory mgmt., file system, storage mgmt., disk controller, storage device, with (a) internal content directory and (b) external content directory.

**Figure 4-3**   Media server's distribution options.

The architecture and work in [TF95] provide an analysis of options for distributing parts of a video server. Especially important is the generalization of the content directory's position. Obviously, the content directory must always be consistent and have all the knowledge available in order to answer requests correctly. There exist two different approaches to generalize the component distribution and maintain the content directory consistency as shown in Figure 4-3. Figure 4-3 (a) uses an *internal content directory* which, for consistency reasons, can exist only once per media server. However, although the content directory appears consistent to all other components, it may still be distributed internally and achieve the appearance of a single component by presenting the same interface to all nodes of the media server. Figure 4-3 (b) shows all options for distributing components when the approach of an *external content directory* is adopted. A client of such a system contacts the external content server first to identify itself and to issue the request.

After that initial request, two alternatives for proceeding with the retrieval operation are possible. If the response of the content server is returned to the client and the client is responsible for issuing the actual request for data in another call (Figure 4-4 (a)), additional security mechanisms must be applied because authentication of the client is checked by the content server. Alternatively, the content server can accept all requests directed to the media server, but instead of answering itself, it can immediately order the appropriate nodes of the media server to deliver the content data (Figure 4-4 (b)). This approach is limited because it requires one of two things: either the client must be able to receive the content data from a different server than the target of its request, or each server node must deliver the content using the address of the content server.

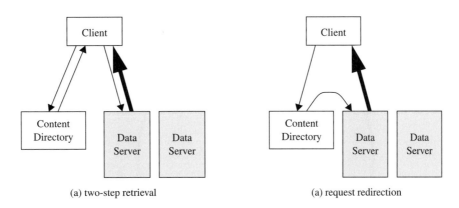

(a) two-step retrieval          (a) request redirection

**Figure 4-4** External content retrieval options.

## 4.2 Storage Devices

The *storage subsystem* is a major component of any information system. Due to the immense storage space requirements of continuous media, conventional magnetic storage devices are often not sufficient. Tapes, still in use in some traditional systems, are inadequate for multimedia systems because they cannot provide independently accessible streams, and random access is slow and expensive.

### 4.2.1 Disk Layout

The *layout* of disks determines the way in which content on a disk is addressed, how much storage space on the media is actually addressable and usable and the density of stored content on the media. This has a major influence on the speed of read and write disk operations as well as on the capacity of the disk.

Since disks are typically used as random-access media, it would be inefficient to organize data in a single track -a single spiral of data- as it has been the case for CD-ROMs until just recently. The single-track technique requires all accessible information to be recorded in terms of distance from the track start, and an access mechanism requires a translation of this number to the position that the read head of the disk has to assume, which must be expressed as a combination of distance from the center or the edge of the disk, to which the head must be moved, and the angular distance, which requires a partial rotation of the disk below the head before the data can be accessed. An additional drawback is the complex handling of operations on files such as delete or append operations. Due to the serial nature of the single-track approach, deletion of files leaves empty space in the track that can hardly be filled with an identically-sized new file. Similarly, data written in append operations is probably located far apart from the original pieces of the file. Segmentation of the medium and a continuous degradation of performance for read and write operations are the result.

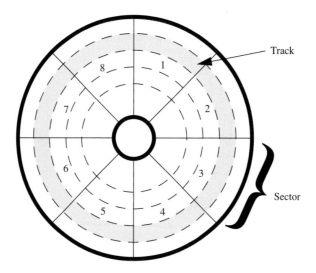

**Figure 4-5**   Tracks and Sectors.

The storage location of a file is more easily expressed by partitioning the medium in tracks and sector as depicted in Figure 4-5. The granularity of disk access is restricted to one sector on one track. The advantage of this scheme is the easy mapping of location information to head movement and disk rotation, and with this scheme the disk can also hide defective parts of the media by reassigning tracks to spare regions of the medium. This scheme has a disadvantage as it looses storage space. When files are generally much smaller than the chosen sector size, large parts of the sector remain unused unless data is appended to the file. If such an append operation is executed, however, it can be handled efficiently.

Additionally, constant rotation speed as well as constant recording and reading speed are typical for both single-track and multi-track disk layout schemes. This does not take into account the fact that the storage capacities of the medium are the same for identically-sized areas in the inner and the outer regions of the disk. Since both rotation and recording speed are kept constant, a sector in track 1 holds the same amount of data as a sector in track 200 although the capacity of the area covered by the sector in track 200 is twice the capacity of the area covered by track 1. Early microcomputers' floppy disk drives addressed this issue by varying sector sizes or by variable rotation speed. For disk drives, neither approach is followed.

### 4.2.2 Zone Bit Recording

The current solution to overcome the above discussed problem is the *Zone Bit Recording* approach. This approach recovers some of the lost space by using the same sector sizes and keeping the rotation speed constant. Figure 4-6 shows a sketch of the distribution of sectors on a disk when ZBR is used.

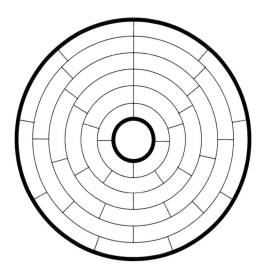

**Figure 4-6**   Sector arrangement on a Zoned disk.

The fact, that the rotation speed remains constant while more equally-sized sectors are present in the outer tracks of the disk, requires a variable reading and writing speed of the disk. The figure is slightly misleading because it hides the fact that zoned disks do not have different numbers of sectors for each track, but only a small number of zones with different layouts.

ZBR disks have the advantage of using the physical medium on the disk more efficiently, when considered for typical discrete data storage. Access to data on the outer tracks remains equally fast as access to content on the inner tracks, and since sector sizes remain constant, no additional complexity is visible. When the disks are considered for the delivery of continuous media streams such as video, additional considerations are necessary.

Assuming that the ZBR disk holds videos of various popularity [BGW97] (for more information on popularity issues, see Section 4.4.1), the placement of popular video files onto the outer tracks can reduce the average seek time when multiple users retrieve videos and thus, increase the number of video streams that can be delivered concurrently. The reason for this is that an outer track is read as fast as an inner track but that the amount of sectors of an outer track is higher than that of an inner track.

In [KLC97], the allocation of complete tracks to videos in this way is proposed. This allows for the fast transfer of frequently requested data from the outer zones to main memory buffers and it is consistent with the approach of storing video contiguously on disk to reduce seek times. However, from these buffers, a continuous playout must be guaranteed and thus, this video data must be kept in memory until it is delivered to the network. This raises the question whether this approach wastes buffer space. The more relevant effect of storing blocks of popular videos in outer tracks is gained in conjunction with algorithms such as SCAN or SCAN-EDF (see Section 4.4.3). Since most popular videos are stored in outer tracks, the probability that data must be retrieve from inner tracks as well as the average distance of disk head movements is reduced.

Alternatively, *track pairing* is proposed in [Bir95]. In this approach, two consecutive parts of a video data are stored first on an outer and than an inner track. A pair of outer and inner tracks forms a logical track, where all logical tracks on a disk have identical average throughput. In [CT97], this approach is modified to *segment group pairing* scheme, in which identically-sized I/O units of a video are stored in outer and inner zones of the ZBR disk in such a way that the average throughput of a pair of groups remains constant (e.g., [PAA$^+$03]).

The *variable block size scheme (VARB)*, introduced in [GKS95], is another scheme to exploit zoned disks. The main difference is the ignorance of disk sector size in favor of self-defined blocks. Blocks of a content file are stored on disk in a round robin manner in such a way that the time for reading a block is always the same. This implies that blocks are larger in the outer zones, where segments are read faster than in the inner zones. As a result of this arrangement, assuming that data has to be delivered to the client in a constant bit-rate manner, the time between retrieval operations on a single stream become variable. The *fixed block size scheme (FIXB)* was also introduced in

[GKS95]. This scheme uses zoned disks but in this case, blocks of the same size are stored in all zones. Another scheme using constant speed has been described in [TL00].

### 4.2.3   File Structure

We commonly distinguish two methods of file organization, the *contiguous placemen*t and the *non-contiguous placement*. In *sequential storage*, using the contiguous placement, each file is organized as a simple sequence of bytes or records. Files are stored consecutively on the secondary storage media as shown in Figure 4-7.

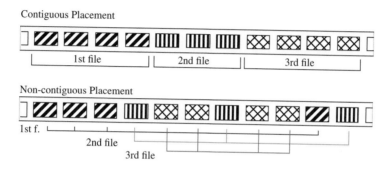

**Figure 4-7**   Contiguous and non-contiguous storage.

They are separated from each other by a well defined "end of file" bit pattern, character or character sequence. A file descriptor is usually placed at the beginning of the file and is, in some systems, repeated at the end of the file. Sequential storage is the only possible way to organize the storage on tape, but it can also be used on disks. The main advantage of contiguous placement is its efficiency for sequential access, as well as for direct access [Kra98], and minimized disk access time for reading and writing. The disadvantages of this approach are the low disk utilization, disk fragmentation and the difficulty of finding contiguous space when files are growing. The *non-contiguous placement* places files where free blocks are available. This placement must use file allocation tables (FAT) or other directory or index structures to keep track of placed blocks scattered across the disk. The main advantage of this approach is its high utilization of the storage space because each error-free disk block can be used by a file. The disadvantage of this approach is the unpredictable access time to each block.

With multimedia data, neither contiguous placement nor non-contiguous placement of disk blocks is an optimal solution. Contiguous placement can be implemented easily but has the drawbacks of creating large empty arrays and thus, fragmentation on the disk. Insertion and deletion operations are extremely costly when data is moved to keep continuity and defragment the disk. This makes contiguous placement unaffordable for media servers that are also used in editing or frequent upload operations. Note that for media servers, which provide playback functionality only, the contiguous placement is desirable. Random non-contiguous placement, in contrast, implies that random seeks from one file block to the next must be made very often, even when only a small amount of data is required.

A few approaches address this problem. One approach is the selection of large block sizes. Since continuous media content is typically large, the percentage of lost space due to partially unused blocks at the end of the file is acceptable. The media server takes advantage of this by the reduced management for all operations because less addressing information needs to be kept, and because big amounts of data can be transferred to the main memory without seek penalties. In [RW94], Reddy and Wyllie introduce *constrained placement* (at the disk controller or storage management level), which introduces the technique of placing blocks on disk in such a way that they are in a reasonable distance from each other, meaning that the seek-time between a block and its consecutive block is within acceptable bounds.

## 4.3   Disk Controller

### 4.3.1   Data Placement

#### 4.3.1.1   Striping

If a system grows large enough to make the usage of multiple disks affordable, the issue of accessing these disks must be taken into account. This problem is especially important nowadays for home PC users. The simple approach is to arrange file systems in a convenient way on either of the disks and gain performance by putting the more frequently used data on the fastest disks. Although this is sufficient if the amount of disk space is the only concern, it is not the most effective way in which multiple disks can be used. *Striping* techniques have been developed that take more than just the amount of available space into account.

**RAID**   The original way of combining disks in a more efficient way is the *"Redundant Arrays of Inexpensive Disks"(RAID)* [PGK88]. RAID addresses both performance and fault tolerance problems to different extents in its various sub-specifications, which are called *RAID-Levels.* As shown in Figure 4-8, seven RAID levels are defined (0-6), each of which makes a different approach at combining performance enhancement with security enhancements. Some of these levels can be implemented in software while others require hardware support

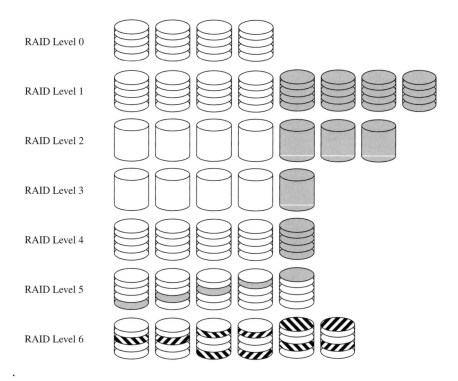

RAID Level 0

RAID Level 1

RAID Level 2

RAID Level 3

RAID Level 4

RAID Level 5

RAID Level 6

**Figure 4-8**   RAID levels [LGKP94].

- A **RAID-0** disk array is nonredundant, so basically, the name RAID is even mis-leading in this case. It is a purely performance-oriented RAID-level. It does not introduce any redundancy (or security) into the system but allows file systems to spread out across multiple disks, e.g. to achieve higher throughput for the delivery of data to applications that can consume data quickly but are throttled by the read-performance of a single disk.

- **RAID-1** implements mirroring or shadowing by storing all data twice. This is the traditional approach to data reliability and fault tolerance. Whenever data is writ-ten to the RAID system, each block is stored on two disks that are mirrors of each other. When data is retrieved, this system can be used to retrieve data from the disk with the lower access delay. In case of a disk failure, all requests are handled by the mirror of that disk. The recreation of a mirror disk after a failure is a copy operation from the remaining disk. The storage efficiency is low in this level, but the number of read transactions is high.

- **RAID-2** implements error correcting codes similar to ECC memory. For all of the primary data disks, the Hamming codes [PW72] are computed and stored on addi-tional parity disks. When a disk fails, the parity information on multiple parity disks identifies correctly the failed disk and in conjunction with all remaining data disks, the data of the failed disk can be reconstructed with a single parity disk. Since parity information must be modified on multiple parity disks at each write operation, this is a rather expensive RAID level and must be implemented in hardware.

- **RAID-3** implements bit-interleaved parity, which requires only a single parity disk. In this scheme, the fact is exploited that the disk controller can easily detect when a disk fails. Thus, the identification of the failed disk, that is possible with level 2, is not needed and only the recreation of lost information remains an issue. This recreation is possible after the failure of one data disk by computing the sum of each bit on all of the remaining data disks and the parity disk modulo 2. As in level 2, the constant maintenance of this parity information restricts the write performance to that of the parity disk and requires hardware support for the parity calculation.

- **RAID-4** is named block-interleaved parity. Instead of looking at each bit individually, the term *striping unit* is introduced for this RAID level. A stripe extends across all data disks of the disk array and is composed of data blocks of arbitrary size, the striping unit, on each disk. If a write operation is smaller than the striping unit, all data is written to one disk, otherwise striping units of more disks are modified. A block of new parity data on the parity disk is than computed from all striping units in the affected stripe. As with level 3, this RAID level is bound by the performance of the single parity disk that is affected by all write operations.

- **RAID-5** reduces this performance bottleneck by implementing block-interleaved distributed-parity. Instead of keeping the parity information of a stripe on a specific parity disk, parity blocks are equally distributed over the disks in the stripe units. The decision for placement of these parity blocks affects the performance of the system, as shown in [LK91]. In case of a disk failure, the missing data can be reconstructed as in level 4, without any additional consideration whether the reconstructed data is original data and parity data.

- **RAID-6,** called P+Q redundancy, uses Reed-Solomon codes to protect against the failure of two disks by increasing the basic size of the array by two redundant disks.These codes provide a better means of reconstructing the original data in case of a disk failure. This is relevant because the parity-protected levels require that no reading errors occur until the failed disk has been replaced. However, in large installations, additional errors become more probable, and protections against this are necessary. Level 6 provides this protection for a failure of up to two complete disks by distribution redundant data in a similar way to level 5.

The performance of the various RAID levels is shown in Table 4-1.

| RAID level | small read | small write | large read | large write | space usage |
|---|---|---|---|---|---|
| 0 | 1 | 1 | =small read | =small write | 1 |
| 1 | 1 | 1/2 | =small read | =small write | 1/2 |
| 2 | (G+1)/2 | (G+1)/2 | =small read | =small write | (G+1)/2G |
| 3 | 1/G | 1/G | =small read | =small write | (G-1)/G |
| 4 | 1/G | 1/G | (G-1)/G | (G-1)/G | (G-1)/G |
| 5 | 1 | max(1/G,1/4) | 1 | (G-1)/G | (G-1)/G |
| 6 | 1 | max(1/G,1/6) | 1 | (G-2)/G | (G-2)/G |

**Table 4-1**    Throughput and storage efficiency of RAID levels.

RAID was not developed to support multimedia applications, although the higher throughput of striped disks is an asset in that case. For the scalability of a media server, however, the throughput is only one issue among many. An increase in the scale of throughput is typically not necessary for a media server to handle new data formats and to deliver that data as quickly as possible to a client. Rather, the number of clients, that are requesting data concurrently, increases. This behavior increases not only the amount of data that has to be delivered, but also the number of files that have to be retrieved in parallel.

This implies an increased number of seek operations per unit time, a scaling issue which is not covered by RAID technology. Similarly, since multimedia data requires time-conforming delivery of data streams, the buffer requirements at the server grow when disk throughput is considerably higher than the delivery rate. A buffer allocated for each single client is filled in a short read burst due to the high throughput of the parallel disks, and subsequently, this data is delivered at the requested rate from that buffer. With an increasing number of disks to support more clients, the larger data blocks delivered per read burst as well as the increased number of parallel streams contribute to a quick increase in buffer requirements.

Figure 4-9 illustrates the increase of buffer sizes that have to be made available to buffer a single retrieval operation when the size of a RAID stripe group grows. A variety of techniques has been developed to address also this issue such as *multiple RAID, declustering, dynamic declustering, weighted striping, split-striping retrieval, and cyclic retrieval* as shown in Figure 4-10.

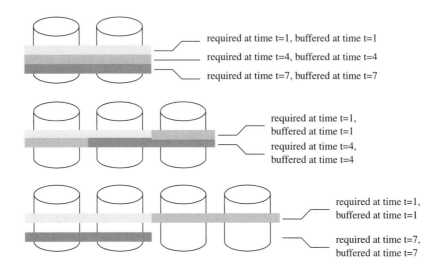

**Figure 4-9**   Growth of buffer requirements.

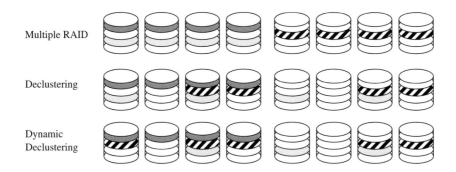

**Figure 4-10**   Varieties of group creation.

### 4.3.1.2    Multiple RAID

The most intuitive of these techniques is the creation of subgroups of disks into independent logical disk arrays. This limits the number of disks across which a file is striped to the size of such a group.

### 4.3.1.3    Declustering

In *declustering*, groups are not made up of complete disks. Rather, the stripe units of each disk are considered. Stripe units are logically connected into a stripe that spans only a subset of the disks (using the typical RAID protection mechanism). The number of disks for any such stripe is fixed and of the same size, but the disks on which a stripe is located differs. In such a way, the overall load is better distributed than in case of Multiple RAID approach, and the I/O throughput of all disks is exploited even if only a limited number of stripes is accessed.

#### 4.3.1.4 Dynamic Declustering

In *dynamic declustering*, this scheme is extended to assign stripes not statically to a set of disks, but rather to decide for each file the size and location of the stripes used. This scheme has two drawbacks. First, it is a very management-intensive scheme and it can not be used with protection mechanisms. It is a lot more management-intensive than the other schemes because a selection of a stripe must be made for each write operation. This selection must be augmented by the application because the file system disk controller is not aware of the throughput requirements of a content file. However, this scheme allows for an adaptation of the buffer size to the bandwidth requirements of the content file. When a server is supposed to deliver a mixed workload which ranges from bulk data to various continuous media formats, this can be worthwhile. A second drawback is that the group assignment in software makes it difficult to compute parity information in the disk controller. Special hardware and special interfaces would be necessary.

#### 4.3.1.5 Weighted Striping

*Weighted striping* [WD97] takes into account that it is unlikely for a real-world system to operate a multimedia server for a long time without adding or replacing part of the disks with newer or cheaper models. Since this introduces an inhomogeneity in the performance of the disks in the system, the throughput of a stripe may be limited by the least performing disk. In the *variable size weighted striping*, the size of stripe units are varied depending on the throughput of each disk in the stripe group. However, the replacement of a single disk with a new disk, with different performance characteristics, requires a memory-intensive restriping of all data bytes of the stripe rather than the reconstruction of a single stripe unit. Because of this, the *constant size weighted striping* is also proposed, which intends to level the throughput demands on single disks in the stripe in the long term. A video is split into units as large as one stripe unit, and these units are distributed onto the disks in such a way that disks with a higher throughput hold more units than disks with a lower throughput. The number of assigned units is equivalent to the throughput of the disks.

#### 4.3.1.6 Split-Stripe Retrieval

*Split-Stripe retrieval method*, introduced in [TF95], aims to address the problem of buffer requirements by allowing read operations for more than one stream in a single read operation to a stripe, i.e. while a full stripe is read in every cycle, the results of this read operation do not necessarily fill only the buffer for a single stream. Figure 4-11 gives a sketch of the retrieval operations. While the smallest addressable unit in RAID is the stripe. Split stripe retrieval requires the addressing of the stripe unit, which may be as small as a single sector on a single disk.

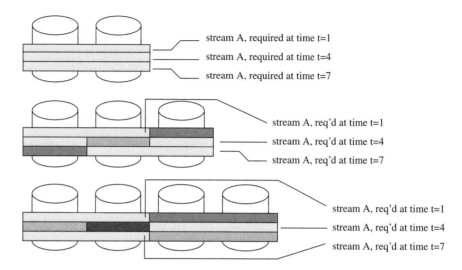

stream A, required at time t=1

stream A, required at time t=4

stream A, required at time t=7

stream A, req'd at time t=1

stream A, req'd at time t=4

stream A, req'd at time t=7

stream A, req'd at time t=1

stream A, req'd at time t=4

stream A, req'd at time t=7

**Figure 4-11**   Split Stripe retrieval.

### 4.3.1.7   Cyclic Retrieval

An enhancement of the split-stripe technique is to allow, in addition to reading independent full stripe units, also read operations on stripe units without the need of retrieving full stripes in one operation. This cyclic retrieval technique allows for a much smaller buffer per stream because the maximum required buffer size per stream is not the size of a full stripe but that of a single stripe unit.

## 4.3.2   Reorganization

The addition of new disks to a media server can result in an overall performance increase for that server if the I/O bandwidth of those new disks can be exploited. For quite a while now, hot-swappable and hot-pluggable disks are available from hardware vendors. Since the newly added disks can be considered initially empty, a reorganization of content that is already located on the server must be initiated in that case. In the best case, such a reorganization is handled without disrupting the service.

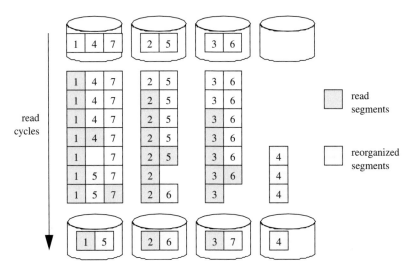

**Figure 4-12**   Lazy reorganization of stripe groups.

One scheme for reorganizing a media server, after the addition of a disk $(n+1)$ to a stripe group $(1 ... n)$ without disrupting the service, is the movement of segments of a content file to rearrange them in such a way that consecutive segments are ordered according to the index of the disk in the stripe group (modulo $n+1$). [GK96] presents *lazy* and *eager* on-line reorganization. Lazy reorganization is activated only when a content file is retrieved by a client. If a segment of the content file is retrieved, which should be relocated to the new disk based on the placement formula for segments in stripe groups, a write operation to the new disk is performed in the cycle following the read operation. Figure 4-12 visualizes the rearrangement. This scheme has the drawback that the reorganization is executed only for those content files that are accessed by a client. If a file is never retrieved, it is also never reorganized. With eager reorganization, idle time of the system is used to reorganize content. Since the order to segments in this approach is not bound by the playout order, multiple segments can be rearranged at a time, if sufficient buffer space in main memory is available.Assuming sufficient buffer space, the reorganization would be performed as shown in Figure 4-13. The time that is necessary to perform the reorganization can further be reduced by preloading the segments that are targeted at the new disks before the insertion of those disks into the system. The original segments are then removed from their previous location and the other blocks are reorganized.

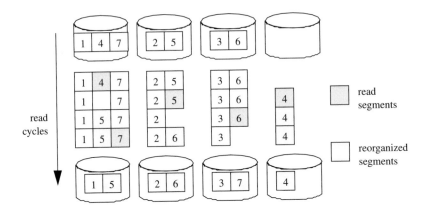

**Figure 4-13**   Eager reorganization of stripe groups.

The *random duplicated assignment* approach proposed in [Kor97] is based on the assumption of a system which is built on a growing number of heterogeneous disks and delivers variable bit-rate data streams. Such a system is on average not degraded by randomly placing blocks two times on different disks of the system and retrieving them from the less loaded disk. In case of replacement of a single disk, content can be reconstructed by replicating data blocks onto that disk when only a single copy of these blocks is available in the system, in case of adding a new disk, blocks can be from any of the disks that are already available in the system and they can be moved to the new disk in case that they have not been moved there from a different disk earlier.

## 4.4   Storage Management

Whereas strictly sequential storage devices (e.g., tapes) do not have a scheduling problem, for random access storage devices, every file operation may require movements of the read/write head. This operation, known as the *access operation*, is very time consuming. Disk management aims to reduce the effects of such access operations [HPG03b]. Still, the actual access time to read or write a disk block is determined by three time components:

- The *seek time* (the time required for the movement of the read/write head).
- The *latency time or rotational delay* (the time during which the transfer cannot proceed until the right block or sector rotates under the read/write head).
- The actual *data transfer time* needed for the data to copy from disk into main memory.

Usually the seek time is the largest factor of the actual transfer time. Most systems try to keep the cost of seeking low by applying special algorithms to the scheduling of disk read/write operations. The access of the storage device is a problem greatly influenced by the file placement methods and disks scheduling algorithms. For instance, a program reading a contiguously allocated file generates requests which are located close together on a disk. Thus head movement is limited. Linked or indexed files with blocks, which are widely scattered, cause many head movements. In multi-programming systems, where the disk queue may often be non-empty, fairness is also a criterion for scheduling. The approaches to optimize the access time are *disk scheduling algorithms*. In this subsection we present related issues such as file placement and disk scheduling that have impact on access operations in media servers.

### 4.4.1 Disk Management

#### 4.4.1.1 Disk Access and File Placement

Disk access is a slow and costly transaction. In traditional systems, a common technique to reduce disk access is to use *block caches*. Using a block cache means that blocks are kept in memory because it is expected that future read or write operations access these data again. Thus, performance is enhanced due to shorter access time to the block cache instead of to the physical disk block. Another way to enhance performance is to reduce disk arm motion. Blocks that are likely to be accessed in sequence are *placed together on one cylinder*. To refine this method, rotational positioning can be taken into account. Consecutive blocks are placed on the same cylinder, but in an interleaved way as shown in Figure 4-14.

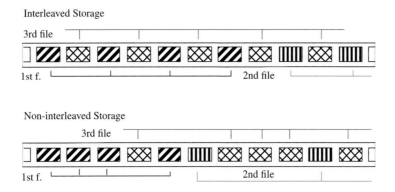

**Figure 4-14**    Interleaved and non-interleaved storage.

Another important issue is the placement of the mapping tables (e.g., I-nodes in UNIX) on the disk. If they are placed near the beginning of the disk, the distance between them and the blocks will be, on average, half the number of cylinders. To improve this, they can be placed in the middle of the disk. Hence, the average seek time is roughly reduced by a factor of two. In the same way, consecutive blocks should be placed on the same cylinder. The use of the same cylinder for the storage of mapping tables and referred blocks also improves performance.

If multiple multimedia files are considered to be stored on a media server, it is important to search for efficient storage of the most frequently accessed multimedia file(s). If files are stored randomly, the time will be wasted when moving disk head from one file to another. We can improve the access time to individual files, if we observe which multimedia files are the most popular ones and take the *popularity* into account when placing the files on the disk. The popularity pattern of books, rented movies and other objects and behaviors, was discovered by the Harvard professor of linguistics, George Zip and it is called the *Zipf's law* [Tan01]. The Zipf's law specifies that if popularity objects such as multimedia files are ranked according to their popularity, then the probability that the next customer chooses the $k^{th}$ item on the list is $C/k$, where C is the normalization constant. Furthermore, if there are $N$ multimedia files, then $C/1 + C/2 +... + C/N = 1$ is true. This equation yields the calculation of $C$ for any number of files. For example, if we consider two multimedia files (N=2), then C = 2/3 = 0.66, and the access probabilities for the two files are 0.666/1=0.666 and 0.666/2=0.333. For N=10 and C= 0.341, the access probabilities for the top two movies are 0.341 and 0.1705. The Zipf's law distribution falls off fairly quickly at the beginning, but it also has a long tail.

The relative popularity makes it possible to consider a simple and distribution independent strategy to place multimedia files, called the *organ-pipe algorithm* [GS73] [Won83]. This strategy places the most popular file in the middle of the disk with the second and third most popular file on either side of the first one. Similarly, the $4^{th}$ and $5^{th}$ files are placed on either side of the $2^{nd}$ and $3^{rd}$ movie, etc. The reason for the best access time of the most popular file placed in the middle of the disk, is that the distance between any position of a disk and the middle position is the shortest. This placement algorithm works best if each file uses the contiguous placement, but can be also used if each file uses only narrow range of cylinders.

As it was discussed above, media servers have mostly multiple disks to allow for parallel access in order to speed up the access time as well as increase throughput of the media server. If multimedia files are placed on multiple disks, they may use RAID techniques or other techniques as discussed in Section 4.3.

### 4.4.1.2    File Structure

In conventional storage management systems, the main goal of the file organization is to make efficient use of the storage capacity (i.e., to reduce internal and external fragmentation) and to allow arbitrary deletion and extension of files. In multimedia systems, the main goal is to *provide a constant and timely retrieval of data*. Internal fragmentation occurs when blocks of data are not entirely filled. On average, the last block of a file is only half utilized. The use of large blocks leads to a larger waste of storage due to this internal fragmentation. External fragmentation mainly occurs when files are stored in a contiguous way. After the deletion of a file, the gap can only be filled by a file with the same or a smaller size. Therefore, there are usually small fractions between two files that are not used, storage space for continuous media is wasted.

As mentioned above, the goals for multimedia file systems can be achieved through providing enough buffer for each data stream and the deployment of disk scheduling algorithms, especially optimized for real-time storage and retrieval of data. The advantage of this approach (where data blocks of single files are scattered) is flexibility. External fragmentation is avoided and the same data can be used by several streams (via references). Even using only one stream might be of advantage; for instance, it is possible to access one block twice, e.g., when a phrase in a sonata is repeated. However, due to the large and unpredictable seek times of access operations during playback, even with optimized disk scheduling, large buffers must be provided to smooth jitter during the data retrieval phase. Therefore, there are also long initial delays during the retrieval of continuous media.

The much greater size of continuous media files and the fact, that they will usually be retrieved sequentially due to the nature of the operation performed on them (such as play, pause, fast forward, etc.), is the reason for an optimization of the disk layout. Our own application-related experience has shown that continuous media streams predominantly belong to the write-once-read-many nature, and streams that are recorded at the same time are likely to be played back at the same time (e.g., audio and video of a movie, [LS93]).

### 4.4.2   Traditional Disk Scheduling

Most traditional storage systems apply one of the following scheduling algorithms:

### 4.4.2.1   First-Come-First-Served (FCFS)

With this algorithm, the disk driver accepts requests one-at-a-time and serves them in incoming order. This is easy to program and an intrinsically fair algorithm. However, it is not optimal with respect to head movement because it does not consider the location of the other queued requests. This results in a high average seek time. Figure 4-15 shows an example of the application of FCFS to a request of three queued blocks.

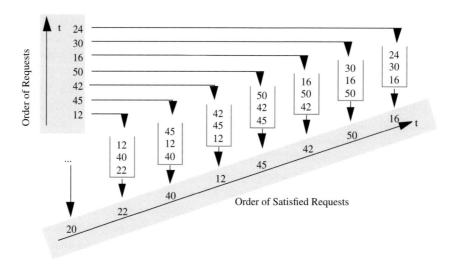

**Figure 4-15**   FCFS disk scheduling.

### 4.4.2.2    Shortest-Seek-Time First (SSTF)

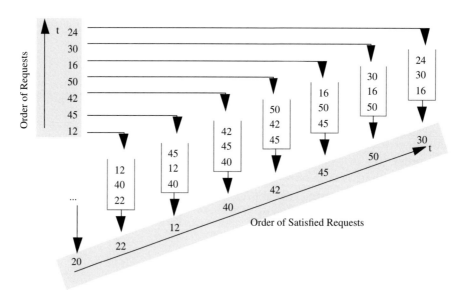

**Figure 4-16**   SSTF disk scheduling.

At every point in time, when a data transfer is requested, SSTF selects among all requests the one with the minimum seek time from the current head position. Therefore, the head is moved to the closest track in the request queue. This algorithm was developed to minimize seek time and it is in this sense optimal. SSTF is a modification of Shortest Job First (SJF), and like SJF, it may cause starvation of some requests. Request targets in the middle of the disk will get immediate service at the expense of requests in the innermost and outermost disk areas. Figure 4-16 demonstrates the operation of the SSTF algorithm.

### 4.4.2.3    SCAN

Like SSTF, SCAN orders requests to minimize seek time. In contrast to SSTF, it takes the direction of the current disk movement into account. It first serves all requests in one direction until it does not have any requests in this direction anymore. The head movement is then reversed and service is continued. SCAN provides a very good seek time because the edge tracks get better service times. Note that middle tracks still get a better service then edge tracks. When the head movement is reversed, it first serves tracks that have recently been serviced, where the heaviest density of requests, assuming a uniform distribution, is at the other end of the disk. Figure 4-17 shows an example of the SCAN algorithm.

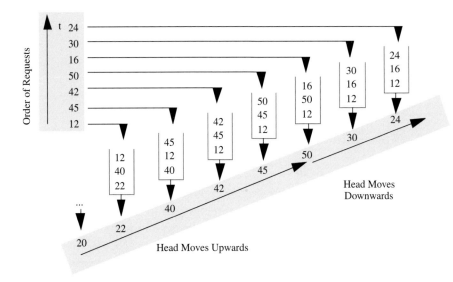

**Figure 4-17**   SCAN disk scheduling.

### 4.4.2.4    N-Step-SCAN

This variation of the SCAN tries to reduce delays that are introduced into the SCAN scheme by requests that arrive after the SCAN has started. As a result of this, incoming requests may have to wait although the disk head passes by the requested position on the disk. The *N-Step-SCAN* approach gains fairness for the requests to data on outer tracks for a lower average response time. The scheme can be modified to move the disk head to the outermost position that is requested for the next SCAN instead of starting the next SCAN from the position of the last read track of the previous SCAN. One effect is that SCAN is not always performed in upwards-downwards order, but the direction of the movement can change. Another issue is that this approach, called Pre-seek-Sweep-Scheduling, yields a lower average seek times. Figure 4-18 shows an example of the SCAN algorithm.

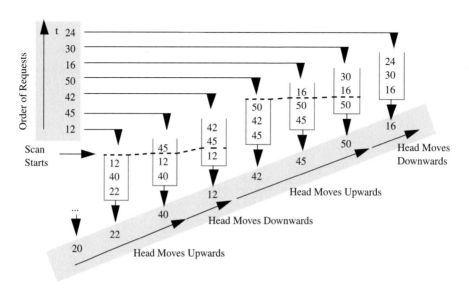

**Figure 4-18**   N-Step-SCAN disk scheduling.

### 4.4.2.5   C-SCAN

C-SCAN also moves the head in one direction, but it offers fairer service with more uniform waiting times. It does not alter the direction, as in SCAN. Instead, it scans in cycles, always increasing or decreasing, with one idle head movement from one edge to the other between two consecutive scans. The performance of C-SCAN is somewhat less than SCAN. Figure 4-19 shows the operation of the C-SCAN algorithm.

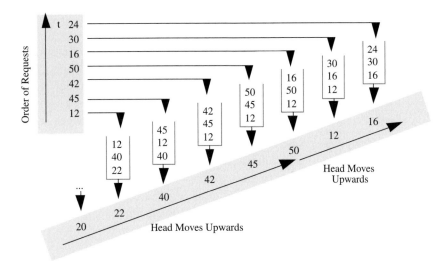

**Figure 4-19**  C-SCAN disk scheduling.

### 4.4.2.6  T-SCAN

T-SCAN uses a method, called *period transformation*, to prevent blocking of individual requests. Such a period transformation is actually a modification of the sizes by which individual requests are serviced. With the goal of supporting media streams without blocking, T-SCAN uses one stream's request behavior as a reference to service all requests. That implies that, if the reference stream's requested rate is $R_1$, the block size that is requested per cycle is $B_1$, and another streams requested rate is $R_2$, then other stream is serviced with blocks of size of $B_1*R_2/R_1$, no matter what the actual requests of the application are. In this way, requests are serviced in the order of their arrival using the SCAN mechanism, and all streams will be provided a fair share of the I/O bandwidth. However, without admission control, this scheme affects all serviced streams when the server gets overloaded.

Traditional file systems are not designed for employment in multimedia systems. They do not, for example, consider requirements like real-time which are important to the retrieval of stored audio and video. To serve these requirements, new policies in the structure and organization of files, and in the retrieval of data from the disk, must be applied. The next section outlines the most important developments in this area.

### 4.4.3  Multimedia Disk Scheduling

The main goals of traditional disk scheduling algorithms are to reduce the cost of seek operations, to achieve a high throughput and to provide fair disk access for every process. The additional real-time requirements introduced by multimedia systems make traditional disk scheduling algorithms, such as described above, inconvenient for multimedia systems. Systems without any optimized disk layout for the storage of continuous media depend far more on reliable and efficient disk scheduling algorithms than others. In the case of contiguous storage, scheduling is only needed to serve requests from multiple streams concurrently. In [LS93], a round-robin scheduler is employed that is able to serve hard real-time tasks. Here, additional optimization is provided through the close physical placement of streams that are likely to be accessed together.

The overall goal of disk scheduling in multimedia systems is to meet the deadlines of all time-critical tasks. Closely related is the goal of keeping the necessary buffer space requirements low. As many streams as possible should be served concurrently, but aperiodic requests should also be schedulable without delaying their service for an infinite amount of time. The scheduling algorithm must find a balance between time constraints and efficiency.

### 4.4.3.1   Earliest Deadline First

Let us first look at the *Earliest Deadline First (EDF)* scheduling strategy as described for CPU scheduling, but used for the file system issue as well. Here, the block of the stream with the nearest deadline would be read first.

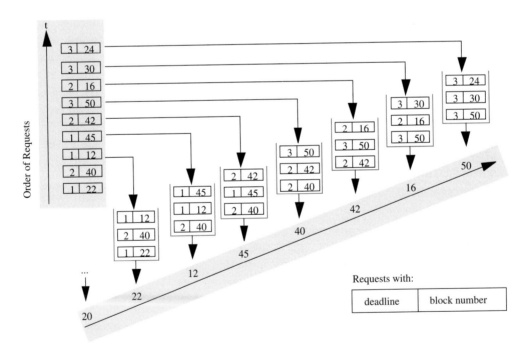

**Figure 4-20**   EDF disk scheduling.

The employment of EDF, as shown in Figure 4-20, in the strict sense results in poor throughput and excessive seek time. Further, as EDF is most often applied as a preemptive scheduling scheme, the costs for preemption of a task and scheduling of another task are considerably high. The overhead caused by this is in the same order of magnitude as at least one disk seek. Hence, EDF must be adapted or combined with file system strategies.

### 4.4.3.2    SCAN-Earliest Deadline First

The SCAN-EDF strategy is a combination of the SCAN and EDF approaches [RW93]. The seek optimization of SCAN and the real-time guarantees of EDF are combined in the following way: like in EDF, the request with the earliest deadline is always served first; among requests with the same deadline, the specific one that is first according to the scan direction is

served first; among the remaining requests, this principle is repeated until no request with this deadline is left.

Since the optimization only applies for requests with the same deadline, its efficiency depends on how often it can be applied (i.e., how many requests have the same or a similar deadline). To increase this probability, the following tricky technique can be used: all requests have release times that are multiples of the period $p$. Hence, all requests have deadlines that are multiples of the period $p$. Therefore, the requests can be grouped together and be served accordingly.

SCAN-EDF can be easily implemented. To do this, EDF must be modified slightly. If $D_i$ is the deadline of task i and $N_i$ is the track position, the deadline can be modified to be $D_i + f(N_i)$. Thus the deadline is deferred. The function $f()$ converts the track number of $i$ into a small perturbation of the deadline, as shown in the example of Figure 4-21. It must be small enough so that $D_i + f(N_i) \le D_j + f(N_j)$ holds for all $D_i \le D_j$, it was proposed to choose the following function [RW93]:

$$f(N_i) = \frac{N_i}{N_{max}}$$

where $N_{max}$ is the maximum track number on disk. Other functions might also be appropriate.

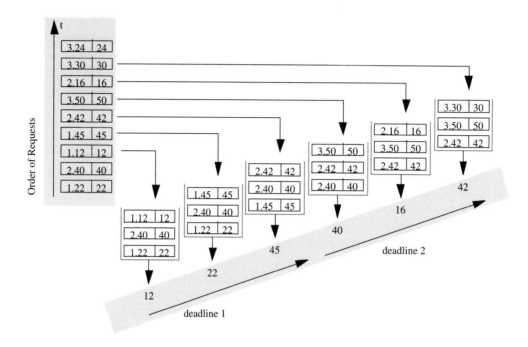

**Figure 4-21**   SCAN-EDF disk scheduling with $N_{max}$ = 100 and f($N_i$) = $N_i$ /$N_{max}$.

We enhanced this mechanism by taking a more accurate perturbation of the deadline which takes into account the actual position of the head ($N$). This position is measured in terms of block numbers and the current direction of the head movement (see also Figure 4-22 and Figure 4-23):

1. If the head moves toward $N_{max}$, i.e., upward, then

    a. for all blocks $N_i$ located between the actual position $N$ and $N_{max}$, the perturbation of the deadline is:

$$f(N_i) = \frac{N_i - N}{N_{max}} \quad for\ all \ \ N_i \geq N$$

    b. for all blocks $N_i$ located between the actual position and the first block (no. 0):

$$f(N_i) = \frac{N_{max} - N_i}{N_{max}} \quad for\ all \ \ N_i < N$$

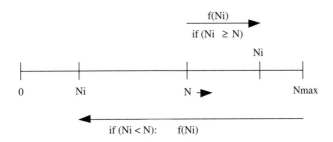

**Figure 4-22**  Accurate EDF-SCAN algorithm, head moves upward.

2. If the head moves downward towards the first blocks, then

   a. for all blocks located between the actual position and $N_{max}$:

$$f(N_i) = \frac{N_i}{N_{max}} \quad for\ all \quad N_i > N$$

   b. for all blocks located between this first block with the block number 0 and the actual position:

$$f(N_i) = \frac{N - N_i}{N_{max}} \quad for\ all \quad N_i \leq N$$

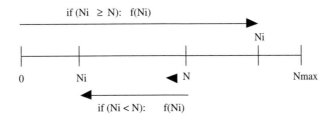

**Figure 4-23**  Accurate EDF-SCAN algorithm, head moves downward.

This algorithm is more computing-intensive than the algorithm with the simple perturbation calculation. In cases with only a few equal deadlines, our algorithm provides improvements and the expenses of the calculations can be tolerated. In situations with many, i.e., typically more than five equal deadlines, the simple calculation provides sufficient optimization and additional calculations should be avoided. SCAN-EDF was compared with pure EDF and different variations of SCAN. It was shown that SCAN-EDF with deferred deadlines performed well in multimedia environments.

### 4.4.3.3    Group Sweeping Scheduling

With Group Sweeping Scheduling (GSS), requests are served in cycles, in round-robin manner [YCK92] [GH94]. To reduce disk arm movements, the set of $n$ streams is divided into $g$ groups. Groups are served in fixed order. Individual streams within a group are served according to SCAN; therefore, it is not fixed at which time or order individual streams within a group are served. In one cycle, a specific stream may be the first to be served; in another cycle, it may be the last in the same group. A smoothing buffer which is sized according to the cycle time and data rate of the stream assures continuity. If the SCAN scheduling strategy is applied to all streams of a cycle without any grouping, the playout of a stream cannot be started until the end of the cycle of its first retrieval (where all requests are served once) because the next service may be in the last slot of the following cycle. As the data must be buffered in GSS, the playout can be started at the end of the group in which the first retrieval takes place. Whereas SCAN requires buffers for all streams, in GSS, the buffer can be reused for each group. Further optimizations of this scheme are proposed in [CKY93]. In this method, it is ensured that each stream is served once in each cycle.

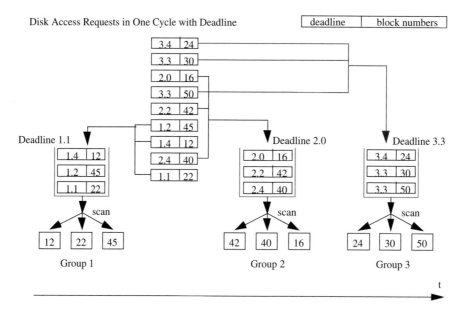

**Figure 4-24**    Group sweeping scheduling as a disk access strategy.

GSS is a trade-off between the optimization of buffer space and arm movements. To provide the requested guarantees for continuous media data, we introduce a *"joint deadline" mechanism*, i.e., we assign to each group of streams one deadline, the "joint deadline". This deadline is specified as being the earliest one out of the deadlines of all streams in the respective group. Streams are grouped in such a way that all of them comprise similar deadlines. Figure 4-24 shows an example of GSS.

### 4.4.3.4 Mixed Strategy

In the literature [Abb84], a *mixed strategy* was introduced based on the *shortest seek* (also called greedy strategy) and the *balanced strategy*.

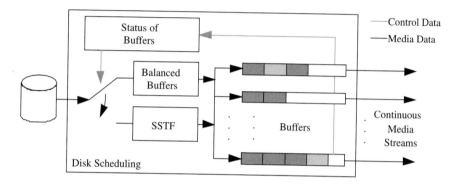

**Figure 4-25** Mixed disk scheduling strategy.

As shown in Figure 4-25, every time data are retrieved from disk they are transferred into buffer memory allocated for the respective data stream. From there, the application process removes them one at a time. The goal of the scheduling algorithm is:

- To maximize transfer efficiency by minimizing seek time and latency.
- To serve process requirements with a limited buffer space.

With shortest seek, the first goal is served, i.e., the process of which data block is the closest one is served first. The balanced strategy chooses the process which has the least amount of buffered data for service because this process is likely to run out of data. The crucial part of this algorithm is the decision about which of the two strategies must be applied (shortest seek or balanced strategy). For the employment of shortest seek, two criteria must be fulfilled: the number of buffers for all processes should be balanced (i.e., all processes should nearly have the same number of buffered data) and the overall required bandwidth should be sufficient for the number of active processes, so that none of them will try to immediately read data out of an empty buffer. In [Abb84], the urgency is introduced as an attempt to measure both. The urgency is the sum of the reciprocals of the current "fullness" (amount of buffered data). This number measures both the relative balance of all read processes and the number of read processes. If the urgency is large, the balance strategy will be used; if it is small, it is safe to apply the shortest seek algorithm. A more recent approach based on mixed strategy has been discussed in [LG03].

### 4.4.3.5 Continuous Media File System Disk Scheduling

*CMFS Disk Scheduling* is a non-preemptive disk scheduling scheme designed for the Continuous Media File System (CMFS) at UC-Berkeley [DPA91]. Different policies can be applied in this scheme. Here the notion of the slack time $H$ is introduced. The slack time is the time during which CMFS is free to do non-real-time operations or workahead for real-time processes, because the current workahead of each process is sufficient so that no process would starve, even if it would not be served for $H$ seconds. The considered real-time scheduling policies are:

- The *Static/Minimal policy* is based on the minimal *Workahead Augmenting Set (WAS)*. A process $p_i$ reads a file at a determined rate $R_i$. To each process, a positive integer $M_i$ is assigned which denotes the time overhead required to read a block covering, for example, the seek time. The CMFS performs a set of operations (i.e., disk operations required by all processes) by seeking the next block of a file and reading $M_i$ blocks of this file. Note, we consider only read operations; the same also holds, with minor modifications, for write operations. This seek is done for every process in the system. The data, read by a process during this operation, "lasts" $\frac{M_i \times A}{R_i}$, where $A$ is the block size in bytes. The WAS is a set of operations, where the data read for each process "lasts longer" than the worst-case time to perform the operations (i.e., the sum of the read operations of all processes is less than the time read data last for a process). A schedule is derived from the set that is workahead-augmenting and feasible (i.e., the requests are served in the order given by the WAS). The *Minimal Policy*, the minimal WAS, is the schedule where the worst-case elapsed time, needed to serve an operation set, is the least (i.e., the set is ordered in a way that reduces time needed to perform the operations, for example, by reducing seek times). The *Minimal Policy* does not consider buffer requirements. If there is not enough buffer, this algorithm causes a buffer over-flow. The *Static Policy* modifies this schedule such that no block is read if this would cause a buffer overflow for that process. With this approach, starvation is avoided, but its use of short operations causes high seek overhead.

- With the *Greedy Policy*, a process is served as long as possible. Therefore, it computes at each iteration the slack time $H$. The process with the smallest workahead is served. The maximum number $n$ of blocks for this process is read; $n$ is determined by $H$ (the time needed to read $n$ blocks must be less than or equal to $H$) and the currently available buffer space.

- The *Cyclical Plan Policy* distributes the slack time among processes to maximize the slack time. It calculates $H$ and increases the minimal WAS with $H$ milliseconds of additional reads; an additional read for each process is done immediately after the regular read determined by the minimal WAS. This policy distributes workahead by identifying the process with the smallest slack time and schedules an extra block for it; this is done until $H$ is exhausted. The number of block reads for the least workahead is determined. This procedure is repeated every time the read has completed.

The *Aggressive* version of the Greedy and the Cyclical Plan Policy calculates $H$ of all processes except the least workahead process that is immediately served by both policies. If the buffer size limit of a process is reached, all policies skip to the next process. Non-real-time operations are served if there is enough slack time. Performance measurements of the above introduced strategy showed that Cyclical Plan increases system slack faster at low values of the slack time (which is likely to be the case at system setup). With a higher system slack time, apart of the Static/Minimal Policy, all policies perform about the same.

All of the disk scheduling strategies described above have been implemented and tested in prototype file systems for continuous media. Their efficiency depends on the design of the entire file system, the disk layout, tightness of deadlines, and last but not least, on the application that is behaving. It is not yet common sense which algorithm is the "best" method for the storage and retrieval of continuous media files. Further research must show which algorithm serves the timing requirements of continuous media best and ensures that aperiodic and non-real-time requests are efficiently served.

## 4.4.4  Admission Control

A media server is required to service multiple client requests simultaneously. Furthermore, the multimedia streams have timing requirements, hence the media server must employ *admission control* algorithms to determine whether a new stream can be serviced (scheduled) without having a negative effect on other streams already being serviced. Consequently, employing admission control has direct dependencies towards resource management as analyzed in [LG03].

To guarantee that a media server meets its guarantees, worst case assumptions must be made about the seek and disk rotation latencies. However, the seek times and rotational latency incur usually shorter than worst case delays, hence a media server may exploit the statistical variation in media block access times from the disk. Also, some applications can tolerate missed deadlines. Hence, in admitting streams, a media server can offer three possible quality of service guarantees [SV02]:

- *Deterministic guarantee*, where all deadlines are guaranteed to be met. In this case, the admission control assumes the worst case.
- *Statistical guarantees*, where deadlines are met with certain probability. To provide such guarantees, the admission control assumes the system's statistical behavior.

• *Best effort guarantees*, where no guarantees are given for meeting deadlines. The server schedules requests only when there is time left over after servicing guaranteed and statistical streams.

To implement the *deterministic service with deterministic guarantees*, different service disciplines may deploy different admission control conditions to accept a single individual request (see for an example of a particular admission control condition the Felini system in Section 4.5.2). In this subsection, we will concentrate on a more generic admission control problem, that allows us to maximize the number of client requests which can be serviced simultaneously [BG87] [HPG03a], and the retrieval of all requested media streams proceeds at their respective guaranteed playback rates. To derive such an admission control [BG87], we assume that the server can service $\tau$ clients, each of whom is retrieving a media stream, and each client retrieves $k_i$ blocks. Each sequence of $k_1, k_2, ...,k\tau$ retrievals represents a service round, and the multimedia server repeatedly executes service rounds until the completion of all requests. The total time, spent retrieving $k_i$ blocks of $i^{th}$ request in a service round, will then consist of (1) $\alpha$: overhead of switching from $(i-1)^{th}$ request to $i^{th}$ request, and then transferring the first block of the $i^{th}$ request, and (2) $\beta$: time to transfer remaining $(k_i-1)$ blocks of the $i^{th}$ request in this service round. If $l_{seek}^{max}$ is the maximum seek and latency time, $R_{dr}$ is the disk rotation rate, $s^i_{mu}$ is the size of $i^{th}$ media unit, $\eta^1, \eta^2, .. \eta\tau$ denote granularities, $l^1_{ds}, l^2_{ds},...,l\tau_{ds}$ denote disk scattering parameters, and $R^1_{pl}, R^2_{pl},...,R\tau_{pl}$ denote the playback rates of the $\tau$ streams, then the continuous retrieval of each request can be guaranteed if and only if the total service time per round does not exceed the minimum of the playback durations of all the requests, i.e., for $i = 1,...,\tau$ :

$$\sum_i (\alpha + \beta) \leq min_i(k_i \times (\eta^i)/(R^i_{pl}))$$

where $\alpha = l_{seek}^{max}(\eta^i * s^i_{mu}/R_{dr})$ and $\beta = (k_i-1)*(l_{ids} + \eta^i * s^i_{mu}/R_{dr})$.

The multimedia server can service all the $\tau$ requests simultaneously if and only if $k_1, k_2, ...,k\tau$ can be determined such that the above admission control equation is satisfied. Since this formulation includes $\tau$ variables and only one admission control equation, we need to determine the values of $k_1, k_2, ...,k\tau$, which requires additional policies. The simplest policy is to assign equal values to $k_1, k_2, ...,k\tau$,yielding a *round robin servicing* algorithm. At the other extreme is an *exhaustive algorithm*, which initially assigns the minimum value 1 to each $k_i$, and then selectively increments the values of each $k_i$ until the continuous retrieval admission control equation is satisfied. An inbetween policy is the *quality proportional multi-subscriber servicing* algorithm, in which the number of blocks retrieved during each service round for each client is proportional to its playback rate.

The implementation of the statistical service is similar to the deterministic service, where instead of the server's worst case values (max values), the admission control uses statistical values. For example, the admission control equation can use an average rotation-delay value that would be expected to occur with a certain probability based on a random distribution of rotational delays.

In servicing streams during a service round, deterministic streams must be guaranteed service before any statistical streams, and all statistical streams must be serviced before best effort streams.

### 4.4.5  Replication

*Content replication* answers two issues at the storage management level: availability in case of disk of machine failures, and limits to the number of concurrent accesses to individual titles because of limits on the throughput of the hardware. The failure handling argument is very similar at the storage management level as at the disk controller level, with the major difference that the storage management can apply various kinds of storage media to store replica (e.g. tapes, disks or main memory). Considerations on this issue have been elaborated in [RW94]. Novel replication schemes have been used, for example, in [OSS03]. The alternatives to using replication, in order to increase the number of concurrent deliveries of one file, however, are increased in this management level.

On-demand applications can be partitioned into two families by the aging characteristics of their content. The content of online archives is assumed to be relatively time-independent and it is accessed based on the current interests of the customers. The content of news-on-demand and video-on-demand systems is expected to exhibit a popularity life-cycle like a newspaper or a movie. For the latter, the existence of a single copy of the content on a media server may not be sufficient to serve the necessary number of concurrent streams for a true on-demand systems from the storage subsystems where it is located.

#### 4.4.5.1    Static replication

The simplest approach to replication that can be taken is the explicit duplication of content files, by storing the file on multiple machines and providing the user with a choice of access points. This is frequently done in the Internet today: the content provider stores copies of the original version up to date on servers closely located to the user. Using the more elaborate manual options, the content is duplicated manually, and an application provides alternating copies of the file under the same name.

Static replication of files for high availability and load balancing in file servers has been proposed in [LGG⁺91] and [SDY93]. A static placement policy that uses such estimated load information for the placement of video objects is proposed in [DS95b].

This static placement policy is complementary to other policies, as it reduces, but cannot eliminate, dynamic imbalances.

### 4.4.5.2 Dynamic Segment Replication

*Dynamic segment replication*, introduced in [DKS95], is designed for content which is accessed read-only and which can be split into equally-sized segments of a size that is conveniently handled by the file system. Fixing segment sizes as well as choosing segments that are large in comparison to a disk block are decisions that are made to keep the implementation overhead low. Since continuous media data is delivered in linear order, a load increase on a specific segment can be used as a trigger to replicate this segment and all following segments to other disks. Such segments are considered temporary segments in contrast to the original segments, which are permanent segments. One of the major advantages of this replication policy is that it takes not only the request frequency of individual movies into account. Rather than this, the load of the disk is also considered. Specifically, the decision is made in the following way: each disk $x$ has a pre-specified threshold for the number of concurrent read requests $B_x$ that must be exceeded by the sum of all segments' read operations in the current read cycle of the disk (where 'cycle' means the playout time of one segment) as well as by next read cycles to initiate the replication algorithm.

To simplify the calculation, the read requests are considered uniformly distributed over all replicas rather than taking requests to other segments on the same disk into account. In this way, the future load in $t$ cycles for the $i$-th segment is predicted as $n_{i-t} / r_i$ where $n_{i-1}$ is the number of viewers of segment $i$-$t$ and $r_i$ is the number of current replicas of the segment. For all segments $j$ ($j<t$), it is assumed that the current arrival rate $n_1/r_i$ will be maintained in the future. If the sum of the expected load for all segments on a disk exceeds $B_x$, the replication is triggered. Then, the algorithm must identify a segments for replication. Since the approach replicates segments only when they are retrieved from disk because of a client request, in order not to add additional load, replication can start only when a stream starts reading a new segment. Hence, if the disk load exceeds $B_x$ at a segment boundary crossing, we must decide whether it is desirable to replicate this segment. Not in any case, but only if the replication of this segment has the highest estimated payoff among all the segments on the disk, it is replicated. If the gain in replicating a different segment is considerable, a boundary crossing to that segment is awaited. The estimated payoff $p_i$ is computed as

$$p_i = \left( \frac{1}{r_i} - \frac{1}{r_i+1} \right) \sum_{j=0}^{i-1} n_j w^{i-j-1}$$

where $w$ is a weighting factor. $w$ can be chosen big to put a stronger weight on long-term predictions; this is a good selection when the load on individual segments stays similar for a relatively long time. If the load on segments is fluctuating strongly, the expectation of future behavior is unreliable and should have less relevance, expressed by a lower weight $w$.

### 4.4.5.3   Threshold-Based Dynamic Replication

The threshold-based dynamic replication, introduced in [LLG98], considers whole movies rather than movie segments, and it takes all disks of the system into account to determine whether a movie should be replicated. It is assumed for this approach that the term 'disk' does not necessarily mean a single physical disk but a logical disk which may also be an array of physical disks with a single representation to the storage management. Still, it is assumed that the media server is large and consists of many such logical disks. The service capacity in number of concurrent streams of such a disk $x$ is called $B_x$, the average service capacity of all disks is called $\bar{B}$.

A replica of a movie is assumed to be stored completely on one of these disks. For each movie $i$ of length $m_i$, a probability to be selected in a new request $P_i$ as well as a request arrival rate $\lambda$ must be computed from earlier requests. The replication threshold $T_i$ is than computed as $T_i = min(p_i \lambda m_i, h\bar{B})$, where $h$ a constant value to limit the probability of replication. For each disk $x$, the measured current load $L_x$ is taken into account to compute the current available service capacity $A_i$ for serving video $i$ by calculating

$$A_i = \sum_{x \in R_i} (B_x - L_x)$$

where $R_i$ is the set of disks that carry replicas of $i$. If $A_i < T_i$, a replication of movie $i$ is triggered. Similarly, [LLG98] proposes a decision for discarding replications when the number of concurrent requests $n_{ix}$ on a movie $i$ at disk $x$ decreases. The following condition is checked before a replica is removed:

$$\sum_{y \in R_i \backslash x} (B_y - L_y) - n_{ix} > T_i + D$$

This inequality integrates two important conditions. The inequality

$$A_i = \sum_{x \in R_i} B_x - L_x > \sum_{y \in R_i \backslash x} (B_y - L_y) - n_{ix} > T_i + D > T_i$$

implies that the replication is not triggered again immediately after a de-replication, and

$$\sum_{y \in R_i \backslash x} (B_y - L_y) - n_{ix} > T_i + D > 0$$

guarantees that all streams on disk $x$ can be served from the remaining replicas. $D$ is an additional threshold to reduce the probability of an oscillation between replication and de-replication further.

The approach includes also the proposal to replicate a movie from the least loaded disk to the destination disk because an overhead may be induced by an additional read operation on the source disk. For the selection of the destination disk out of the set of disks that do not yet hold a replica of the movie in question, multiple approaches are considered. The most complex one takes the number of current streams into account, but assumes that all ongoing replications are already finished and the streams are distributed onto the disks as if the replicas were already active. For the replication itself, various policies are proposed.

*Injected Sequential Replication* adds additional read load to one disk because it behaves like an additional client, by copying the movie at the normal play rate from the source disk to the target disk.

*Piggybacked Sequential Replication* is identical to the replication used in the Dynamic Segment Replication: the movie is written to the destination disk while it is delivered to one client from the same memory buffer. Since this scheme makes replication decisions for a movie always during admission control for new clients, this does not add complexity to identify the source copy of the operation. However, the copy operation is affected when VCR operations on the movie are performed.

*Injected Parallel Replication* uses a multiple of the normal data rate of the movie to replicate the movie faster from the source disk to the destination disk. In order not to inhibit admission of new customers, this multiple of the normal data rate is limited.

*Piggybacked Parallel Replication* copies at the normal rate of the movie, but not only from the position of the newly admitted client. Instead, later parts of the movie are copied at the same time from the buffers which serve clients that are already viewing the movie. Obviously, this approach needs unusually low level support because data is written in parallel to different positions in a not-yet complete file.

*Piggybacked and Injected Parallel Replication* combines the other parallel replication approaches to replicate parts by the injected approach of the movie that would have to be copied late in a piggybacked parallel replication mode because no client is expected to view those parts in the near future.

### 4.4.6  Supporting Heterogeneous Disks

Approaches of measuring the performance of disks and assigning data to them based on their performance characteristics becomes relevant when large-scale systems are considered. Such systems are assumed to grow over a long period of time, and considering the availability of time for which a specific series of hard disks is produced today, the chance to maintain a server that consists of homogeneous disks is low. The simple approach is to identify the disks with the smallest I/O-bandwidth and make this the reference bandwidth for all calculations. This approach would not collide with typical buffer management strategies since the strategies to keep the playout buffers filled is so resource-conservative that even disk read times are taken into account for refill operations.

Since both disk space and bandwidth have increased considerably in the past, the simple approach may be extremely pessimistic when the number of potentially supported streams is calculated. For example, an SSA storage system may deliver data at a rate of 100 MByte/s, while an typical SCSI-II fast/wide RAID system connected to the same media server delivers only 20 MByte/s. Various means can be applied to reduce the impact of heterogeneous storage systems.

#### 4.4.6.1 Bandwidth to Space Ratio

In the literature (see [DS95b]), not only the raw throughput of such logical disks is considered, but rather the ratio of throughput to storage capacity (*bandwidth to space ratio*, or *BSR*). This approach assumes that approaches to replication such as the dynamic segment replication policy mentioned above take care of a smoothing the average number of concurrent streams from the same movie. However, if throughput requirements of movies' copies (the product of data rate and number of concurrent viewers) differ, the throughput requirements for equally-sized segments of that video differ, too, and locating popular, high data-rate movies on large but throughput-restricted disks wastes space in comparison with storing them on smaller or faster disks. The same argument holds for variable-sized movies if the threshold-based dynamic replication is used. The decision to replicate a video according to the BSR scheme is identical to that of the dynamic segment replication, but the destination disk is chosen according to least expected deviation of the movie's BSR (data rate*concurrent viewers/length) from the disk's BSR (maximum throughput/size). Figure 4-26 illustrates this BSR deviation.

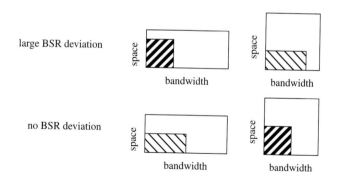

**Figure 4-26** Bandwidth to space ratio deviation.

It is a interesting detail of the BSR approach that as many replicas as possible are created to approach as close as possible the identity of used to available throughput ratios among all disks of the system. When the number of viewers for a movies changes, the best distribution is again recalculated.

## 4.5   File Systems

The *file system* is said to be the most visible part of an operating system. Most programs write or read files. Their program code, as well as user data, are stored in files. The organization of the file system is an important factor for the usability and convenience of the operating system. A file is a sequence of information held as a unit for storage and use in a computer system [Kra98].

Files are stored in secondary storage, so they can be used by different applications. The life-span of files is usually longer than the execution of a program. In traditional file systems, the information types stored in files are sources, objects, libraries and executable of programs, numeric data, text, payroll records, etc. In multimedia systems, the stored information also covers digitized video and audio with their related real-time "read" and "write" demands. Therefore, additional requirements in the design and implementation of file systems must be considered.

The file system provides access and control functions for the storage and retrieval of files. From the user's viewpoint, it is important how the file system allows file organization and structure. The internal, i.e., the organization of the file system, deals with the representation of information in files, their structure and organization in secondary storage.

### 4.5.1   Traditional File Systems

Although there is no such term as a traditional file system, a couple of file systems can be considered traditional for their wide-spread use in computer systems for all-round operations. In the operating system family stemming from MS-DOS, the FAT file system is the original one, in the family of Unix (-like) operating system, the Berkeley Fast FileSystem is a typical representative. Log-structured file systems provide some additional functionality but must be counted among these all-round file systems rather than multimedia file systems.

### 4.5.1.1   FAT

One way to keep track of scattered file blocks on a disk is to use linked blocks, where physical blocks containing consecutive logical locations are linked using pointers. The file descriptor must contain the number of blocks occupied by the file, the pointer to the first block and it may also have the pointer to the last block. A serious disadvantage of this method is the cost of the implementation for random access because all prior data must be read. In MS-DOS, a similar method is applied. A *File Allocation Table (FAT)* is associated with each disk. One entry in the table represents one disk block. The directory entry of each file holds the block number of the first block. The number in the slot of an entry refers to the next block of a file. The slot of the last block of a file contains an end-of-file mark [Tan01].

### 4.5.1.2    Berkeley FFS and relatives

Another approach is to store block information in mapping tables. Each file is associated with a table where, apart from the block numbers, information like owner, file size, creation time, last access time, etc., are stored. Those tables usually have a fixed size, which means that the number of block references is bounded. Files with more blocks are referenced indirectly by additional tables assigned to the files. In UNIX, a small table (on disk) called an i-node is associated with each file (see Figure 4-27). The indexed sequential approach is an example for multi-level mapping; here, logical and physical organization are not clearly separated [Kra98].

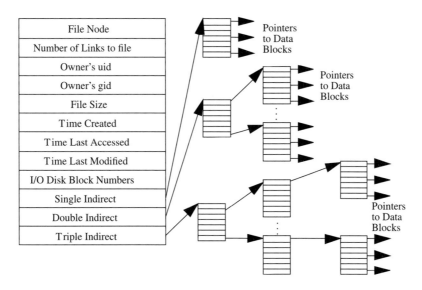

**Figure 4-27**   The UNIX i-node [Kra98].

### 4.5.1.3    Log-structured file system

The log-structured file system was devised to ensure fast crash recovery, increased write performance and an option for versioning in the file system. The basic approach is to write data always asynchronously to free space on the disk and to keep a log of all write operations on the disk. This ensures that in case of a machine crash, the information that was last written to disk can be identified from the log file, and the blocks that have most likely been corrupted can be checked explicitly rather than checking the whole disk. If the block can not be recovered, a consistent state can always be recovered in spite of this by examining the log; even in case of a modify operation, the old block is still present on the disk and can be identified by the log. The effect of writing always target write operations to a contiguous free space on the disk makes writing to the disk also more efficient since head movement is large reduced. In case of a small number of concurrent write operation, this results also in largely contiguous files.

Various ways to use a log-structured file system are conceivable. Figure 4-28 shows in-band logging as it was presented in [OD89] and a variation that uses a separate log partition, which was mentioned by [OD89] as an alternative approach.

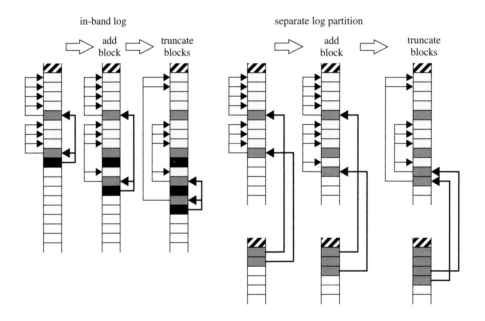

**Figure 4-28**   Disk operations in log-structured file systems.

Obviously, write operations in in-band logging are faster because no seek operation to the log partition is necessary. On the other hand, log partitions may be located on separate disks, close to the logged partition, or the log records can be kept in memory until sufficiently large block of log information has been collected to make the seek operation feasible. While in-band logging provides faster write operations, it suffers from the complexity of necessary compression operations that perform similar to a garbage collection. Using a separate log partition, superseded information from an earlier write operation can be flushed every time a new log information block is write and the log can be compressed to contain only the remaining relevant information.

#### 4.5.1.4    Directory Structure

Files are usually organized in *directories*. Most of today's operating systems provide tree-structured directories, where the user can organize the files according to his/her personal needs. In multimedia systems, it is important to organize the files in a way that allows easy, fast, and contiguous data access.

### 4.5.2  Multimedia File Systems

Compared to the increased performance of processors and networks, storage devices have become only marginally faster. The effect of this increasing speed mismatch is the search for new storage structures, and storage and retrieval mechanisms with respect to the file system [SGV02a] [GSYZ02]. Continuous media data are different from discrete data in:

- Real Time Characteristics

  As mentioned previously, the retrieval, computation and presentation of continuous media is time-dependent. The data must be presented (read) before a well-defined deadline with small jitter only. Thus, algorithms for the storage and retrieval of such data must consider time constraints, and additional buffers to smooth the data stream must be provided.

- File Size

  Compared to text and graphics, video and audio have very large storage space requirements. Since the file system has to store information ranging from small, unstructured units like text files to large, highly structured data units like video and associated audio, it must organize the data on disk in a way that efficiently uses the limited storage. For example, the storage requirements of uncompressed CD-quality stereo audio are 1.4 Mbits/s; low but acceptable quality compressed video still requires about 1 Mbit/s using, e.g., MPEG-1.

- Multiple Data Streams

  A multimedia system must support different media at one time. It does not only have to ensure that all of them get a sufficient share of the resources, it also must consider tight relations between different streams arriving from different sources. The retrieval of a movie, for example, requires the processing and synchronization of audio and video.

There are different ways to support continuous media in file systems. Basically, there are two approaches. The first approach preserves the organization of files on disk as it is. The necessary real-time support is provided through special disk scheduling algorithms and sufficient buffer to avoid jitter. In the second approach, the organization of audio and video files on disk is optimized for their use in multimedia systems. Scheduling of multiple data streams still remains a research issue.

In the following subsection, we discuss the different approaches via examples of existing prototypes. Architectural considerations have also been discussed in [SGV02b].

### 4.5.3   Example Multimedia File Systems

#### 4.5.3.1   Video File Server

The experimental *Video File Server,* introduced in [Ran93], supports integrated storage and retrieval of video. In this multimedia file system, continuous media data are characterized by consecutive, time-dependent logical data units (LDUs). The basic data unit of a motion video is a frame. The basic unit of audio is a sample. Frames contain the data associated with a single video image, a sample represents the amplitude of the analog audio signal at a given instance. Further structuring of multimedia data can be considered in the following way [RV91] [Ran93] [SF92]: LDUs can be grouped into a strand, where a *strand* is defined as an immutable sequence of continuously recorded video frames, audio samples, or both. It means that it consists of a sequence of blocks which contain either video frames, audio samples or both. Most often it includes headers and further information related to the type of compression used. The file system holds primary indices in a sequence of *Primary Blocks.* They contain mapping from media block numbers to their disk addresses. In *Secondary Blocks* pointers to all primary blocks are stored. The *Header Block* contains pointers to all secondary blocks of a strand. General information about the strand like, recording rate, length, etc., is also included in the header block.

Media strands that together constitute a logical entity of information (e.g., video and associated audio of a movie) are tied together by synchronization to form a multimedia rope. A rope contains the name of its creator, its length and access rights. For each media strand in this rope, the strand ID, rate of recording, granularity of storage and corresponding block-level are stored (information for the synchronization of the playback start for all media at the strand interval boundaries). Editing operations on ropes manipulate pointers to strands only. Strands are regarded as immutable objects because editing operations like insert or delete may require substantial copying which can consume significant amounts of time and space. Intervals of strands can be shared by different ropes. Strands that are not referenced by any rope can be deleted, and storage can be reclaimed [RV91]. The following interfaces are the operations that file systems provide for the manipulation of ropes:

* RECORD [media] [requestID, mmRopeID]

  A multimedia rope, represented by mmRopeID and consisting of media strands, is recorded until a STOP operation is issued.

* PLAY [mmRopeID, interval, media] requestID

  This operation plays a multimedia rope consisting of one or more media strands.

- STOP [requestID]

  This operation stops the retrieval or storage of the corresponding multimedia rope.

- Additionally, the following operations are supported:

```
INSERT [baseRope, position, media, withRope, withInterval]
REPLACE [baseRope, media, baseInterval, withRope,
         withInterval]
SUBSTRING [baseRope, media, interval]
CONCATE [mmRopeID1, mmRopeID2]
DELETE [baseRope, media, interval]
```

Figure 4-29 provides an example of the INSERT operation, whereas Figure 4-30 shows the REPLACE operation.

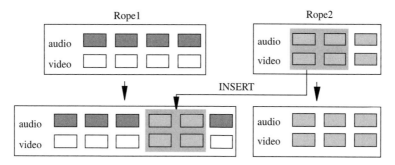

**Figure 4-29**  INSERT operation.

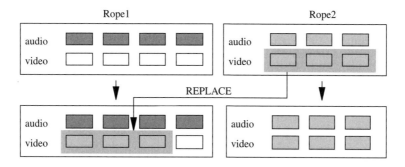

**Figure 4-30**  REPLACE operation.

The storage system of the Video File Server is divided into two layers:

- The *rope server* is responsible for the manipulation of multimedia ropes. It communicates with applications, allows the manipulation of ropes and communicates with the underlying *storage manager* to record and play back multimedia strands.

It provides the rope abstraction to the application. The rope access methods were designed similarly to UNIX file access routines. Status messages about the state of the play or record operation are passed to the application.

• The *storage manager* is responsible for the manipulation of strands. It places the strands on disk to ensure continuous recording and playback. The interface to the rope server includes four primitives for manipulating strands:

1. "PlayStrandSequence" takes a sequence of strand intervals and displays the given time interval of each strand in sequence.
2. "RecordStrand" creates a new strand and records the continuous media data either for a given duration or until StopStrand is called.
3. "StopStrand" terminates a previous PlayStrandSequence or RecordStrand instance.
4. "DeleteStrand" removes a strand from storage.

The "Video Rope Server" presents a device-independent directory interface to users (Video Rope). A Video Rope is characterized as a hierarchical directory structure constructed upon stored video frames. The "Video Disk Manager" manages a frame-oriented motion video storage on disk, including audio and video components.

### 4.5.3.2   Fellini

The *Fellini Multimedia Storage Server* [MNO$^+$96] [MNOS97] was developed in Bell Labs and has the goal to support real-time as well as non-real-time data, but its file system is dedicated to the storage and retrieval of continuous media data. It organizes data similarly to the Unix system, from which it is derived, but data and meta-information about the data are stored separately.

The Felini *process architecture* consists of (1) processes at the server machine such as the network process, peer client process, local client process and server process which communicate through buffer cache (shared memory), and (2) processes at the remote client machine such as the remote client processes. The server process runs on a dedicated machine and is responsible for data transfer between disks and the server machine. The server process includes the admission controller, cache manager and storage manager. The network process waits for connection requests and spawns new peer client processes at the server machine. The buffer cache is common to the server process and all peer client processes at the server machine. Peer client processes communicate with remote clients to mediate reads and writes.

The *admission control* in the server process ensures that the server has enough available data for each client. Data for client requests are retrieved in cycles $T$ which is referred to as the common period of the system. If a real-time client has the consumption rate $r_i$ and there are $d$ bits in the buffer at the start of a cycle, then the number of retrieved bits is

$$min((2 \times T \times r_i - d), T \times r_i).$$

The admission controller checks at the beginning of each subsequent cycle if

$$d \leq T \times r_i.$$

This means that the admission controller ensures that the server in time $T$ of a cycle always has $T*r_i$ bits available for each client in order to meet the rate guarantees for all admitted real-time clients.

Performance of a file system, which frequently accesses disk storage while manipulating data, depends on the *buffer cache*. The data, stored on disk, uses the raw disk interface and it is addressed both in main memory and on disk in terms of pages. Hence, the cache management maintains pages, deals with cache misses, maximizes cache hits and minimizes the cache misses. The requirements on the cache management, coming from multimedia systems, are (1) to allow real-time clients to access continuous media sequentially for playback, and (2) to allow several clients to access the data simultaneously. Therefore, the goal of cache management is to have the right policies so that the right pages get tossed out as replacement victims.

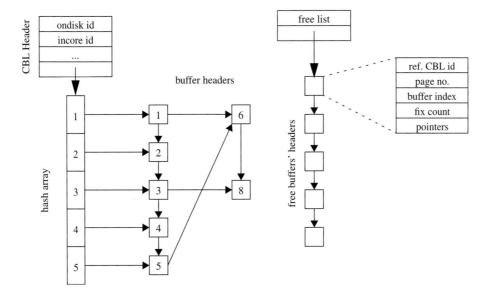

**Figure 4-31**   Fellini's Current Buffer List.

The cache management works with the buffer cache, *current buffer list* (CBL) and free list information to provide the above discussed goal. The buffer cache consists of buffer headers. Each buffer header points to a page in the buffer cache that contains data on the disk. The buffer header includes information such as buffer index, logical page number, dirty bit and fix count that determines the number of clients that access an appropriate location on the hard disk. The CBL is a set of pages containing data of cached files. These pages are countable and they are sorted, intuitively, in the order of a normal forward playout. Figure 4-31 shows the connection of buffer headers and the Current Buffer List (CBL).

For each file on disk, one CBL exists as a representation of that file. The CBL header contains an *ondisk id*, representing the file uniquely to all clients, and an *incore id*, containing the open file handle of the file on disk. This abstraction is necessary because a file should be opened only once for all concurrent accesses. Besides other information, the CBL header refers to a hash array that allows quick access to the buffer headers representing pages which are currently in main memory. At startup time, the Fellini server allocates free buffers in main memory, pins[1] them and stores their headers, with a 0 fix count, in the free list.

When a page is requested by a client for the first time, a buffer from the free list is chosen, inserted into the appropriate CBL list, and its fix count is increased to 1. When it is allocated again by another client, its fix count is increased. In order to share the buffers between the server process and its peer client processes, the buffer headers and buffers are located in shared memory. When a client stops using a page, its fix count is decreased. When the fix count reaches 0, the page is not automatically deallocated. Only if a new page is requested and the free list is empty, the CBL which has had not active clients for the longest time (a so-called aged CBL) is forced to release their page with the highest logical page number (the one that would be the last to be accessed by a new client that plays the file from the beginning to the end). If no aged CBLs are available, all CBLs are checked for unfixed pages. A page is selected (1) according to a weighting calculation that aims at identifying the pages that will not be used any more by any of the clients that are already in the system, and (2) from that set with the highest page number (the one that would be last to be accessed by a newly arriving client at its queue at the given time). It means that the cache management uses a *global victim selection* policy.

The management of the data on disk is handled in a way that makes the use of multiple disks transparent to the user. The Felini system uses striping to distribute workload uniformly across all disks, where consecutive blocks of a file are stored on successive disks, and the access of data is performed in a round robin fashion with block size being $T*r_i$ for a file with data rate $r_i$. The information about the location of the data is maintained in file control blocks (FCBs) that are similar to Unix file i-nodes at the root of the directory tree. Subdirectories are not supported. All FCBs of the

---

[1] A memory page is said to be pinned when the OS is forbidden to swap it out of the main memory.

system are stored in a single Unix file. This file is big enough to store FCBs for the entire space that is available to the Fellini server.

| Unix API | Fellini RT-API | Fellini non-RT-API |
| --- | --- | --- |
| open | begin_stream | fe_nr_open |
| read | retrieve_stream | fe_nr_read |
| write | store_stream | fe_nr_write |
| seek | seek_stream | fe_nr_seek |
| close | close_stream | fe_nr_close |

**Table 4-2**    Identification of UNIX and Fellini APIs

To the rest of the system, the Fellini server offers an API that is very similar to the Unix file system API for convenience. Table 4-2 identifies the Fellini function calls with their Unix couterparts.

### 4.5.3.3   Symphony

The *Symphony file system* [SGRV98] was developed at University of Texas, Austin, and it is an integrated multimedia file system designed for the storage and delivery of heterogeneous data types. Particularly, Symphony addresses the following issues:

- support real-time as well as non-real-time requests
- support multiple block sizes and control over their placement
- support a variety of fault-tolerance techniques
- provide a two-level meta data structure that all type-specific information to be attached to each file

To support heterogeneous data types, the file system is divided into a data-type specific and a data-type independent layer. The data-type independent layer consists of a resource manager, disk subsystem and buffer subsystem. The resource manager includes a scheduler that uses a modified SCAN-EDF approach to schedule real-time requests and adds non-real-time requests according to C-SCAN as long as no deadlines for the real-time requests are violated. To provide timing guarantees, the resource manager supports admission control and resource reservation for scheduling activities. The data independent layer also offers to the data-type specific layer variable block sizes that are multiples of a minimal basic block size that is defined at file system creation time and an option to express a preferred, but not guaranteed, location of blocks in terms of disk and location on that disk. To locate variable-sized blocks on disk efficiently, each block is addressed through an indirection as shown in Figure 4-32. Finally, the fault tolerant layer can optionally use parity information to deliver verified data, or skip this check in favour of speed.

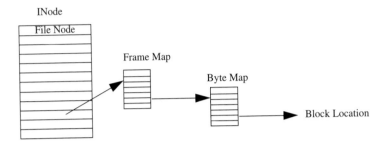

**Figure 4-32**  Symphony's indirect block location.

The data-type specific layer offers a set of modules (audio, video and text) for different kinds of data, where each of the modules makes use of the features provided by the underlying layer according to its requirements.

For example, the video module implements variable size data blocks by observing a video stream at writing time and by deriving an approximation of a maximum block size from the start of the stream. This block size is negotiated with the data-type independent layer, and subsequently, space that remains unoccupied because the actual block was smaller than the maximum block size is filled with data from the following block until the buffer space of a full block is saved. This allows for the continuous write as well as read operations at the cost of buffering one additional block size of memory per stream in the worst case. Concerning the placement policy, the video module prefers to stripe a file over as many disks as possible to maximize the utilization of I/O bandwidth for the case of parallel retrieval operations. In addition to this, during retrieval operations it starts to cache video blocks in main memory for efficiency according to the Interval Caching Policy.

Symphony supports the typical Unix file operations and extends this interface by function calls that are necessary to support quality of service. These additional functions are *ifsPeriodRead()*, *ifsPeriodicWrite()*, *ifsQoSNegotiate()*, *ifsQosConfirm()* and *ifsgetMetaData()*.

## 4.6  Memory Management

Memory management in media servers is mainly concerned with the assignment of part of the media server's main memory to the delivery of a multimedia stream. While straightforward implementations of media servers do not exploit all content's movement through the main memory of the media server but rather rely on the file system implementation to allocate sufficient bandwidth for a smooth delivery of each stream, a couple of approaches exist for the exploitation of this phase of data delivery. One approach was demonstrated earlier with the Fellini server's file system. Others are listed in the following.

### 4.6.1   Interval Caching Policy

Dan and Sitaram in [DS93a] introduce partial replication of multimedia files for load-balancing in multimedia systems. It is based on the observation that if there were a number of consecutive requests for the same video, and if the blocks read in by the first request were copied to another disk, it would be possible to switch the following requests to the partial replica just created. The *Interval Caching Policy*, proposed in [DS93a], therefore exploits the movement of data through the main memory of a video server by keeping the data of time-wise close streams in memory.

### 4.6.2   Generalized Interval Caching Policy

The Interval Caching Policy is refined and generalized in [DS95a]. The *Generalized Interval Caching Policy* takes into account that the interval caching policy does not handle short files appropriately when the media server is handling a mixed workload rather than videos only.

### 4.6.3   Batching

*Batching* is an approach introduced in [DSST94] to exploit the memory bandwidth and to save disk bandwidth in media servers by defining temporal cycles, called batching windows. All requests that arrive within such a cycle are collected and at the end of the cycle, all requests to the same content are serviced from the same file and buffer. This approach weakens the on-demand idea in comparison to the interval caching policy, but it recovers potentially large amounts of main memory because content can be discarded from the main memory immediately after playout and it will be re-loaded only after the next cycle. [DSS94] modifies this approach towards dynamic batching, which services requests as soon as a stream becomes available. Two selection policies to serve requests can be considered: the First Come First Serve (FCFS) policy and the Maximum Queue Length (MQL)policy, where queue length is defined by the number of user who requested that file. The comparison results between these two policies show that FCFS performs better than MQL.

### 4.6.4   Piggybacking

The aggregation of streams, that delivers the same content in close sequence without the use of batching window, was proposed using *piggybacking* [GLM96]. It means that one stream of a content file that is shortly preceding another stream of the same file will be joined with the later one by piggybacking the later stream onto the earlier stream. The general approach to do this is to increase the speed of the later stream and/or decrease the speed of the earlier stream until they join. Various strategies for joining more than a pair of streams are then investigated in detail in [GLM96].

### 4.6.5   Content Insertion

For the video-on-demand special case, [VL95] proposes the most radical extension of that scheme to date by offering *content insertion* to force larger numbers of streams into a time window which is small enough to allow the use of the piggybacking technique to join them into a single stream. Such inserted content from a content loop like an eternal advertisement show or from a continuous news show might be acceptable to the user to stay tuned. Alternatives might be a lengthening or shorting of introducing scenes of a movie. In [KVL97], it is then offered that this technique can also be used for providing a just as pragmatic and radical solution to problems such as server overload or partial server failure by diverting users into an advertisement loop or presenting other fill-in content until the problem can be fixed or until an aggregation with an action stream can be performed.

# Networks

Anetwork-enabling multimedia system lets you exchange discrete and continuous media data between devices, which generate and process these types of data. This communication requires appropriate services and protocols for data transmission.

## 5.1  Services, Protocols, Layers

To reduce their design complexity, most networks are organized as a series of *layers* or levels, each one built upon the one below it. The number of layers, the name of each layer, the contents of each layer, and the function of each layer differ from network to network. However, in all networks, the purpose of each layer is to offer certain services to the higher layers, shielding those layers from the details of how the offered services are actually implemented.

The rules and conventions used in this scenario are collectively known as the *protocol* of the respective layer. Basically, a protocol is an agreement between the communicating parties on how communication is to proceed. This agreement specifies the format and meaning of messages computers exchange. Application programs that use a network do not interact directly with the network hardware. Instead, an application interacts with protocol software that follows the rules of a given protocol when communicating. A protocol includes the format (syntax) and meaning of the data units to be exchanged; these are the so-called *protocol data units* (*PDUs*).

The function of each layer is to provide *services* to the layer above it. Logically relating services are grouped into individual layers and defined in reference models, such as the OSI Reference Model. These services describe the behavior of the respective layer and its service elements (*Service Data Units* — SDUs). The specification of a service does not describe how that service is implemented.

### 5.1.1  Requirements to Services and Protocols

The requirements services and protocols of a multimedia communication have to meet vary from layer to layer:

- Depending on the application, audio and video data have to be processed within a certain *delay* or during a defined *time interval*. Data have to be transmitted (from application to application) within this interval.
- The end-to-end delay should be as small as possible, in particular for applications working in dialog, similar to the conventional telephone.
- All guarantees required to ensure that data are transmitted within a defined time interval have to be maintained. This concerns, among other factors, the required processor performance and the storage required to process the protocol.
- Cooperative work and conference systems, using several media, are one of the main applications of communicating multimedia systems. This means that multicast connections should be supported to avoid a waste of resources. For example, the sending instance can change several times during a conference. Additional communication partners may join the conference, or other members may leave the conference. It should be possible for members of a multicast group to join or leave the conference without the need to terminate and reestablish the connection.
- The services should offer mechanisms to synchronize different data streams, or they should allow synchronization, if synchronization is handled by another component [Sal89].
- The communication is based on the compatibility of the communication systems used. All communication systems have to use the same protocols in different computers. Many of the more recent multimedia communication systems are proprietary implementations, which are not based on a (de-jure or de-facto) standard.
- Due to the preferred or guaranteed transmission of audio and video data, the communication of the remaining data should not be impaired. Discrete data have to be transmitted without interference.
- The fairness principle should be applied between the communicating applications, users, and stations.

The actual information rate for audio and video data vary strongly. This leads to fluctuations in the data rate. Figure 5-1 shows an example of the data rate that forms in three different situations: We see a difference between uncorrelated images, people in a room, and a news speaker. Despite the strong fluctuations, in average, we can see relatively low values. The information shown in Figure 5-1 refers to an encoding method according to CCIR 601 (see Volume 1 Section 5.3).

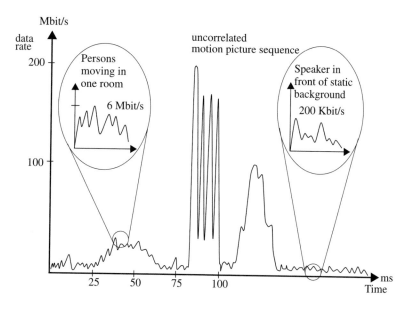

**Figure 5-1** Typical information and data rate while encoding the motion image of a scene.

## 5.1.2 The Layers of the ISO-OSI Model

The requirements described so far apply to different components of a communication system. For this reason, to complete this introduction to multimedia communication systems [Sha99], we describe the meaning of the individual layers based on the ISO-OSI Reference Model with regard to multimedia in short:

The ISO model has been popular because it provides a simple explanation of the relationships among the complex hardware and protocol components of a network. In the ISO model, the lowest layer corresponds to hardware, and successive layers correspond to firmware or software that uses the hardware. This section summarizes the purpose of each layer:

1. The *Physical Layer* is concerned with transmitting raw bits over a communication channel. This layer corresponds to basic network hardware. For example, the specification of LAN hardware, or modulation methods and bit synchronization. The propagation speed in the transmission medium, in the electric circuits used, cause delays relating to the respective modulation method when data propagate. Among other factors, they also determine the bandwidth the communication channel can provide. Normally, the delay has to be minimized for audio and video data, and a relatively high bandwidth has to be available.

2. The main task of the *Data Link Layer* is to take a raw transmission facility and transform it into a line that appears free of undetected transmission errors to the

network layer. The protocols of this layer specify how to organize data into frames and how to transmit frames over a network. For example, error detection and error correction, flow control, and block synchronization are defined in this layer. Access protocols depend strongly on the underlying network. Two categories of networks are known: First, networks that use point-to-point connections, and second, networks that use broadcast channels. Broadcast channels are also called *multi-access channels* or *random-access channels*. In a broadcast network with concurrent access, we need to define who can access the channel. To solve this problem, the *Medium Access Control* (*MAC*) sublayer has been introduced. Additional protocols were defined for this sublayer, including the *Timed Token Rotation Protocol* or the *Carrier Sense Multiple Access with Collision Detection* (*CSMA/CD*) protocol. The MAC sublayer is particularly important in local networks (LANs) that typically use multi-access channels as a basis for communication.

Continuous data streams require the reservation and guarantee of the throughput over a connection path. To avoid long delays, an appropriate error handling scheme can be implemented because, in most cases, retransmission is not desirable. The low error rate of modern networks, in particular with regard to optical fiber technology, favors its use to transmit multimedial data. In addition, message blocks with a fixed length (cells), e.g., in Asynchronous Transfer Mode (ATM) networks, allows efficient implementation of protocols, which offer reservation and guaranteed quality of service.

3. The *Network Layer* is concerned with controlling the operation of the subnet. A key design issue is to determine how packets are routed from a source to a destination. Protocols in this layer specify how addresses are assigned, and how packets are forwarded from one end of the network to another. Functions such as addressing, switching, routing, error handling, network management (congestion control), and package sequencing, belong to this layer.

Continuous media require the reservation of resources and guarantees of transmission in this layer. A reservation requirement with a subsequent guarantee of resources, is defined by quality-of-service parameters that comply with the requirements of a continuous data stream to be transmitted. The reservation has to be done along the path between the communicating stations. This problem is normally solved by a connection-oriented approach, which reserves resources during the establishment of a connection. In a connectionless environment, the reservation status in the network has to be adapted to the path used in a data transmission. As this adaptation cannot be done directly, so that some packets may follow an unreserved path. Therefore, no deterministic guarantees can be given. In any case, the use of the reservation approach allows an end-to-end delay with small variance and the observance of the correct sequence of packets. In an internetworking environment, there is the additional factor that packets may be duplicated, depending on the different communication structures of broadcast or multicast connections, which introduce additional complexity to the reservation process. The quality of service in the network with regard to a connection should be negotiated in this layer.

4. The *Transport Layer* offers process-to-process connection. More specifically, quality-of-service characteristics are negotiated and guaranteed. Large packets are segmented in this layer and reassembled to their original size at the receiving end. Error handling is based on process-to-process communication.

The required quality-of-service parameters in this layer have to refer to continuous media. An error handling scheme can normally not include the retransmission of data, because this would lead to high end-to-end delays and high jitter. A synchronization method that allows to maintain time relationships between LDUs—and thus also between SDUs—belonging to different connections can be considered an integral part of this layer.

5. The *Session Layer* allows users on different machines to establish sessions between them. A session allows ordinary data transport, as does the transport layer, but it also provides enhanced services useful in some applications. For example, a session can be used to allow a user to log into a remote timesharing system or to transfer a file between two machines. Protocols of this layer specify how to establish a communication session to a remote system (e.g., how to login to a remote timesharing computer). Specifications for security details, such as authentication using passwords, belong in this layer.

Automatic reestablishment of active connections is not always meaningful in sessions where continuous data are transmitted. In this respect, the definition of a suitable semantics method for multimedia sessions can be a better alternative. Another aspect concerns data encoding. When a connection is activated, it is very important for an application to know when an LDU is ready, which has been compressed for example as an intra-frame. The presentation cannot start, unless such a data unit is available [Mey91].

6. The *Presentation Layer* performs certain functions that are requested sufficiently often to justify a general solution for them, rather than letting each user solve the problems. In particular, unlike all the lower layers, which are just interested in moving bits reliably from here to there, the presentation layer is concerned with the syntax and semantics of the information transmitted. Protocols of this layer specify how to represent data. Such protocols are needed because different brands of computers use different internal representations for integers and characters. Thus, presentation layer protocols are needed to translate from the representation on one computer to the representation on another.

7. The *Application Layer* contains a variety of protocols that are commonly used. For example, there are hundreds of incompatible terminal types in the world. To solve this problem, virtual terminal software is normally used in the application layer. Another application layer function is file transfer. Each protocol of this layer specifies how a particular application uses a network. The protocol specifies the details of how an application program on one machine makes a request (e.g., how to specify the name of the desired file), and how the application on another machine responds. The application layer considers all application-specific services, e.g., the *File Transfer Protocol* (*FTP*) and electronic mail. Tasks on this layer with regard to audio and video data could be, for example, a remote database access with concurrent representation. This means that the presentation, including the specified parameters, is transmitted in real time. An application like video-on-demand requires special services to be implemented on a video server that supports real-time access to a database [RVG+93].

Later, the layers 5, 6, and 7 were grouped to form one application layer. We will follow this development in this book.

The following sections describe the principles of various networks built on the five layers of the reorganized reference model (i.e., the physical layer and the data link layer and its sublayers). The other layers (i.e., network layer, transport layer, session layer, presentation layer, and application layer) will be described in Chapter 7 in connection with group communication. Our discussion will concentrate on the important characteristics in relation to audio and video transmission. We will begin with an analysis of a few important networks with regard to their multimedia-enabling capabilities. In this discussion, we assume that the readers have a basic knowledge of these networks, and we refer the readers to computer networking textbooks, e.g., [Tan96, Sta92, BG87, Pry93, Par94b].

## 5.2  Networks

An integrated distributed multimedia system transmits the data of all media involved over the same network. The following section discusses various networks with regard to their capabilities to transmit multimedia data.

Networks are divided into three categories with regard to the distance of the endpoints (stations/computers):

- Local area networks (LANs)
- Metropolitan area networks (MANs)
- Wide area networks (WANs)

These network types will be briefly discussed in the following subsections.

**Local Area Networks (LANs)**    A *local area network* (*LAN*) is characterized by the distance it covers, which is a few kilometers, and its high data rate. The number of hosts it can connect is limited, with a typical value being a few hundred stations (within a campus or company). Several LANs can be interconnected to form larger networks for a higher number of connection stations. The communication basis in LANs is the so-called *broadcasting* over a broadcast channel (multi-access channel), which means that the MAC sublayer is particularly important for these networks.

**Metropolitan Area Networks (MANs)**    A *metropolitan area network* (*MAN*) normally covers an urban area, or a city, and has a higher data rate than LANs, i.e., more than 100 Mbps. A MAN is normally owned and managed either by a public or private carrier. The number of connections is typically in the range of several thousand. MANs are often used to interconnect several LANs.

**Wide Area Networks (WANs)**    A *wide area network* (*WAN*) can cover larger distances and several countries or even continents. Its data rates are lower, i.e., less than 2 Mbps. This will change with the advent of broadband ISDN. A WAN connects many organizations, companies and individuals. The network carriers are normally private or public telecommunication companies.

Conventional, widely used LANs (e.g., token ring or Ethernet) have not been designed for data traffic under real-time conditions. Normally, modern LANs take the properties required for the communication of audio and video data into account, but they are less common. In contrast to LANs, WANs are mainly used for the transmission of voice and data. This means that these networks, originating from the telecommunication industry, are designed for transmissions under real-time conditions. However, language-specific characteristics that are not suitable for video and other data transmissions are also integrated. One example would be the relatively long connection establishment.

### 5.2.1   Ethernet

Ethernet is a well-known and widely used network technology that employs a bus topology. The original Ethernet hardware operated at a rate of 10 Megabits per second (Mbps); a later version known as *Fast Ethernet* operates at 100 Mbps, and the most recent version, which is known as *Gigabit Ethernet*, operates at 1000 Mbps or 1 Gigabit per second (Gbps). Because it uses a bus topology, Ethernet requires multiple computers to share access to a single medium. A sender transmits a signal, which propagates from the sender towards both ends of the cable.

The most interesting aspect of Ethernet is the mechanism used to coordinate transmission. An Ethernet network does not have a centralized controller that tells each computer how to take turns using the shared cable. Instead, all computers attached to an Ethernet participate in a distributed coordination scheme called *Carrier Sense Multiple Access* (*CSMA*). The scheme uses electrical activity on the cable to determine status. To determine whether the cable is currently being used, a computer can check for a carrier. If no carrier is present, the computer can transmit a frame. If a carrier is present, the computer must wait for the sender to finish before proceeding.

To ensure that no other computer transmits simultaneously, the Ethernet standard requires a sending station to monitor signals on the cable. Whenever a collision is detected, a sending station immediately stops transmitting. Technically, monitoring a cable during transmission is known as *Collision Detect* (*CD*), and the Ethernet mechanism is known as *Carrier Sense Multiple Access with Collision Detect* (*CSMA/CD*).

One of the problems in building any type of high-speed Ethernet based on CSMA/CD and using optical fiber as its transmission medium is to implement reliable collision detection. Various methods using a passive star configuration have been proposed (e.g., Power Sensing, Directional coupling) [RJ85]. Fibernet II of Xerox [SRN+83] uses an active star configuration to detect collisions. Another problem results from high data rates and the related decrease of time available to transmit data, resulting in a dramatically reduced diameter of the CSMA/CD network.

### 5.2.1.1   Use of Ethernet for Audio and Video Transmission

The communication of continuous data requires a maximum end-to-end delay to be maintained, which can normally not be guaranteed by Ethernet. For this reason, various efforts have led to the development of a number of options enabling an Ethernet-LAN for audio and video data transmission:

1. One variant handles continuous data without exception handling. If the maximum load is kept within a certain limit, then the volume of data arriving too late is extremely low. This is currently the most common solution, because it does not require additional cost. However, it is not satisfactory due to errors.
2. To avoid these errors, the data traffic of continuous media can be dynamically adapted when the network is congested. In a congested network, the rate of the data streams of continuous media would be dynamically reduced. A scalable encoding method is used to reduce this rate. However, this does not prevent errors from occurring either.
3. A third variant can enable an Ethernet LAN especially for the transmission of continuous data. The solution requires an additional protocol and at least two separate networks between all communicating multimedia computers: one network for continuous data and a second one for all remaining data. This approach is meaningful for experimental systems, but would be too costly for a practical solution. A similar solution consists of a LAN that works as a digital network and transmits control information and discrete data, and another network that operates as an analogous network and transmits video and audio data. This approach was implemented in *MediaSpace* developed at Xerox Parc [BBI93], and in *Cruiser Environment* developed by Bellcore [FKRR93].

4. A rather pragmatic solution originates from installed network configurations. Normally, the Ethernet cables are not installed in a building in the form of a bus system, but are laid from each station to a central room, forming a star topology, where they are connected to an Ethernet bus. In such a case, instead of configuring a bus, each station could be connected to a *switch*. Each station would be connected to this switch over an independent Ethernet. This means that each station can use the full 10 Mbps, so that it is not absolutely necessary to install a new multimedia-enabling network. The only additional cost in this approach arises for the switch. This solution is based on data rates of less than 10 Mbps. Note, however, that a file transfer application could disturb the audio and video data transmission.

5. Fast Ethernet, also known as *100Base-T*, offers a throughput of up to 100 Mbps, and allows the user to enjoy low-cost use of this high-speed technology. Fast Ethernet supports three media options: 100Base-T4 for half-duplex operation over four UTP (Unshielded Twisted Pair) cable pairs, 100Base-TX for half-duplex and full-duplex operation over two pairs of UTP or STP (Shielded Twisted Pair) cable pairs, and 100Base-FX for half-duplex or full-duplex operation over optical fiber. Like 10-Mbps Ethernet, 100-Mbps Fast Ethernet can also be configured in switched or shared media implementations. Full-duplex requires a switch able to support several nodes to transmit and receive data simultaneously. Full-duplex Fast Ethernet switches increase the throughput of networks effectively to up to 200 Mbps [Mel94]. Fast Ethernet requires the use of new adapter cards in workstations and new hubs or switches, quipped with 100-Mbps transceivers. On the other hand, no changes have to be made to existing Ethernet applications. Another benefit of Fast Ethernet is that it easily interconnects to other networks, using shared media and switched 10Base-T (10 Mbps Ethernet).

## 5.2.2  Gigabit Ethernet

*Gigabit Ethernet* expands the approach of Fast Ethernet, offering a throughput of up to 1 Gbps, while still using the traditional Ethernet technology. However, this is possible only to a certain degree. In fact, the differences to its predecessor are more important than their similarities. First, Gigabit Ethernet uses a modified medium-access layer, as far as the size of the network and its use are concerned. Second, there are different requirements to the cabling system. The primary medium it uses is optical fiber, but UTP category 5 can also be used.

One of the key factors in Gigabit Ethernet is the maximum *size of the network*. Compared to Fast Ethernet, Gigabit Ethernet offers the tenfold clock speed, which means that it covers a maximum distance of approx. 20 meters, because higher clock speeds mean reduced network diameters. A network with this kind of diameter is not usable. For this reason, one of the IEEE workgroups proposed a mechanism that uses a

200-meter collision domain of Fast Ethernet. In fact, the MAC layer was redefined for Gigabit Ethernet. The mechanism that allows a network to extent to a diameter of 200 meters in Gigabit Ethernet is called *carrier extension*. During each transmission of a frame over an adapter within a Gigabit network, the Gigabit layer sends a special signal (while the collision detection continues). The expansion of a frame and the carrier is at least 512 bytes. This means that all packets are padded to a minimum length of 512 bytes. Due to the constraint that only one repeater hop is permitted, instead of two like in Fast Ethernet, and due to the limitation of temporal specifications, Gigabit Ethernet achieves almost the same network coverage like Fast Ethernet.

Although the carrier extension technique allows a Gigabit Ethernet to scale to a useful size, this method has a major drawback. No payload data can be put in the part of a frame which is shorter than 512 bytes, representing the expansion of the carrier. This leads to an inefficient utilization of the bandwidth. In network traffic consisting exclusively of 64-byte frames (i.e., in the case where one would reach the full capacity of Fast Ethernet), the effective throughput of Gigabit Ethernet would drop to 125 Mbps. However, the carrier expansion would be required only if Gigabit Ethernet is operated in half-duplex mode, like its predecessor. Switching to full-duplex operation makes the use of CSMA/CD superfluous. The stations would then send and receive data over different line pairs, so that no collisions can occur, and there would be no need for a station to wait before it can transmit. Full-duplex mode works only over point-to-point links.

As mentioned before, the use of optical fiber as transmission medium is another particularity where Gigabit Ethernet deviates from its slower predecessors. Multi-mode optical fiber allows to transmit in speeds within the gigabit range over a distance of at least 550 meters, or up to three kilometers when single-mode fiber is used. With regard to *copper* as a transmission medium, there are still issues to be solved relating to the electrical design. In fact, these problems prevent Gigabit Ethernet from operating over UTP (Unshielded Twisted Pair), including category-5 cables.

Finally, it should be noted that Gigabit Ethernet (like its predecessors) does not make QoS guarantees of the kind required by multimedia applications. Ethernet was originally designed to move data so that no capabilities for the use of QoS or priorities were integrated in the technology. The method guarantees merely that the same access rules apply to all nodes in a network. This holds also true for Gigabit Ethernet.

### 5.2.3  Token Ring

*Token ring* is a LAN with a data transmission rate of 4 Mbps or 16 Mbps. It is based on an ordered access mechanism. Computers attached to a token ring network use a special, short message called *token* to coordinate access to the ring. One token rotates in the ring at any time. To send data, a computer must wait for the token to arrive, transmit exactly one frame, and then transmit the token to the next computer. When no computers have data to send, the token cycles around the ring at high speed.

All stations in the network are connected to a logical ring as shown in Figure 5-2. Each packet includes the sender address (SA) and the destination address (DA) as depicted in Figure 5-3.

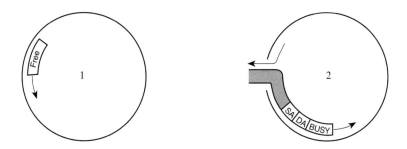

**Figure 5-2**   Transmitting data over a token ring; first phase, showing the principles with labels according to the standard.

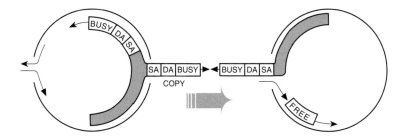

**Figure 5-3**   Transmitting data over a token ring, showing the last two phases.

If the destination address matches the address of a station, then that station removes this message from the network and copies it to its local storage. This event is reported to the local *LLC* (*Logical Link Control*), and an acknowledge (ACK) message or error field is modified accordingly. In this case, the A and C bits of the error field are verified. The following three combinations are valid:

- A = 0, C = 0: receiver does not exist, or is not active.
- A = 1, C = 0: receiver exists, but rejected the frame.
- A = 1, C = 1: receiver exists and copied the frame.

Subsequently, the message is forwarded to the neighboring station. The sending station removes its message and interprets the ACK fields. To obtain the right to send, a station has to obtain the token. This can be reserved in advance by any station with a certain priority. Only the station with the highest reserved priority will obtain the right to transmit. These priorities, together with the defined maximum cycling times of a packet, allow a guaranteed data transmission of continuous media.

The IEEE 802.5 protocol includes a sophisticated scheme using *multiple priorities*. The token includes a field to specify a priority, i.e., the priority of a frame is specified in the Access Control (AC) field of the frame header. When a frame is transmitted, it inherits this priority from the token, which was removed from the ring. The priority of the token is stored in the AC field. Priority operation functions as follows: A station can transmit a frame with a predefined priority, by using an available token with a priority smaller than or equal to the priority of the frame. If no suitable token is available, then the station can reserve a token with the desired priority, when a suitable token or frame passes the station. This reservation involves the following steps:

- When another station has reserved the same or a higher priority in a passing token or frame, then the station cannot use this token or frame to make a reservation.
- When the reservation bits were not set, or if they were set to a lower priority than the one required by a station, then the station can set the reservation bits to the desired priority.

When a station removes its frame from the token ring and finds that the values in the reservation bits are unequal 0, then it has to generate a token with the priority specified in the reservation bits. The token ring technology implements a so-called *fairness scheme* to prevent a misbehaving station from permanently sending priority frames. Although a priority setting can be overwritten by a higher-priority requirement at any given time, the priority has to be set to a lower level, once the highest priority has been served. Priorities are ordered according to their importance (see Table 5-1).

| Priority | Application |
|----------|-------------|
| 0 | free usability; used my most applications |
| 1-3 | free usability |
| 4 | used by bridges |
| 5-6 | reserved, but unused |
| 7 | used by ring management |

**Table 5-1**   Priorities used in a token ring network.

The priority scheme and the maximum possible propagation delay of a frame in the token ring allow the support of data transmission guarantees for continuous media. The main strength of this method is that expected transmit actions of a station can be predicted. The worst case, which is equal to the longest time a station has to wait until it obtains a token, is deterministic and can be calculated. Consider a ring with $N$ stations, as described in [BPSWL93], then the *token rotation time*, $t_{trt}$, can be characterized as

$$t_{trt} = \tau_l + \sum_{i=0}^{N-1} \tau_i$$

where $\tau_1$ is the delay introduced by the ring (the fixed delay due to the physical length of the ring and the fluctuating connection delays), and $\tau_i$ is the time a station $i$ holds the token. The maximum frame size is 16 Kbps, and the maximum token holding time, $\tau_{max}$, is 10 ms. Today, most connections normally require $\tau_{max} = 2$ ms. This means for the worst case that a station has to wait $(N-1)\ \tau_{max} + \tau_1$ seconds between two data transmission opportunities. Note that $\tau_1$ versus $(N-1)\ \tau_{max}$ is normally negligible.

A reservation mechanism is meaningful to limit the access delay for high-priority traffic. If only one station wants to send a high-priority packet at any time, the worst-case delay is limited by

$$t_{access} \le 2\tau_{max}.$$

The upper limit is higher when stations transmit a larger number of high-priority frames. If we consider $M$ stations that are transmitting high-priority frames, then the maximum delay is limited by

$$t_{access} \le (M-1)\tau_{mm} + 2\tau_{max}$$

where $\tau_{mm}$ is the time required to transmit high-priority multimedia data. The component $2\tau_{max}$ designates the potential waiting time in one cycle ($\tau_{max}$) for priority data to be able to reserve the token when the priority field of the token is unused, plus the waiting time for another cycle ($\tau_{max}$) required to obtain the token. The meaning of the term $(M-1)\tau_{mm}$ designates the potential waiting time of $(M-1)$ cycles, i.e., the $M^{th}$ high-priority station has to wait to reserve the priority token in the worst case.

### 5.2.3.1 Use of Token Ring for Audio and Video Transmission

In a token ring network, just like in Ethernet, various variants relating to integrated communication have to be considered, and some of the variants described for Ethernet also apply to token ring. For example, scaling for encoding can be implemented, or an isochronous token ring can be defined. In addition, the following options are available:

1. The existing priority mechanism can be used in token ring networks to transmit continuous media without having to modify its communication components. Continuous data streams get a much higher priority than discrete media streams. With a high share of continuous media traffic to be transmitted over a token ring network, however, the dta frames will be exposed to undesirable delays. To achieve an acceptable performance, one could use a simple form of bandwidth management to limit the number of multimedia sessions that are concurrently active in a

token ring segment. For example, when a high-priority application transmits multimedia data in MPEG-1 format at a maximum transfer rate of 1.8 Mbps, then a maximum of 13 multimedia sessions is possible, regardless of the data traffic flowing over the token ring network. Various test results have shown that the use of the existing priority mechanism, together with separate queues maintained in the stations for each of the frame priorities, reduce the delay of multimedia traffic. Several queues need to be used when the network is congested to reduce the delay. In addition, priority access mechanisms help reduce the delay, particularly when the network is not congested.

2. We can distinguish continuous data streams by their basic importance: audio connections obtain a higher priority level than all other continuous data streams. For this purpose, two high-priority levels have to be used. This principle has proven in studies conducted by the author. However, errors will still occur when there is a large number of audio-only connections.

3. Another option is to allow high priority for both audio and video data traffic and to introduce an additional resource reservation scheme for these connections. The following three approaches are widely used for this purpose:

   a. *Static reservation of resources*: Static reservation means that the resources are defined in advance. One example would be to allow eight multimedia stations to send continuous media data for up to a maximum of 1.8 Mbps each. Note, however, that this approach works fine only in a small environment, where the throughput demand of the applications is known.

   b. *Dynamic, centralized reservation of resources*: As an alternative, each station could use a central management facility during the establishment of a connection to negotiate and assign scarce resources. The data are subsequently transmitted on the basis of this negotiation. This central management could be a *bandwidth manager*, which knows the required information, so that it can distribute a requested resource capacity (i.e., the required bandwidth). There are several practical protocols for this type of bandwidth management. Such a management facility could also be used to reserve network resources across the domains of local networks, although the establishment of a connection would take much longer than in a local network, because a centralized solution has obvious restrictions with regard to scalability. The problem with the reservation of resources also concerns operating system issues (see Chapter 3). Reservation experiments for non-interruptible scheduling methods with regard to token ring networks are discussed in the literature, e.g., in [NV92]. These techniques can also be applied to the reservation of operating system resources, just as well as to the reservation of the network bandwidth.

c. *Reservation of dynamically distributed resources*: Distributed bandwidth management can reserve a required connection resource faster than a centralized solution. The following subsections describe a time-optimized technology in detail as a representative example [Ste93].

Each multimedia station has an internal table, the so-called *available resource table* (ART). This table contains entries with the available bandwidth of the network, together with the bandwidth already used for active audio and video connections. Assume for example that, to initialize all stations, the entire real bandwidth is reduced to an available bandwidth of 80% (resulting in 3.2 Mbps, or 12.8 Mbps for token ring). The remaining 20% are used for administrative traffic in the ring (this share would be approx. 3% in real-world applications), running on the highest priority level. This means that there will always be some capacity left for other media. The value of 80% is an experience values, which can be adapted to other situations.

The resource managers of all multimedia stations belong to one group with a common address in the token ring. This means that each of these resource managers can send messages to all other managers. *Functional addresses* in the token ring network can be used for this purpose.

To start establishing a connection, the local resource manager compares the required capacity with the currently available capacity. If the available bandwidth found in the ART table is less than the desired amount, then the connection request is rejected and an appropriate notification is sent. If the local ART shows that there is sufficient capacity to meet the connection request, then the request is forwarded to all resource managers of the group.

As an example, assume that a capacity request for 1.41 Mbps was sent to all members of the group. Let us further assume that the currently available capacity is 10 Mbps. Then the requesting station would first adapt its local ART to the available capacity. In this example, the station would reduce the value of 10 Mbps to 8.59 Mbps. In the next step, the requesting station would send its capacity reservation request (-1.410.000) to the group. This information is then used by all other stations to update their ART tables.

The packet (which is called *frame* in the token ring terminology) that contains the reservation request returns to the requesting station after a full cycle. This way, the requesting station knows that all members of the group were informed and have adapted their local ART tables accordingly.

If the ART of the requesting station was set to a negative value between the transmission of the reservation request and the completion of that request, then the reservation request is rejected and all members of the group are informed accordingly. Otherwise, the reservation request is deemed to have been accepted and the actual high-priority data transfer can begin. A reservation request can be rejected (when a negative value is found in the local ART of the requesting station) in multiple stations that send connection requests at the same time due to the early-token release method. To allow a station to access the available bandwidth in case of a collision, a pattern can be used, which functions similar to the mechanism in Ethernet. For example, the station could be allowed to make up to three access attempts and distributes them by a specific stochastic value. This ensures a dramatic reduction of the probability of more collisions.

If a connection is to be torn down, all stations have to be informed, so that they can reset their local ART tables. In the above example, (+1.410.000) would be sent to the entire group.

All local ART tables of the other members in the ring are polled, if a new station is added. Once all stations have returned their entries (within a specific time), and if all these tables contain the same value, then the new station is initialized to this value. Inconsistencies are detected and removed by use of an additional administrative protocol.

Note that this method can also work with variable bit rate streams. In this case, the maximum value is normally specified for reservation. Note that no resource capacity would be wasted, because all discrete data fill the *gaps*.

It should be noted that this method is suitable not only to reserve bandwidth, but also for all other resources within a ring, e.g., the limited number of available functional addresses in a token ring network.

The method assumes that each multimedia station uses only the capacity specified in the reservation request. This means that an appropriate monitoring component should be implemented additionally to ensure that negotiated capacities are maintained.

### 5.2.3.2    Bit Length

The most important—and usually scarce—resource in networks is the *bandwidth*, which can be allocated by using the above described methods. An increase in bandwidth means that a larger volume of continuous data streams can be transmitted. An important criterion for the effectiveness of the access protocol used is the *bit length*, referred to the distance covered by the physical network. The following example should explain this issue: At 100 Mbps, one bit has the following propagation over optical fiber:

$$length \approx \frac{velocity\ of\ propagation\ in\ optical\ fiber}{data\ rate}$$

$$length = \frac{2.5 \times 10^8 m/s}{100 \times 10^6 bit/s} = 2 m/bit.$$

In contrast, with a data transfer rate of 64 Kbps over copper cable, the propagation of each bit is:

$$length \approx \frac{velocity\ of\ propagation\ in\ copper\ cable}{data\ rate}$$

$$length = \frac{2.5 \times 10^8 m/s}{64 \times 10^3 bit/s} = 3.9 km/bit$$

Note that each station buffers at least 64 bits internally during the forwarding process. This means that several frames can be in a ring concurrently when the data rates are higher. This transition to higher data rates has led to the introduction of a principle called *early token release*. It means that several consecutive packets can be present in the ring. Once a station has sent its data, it will put the token back into the ring, so that all stations get a chance to send their packets.

### 5.2.4 100VG AnyLAN

The 100VG AnyLAN standard was developed by the IEEE 802.12 workgroup. Similar to Fast Ethernet, its 100-Mbps competitor, it also operates in *shared* media and *switched* implementations. Another similarity is that 100VG AnyLAN can use the existing network topology without extensive reconfiguration. In contrast to Fast Ethernet, however, 100VG AnyLAN does not require any significant network distance constraints, which would inherently be more restrictive than those of the conventional Ethernet. Compared to 100Base-T, 100VG AnyLAN offers the following benefits:

1. As its name suggests, 100VG AnyLAN can use both Ethernet and token ring frames, but not in the same network. A *router* is used to connect a 100VG Ethernet to a 100VG token ring network.
2. 100VG prevents collision of packets and allows efficient utilization of the network bandwidth. Both is achieved by a so-called *demand priority* scheme instead of the CSMA/CD scheme used in 10Base-T and Fast Ethernet.
3. The demand priority scheme allows a straightforward implementation of a priority method for time-critical traffic, e.g., real-time voice and real-time video. This makes 100VG a suitable candidate for multimedia applications.

However, 100VG has a few drawbacks. Although 100VG is transparent with regard to the network software, it causes considerable administrative cost. 100VG requires a four-wire (voice grade—VG) UTP (Unshielded Twisted Pair) cable category 3, 4, or 5, so that new cabling is required, in addition to investments in new adapter cards and hubs.

The main characteristic of 100VG AnyLAN is its special medium access (MAC) layer. The demand priority access scheme defined in the IEEE 802.12 standard replaces CSMA/CD. Instead of collision detection or a rotating token, the demand priority method uses a *round-robin* polling scheme, which is implemented in a hub or switch. In contrast to the conventional Ethernet, 100VG is a "collision-free" technology. Using the demand priority scheme enables the 100VG hub or switch to allow only one connected node access to the network segment at a time, so that collisions are avoided. When a node needs to transmit data over the network, it has to send a request to the hub (or switch). The hub (or switch) polls all nodes of a segment sequentially. If a node has data to send, then it obtains permission from the hub (or switch). Otherwise, the hub (or switch) continues polling the next node. Each round-robin polling sequence allows each port of a network node to send exactly one — and only one — packet. All nodes wishing to send data are served in each round, which means that all nodes get fair access to the network. If a multi-port hub or a multi-port switch is considered to be a node of a larger 100VG network, then it also has to obtain permission to access the network from a level one step higher within the network hierarchy. Such a device is also called *root hub*. When the root hub grants access to a larger network, then the multi-port node can transmit one packet from each port it supports. 100VG networks based on the token ring technology use the same method. In this case, the VG100 hub or VG100 switch acts basically as a rotating token. Instead of a waiting time to obtain a token, a node waits until it obtains permission from the hub or switch. Similar to traditional token ring systems, only one station at a time may transfer its data over a network segment.

In addition to regulating network nodes by a democratic polling method, the demand priority scheme allows straightforward priority settings for LAN traffic. Time-critical network applications, e.g., voice and video, can be marked as high-priority data. When the 100VG hub or switch distributes access rights, it first serves high-priority traffic and then less time-critical traffic. 100VG allows traffic division into two classes: high-priority and regular traffic. The applications of the higher layers in the network nodes set the priorities for data. This information is passed down to the MAC sublayer in the 100VG protocol stack. A packet with no priority set is handled as regular traffic. Each hub manages information about high-priority requests. When a high-priority request arrives, then the hub or switch terminates the current transmission and serves this request. When a hub (or switch) receives more than one high-priority request at once, then these are handled in the order of the ports, i.e., in the order in which regular traffic is handled. The hub (or switch) returns to the mode it uses to handle regular priority traffic once all high-priority requests have been served. Timeouts and bottlenecks will occur when a large number of high-priority requests arrive at the hub (or switch), so that it cannot handle regular traffic over an extensive period of time. To avoid this problem, the VG100 hub or VG100 switch manages the time between the request for a service by one node and its handling automatically. If too much time elapses, then the hub automatically increases the priority setting for regular requests.

One issue of critic about the demand priority scheme is that the hub or switch has to be equipped with excessive intelligence to handle its tasks. On the other hand, the demand priority scheme is a deterministic protocol, so tht it allows the definition of guarantees for a maximum delay for multimedia application. This is not supported in CSMA/CD. This means that VG100 is better suitable for multimedia communication than Fast Ethernet. Currently, 100VG has not been implemented by many hardware manufacturers.

## 5.2.5   Fiber Distributed Data Interface (FDDI)

One of the chief disadvantages of the token ring networks arises from their susceptibility to failures. Several ring network technologies have been designed to overcome severe failures. For example, *Fiber Distributed Data Interface (FDDI)* is a token ring technology that can transmit data at a rate of 100 Mbps, ten times faster than the original Ethernet. To provide such high data rates, FDDI uses optical fibers to interconnect computers instead of copper cables. FDDI was proposed as an expansion of token ring with regard to the IEEE 802.5 protocol it uses. This standardization effort was initiated by the X3T9.5 workgroup of the American Standards Institute (ANSI) in 1982. The basic features of this technology are optical fibers with an immanently lower error rate and attenuation, allowing a larger distance between active stations.

While token ring runs in 4 Mbps or 16 Mbps, FDDI was designed for 100 Mbps from the beginning. FDDI serves up to 500 stations; a token ring typically connects between 50 and 250 stations. By standard, the length of an FDDI ring is a maximum of 100 km in duplex operation, and the distance between any two stations must not exceed 2 km. These values show the benefits of FDDI versus its predecessors clearly.

FDDI can operate in various transmission modes (see Figure 5-4), which are relevant for multimedia data communication. The synchronous mode allows reservation of the bandwidth, while the asynchronous mode behaves similar to the token ring protocol. Many current implementations support only the asynchronous mode. We will describe the topology and the components, and then discuss the modes supported by FDDI. Interested readers are referred to the standard documentation, or [MK93].

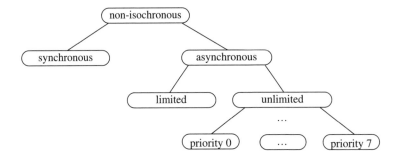

**Figure 5-4**  Communication options in FDDI; overview of the data transfer modes.

The specification of the FDDI design suggests a maximum bit error rate of $2.5 \times 10^{10}$ bits. Many implementations work with lower bit error rates. The following sections will discuss the topology and components of FDDI.

### 5.2.5.1    The FDDI Topology

The most important feature of the FDDI topology is that it is based on two counter rotating rings, i.e., FDDI uses a pair of counter rotating rings. One ring is used to transmit data. When a failure occurs that breaks the ring, stations adjacent to the failure automatically reconfigure, using the second ring to bypass the failure. FDDI classifies several types of stations:

- A *dual attachment station* is also called a *class A* station. Such a station is connected to the primary and secondary ring either directly at the trunk ring, or over a concentrator.
- The *single attachment station*, also called *class B* station, is connected to the primary ring over a concentrator. The concentrator station can connect more than two stations, while it is always connected to the primary and secondary ring. Figure 5-5 shows a complete configuration with various stations in the form of a dual ring with trees. If a failure occurs, then the FDDI ring is reconfigured, where some stations are configured for transparent switch-through function.

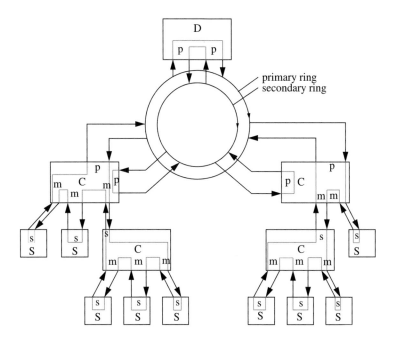

**Figure 5-5** A possible connection of various FDDI stations, forming a dual ring with several trees.

### 5.2.5.2 FDDI Reliability

In addition to the fault tolerance ensured by the dual ring (secondary ring), an FDDI station offers high reliability by the use of a so-called *bypass switch* or *concentrator* (CON). A station equipped with such a bypass switch is taken from the ring as soon as a failure is detected, e.g., a power failure. A CON allows to connect the stations to the ring, and it is also responsible for disconnecting faulty stations. The use of reliable CONs to connect stations is the core of the so-called *dual-homing* configuration. In most cases, dual homing is more reliable than the dual ring principle alone. However, this is the case only provided that the following conditions are met:

- At least four dual stations have to be connected.
- The reliability of the line, defined as the difference probability (1 − error probability of the line) should be at least $\sqrt{2}/2$.
- The CONs forming the primary ring have to be reliable.
- The number of CON pairs in the primary ring should be as small as possible.

Another approach that makes complex FDDI networks more reliable is the use of creative topologies. A *creative topology* consists of configurations that reduce the vulnerability of a connection and/or use redundant resources. This type of approach is the co-called *concentrator tree*. In such a topology, the concentrators are connected in such a way that the *A* and *B* ports of each concentrator connect to the *M* ports of the same concentrator, which is located higher in the tree hierarchy. The concentrator tree alone does not work more reliably than other approaches, e.g., dual homing, because each line failure will always cause an isolation. For a few applications, some mechanisms are of particular interest, because they continue working even when two or more lines fail. One known technology uses a concentrator tree, where the upper and lower ends are connected. This configuration is also called *concentrator tree with loopback* [MK93].

### 5.2.5.3    FDDI Components

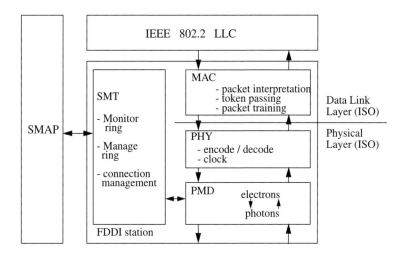

**Figure 5-6**   The FDDI reference model.

FDDI is composed of the following components, as shown in Figure 5-6:

- PHY (Physical Layer Protocol) specified in ISO 9314-1 "Information Processing Systems: Fiber Distributed Data Interface - Part 1: Token Ring Physical Protocol".

- PMD (Physical Layer Medium Dependent) specified in ISO 9314-3 "Information Processing Systems: Fiber Distributed Data Interface - Part 1: Token Ring Physical Layer, Medium Dependent".

- SMT (Station Management) defines management functions of the ring as specified in "ANSI Preliminary Draft Proposal American National Standard X3T9.5/ 84-49 Rev. 6.2, FDDI Station Management".

- The network is accessed over a MAC (Media Access Control) component specified in ISO 9314-2 "Information Processing Systems: Fiber Distributed Data Interface - Part 2: Token Ring Media Access Control".

The physical layer (PMD, PHY) is responsible for an adaptation to an optical fiber. Today, Multi-mode fibers with a diameter of 52.5 mor mono-mode fibers with a diameter of 125 mare used. An LED with a wavelength of 1.320 nm serves as a sender. On this lowest layer, a 4-bit to 5-bit encoding is implemented, where 4 out of 5 encodes each group of 4 MAC symbols (zeros, ones, and various non-data symbols, e.g., the beginning of a frame) into a group of 5 bits (4 bits for encoding of the 4 MAC symbols and an additional non return to zero inverted (NRZI) bit). This scheme increases the physical data rate to 125 Mbps.

The station management (SMT) controls, monitors, and manages the stations connected to the network. For the stations, this includes initialization, activation, monitoring of services, and error handling. For the network itself, this management includes addressing, reservation of bandwidth, and configuration.

The MAC-LAN access component regulates access to the ring by stations. It reads the address and inserts or removes frames into and from the network, respectively. In FDDI, a packet is called *frame*. The length of this packet can vary, but it never exceeds 4,500 bytes. The addressing supports point-to-point, multicast, and broadcast communication.

### 5.2.5.4    The Timed Token Rotation Protocol

The *Timed Token Rotation Protocol* is the access protocol used by FDDI. It basically offers t two services, namely *synchronous* and *asynchronous* services. Each station can reserve a certain share of the bandwidth available in the network to transmit synchronous data. When a station obtains a token, it can transmit synchronous data over the period it requested previously. This is also called *synchronous capacity*. Subsequently, the station releases the token and passes it on to the next neighboring station. Messages in asynchronous mode are transmitted only if specific requirements are met.

The *Target Token Rotation Time* (*TTRT*) was added to implement these services. This scheme represents a typical and desired time required by a packet to complete one cycle around the ring. The TTRT value is determined during the initialization phase of the ring, by sending a request to all SMT components of the stations connected to the ring. Each station stores this value. Based on the FDDI specification, the value range for TTRT is between 4 ms and 165 ms. A typical TTRT is approx. 50 ms. Such a value is typically achieved in congested networks and 75 connection stations using approx. 30 km of optical fiber.

### 5.2.5.5    The Token Rotation Time

Each station measures continuously the real rotation time of a token and stores the result as the *Token Rotation Time* (*TRT*). TRT indicates the duration measured last, referred to the respective station that required a token for this last rotation. This method is based on the following rules:

• *Asynchronous traffic*: Asynchronous traffic can be sent only provided that there is free capacity on the network. The criterion for this free capacity is the comparison between the respective TRT and TTRT values. A station can always send asynchronous data as long as the TRT < TTRT ratio is true. This means that asynchronous traffic can occur in the LAN for a maximum duration TTRT. Several other methods describe the possible coexistence of asynchronous and synchronous traffic, without excessive delays. Non-real-time messages are transmitted before real-time messages, unless there is an absolute necessity to break this rule. Real-time messages are transmitted first to guarantee their timely arrival [HR93]. In this case, it is necessary for a station to determine whether the transmission of real-time messages can be delayed without risking late delivery. The use of a restricted token (see Figure 5-2) means that the total asynchronous bandwidth is reserved for the dialog between two stations. More specifically, the sending station informs the receiving station about its wish to transmit. To inform the station the sending station uses non-restricted asynchronous traffic. Next, the corresponding packets are transmitted as additional packets together with the restricted token. At this point, no other station may use the asynchronous bandwidth. The receiving station can now continue the dialog. The dialog is terminated when the sending station replaces the restricted token by an unrestricted token. Asynchronous traffic with restricted token is based on several priorities, similar to the scheme used in token ring.

• *Synchronous traffic*: To maintain the time limits of synchronous messages, all network parameters, including synchronous bandwidth, TTRT, and buffer size, have to be carefully selected [MZ93]. The synchronous bandwidth is the most sensitive parameter to determine whether or not time limits for messages are observed. Each station can use SMT procedures to reserve bandwidth for synchronous data transfer. This reservation of bandwidth is also called *synchronous allocation* (*SA*). When there is not enough synchronous bandwidth available, then a network node does not have sufficient access time to transmit its data in time. In contrast, large synchronous bandwidths can result in a long TRF, which means that the time limits for transmissions cannot be maintained. A suitable choice of TTRT is also important, because the amount of time of all synchronous connections must not exceed the TTRT value. A smaller TTRT results in a poor utilization of the network, thus limiting the network capacity. On the other hand, if the TTRT is too large, the time limits may not be guaranteed, because the token may not pass a station often enough. Each node has a buffer for outgoing synchronous messages. The size of this buffer also influences the real-time performance of the system, just as well as the size of the buffer for incoming messages. For this reason, the receiver should be able to receive all transmitted messages. If the buffer size is too small, then messages may be lost, resulting in a buffer overflow. If the selected buffer size is too large, then storage space is wasted.

Based on the synchronous and asynchronous traffic shown in Figure 5-4, the TRT value in this example is at most twice the TTRT value. In our example with a TTRT value of 50 ms, the maximum rotation time is restricted to 100 ms, where the TRT is also a measure for the current load in the ring.

### 5.2.5.6    Audio and Video Transmission over FDDI

The transmission of audio and video data can be efficient in synchronous mode. However, the times for the reservation of bandwidth should not be neglected. During a data transmission, the following cases could occur, depending on the TRT to TTRT ratio:

1. In the case shown in Figure 5-7, the TRT < TTRT ratio applies, which means that this station can continue sending data as long as the local TRT counter does not exceed the TTRT value. If this happens, the station can transmit only its synchronous data.

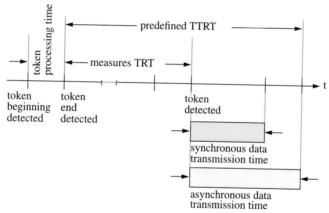

**Figure 5-7**   Synchronous and asynchronous traffic with TRT < TTRT over FDDI.

2. In the case shown in Figure 5-8, the TRT > TTRT ratio applies, which means that this station can transmit only its synchronous data.

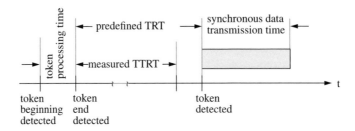

**Figure 5-8**   Synchronous traffic with TRT > TTRT over FDDI.

Finally, we will use the following example to explain the Timed Token Rotation
Protocol. Assume that the TTRT is 8 time units, and that three stations are connected to
the FDDI ring. Each station has reserved one time unit (SA) for synchronous traffic,
which it actually transmits. All stations want to transmit as much non-restricted asynchronous traffic as the network allows. Table 5-2 shows the values of the respective
TRT counters per station together with the transmitted units. After station 1, station 2
receives data, then station 3, then station 1 again, and so on, which results in the
interplay shown in Table 5-2.

| Station 1 | | | Station 2 | | | Station3 | | |
|---|---|---|---|---|---|---|---|---|
| TRT | syn | asyn | TRT | syn | asyn | TRT | syn | asyn |
| 0 | 1 | 8 | 9 | 1 | | 10 | 1 | |
| 11 | 1 | | 3 | 1 | 5 | 8 | 1 | |
| System has "settled down"; first cycle starts: | | | | | | | | |
| 8 | 1 | | 8 | 1 | | 3 | 1 | 5 |
| 8 | 1 | | 8 | 1 | | 8 | 1 | |
| 3 | 1 | 5 | 8 | 1 | | 8 | 1 | |
| 8 | 1 | | 3 | 1 | 5 | 8 | 1 | |
| Cycle starts again: | | | | | | | | |
| 8 | 1 | | 8 | 1 | | 3 | 1 | 5 |
| ... | | | | | | | | |

**Table 5-2**   TRT counter per section, divided into traffic types.

### 5.2.5.7   Other FDDI Features

FDDI supports all requirements with regard to group addressing for cooperative multimedia applications. The synchronization between different data streams is not part of

the network, which means that is has to be solved separately. The relationship between synchronous and asynchronous data transmissions are particularly relevant in this respect. A time reference existing at the sender does not necessarily exist any longer at the receiver due to the Timed Token Rotation Protocol.

The packet size can have a direct impact on the delay of data between two applications, when the transmitted data are composed of small LDUs. For voice data with a sampling rate of 8 KHz and a data transfer rate of 64 Kbps, packets have to be collected or accumulated until an FDDI packet is complete. It would be desirable to have a smaller FDDI packet size.

Unfortunately, many FDDI implementations do not support the synchronous mode, which would be well suited for the transmission of continuous media data. In asynchronous mode, the same methods as in token ring can be applied. However, a synchronous data transmission always interfers with the continuity of the asynchronous traffic. This means that, in contrast to token ring, guarantees can be given only if no station uses the synchronous mode.

If only two stations transmit continuous data at a time, then the asynchronous mode with restricted token could be used. This leads to less end-to-end delays, but it hinders any other asynchronous traffic in the LAN. This means that this mode is suitable for the transmission of continuous media data only to a limited extent.

## 5.2.5.8    FDDI Successors

To use the synchronous mode, considerable delays have to be taken into consideration for the reservation of synchronous bandwidth. In addition, it should be noted that the synchronous mode guarantees bandwidth together with a maximum delay. This delay never exceeds twice the TTRT value. However, in synchronous mode data could arrive much earlier at the receiver end. The fluctuations in the delay depend on the ring load. This means that the delay has to be set to the maximum value within a range of 100 ms, which is considerable for dialog applications. In addition, data arriving too early have to be buffered, which requires a buffer for the duration of one TTRT at the receiver. For this reason, FDDI II was introduced with an additional isochronous mode (see Figure 5-9). Note, however, that [ZK91] uses the original FDDI for audio data transmission.

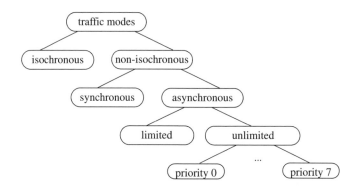

**Figure 5-9** Communication options in FDDI II; overview of the data transmission modes, using the terms introduced in the literature.

The development effort for FDDI II began in 1984 and was intended to serve as an FDDI extension for a hybrid high-speed LAN (HSLAN). The most important aspect of this effort is the combination of services with a guaranteed bandwidth for isochronous data streams (voice and video) with (asynchronous and synchronous) packet services, similar to those supported by FDDI on the same physical medium. Although packet-switched service is still connectionless, the new FDDI version runs a connection-oriented circuit-switched service.

FDDI II is well suited for the transmission of continuous media data, but it is less popular than the original FDDI for real implementations. One reason may be that the two systems are incompatible, i.e., existing FDDI systems cannot be directly connected to an FDDI-II LAN; they have to be replaced.

### 5.2.6   ATM Networks

This section discusses the characteristics of the *Asynchronous Transfer Mode* (*ATM*) and its architecture. Subsequently, we will introduce some properties of local ATM networks. Section 5.4 discusses the switching properties of ATM-WAN networks.

### 5.2.6.1   ATM Characteristics

The Asynchronous Transfer Mode (ATM) is a switching technology designed for minimum network functionality, where a packet is called a *cell*. The ATM concept uses cells with a fixed size (53 bytes), of which 48 bytes are used for payload data and 5 bytes for heater information (see Figure 5-10).

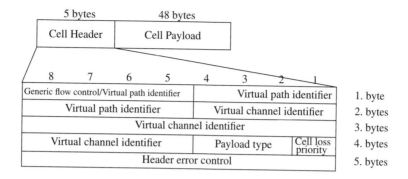

**Figure 5-10** The structure of an ATM cell.

ATM operates with much higher data rates than other packet-switching systems. This high rate is achieved thanks to the following properties:

1. *No error handling or flow control on link-to-link basis*: ATM does not implement any special error handling method (e.g., transmission errors or temporary congestion leading to packet loss) over the paths of a connection (either the connection from the user to the network, or a connection between two ATM switches). This means that this type of errors does not cause the retransmission of packets, as is usually the case in packet-switched networks. This means that there is no error correction within a network. The ATM network is based on end-to-end protocols.

2. *ATM operates in a connection-oriented mode*: Before data can be transferred from a multimedia terminal to the network, a logical/virtual connection establishment phase has to be made to reserve the required resources. If the requested resources are not available, then the connection is rejected and the terminal is notified. Upon completion of a data transfer, the resources used by that transfer are released. This connection-oriented mode ensures minimum cell loss rate in the network (in any case).

3. *The header functionality is strongly restricted*: ATM headers have a strongly restricted functionality to ensure fast processing in the network. The most important task of the header is to identify a virtual circuit by use of an identifier, which is selected during the establishment of a connection; it guarantees the routing of all packets through the network. In addition, it supplies a simple multiplexing function of several virtual circuits over one single physical channel.

In addition to the identification mechanisms of a circuit, i.e., the *Virtual Path Identifier* (*VPI*) and the *Virtual Channel Identifier* (*VCI*), the ATM header uses a heavily reduced number of functions, most of them dealing with management tasks. This simple functionality of the header facilitates the implementation of the functions processed by the headers in ATM nodes and at high speed (155 Mbps to several Gbps), so that both the processing and the buffer delays are reduced.

4. *Relatively small field to carry information*: To reduce the number of internal buffers in the switching nodes and to limit the delay introduced by their processing time, the field that carries the information is relatively small. This ensures a small end-to-end delay, which may be caused by the packetizing of audio and video data into ATM cells.

The ATM concepts offers a way to transport data independent of their characteristics, such as data rate, quality requirements, or switching-specific properties. ATM networks are able to offer a connection service for multimedia traffic with various quality requirements thanks to their speed and bandwidth. This property was one of the main motivation for ITU-T (former CCITT) to propose ATM as a transmission mode for the future Broadband-ISDN.

### 5.2.6.2   The ATM Architecture

The ITU-T standard I.321 proposes a hierarchical architecture for B-ISDN over ATM, similar to the OSI architecture (see Figure 5-11).

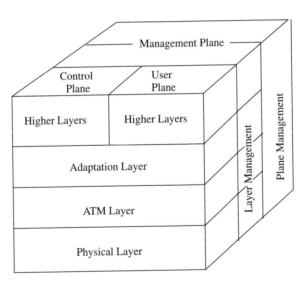

**Figure 5-11**   Reference model for the B-ISDN-ATM protocol.

ITU-T specifies the lower layers of B-ISDN. The B-ISDN protocol model for ATM consists of three layers: the *user plane*, which transports user information; the *control plane*, which deals mainly with signaling information; and the *management plane*, which is used to maintain the network and run operational functions. Each of these layers uses a layering concept to ensure independence between the layers. In addition, ITU-T specifies three sublayers:

- The *PHYsical Layer* (*PHY*) transports data (bits/cells). This layer consists of two sublayers: the *physical medium* (PM) sublayer, which runs media-specific functions, and the *transmission convergence* (TC) sublayer, which converts ATM cell streams into bits to be transported over the physical medium. Optical fiber is the medium best suitable for a full-duplex transmission in 155.52 Mbps or 622.08 Mbps, respectively. The structure used for transmission (at a data rate of 155.52 Mbps) used to multiplex various cells from several virtual channels can be either a *continuous cell stream* with no multiplex frame structure at the interface, or enveloping cells in a *synchronous "envelope"* that works by the time division multiplexing principle. In this case, the bit stream at the interface uses an external frame, based on the *Synchronous Digital Hierarchy* (*SDH*). In the USA, this structure is called SONET (Synchronous Optical NETwork). The SDH standard G.709 defines a hierarchy of data rates, which are a multiple of 51.84 Mbps.

- The *ATM layer* is totally independent of the PHY layer. It assumes several important functions: Multiplexing and demultiplexing of cells from various virtual circuits into one single cell stream for the physical layer; translating the identifier of received cells into outgoing cells; implementing one of several possible service classes; management functions; extracting (adding) a cell header; and implementing a flow control mechanism at the user network interface.

- The *ATM Adaptation Layer* (*AAL*) expands the services offered by the ATM layer and runs functions for the user, control and management planes, or maps the ATM layer to the next higher layer. The AAL consists of the *Segmentation And Reassembly* (*SAR*) sublayer, which segments the information from the higher layer at the sender into a cell stream, or reassembles the data units of the higher layers at the receiver. In addition, the AAL includes the *Convergence Sublayer* (*CS*), which identifies messages and restores the time/clock, among other functions.

Several AAL types were defined to support various services (e.g., voice, video, data) and to address their different transport properties. Currently, four AAL classes are defined to support connection-oriented or connectionless, variable bit rate (VBR), and constant bit rate (CBR), real-time, and non-real-time services:

- *AAL1* supports CBR services once a virtual circuit has been established. This service class is suitable mainly for high-quality audio and video data with constant bit rate, because it offers mechanisms for synchronization, variance control of the cell delay (jitter), detection of lost or out-of-order cells, and optionally a forward error correction.

- *AAL2* offers data transfer with VBR. In addition, it exchanged time information between the source and the destination. The CS sublayer provides the following functions: retrieve the clock (e.g., tokens), handle lost or corrupted cells and Forward Error Correction (FEC) for audio and video services.

- *AAL3/4* was intended for the transfer of data that are sensitive to loss, but not to delays. This AAL layer can be used for connection-oriented and connectionless data communication (e.g., multimedia file transfer or multimedia e-mail).

- The ATM Forum defined another AAL layer for high-speed data transfer (e.g., to transfer transactions) called *AAL5*. An AAL5 packet includes a much smaller overhead than AAL3/4. In addition, this layer minimizes the cell computing cost in the computer. AAL5 behaves similar to traditional data communication interfaces for Ethernet and FDDI, so that existing data communication software can be easily adapted to ATM.

### 5.2.6.3    ATM Cell Information

Both the ATM services and the ATM capabilities are implemented by use of the information contained in the ATM cell header. We will describe some of the information contained in this header, because it is important with regard to the transmission of multimedia data:

- *Virtual circuits*: Information such as the address of the sender or receiver, or the sequence number, do not have to be part of an ATM cell. Each virtual circuit is identified by a number, which has only local significance in a transmission path. A virtual circuit is identified by two header fields: the *Virtual Channel Identifier* (*VCI*) and the *Virtual Path Identifier* (*VPI*).

- *Virtual channel*: ATM is a connection-oriented technology, so that a *Virtual Channel Identifier* (*VCI*) is assigned to each circuit during the establishment of the connection. A VCI has only local significance for each circuit between two ATM nodes. The VCI is translated in each ATM node along the route from the sender to the receiver. When a circuit is closed, then the VCI values of the participating paths are released and can be reused for other virtual circuits.

An important benefit of the VCI principle is the use of several VCI values for services consisting of several components (e.g., video telephony or digital TV). For example, a video telephone call can use three communication streams — voice, video, and data, where each is transported over a separate VCI. The network can add or remove streams during the transmission. This means that the video telephony service can begin with just voice (one single VCI), and a video stream can be added (and removed) later over a separate VCI. Signaling to manage the different set of circuits is transported over a separate VCI. The VCI principle has an impact on the connection establishment and the connection management in the higher layers, where the call can be mapped to three virtual circuits between the sender and the receiver (one logical call connection), depending on the media the sender or receiver wants to use for communication.

- *Virtual path*: The future broadband networks will support semi-permanent connections between endusers. This concept is called *virtual path* or *virtual network*. To implement such a virtual network, an additional header field—the *Virtual Path Identifier* (*VPI*)—is used. The VPI allows the use of backbone switches, so-called *cross connectors*, which forward cells exclusively on the basis of VPI values. This approach reduces the size of the switching tables in the cross connectors of a large ATM network and improves scalability.

- *Priorities*: The ATM header allows a differentiation of logical connections by use of various priorities. Basically, there are two priority types: the *temporal* and the *semantic* priority. A system that uses temporal priorities assumes that some cells will dwell longer in the network than others. A system that uses semantic priorities assumes that some cells will have a higher loss probability, resulting in a higher loss rate in the network.

  The ATM layer uses a simple mechanism to set semantic priorities, the so-called *Cell Loss Priority* (*CLP*) bit. When a congestion occurs in an ATM network, then cells with the CLP bit set are dropped first. The CLP bit can be assigned either on a per-circuit or per-cell basis. When the first option is used, all cells of a virtual channel/path have the same priority. In the second case, cells of a virtual channel/path can have different priorities. Optimum utilization of resources is achieved when priorities are avoided, but this is at the trade-off that services with different quality requirements cannot be differentiated.

- *Maintenance*: Additional bits are required to maintain the network and to control the performance of ATM circuits (including media quality monitoring). The *Payload Type Identification* (*PTI*) identifies the data types (e.g., video, data, control messages) transported in an ATM cell based on the PTI field.

- *Header error protection*: The header of an ATM cell has to be particularly well protected against errors. This includes single-bit errors and ideally also block errors. To protect a header, an encoding principle based on a generalization of the Hamming encoding, the so-called *BCH* encoding (Bose-Chadhuri-Hocquenghem) is used [Pry93].

### 5.2.6.4    ATM Circuits between Traditional LANs and ATM Networks

The use of ATM-WANs expands the availability of ATM connection options in LANs, because this type of ATM-LANs can communicate over certain distances. There are several options to implement the connection of a traditional LAN (e.g., Ethernet, FDDI, token ring) over ATM networks:

• The introduction of additional functionality in the gateways between LAN and ATM-WAN and in the ATM hubs (bridges) between traditional LANs and an ATM-LAN shown in Figure 5-12 is one possible topology of this type.

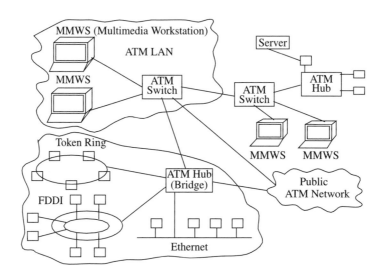

**Figure 5-12**   ATM interconnecting traditional LANs and an ATM-LAN.

In ATM, intelligent hubs support LAN segments of various LAN types (e.g., Ethernet, token ring, FDDI), offering a bridge or routing functionality. In addition, the high switching capacity of the hubs offer the full capacity to each terminal.

• Implementation of additional ATM software in the endpoints above the traditional LAN protocol stack [AA93], e.g., to emulate the ATM concept between two Ethernet interfaces. In this approach, the ATM cells are encapsulated in Ethernet packets.

• A network architecture consisting of at least one LAN/optical fiber switch node, which switches cells between physical intranet connections and an external B-ISDN optical fiber line; this approach was proposed in [AA93].

### 5.2.6.5    Local ATM Networks

An ATM-LAN connects ATM multimedia terminals, i.e., workstations or servers, to an ATM host interface, either over a private *User Network Interface* (*UNI*) through a private ATM switching center, or over a public UNI in a public ATM network (see Figure 5-13).

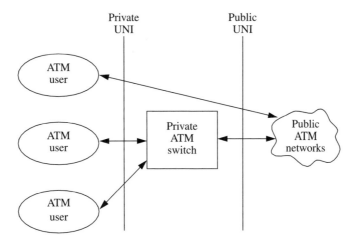

**Figure 5-13**   A local ATM network.

A local ATM network is configured as a simple star, which does not required the definition of a MAC protocol, like in other local high-speed networks. We merely define a point-to-point interface in this star-shaped architecture.

An ATM-LAN can cover both a small and a large geographic distance. It can be composed of a small or large number of terminals. Both factors depend exclusively on the size of the ATM-LAN switching node and the use of interfaces. There are some differences between the service requirements of ATM-LAN switching nodes versus those of ATM switching nodes for B-ISDN:

- An ATM-LAN switching node offers a more limited number of ports (typically less than 1,024 ports), because the number of stations connected to a LAN is limited.
- Delays in the switching centers can dominate the connection delays. To determine a total delay comparable to a traditional LAN, the switches have to minimize this value. For this reason, the delay introduced by the switching center is more important in ATM-LANs than in comparable WANs.
- Some LAN applications require data that are exchanged between all or a set of stations. For this reason, a switch in an ATM-LAN has to provide mechanisms for multicast and broadcast.
- A WAN that transports voice data has to operate very reliably. In ATM-LANs, this type of restrictive constraints may not be met.
- The establishment of a connection in a WAN is similar to the telephone paradigm, where a user may have to wait for a connection. This is difficult to achieve in LANs, because immediate data transmissions are the rule. Therefore, ATM-LANs

should keep the duration of the connection establishment phase as short as possible.

Both ATM-LANs and ATM-WANs are based on ATM switching, ATM routing, and multicast properties. The endpoints in an ATM-LAN require very efficient end-to-end protocols, because the delays in the endpoints dominate the connections and the switch delay. As mentioned before, AAL5 can be used to transmit signaling information. User data use AAL1 and AAL2 for voice/video services, and AAL3/4 or also AAL5 for other services.

## 5.3  Metropolitan Area Networks (MANs)

A *Metropolitan Area Network* (*MAN*) is a network that falls between a LAN and a WAN with regard to the distance it covers, e.g., a MAN can span an entire university campus, or an entire city. In addition, a MAN can carry different types of traffic simultaneously, such as data, voice, and video. These characteristics make the MAN complementary to the definition of B-ISDN, so that it may be considered as a large advantage for a MAN of being compatible with ATM as defined by CCITT.

The two basic characteristics of a MAN (medium distance and large service range) distinguish it from currently used and installed LANs. A MAN must be able to transport all kinds of services, including voice and video. In addition, a MAN is able to interconnect LANs, but it can also connect high-performance workstations, hosts, file servers, etc., directly.

To interconnect all these devices, a MAN can use different topologies, such as a star, bus, or ring. The option chosen for the MAN is to use a shared medium with distributed switching and medium access control (MAC). This is different from the ATM-LAN solution, where a star topology is preferred, since this requires only the standardization of transmission intelligence in a single box with centralized operation. MANs offer the following services:

- *Interconnecting several LANs*: To connect several LANs, a network bridge offers functions, such as the protocol conversion, address mapping, or access control. This functionality depends on whether or not, or to what extent the interconnected LANs are compatible. LANs normally operate in a connectionless mode, so that a MAN that interconnects several LANs should also support connectionless operation. This implies that no resources are normally used in a MAN. However, the transmission of continuous media requires guarantees, which can be implemented only if resources can be reserved.

- *Host-to-host communication*: A MAN can offer a semi-permanent point-to-point connection with high throughput and high reliability between hosts [Pry93]. This service is equivalent to a high-speed private/leased line. In this case, a connection is established during the installation, and it ensures that enough resources are available in the MAN. The operation mode is thus connection-oriented, with a semi-permanent assignment of resources. In addition, a MAN can offer a number of isochronous slots, requested on demand by signaling. This solution is similar to a circuit-switched solution, where *Time Division Multiplexing* (*TDM*) is the enabling approach. The time slots are allocated on demand by a signaling procedure. This functionality may not be available in all MANs. Finally, a MAN can offer a number of non-isochronous slots. In this case, resources of the MAN are only used when information has to be transported, and information is transported in a connectionless way.

- *Voice and video communication*: Voice and video communication may also be offered in a MAN. The three alternatives described above can be used for these services, depending on the quality requirements. If voice and video are offered either by solution 1 (semi-permanent point-to-point connection) or solution 3 (non-isochronous slots), then the jitter introduced by the MAN has to be removed at the receiving terminal. In addition, a MAN can offer broadcast and multicast services.

In an effort to standardize MAN technologies, two standardization organizations have worked on MAN standards: The ANSI with the *FDDI* (Fiber Distributed Data Interface) proposal and IEEE 802.6 with the *DQDB* (Distributed Queue Dual Bus) proposal. A separate standardization in Europe led to a MAN mechanism called *Orwell*, which was developed by British Telecom. However, Orwell was not successful in developing into a widely accepted standard.

### 5.3.1 Distributed Queue Dual Bus (DQDB)

The token passing mechanism is not very effective for modern networks with data rate of more than 100 Mbps and a geographic coverage of over 100 km [RB90]. The reason is the delay introduced by the bus or ring, resulting from the rotation of the token to the next active station and along the entire ring or bus. This means that the larger the geographic expansion of a network, the longer the time until the token will return to the sending station and released again by that station. This fact motivated the development of another network, which was initially called *Queued Packet Synchronous Exchange* (*QPSX*) [NBH88]. It originates from a joint effort between the University of Western Australia and Telecom Australia. Due to naming conflicts, the standard was later renamed in *Distributed Queue Dual Bus* (*DQDB*).

This MAN standard was adopted by IEEE and defined as IEEE 802.6 standard; it is characterized by a bus with a data transfer rate of $2 \times 150$ Mbps, which can use various cable types. Figure 5-14 shows that DQDB is based on two unidirectional busses with work in opposite direction. In contrast to FDDI, both busses carry information, which means that one bus is not exclusively dedicated to fault tolerance. Similar to FDDI II, this bus creates frames with a length of 125 m.Each frame contains additional slots with a fixed length. The slots transport the data between the nodes. This means that the bus capacity is allocated in so-called *Access Units* (*AUs*) with a size of 53 bytes each, which are used by a user terminal to gain access. The data flow starts and ends at the two head-ends, where the frames are generated and later resolved.

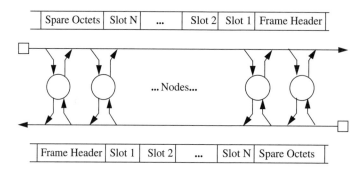

**Figure 5-14**   Basic DQDB topology with labeling as used in the standard specification.

The MAC mechanism used in DQDB is basically different from most other LAN/ MAN protocols based on distributed network access. Most other mechanisms use one single protocol to manage the network status in the nodes. In these networks, a status information has to be derived from the medium directly before the access. This means that the performance of these systems is closely tied to the network size. For example, FDDI uses the *Distributed Queuing* algorithm, which stores current status information about the network in each node, so that each node knows the exact number of DQDB segments, while waiting to access the bus. When a node has to transmit a time slot, it uses local information stored in a counter to determine the position of the segment.

The DQDB standard includes the specification of a connectionless packet service for asynchronous data transmission, an isochronous service, and the so-called *Guaranteed Bandwidth* (*GBW*) protocol for connection-oriented data services. These are two expansions to the original specification that defined only the connectionless packet service.

### 5.3.1.1   Asynchronous Data Transmission

Asynchronous data transmission works by the *Distributed Queuing* algorithm based on distributed queues. More specifically, each station continually listens to the network. To make a request for transmission, the station sets the *Request* field. For each direction, each station implements its own queue by using a counter, where priorities may also be set. The following four steps explain this process:

1. Each station that does not have data to transmit (node in Figure 5-14) counts all requests arriving from the right side towards the bus at the bottom. These requests

are stored in a queue (or in the counter). As soon as a free time slot appears in the upper bus, the oldest request in the queue is served, which means that this entry is removed from the queue. The queue will then contain all other transmit requests arriving from the right side to be transmitted over the upper bus. The same principle applies to the lower bus, with stations arranged towards the left side, and using a second queue.

2. A station with data to send waits for a free time slot on the lower bus. Then it marks its request by setting the Request field in the lower bus and puts its send request into the queue for the upper bus.

3. The station ready to send waits to send its data in asynchronous mode. It can always place at most one request in the queue. It also has to remove requests continually from the queue as time slots become free, as described in point 1. In addition, it adds requests as they arrive from the lower bus.

4. The station sends its data. This request is the top request in the queue. These data are transmitted with the first free slot in the upper bus and removed from the queue. The free slot is now marked *busy*. In addition, incoming requests are added to the queue and processed as described above.

In summary, we can state that the DQDB protocol is based on counters acquiring the requests from the stations connected and ensuring that a station will not send until the reservations waiting in the queue before its request have been served.

The standard requires that priorities for transmission requests be distinguished by use of various request bits. These bits are stored in several priority queues. In addition, the standard requests that the connectionless service may be used only in low priority. This means that connectionless traffic can be transmitted only if the higher-priority queues are empty. Unfortunately, not all implementations follow this approach for the use of queues with several priorities.

## 5.3.1.2    Isochronous Data Transmission

Isochronous data transmission is important for continuous data and implemented by use of a so-called *Pre Arbitrated function*. For this purpose, certain slots are marked in the head stations, i.e., they are set to a value of 1 in the *Slot Type SLT* entry. This means that they are now ready for previously reserved traffic. The slots occur every 125 m; this corresponds to a frequency of 8 kHz. This means that the isochronous mode of DQDB can also be linked to WANs, based on the PCM hierarchy, similar to FDDI II. In addition, all audio and video data can be integrated in this 8-kHz pattern.

## 5.3.1.3    Connection-oriented Data Transmission

Connection-oriented data transmission is provided by the *Guaranteed Bandwidth Protocol (GBW)*. GBW represents an expansion of the basic DQDB protocol; it is tailored to the requirements of Variable Bit Rate (VBR) traffic, which requires bandwidth guarantees. GBW is compatible with priority mechanisms working under the basic DQDB protocol with lowest priority, i.e., it is capable of offering a requested bandwidth for connection-oriented data services with priorities higher than 1 or 2.

By the GBW protocol specification, each queue with a specific priority contains all segments not yet transmitted, but "accepted" for immediate transmission. In this context, *accepted* means that the segment has traversed the *traffic shaper*, which will be described in the next section. The GBW protocol continues using the above described distributed queuing algorithm as follows: Each queue can be thought of as a linked list of zeros and ones, where 1 designates a segment put into the queue by the station itself, and 0 designates a segment requested by a station on the subsequent transmission path for transmission. The queue is refreshed once after the transmission of a segment, when a segment was accepted by the traffic shaper, or when a request was received. By implementing a distributed queue, GBW also allows that several requests be pending.

GBW can *balance* the traffic load, because it limits the rate of segments to be stored for a specific connection to the bandwidth accepted during the establishment of the connection. This method is called *traffic shaping*. To balance the traffic load, GBW uses a variable credit system and the system parameters *income*, *slotcost*, and *creditmax*. For each slot that passes the bus and is ready to be transmitted, the value of the income parameter is added to the current value of the *credit* parameter. A connection may add a segment to a queue, if the value of the credit exceeds the *slotcost* parameter, which can be thought of as an amount of "money" that may be spent for the transmission of segment. When a segment is added to the queue, the value of the *credit* parameter is immediately reduced by the *slotcost* parameter. To avoid peak traffic, the *credit* value is limited by the *creditmax* parameter, i.e., set to an upper limit. The GBW parameters are determined by the network management. When setting higher priorities, the fairness scheme for bandwidth balancing has to be switched off (see below); otherwise, high-priority transmission will not work [As90].

Lower-priority traffic is controlled in another way. GBW allows the transmission of connectionless traffic with a priority of 0 by means of a mechanism which is fully compatible with the DQDB protocol. This ensures division of dynamic bandwidth without the use of bandwidth guarantees.

### 5.3.1.4   Reachability and Fairness

The DQDB method has to deal with the problem of reachability. Each station has to know the bus from which it can reach other stations. In addition, the location of a station with regard to the head stations has an impact on fairness. Stations located near a head-end have a better chance to transmit their data towards this head-end than the other stations. With regard to utilization, it is important that the data are always transported all the way to the head-ends, although the actual data transmission may not require it.

Several solutions have been developed to solve the unfairness problem potentially inherent in DQDB. One solution is *Bandwidth Balancing* (*BWB*), which was specified in IEEE 802.6 draft standard for MANs. This scheme attempts to avoid unfair use of bus capacity by forcing an Access Unit (AU) artificially to pass on a certain part of its bus access allocation. More specifically, this scheme is based on the principle that the smaller the potential unfairness, the larger this part. In general, this scheme achieves fairness, but at the cost of wasted bandwidth.

Another solution to improve fairness in DQDB is the *Reactive DQDB* protocol (*R-DQDB*), where more status information about bus activities is collected over a dedicated control slot. An AU can use this additional information to discover whether or not it works fairly in relation to other users. If this is the case, then the reactive protocol allows the other stations to request additional capacities. This leads to an immediate fair treatment of all stations. The cost of R-DQDB is the periodic collection of status information from the bus to determine the number of active AUs. It was observed that a rate of 100 slots is normally adequate [OF93].

The isochronous mode of DQDB is well suited for the transmission of continuous media data. However, most implementations do not support this mode. The concurrent access to network data by multiple stations also allows an effective, high throughput in large networks.

All networks studied so far offer their services in the upper level of the logical link control layer as specified in IEEE standard 802.2. This layer itself does not have to have additional particularities for the transmission of multimedia data; all it needs to do is to allow effective access to the corresponding MAC services with the required parameters.

### 5.3.2  Orwell

*Orwell* is based on the approach to release the filled slot at the destination. This results in a better performance, since the released slot can be used by another node, located between the destination and the source node. However, when a slot is emptied, the node has to pass it to the next node in the ring. To ensure fairness in the ring and to prevent a node from hogging the ring, access is organized in cycles, also called *reset intervals*. Each node on the ring has a counter, indicating how many slots may be occupied by that node during a cycle.

Two service classes are defined in Orwell: class 1 for isochronous, delay sensitive services, and class 2 for asynchronous delay tolerant services.

The rate at which reset slots rotate in the ring gives a measure for the occupancy of the ring. When the reset rate becomes too small, the occupancy is too high. This information can be used by every node to decide whether or not a new call will be accepted. If the call is accepted, the new virtual reset rate can be calculated and checked against the allowable rate.

Four priority levels are provided in Orwell, implemented by four independent queues in each node. This is also reflected in the Orwell slot header.

In order to increase the bandwidth of the Orwell ring, several rings can be arranged in parallel, where each ring acts as an independent Orwell ring. This solution is a flexible means to increase the network capacity,, i.e., by adding new rings as required, which also provides for higher network reliability.

The principle of the Orwell ring (slotted ring) does not impose any information field length. This means that the slot length can have any size, but once determined for an Orwell ring, it is fixed for the complete ring and all nodes connected to it. However, for practical reasons, it should not be too long, or too many slots may circulate in the ring.

An Orwell ring performs very well, mainly thanks to the destination deletion principle. Since the slots are already released at the destination, it is possible that more than the physical bit rate can be effectively used in the ring. In fact, an Orwell ring can support up to 240 Mbps, however at the cost of a considerable delay in the ring [Pry93].

### 5.3.3  MAN Connection to ATM Networks

Several remote MANs are normally connected over a WAN, and ATM is one of the preferred technologies for this end. Unfortunately, if FDDI-MANs are to be connected over ATM, a considerable amount of incompatibility has to be solved. To solve this problem, adaptation functions are normally used at the network transition points. The cell size of ATM and the frame length of FDDI are incompatible. This means that the unit connecting the networks has to segment and reassemble packets, which introduces additional end-to-end delay. Moreover, considerable processing capacities are required to ensure high throughput. This segmentation and reassembly can be implemented in the ATM-AAL3/4 layer.

Both DQDB and Orwell were specified in parallel to the ATM specification, so that it is easier to connect these network types. The DQDB protocol uses a slot-based transmission method, where the slot size (53 bytes) corresponds to the ATM cell size. DQDB is also called *Shared Medium ATM*, but the similarity of these two technologies is limited to the length of the payload field.

*Internetworking*, i.e., connecting several different networks, means here that DQDB slots are mapped to ATM cells, and vice-versa. Several solutions have been studied in laboratory environments for this purpose, e.g., the *Cell-to-Slot Internetworking* or *Frame Internetworking*, proposed for the connection-oriented mode of DQDB. The cell-to-slot internetworking converts ATM cells into DQDB slots, and vice-versa. Frame internetworking reassembles cells/slots and converts AATL frames into initial DQDB-MAC protocol data units, and vice-versa. Both modes have been studied and compared by using aggregate traffic of B-ISDN and high-priority transmissions, controlled by the GBW protocol to the DQDB access. The cell-to-slot mode was found to yield better results and appears to be more promising [MR93]. Internetworking over ATM has the following characteristics:

- *Semi-permanent basis*: DQDB was primarily designed for connectionless asynchronous service. Several preparations have to be made for the connectionless mode, because ATM is based on a connection-oriented concept. For example, semi-permanent connections have to be installed by using virtual paths, transporting various virtual channels between all MANs to be interconnected. Other preparations are the use of special message IDentification (MID) values in the AAL, and the use of a very fast connection establishment [Pry89], the so-called *Fast Reservation Protocol* [TBR92].

- *Connectionless server*: Due to the connectionless transport in MANs, one or several servers capable of delivering connectionless data could be interconnected instead of virtually connecting all MANs. For example, a server based on the *Switched Multimegabit Data Service* (*SMDS*), or on the *Connectionless Broadband Data Services* (*CB-DS*) could be used [HL90].

- *Direct ATM connection by means of an ATM-LAN*: The traffic volume in networks can continue until each device accessed by users will have its own connection to the WAN over an ATM-LAN. The result would be a topology in the form of a complete star, where each user is directly connected to the ATM network and has maximum access to the B-ISDN functions.

In principle, DQDB is well suited for continuous multimedia traffic. Orwell is an experimental MAN, basically suitable for the transport of multimedia data. However, it remains to be seen whether or not Orwell will be accepted in practice. While the necessity of MANs has been an issue of discussion only a few years ago, there is agreement today that the current high-speed LANs and ATM-WANs may mean that MANs will become insignificant.

## 5.4   Wide Area Networks (WANs)

*Wide Area Networks* (*WANs*) normally extend over countries and even continents. In contrast to the early versions, current WANs support data rates similar to those of LANs and MANs. For example, the current backbone of the Internet, the so-called *very High-Speed Backbone Network Service* (*vBNS*) offers a data rate of 622 Mbps. The "ownership" of these networks can be split among many organizations, including telecommunication companies who may own the communication subnetwork, while users own hosts. WAN communication is normally based on point-to-point connections, with the exception of satellite networks.

Two types of WANs are normally used for the transmission of multimedia data: traditional *computer networks*, like the Internet, and enhanced implementations of the conventional telephone networks in the form of ISDN and *Broadband-ISDN* (*B-ISDN*), i.e., ATM. This section describes the basic mechanisms and principles of these WAN systems below the network layer, which is relevant for multimedia data transmission. With regard to traditional WAN systems, we will discuss aspects about their interconnecting capabilities and give a short overview of the global Internet precursor network. Subsequently, we will discuss some functions of the Internet, including multicasting and routing in the network layer, which are of particular relevance for multimedia applications, e.g., collaborative computing. With regard to B-ISDN over ATM, we will introduce switching functions, routing, and the so-called host interfacing.

## 5.4.1 Traditional WANs

### 5.4.1.1 Internetworking

The internetworking capabilities of various local networks over a large distance represent an important aspect of WANs. This function allows users to run networked multimedia applications, e.g., for collaborative work in a project. The internetworking capability of systems can be implemented on three layers:

- *Physical layer and Data Link layer*: These layers offer the function of basic internetworking capabilities of transmission paths. This is normally achieved by common use of such paths, or by use of the infrastructure of public packet-switched data networks, which often base on X.25 and Frame Relay, but these technologies will most likely be replaced by ATM. In May 1993, the *National Science Foundation* (*NSF*) proposed a new architecture for data communication within the US. This architecture consists of a high-speed backbone network (very High-Speed Backbone Network Service — vBNS) to the network access points (NAPs) and many network service providers (NSPs). vBNS was taken into operation in 1995 as a result of a cooperative effort between MCI and NSF. The same research team is currently working on the Internet-2 project. The data rate will be increased and the service quality optimized for multimedia data traffic.

Transmission paths between the US and Europe are interconnected as follows:

- *Dedicated connections*, normally operating at relatively low bit rates, which are intended to meet special requirements. For example, the German Research Network (Deutsches Forschungsnetz—DFN) is connected to vBNS over two 45-Mbps paths.
- *High bandwidth paths* (*fat pipes*) with a higher bandwidth (typically from 155 Mbps and up), spread among various networks. One example is an OC-3 link (155 Mbps), e.g., of Teleglobe, as a service to connect to the *Multicast Backbone* (*MBone*) [MB94]. MBone is a virtual network using the same physical media like the Internet. It serves as a basis for multicast group communication.

• *Network layer*: The next layer for internetworking offers a network connection to implement end-to-end communication. This connection layer is normally implemented by use of one single protocol stack. Another challenge is the support for multicast functions in the Internet routers, when continuous media have to be transmitted. Today, MBone supports multicast, where a network of routers (MRouters) is used to provide all multicast functions. One argument in favor of supporting such functions for the transmission of continuous media is the required bandwidth. A multicast stream is *bandwidth-efficient*, because one packet (not many) reaches all computers connected to a network. For example, a 128-Kbps video data stream (typically 1 to 4 images per second) uses the same bandwidth, regardless of whether or not it is sent to one or 20 computers.

• *Transport layer and Application layer*: These layers offer user services, e.g., electronic mail, conference applications, and distributed applications. This is achieved by "connecting" similar services for different protocol families. This implementation normally uses so-called *application gateways* (e.g., to translate packet formats between OSI and TCP/IP services). One example that explains the application-to-application link is the set of MBone applications that connect users around the globe. MBone applications, such as *Net Video* (*nv*), *Visual Audio Tool* (*vat*), and *Whiteboard* (*wb*), are based on IP multicasting; some use the Real-Time Protocol (RTP) on top of a combination of UDP/IP. These applications allow the interconnection of users for multimedia conference applications over a WAN, using the MBone tools on different computers and different operating systems.

### 5.4.1.2    The Internet

The Internet experiment of DARPA conduced in 1973 led to the development of a system of networks, the global Internet, with a growth rate of currently more than 10 percent. The Internet is based on a layered structure, similar to the OSI reference model. Table 5-3 shows the Internet layer model with examples of applications for each layer.

| Layer | | Examples |
|---|---|---|
| Application | | FTP, Telnet, SMTP, X-Window |
| Transport | | UDP, TCP |
| Network | Internet | ICMP, IP, CLNP |
| Data Link | Subnetwork | Ethernet, X.25, FDDI, Token Ring |
| | Link | HDLC, PPP, SLIP |
| Physical | | RS-232, V.35, 10Base-T, optical fiber |

**Table 5-3**    The Internet layer model.

The Internet is based on the packet-switched technology, which is implemented in the *Internet Protocol* (*IP*) environment, providing for internetworking. Application-to-application communication is provided for by the *Transmission Control Protocol* (*TCP*) as well as by other transport protocols (e.g., UDP), and higher-layer protocols (e.g., RTP).

The Internet offers services like electronic mail and file transfer. Special procedures for electronic mail are used to support modern applications and blackboards. Modern Internet applications support audio (e.g., vat) and video (e.g., nv), conference applications, or distributed applications (e.g., wb). However, there is no doubt that the most popular application of the Internet is the *World Wide Web* (*WWW*).

### 5.4.2   B-ISDN over ATM

*Broadband Integrated Services Digital Network* (*B-ISDN*) is an expansion of *Narrowband-ISDN* (*N-ISDN*).

#### 5.4.2.1   Transmission Modes

Until 1987, B-ISDN was based on the *Synchronous Transfer Mode* (*STM*). Since 1988, it is based on the *Asynchronous Transfer Mode* (*ATM*) [HH91, Sta92].

- *Synchronous Transfer Mode*: Within the connection-oriented mode, STM has a permanently assigned bandwidth. For this reason, the lower layers can support a guaranteed transmission with a fixed bandwidth (like in ISDN), where there are only low end-to-end delays. A time window is called a *slot* in this context. These slots are reserved for the duration of a transmission. They are embedded in periodically repeating structures, the so-called *frames*. Figure 5-15 shows an example for slots and frames.

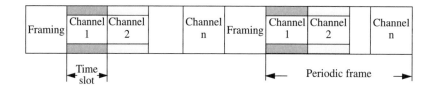

**Figure 5-15**   Allocation of slots in STM, using time-division multiplexing.

Each slot has a fixed duration, which means that STM adapts well to PCM transmission hierarchies and ISDN. Table 5-4 shows a summary of the channels and their corresponding data rates.

| Channel | Bandwidth |
|---------|-----------|
| B | 64 Kbps |
| $H_0$ | 385 Kbps |
| $H_1$ | 1,920 Kbps (Europe), 2,048 Kbps (USA) |
| $H_2$ | 32,768 Kbps (Europe) |
| $H_4$ | 132,032 - 139,265 Kbps |

**Table 5-4** Channels and their data rates.

This approach is relatively inflexible, because fixed data rates are used and the bandwidth for each connection is fixed in advance. There are various solutions to increase flexibility:

- *Compression methods*: For example, the video compression methods described in Volume 1 Chapter 7 can be used. Many multimedia systems use compression methods that allow scaling.

- *Additional slots*: This solution uses a large number of slots, i.e., 2,048 8-bit slots for 15 Mbps. The drawback of this solution is its additional administrative cost due to the large number of possible combinations.

- *Container solution*: As a compromise, a so-called container solution has been proposed to allow limited number of partitions. For example, they could be $H_4 + 4 \times H_1 + n \times B + D$ with containers in the $H_1$ and $H_4$ channels. This solution also uses the static STM mechanism. The remaining bandwidth is not utilized in a continual way due to this partial reservation.

The STM approach is well suited for situations where data have to be transmitted in a fixed data rate that does not change. In addition, it has the benefit of low end-to-end delay in interactive multimedia applications.

- *Asynchronous Transfer Mode (ATM)*: ATM was introduced in Section 5.2.6. The ATM approach is more efficient and more flexible than the STM approach for the transmission of data streams with variable bit rates, because the overall bandwidth utilization is better.

The next sections discuss mainly ATM-WAN properties, e.g., switching and ATM host interface to multimedia workstations, offering the functionality for interconnection to multimedia communication systems. We will also describe some properties of the cell data transport and the ATM service model.

### 5.4.2.2    Switching

The switching requirements for ATM can be derived from the fact that different types of data have to be transmitted, including voice and video data (for image telephone, conferences, and TV-quality data), control data, and data from conventional data processing applications. As described earlier, these services have different requirements with regard to the bit rate (from a few Kbps to several hundred Mbps), the temporal behavior (constant or variable bit rate), the semantic transparency (cell loss rate, bit error rate), and the temporal transparency (delay, delay fluctuations). We will discuss some of the most important of these requirements below.

- *Bandwidth*: The usual bit rate in current networks operating over ATM-WAN switching centers is approx. 155 Mbps, or 622 Mbps for the data transfer between switching centers. Increasingly, 2.4 Gbps and higher data rates are required (in the backbone). This does not imply that ATM switching centers have to operate internally at 155 Mbps and more. The switching of a single path can be in parallel, so that a smaller speed can be used internally. On the other hand, several 155-Mbps paths can be operated over some connections with higher data rates by using a multiplexing method, so that higher rates have to be used internally.

- *Broadcast/Multicast*: Traditional ISDN and packet-switched networks support only point-to-point connections, although data have to be switched from one logical source to several logical sinks. For this reason, it was found that broadband networks should have multicast and broadcast functionality in the future, and several development efforts were initiated. Currently, there are many ATM switching centers that offer this functionality already. This type of services is required for applications like conferencing and digital television.

- *Performance parameters*: The following performance parameters play an important role for multimedia applications:

  - *Throughput and bit error rate*: In ATM switching centers, the throughput and the bit error rate depend mainly on the hardware technology (CMOS, BICMOS, or ECL), where current bit rates can be many hundred Mbps to several Gbps, with an acceptable residual error rate.

  - *Link blocking probability*: This concerns the probability when there are sufficient resources available between the source ($m$) and the sink ($n$) to guarantee the quality of all active connections and a new connection.

  - *Cell loss probability*: It may happen that several cells arrive at the same time, which means that they compete for the existing buffer space. Consequently, some cells will be dropped, so that data are lost. Typical values for the cell loss probability in an ATM network are between $10^{-8}$ and $10^{-11}$. Note, however, that these values are considered harmless, because the header of a cell is protected by a *Forward Error Correction* (*FEC*) scheme.

- *Inserting cells in other links*: It could happen that some ATM cells are not properly switched in the switching center, so that they are misrouted and arrive in other links. The probability of these cell insertions has to be kept to a certain limit. For this purpose, the literature suggests very small values of $10^{-14}$ and less [Pry93].
- *Switching delay*: The time required to forward an ATM cell in the switching center is highly significant for the end-to-end delay. Typical values for the delay in ATM nodes are between 10 and 1000 s,with a variance of a few 100 s or less [Pry93]. For continuous media applications, an overall end-to-end delay of up to 100 ms is acceptable, so that this delay can be neglected, even in paths with many ATM switching centers.

A so-called *ATM switching fabric* consists of a large number of basic ATM switching elements. In terms of size, such an element can have between two 155-Mbps inputs and outputs and 16 inputs and 16 outputs at 10 Gbps each. A switching fabric consisting of a large number of identical basic ATM switching elements is also called *multi-stage interconnection network*.

The ATM *switching architecture* consists of the control part and the transport part. The *control part* of the switching center controls the cell transport and implements the ATM service model, which will be described later. One of the decisions this part has to make is to select which input should be connected to which output. The control part uses QoS parameters to measure the performance of the services it uses. For example, this includes the establishment of a connection and the ATM transport services (e.g., cell transmission). QoS parameters for the control network refer to the signaling protocols. One example is the time required to establish or tear down a connection. The *transport part* handles the correct transport of cells from an input to an output in the switching center, based on the QoS specifications of ATM. Typical QoS parameters for the transport part are the cell loss rate, the bit error rate, the cell delay, or the cell delay variance.

### 5.4.2.3  Cell Data Transport

The transport of data from an incoming to an outgoing logical ATM channel requires the definition of identifying numbers for the outgoing logical channels. A *logical ATM channel* is characterized by a physical input/output (physical port number) and a logical channel on a physical port (VCI and/or VPI). To support the switching function, two additional functions have to be implemented:

- *Routing as a local switching function*: The routing in an ATM switching center concerns the internal forwarding of a cell from an input to an output.
- *Queuing as a temporal switching function*: Queuing of cells means that a cell is transported from a time slot $k$ to a time slot $l$. An ATM switching center does not use previously assigned time slots, which means that fairness problems can occur

when two or more logical channels compete for the same time slot. To prevent this problem, ATM cells are rearranged on the basis of temporal queuing before they arrive at the input of the switching center.

At this point, it is worth discussing the routing of cells in multi-stage interconnection networks, because this function is closely related to multicasting, which is relevant for multimedia.

ATM is based on a connection-oriented approach. For this reason, the paths (logical ATM channels) from the source to the destination are determined during the connection establishment phase. The header values (VPI/VCI) are allocated and translated in each section of a connection, when they are forwarded from one section to the next (routing of cells). When cells are switched, the header/link is translated from the incoming data header into the outgoing data header.

With regard to the routing decision time and the routing information location, the switching function can be categorized as follows: The *time parameter* determines when a translation decision has to be made, i.e., whether the routing decision is to be made only once for a connection or every time when a cell arrives at a switching center. The *location parameter* specifies where the routing information will be stored.

- *Routing decision time*: The routing translation can be done either once for the entire duration of a connection (connection-based routing), or for each cell separately (cell-based routing). *Connection-based routing* means that the multi-stage interconnection network is connection-oriented internally, or it uses paths defined in advance. This case is better suitable for the transmission of continuous multimedia streams, because the data will arrive at the receiver in the correct order. On the other hand, a problem may arise from concurrent access attempts to the previously assigned path, which increases the end-to-end delay of multimedia data. This problem can be solved by using mechanisms for resource reservation internally in the switching centers. *Cell-based routing* means that the multi-stage interconnection network operates connectionless internally. With the first variant, all cells follow a virtual circuit over the same path through the multi-stage interconnection network, which is not the case in the second variant. In practice, the cell-based mode should be selected when data could arrive at the receiver out of order, or when the data to be transmitted should be transmitted as fast as possible. This mode allows each cell to select a path that disposes of a sufficient quantity of resources to avoid bottlenecks. This implies the use of functions that monitor the availability of resources in the switching centers.

- *Routing information location*: Routing information can be transported either by each cell itself, where so-called *routing tags* are used, or it can be stored in routing tables in the switching elements. *Routing tables* are the preferred technique for multimedia data transmissions, because they can be easily implemented in a multicasting environment, where they are then called *multicast routing tables*. An example of an older ATM switching center that supports multicast in cell-based mode is *Roxane* [Pry93]. Today, most of the available ATM switching centers support multicast.

### 5.4.2.4    The ATM Service Model

The ATM service model was developed in parallel by ITU-T and the ATM Forum, a consortium of service providers and equipment manufacturers, and subsequently standardized. The service model specified by the ATM Forum is more advanced than the ITU-T specification and can be considered as a subset of the ITU-T model, with a few limitations. For this reason, we will describe the ATM service model based on the specification formulated by the ATM Forum.

The basic component of the service model specified by the ATM Forum is the existence of various service categories:

- Constant Bit Rate (CBR);
- Unspecified Bit Rate (UBR);
- Real-time Variable Bit Rate (rt-VBR);
- Non-real-time Variable Bit Rate (nrt-VBR); and
- Available Bit Rate (ABR).

One of the basic assumptions this model makes is that this set of service categories is sufficient to meet all communication needs of all kinds of different applications, including distributed multimedia applications. The ATM service model with its service categories is intended to represent an abstraction to map applications to a mechanism offered by the communication system, so that the QoS required by an application can be guaranteed. Each of the service categories should represent such a set of important applications with specific common requirements and properties.

The service categories of the model specified by the ATM Forum are similar to the ATM *Bearer Capability* (*BC*) classes (i.e., classes A, B, C, and X) defined by ITU-T. The BC model represents a class model built on three properties:

- Fixed data rate (CBR), or variable data rate (VBR) adapted to the data source.
- Temporal synchronization between sender and receiver (i.e., either real-time or non-real-time).
- Connection-oriented or connectionless service above the ATM layer.

While the model specified by the ATM Forum also distinguishes between CBR and BVR, the requirements for real-time conditions are defined depending on whether or not an application makes explicit and quantifiable requests with regard to the delay and its variance. This is a weaker understanding of real-time, compared to the ITU-T model. And finally, the indication of the connection type was excluded from the service model proposed by the ATM Forum, because it was thought to be unnecessary information in the ATM layer [Gar96].

The original model specified by the ATM Forum included best-effort services from the very beginning, which were later divided into two service types, i.e., actual best-effort (UBR) and better best effort (ABR) [Gar96]. The VBR service adopted by ITU-T was later also divided into real-time and non-real-time categories.

When comparing the *traffic management* (*TM*) of the ATM Forum (in Version 4.0), which includes the specification of the service categories, with the corresponding document of ITU-T (ITU-T Rec. I.371), we notice the following:

- I.371 refers to CBR as DBR (Deterministic Bit Rate), and VBR is called SBR (Statistical Bit Rate). However, there is no difference between real-time and non-real-time SBR. In addition, there is no service comparable to UBR, and ABR is not fully specified in I.371.
- With regard to the available quality of service (QoS), it should be noted that the ITU-T model does not provide for negotiation of individual QoS parameters; instead, it only uses QoS classes with fixed QoS values. In this respect, the model specified by the ATM Forum is more flexible as it lets you specify and negotiate individual QoS parameters.

### 5.4.2.5    Traffic and QoS Parameters in ATM

The parameters specifying the characteristics of a certain connection are divided into traffic and QoS parameters.

*Traffic parameters* describe the traffic characteristics of a sender. These parameters are defined by a so-called *traffic descriptor* in the source. The traffic descriptor of a connection and the desired QoS parameters form the basis for negotiations between an application and the network. The characteristics of a connection eventually negotiated are specified together in a so-called *traffic contract*. The service model defined by the ATM Forum specifies the following traffic parameters:

- The *Peak Cell Rate* (*PCR*), which is the highest possible cell rate a source can generate during an active connection.
- The *Sustained Cell Rate* (*SCR*), which is the mean cell rate a source can generate during an active connection.
- The *Maximum Burst Size* (*MBS*), which is the maximum number of cells that can be sent in the Peak Cell Rate.
- The *Minimum Cell Rate* (*MCR*), which is the minimum bandwidth guaranteed for a given connection.

The QoS parameters are part of the traffic contract and describe so-called *performance guarantees* offered to the application by the network. They can be specified individually for each direction of a link, and have to be negotiation in several steps between the network and end systems. In addition to negotiated QoS parameters, the network may also demand QoS parameters not subject to the negotiation process. The following QoS parameters can be negotiated:

- The *maximum Cell Transfer Delay* (*maxCTD*), which is the maximum admissible end-to-end delay for incoming cells, before they are considered to have been arrived late (i.e., lost for real-time applications).
- The *peak-to-peak Cell Delay Variation* (*CDV*), which is the variance of the delay (jitter), corresponding to the difference between the earliest possible arrival of a cell and the maximum admissible delay of a cell (maxCTD).
- The *Cell Loss Rate* (*CLR*), which corresponds to the ratio of lost to completely transmitted cells.

QoS parameters not subject to negotiation include the following:

- The *Cell Error Ratio* (*CER*), which is the ratio of corrupted cells to the sum of successfully transferred cells.
- The *Severely Errored Cell Blocks Ratio* (*SECBR*), which is the ratio of strongly corrupted cell blocks to the total amount of transmitted cell blocks, where a cell block is a sequence of $N$ transmitted cells.
- The *Cell Misinsertion Ratio* (*CMR*), which is the rate of erroneously inserted cells.

The service categories determine how parameters should be interpreted, or which parameters should be used for a special service.

### 5.4.2.6   Simple Services for Real-Time and Non-Real-Time: CBR and UBR

The support of real-time or non-real-time services is considered one of the most important characteristics in which service categories differ [Gar96]. The simplest service for these two categories are CBR for real-time transmissions and UBR for non-real-time transmissions.

**Constant Bit Rate (CBR)**   The CBR service is a very simple, reliable and guaranteed service. It was developed for applications that have to run in real time and do not tolerate any violation of the quality of service, even over short periods. For this reason, agreed qualities of service are always kept, which means that the user obtains a deterministic service for applications bound to real time. The rate to be used is defined by the *Peak Cell Rate* (*PCR*). This implies that a static bandwidth is reserved and continually available during an active connection. This service category is ideal for video and audio data traffic, where they normally generate rather continuous traffic thanks to encoding and compression. Note that CBR would still be an appropriate service for audio or video sources, if they were to send bursty traffic, but the efficiency of available resources would drop in the latter case, depending on the amount of bursty data traffic.

**Unspecified Bit Rate (UBR)**   UBR is a service for applications without real-time reference, i.e., for applications that do not have delay or jitter requirements. UBR does not make any quantitative numeric guarantees. In addition, no fairness can be expected across connections, because FIFO (First In, First Out) is used as a service discipline. Although the Peak Cell Rate is used in UBR, it merely serves as an information source to the network. UBR is normally suitable for traditional applications in computer communication, e.g., file transfer or electronic mail. The traffic generated by these applications can be bursty with regard to the data volume, so that static multiplexing may yield considerable efficiency gains. In addition, although these applications are normally not sensitive to delays, they suffer from data loss. As mentioned earlier, a FIFO method is used in combination with large buffers in the network, so that there is a direct connection between delay and data loss. This means that UBR represents exactly the service model of the current global Internet [Gar96].

### 5.4.2.7   More Complex Services: rt-VBR, nrt-VBR, and ABR

In view of the fact that CBR and UBR cannot meet all aspects requested by applications in a complete or efficient manner, additional service categories, namely rt-VBR, nrt-VBR, and ABR, have been developed. Figure 5-16 shows the relationship between these service categories in the context of the service model specified by the ATM Forum.

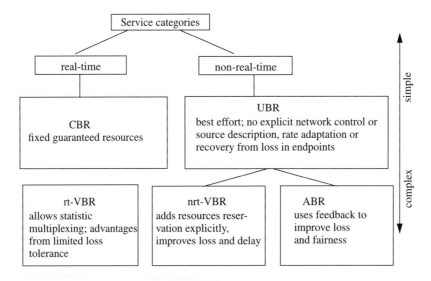

**Figure 5-16**   Relationship between the ATM service categories.

As the name implies, the real-time Variable Bit Rate (rt-VBR) category was designed for real-time applications with special requirements to the delay and delay variance, where a time-variant transmission rate of the source is used. This technology assumes that some applications will not operate in real-time and increase their performance considerably by improving the fairness, the loss, and/or the delay, so that these options, which are not offered by the simpler UBR service category, will be implemented by nrt-VBR and ABR.

**Real-Time Variable Bit Rate (rt-VBR)**  The VBR service should be used for bursty transmission from real-time applications for efficiency reasons. This enables the use of a static multiplexing scheme between real-time media streams with a variable source rate, at least to a certain degree. Static multiplexing leads to minor losses, which have to be compensated by encoding, which means that this service category is not suitable for loss-sensitive applications; these applications should use the more reliable CBR service instead. On the other hand, CBR may waste resources reserved for a variable source. The rt-VBR service uses three traffic parameters—SCR, MBS, and PCR—to describe the varying source rate. The QoS parameters maxCTD, peak-to-peak CDV, and CLR are additionally available. Some authors distinguish between two types of rt-VBR [Gar96], but they are not specified separately in the relevant standards, i.e., the *Peak Variable Bit Rate* (*PVBR*) and the *Statistically Multiplexed Variable Bit Rate* (*SMVBR*).

In PVBR, the traffic data rate varies, but the quality of service remains constant, because the reservation of resources for the peak rate of a media stream always guarantees sufficient resources. This scheme leads to a situation, where only low-priority traffic, e.g., UBR and ABR, may use the remaining bandwidth. In contrast, SMVBR reserves less resources than the peak rate would require, which can cause data loss and delays, temporarily violating the given QoS guarantees. This means that the service is no longer deterministic, but static. However, this less conservative resource reservation strategy allows static mutiplexing between multiple SMVBR streams, normally resulting in a more efficient utilization of available resources.

**Non-Real-Time Variable Bit Rate (nrt-VBR)**  The nrt-VBR service is intended to support applications without real-time reference, characterized by bursty transmissions. Another objective of this service is to improve the loss and delay characteristics of connections based on UBR, which cannot make these service guarantees. This goal is achieved by supplying three traffic parameters, namely Peak Cell Rate (PCR), Sustained Cell Rate (SCR), and Maximum Burst Rate (MBS), or the Cell Loss Rate (CLR) QoS parameter to the application. While the loss characteristics can be specified by use of these parameters, no limits can be determined for the delay. However, as some bandwidth is reserved by the above traffic parameters, the delay should not be excessively large. Note that this is a qualitative statement assumed to be sufficient for applications that are sensitive to delays, but which do not have real-time character.

**Available Bit Rate (ABR)**  The ABR service was developed for applications without real-time reference, which have no particular requirements with regard to the delay or delay variance, but which expect good loss characteristics and fairness across all concurrently active ABR connections. ABR is a service category, where the transfer characteristics may change during the data transfer phase. ABR is based on a flow control mechanism responsible for adapting the source rate in response to changing network characteristics to prevent bottlenecks in the network and resulting high loss rates. One important goal of ABR is to minimize loss and maximize fairness by applying a protocol that uses rate-based flow control. However, fairness is ensured only for connections that actually adapt themselves to the flow control protocol. ABR does not use traffic descriptors, so that it is similar to UBR rather than nrt-VBR [Gar96]. There is no signaled cell loss rate, nor a delay or jitter mechanism in ABR, but it can guarantee a certain minimum bandwidth as it uses PCT (informally), like UBR, and MCR optionally. Figure 5-17 shows a summary of the service categories with the respective traffic and QoS parameters.

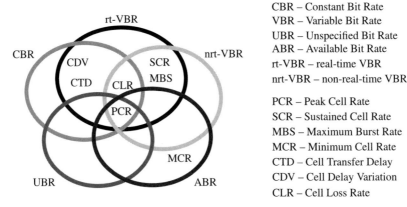

CBR – Constant Bit Rate
VBR – Variable Bit Rate
UBR – Unspecified Bit Rate
ABR – Available Bit Rate
rt-VBR – real-time VBR
nrt-VBR – non-real-time VBR

PCR – Peak Cell Rate
SCR – Sustained Cell Rate
MBS – Maximum Burst Rate
MCR – Minimum Cell Rate
CTD – Cell Transfer Delay
CDV – Cell Delay Variation
CLR – Cell Loss Rate

**Figure 5-17**   Traffic and QoS parameters of various service categories.

### 5.4.2.8   The ATM Host Interface

Another important aspect of ATM is its influence on the end nodes (hosts, multimedia workstations). This section introduces a few options end systems can use to transmit multimedia data effectively within the ATM concept:

• *Support for VBR encoding*: When video signals are encoded by use of a simple pulse code modulation, the resulting bit rate is constant. As soon as a compression algorithm is used, the bit rate varies normally depending on time. In traditional ISDN networks, this fluctuating rate has to be converted into a constant bit rate (CBR), namely into exactly the rate used by the network. This is a rate of 64 Kbps or a multiple of this value for ISDN. This adaptation of the bit rate can be implemented by using an output buffer between the decoder and the network, or by a feedback signal from the buffer to the decoder. ATM networks do not require a limitation of the constant bit rate to be used, so that basically no large buffer is required at the decoder output. Data generated by the decoder can be fed directly into the ATM network, by using AAL2 in combination with a VBR video decoder.

• *Support for medium-dependent hierarchical encoding*: Future WANs will have to support new multimedia services consisting of one or several of the following data streams: audio, standard video, television-quality video data, animation, and regular data. All these components can be transported individually over separate virtual channels. However, a few constraints have to be observed for the virtual channels, resulting mainly from the relative delay introduced by the network.

For example, lip synchronization between voice and video images requires a delay skew of < 80 ms [SM92b]. For this reason, the individual data streams can be divided hierarchically. Each hierarchical level uses information from the next lower level to generate an image in the required quality. With regard to the resolution, this concept is also called *hierarchical encoding*. Sound (e.g., music) and data (e.g., subtitles) are not hierarchically encoded. This implies that a separate VCI/VPI could be assigned to each hierarchical level. One important benefit of this approach is that the different set of services and terminals are compatible. Another benefit is the way cell losses caused by the ATM network can be handled [Pry93]. Still, there is no general, wide acceptance of well defined hierarchical encoding formats.

## 5.5 Closing Remarks

Most cooperative multimedia applications use Ethernet as the underlying network, without changing the existing systems. Video and voice teleconferences have been demonstrated with datagram-based protocols over the Internet (e.g., in [TP91, NS92, CCH+93] and many recent implementations [LLZ03], [WMS02], [Che02]). In fact, it is not true that multimedia communication systems require a bandwidth of at least 100 Mbps to achieve an acceptable performance. The MBone with software for video and audio conferences, e.g., nv or vat, has shown the support of the remote participation in conferences and other technical meetings [Moy93]. Note that augmented nv and vat protocols are currently the main protocols in the Access Grid collaborative applications that connect National Laboratories (e.g., Argonne National Laboratory) and centers in academic institutions (e.g., NCSA—National Center for Scientific Accplications at University of Illinois at Urbana-Champaig).

The network solutions currently available handle multimedia traffic very well, when the network is not congested. However, this situation will change when these applications will become more popular and proliferate accordingly. The number of end users increases continually, which means that the traffic volume rises. Large volumes of this traffic can no longer be processed without handling of various service types in the gateways and routers, or end-to-end protocols. This situation is becoming especially critical in wireless networks carrying multimedia traffic. There is an intensive research going on on Wireless Ethernet 802.11 to assist in multimedia transmission and QoS provisioning (e.g., [KCBN03], [GP01], [ACVS02], [VBG00], [SCN03], [LMCL01]). Furthermore, similar to multimedia operating systems on mobile devices, wireless networks worry in great deal about energy efficiency as well (e.g., [CV02]). The wireless networks including sensor networks and mobile ad-hoc networks are the next types of networks and new frontiers to explore for multimedia networking.

# Communication

T he consideration of multimedia applications supports the view that local systems expand toward distributed solutions. Applications such as kiosks, multimedia mail, collaborative work systems, virtual reality applications and others require high-speed networks with a high transfer rate and communication systems with adaptive, lightweight transmission protocols on top of the networks.

In Chapter 5 on Networks, high-speed network requirements, such as low latency for interactive operations, high bandwidth above 100 Mbps, and low error-bit rate were discussed. Several networks were described that support transmission of multimedia, such as FDDI, High-Speed Ethernet, Token Ring or ATM networks.

In this chapter we discuss important issues related to multimedia communication systems above the data link layer, especially the network and transport layers. Both layers will be considered with respect to multimedia communication and transmission.

We will present not only possible optimizations and extensions to existing protocols, such as TCP/UDP and IP protocols, for multimedia transport, but also new alternative methods and protocols for provision of end-to-end Quality of Service guarantees (QoS) guarantees, such as RSVP, IntServ, DiffServ, RTP and RTCP protocols.

## 6.1  Transport Subsystem Requirements and Constraints

We present in this section a brief overview of requirements and constraints of transport and network protocols, as well as their functionalities, which are used for multimedia transmissions. We evaluate them with respect to their suitability for distributed multimedia applications because they put new requirements on application designers, as well as network protocol and system designers.

### 6.1.1   User and Application Requirements

Networked multimedia applications by themselves impose new requirements onto data handling in computing and communications because they need (1) *substantial data throughput*, (2) *fast data forwarding*, (3) *service guarantees*, and (4) *multicasting*.

- *Data Throughput:* Audio and video data resemble a stream-like behavior, and they demand, even in a compressed mode, high data throughput. In a workstation or network, several of those streams may exist concurrently, demanding a high throughput. Further, the data movement requirements on the local end-system translate into terms of manipulation of large quantities of data in real-time where, for example, data copying can create a bottleneck in the system.

- *Fast Data Forwarding:* Fast data forwarding imposes a problem on end-systems where different applications exist in the same end-system, and they each require data movement ranging from normal, error-free data transmission to new time-constraint traffic types transmission. But generally, the faster a communication system can transfer a data packet, the fewer packets need to be buffered. This requirement leads to a careful spatial and temporal resource management in the end-systems and routers/switches. The application imposes constraints on the total maximal end-to-end delay. In a retrieval-like application, such as video-on-demand, a delay of up to one second may be easily tolerated. On the other hand, a dialogue application, such as a videophone or videoconference, demands end-to-end delays lower than typically 200 msec to ensure a natural communication between the users.

- *Service Guarantees*: Distributed multimedia applications need service guarantees, otherwise their acceptance does not come through as these systems, working with continuous media, compete against analog radio and television services. To achieve service guarantees, resource management must be used. Without resource management in end-systems and switches/routers, multimedia systems cannot provide reliable QoS to their users because transmission over unreserved resources leads to dropped or delayed packets [DHVW93].

- *Multicasting:* Multicast is important for multimedia-distributed applications in terms of sharing resources like the network bandwidth and the communication protocol processing at end-systems.

### 6.1.2   Processing and Protocol Constraints

Communication protocols have, on the contrary, some constraints which need to be considered when we want to match application requirements to system platforms.

A typical multimedia application does not require processing of audio and video to be performed by the application itself. Usually the data are obtained from a source (e.g., microphone, camera, disk, network) and are forwarded to a sink (e.g., speaker, display, network). In such a case, the requirements of continuous-media data are satisfied best if they take "the shortest possible path" through the system, i.e., to copy data directly from adapter-to-adapter, and the program merely sets the correct switches for the data flow by connecting sources to sinks. Hence, the application itself never really touches the data as is the case in traditional processing. A problem with direct copying from adapter-to-adapter is the control and the change of QoS parameters. In multimedia systems, such an adapter-to-adapter connection is defined by the capabilities of the two involved adapters and the bus performance. In today's systems, this connection is static. This architecture of low-level data streaming corresponds to proposals for using additional new busses for audio and video transfer within a computer. It also enables a *switch-based* rather than a bus-based data transfer architecture [Fin91, HM91]. Note, in practice we encounter headers and trailers surrounding continuous-media data coming from devices and being delivered to devices. In the case of compressed video data, e.g., MPEG-2, the program stream contains several layers of headers compared with the actual group of pictures to be displayed.

Protocols involve a lot of data movement because of the layered structure of the communication architecture. But copying of data is expensive and has become a bottleneck, hence other efficient mechanisms for *buffer management* must be found and utilized as discussed in Chapter 3 on Operating Systems.

Different layers of the communication system may have different PDU sizes, therefore, a *segmentation* and *reassembly* occur. This phase has to be done fast, and efficient. Hence, this portion of a protocol stack, at least in the lower layers, is done in hardware, or through efficient mechanisms in software.

Some parts of protocols may use *retransmission error-recovery* mechanism which imposes requirements on buffer space for queues at the expense of larger end-to-end delays.

The new underlying packet/cell networks which work in an asynchronous transfer mode (most of them, although, for example, FDDI offers also an isochronous transfer mode which is best suited for multimedia transmission) put requirements on the protocol design for continuous media. What has to happen is that the higher protocols must provide a *synchronous behavior* to the application, but they rely on an *asynchronous behavior* of the service provider at the packet/cell level. This means introduction of connection-oriented protocols (e.g., ST-II) where, during the connection establishment, preparation for "synchronous transmission" of continuous media has to occur, or some connection-like behavior has to be enforced to provide service guarantees (e.g., RSVP with IP).

## 6.2   Traditional Network Protocols and Their Support for Multimedia

The requirements on the network layer for multimedia transmission are a provision of *high bandwidth*, *multicasting*, *resource reservation and QoS guarantees*, *new routing protocols* with support for streaming capabilities and *new higher-capacity routers* with support of integrated and differentiated services.

The Internet and its traditional protocols go through dynamic changes currently in order to satisfy requirements for rapid increase in the number and functionality of various new applications and services such as multimedia applications and services.

Besides the mostly used traditional Internet Protocol (IPv4), which provides in its current form the support for best-effort service, a number of extensions to the IP protocol itself as well as a number of new protocols were implemented to satisfy the given requirements. Especially of interest are protocols which allow for differentiation of traffic as well as routing and handling of differentiated traffic according to QoS requirements. In this section we will analyze existing IP protocols and their support for multimedia transmission.

### 6.2.1   Internet Protocol Version 4 (IPv4)

Internet is currently going through major changes and extensions to meet the growing need for real-time services from multimedia applications. IP provides for the unreliable transfer of datagrams from a source host to destination hosts, possibly passing through one or more gateways (routers) and networks in the process. We examine some of the IP properties which are relevant to multimedia transmission requirements:

#### 6.2.1.1   Type of Service

IP includes identification of the service quality through the *Type of Service (TOS)* specification. TOS specifies (1) *precedence relation* and (2) services such as *minimize delay, maximize throughput, maximize reliability, minimize monetary cost* and normal service. Any assertion of TOS can only be used if the network into which an IP packet is injected has a class of service that matches the particular combination of TOS markings selected. The assumption is that different networks offer varying classes of service. Different classes may support different media requirements. For example, multimedia conferencing would need service class which supports low delay, high throughput and intermediate reliability. Precedence handling would support priority schemes in a wide area network and therefore support real-time network traffic. Unfortunately, at present, only some commercial routers implement precedence handling in a way that affects the forwarding of packets. In general, routers with IPv4 provide no QoS guarantees.

The TOS capability of IP becomes increasingly important as networks emerge that have the ability to deliver specific classes of services and offer certain service guarantees. The changes, which may need to be specified, are: (a) for multimedia, we may not need a precedence relation, but an *AND* relation; (b) instead of having services, such as *minimize, maximize delay*, etc., lower and upper bounds of a delay should be introduced.

## 6.2.1.2    Addressing

One of the most critical functions of the IP is the addressing, i.e., to establish a global address space that allows every network in the Internet to be uniquely identified. The IP addressing structure is shown in Figure 6-1

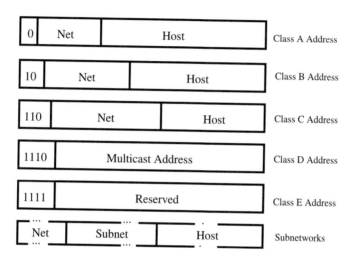

**Figure 6-1**    IPv4 addressing structure.

The network addressing structure was revised to accommodate five classes of address: A, B, C, D and E. *Class A* retained the 24-bit host identifier field, but only seven bits for network number. This address space covers a small number of class A networks. *Class B* with 16 bits for the host identifier and 14 bits for the network number allows a larger number of Class B networks. Class C allocates 21 bits for network number and eight bits for host identifier, therefore many more *Class C* networks are available. A common practice is to assign a class B network address to a collection of LANs belonging to an organization. For example, at Technical University Darmstadt, the Class B IP addresses will range from 130.83.0.0 to 130.83.255.255. The prefix for the network here is 130.83. Inside of a network, further division into subnetworks is possible using subnetwork masks.

The LAN technology brought the concept of convenient *broadcasting* to all end-points on the LAN. LANs also introduced the concept of *multicasting*, in which only a subset of the end-points on the LAN are targeted to receive a particular transmission. This capability allows an application to send a single message to the network and have it delivered to multiple recipients. This service is attractive in a variety of distributed applications, including multi-side audio/video conferencing and distributed database maintenance. This concept is captured in the Internet architecture through special *Internet Class D* addresses, in which multicast-addressed packets are routed (and duplicated at routers when necessary) to all targets that are part of the multicast group.

*Class E* addresses have been reserved for future extensions.

### 6.2.1.3    Routing

A major subject in Internet architecture is the routing of IP packets because the basic model of Internet consists of networks connected by routers. To create an opportunity for further experimental exploration of different routing protocols for global networking, the concept of *Autonomous Systems (AS)* was developed. ASs are collections of routers falling under a common administrative authority. In theory, the routers commonly use the same routing protocol - *Interior Gateway Protocol (IGP)*, within the AS. AS of gateways (routers) exchange reachability information by means of an *Exterior Gateway Protocol (EGP)*.

As the common IGP for the Internet, the *Open Shortest Path First (OSPF)* has been adopted [Moy97]. OSPF protocol can scale to large organizations, uses a link-status algorithm to propagate routing information, and each router participating in OSPF must periodically probe adjacent routers and then broadcast a link status message. Routers that receive the message use Dijkstra's Shortest Path First (SPF) algorithm to compute shortest path. OSPF includes a 32-bit address mask with each address to support classfull option, classless option, and subnets. Furthermore, OSPF allows to authenticate each message to ensure that messages are only accepted from a trusted source, and it allows routers to introduce routes learned from another means such as BGP.

Another IGP protocol is the *Routing Information Protocol (RIP)*. RIP was one of the first routing protocols used with IP and was implemented by the program routed that comes with most UNIX systems. RIP uses a *distance vector algorithm* to propagate routing information. A router running RIP advertises the destinations it can reach along with a distance to each destination; adjacent routers receive the information and update heir routing tables.

For EGP, the *Border Gateway Protocol (BGP)* was developed [RL95]. Version 4 of the BGP protocol (BGP-4) is the current standard and it exchanges routing information among ASs. Furthermore, BGP-4 allows the sender and receiver to enforce policies, to provide facilities for transit routing, and it uses TCP for all communication to ensure reliable transport. ISPs use BGP-4 to obtain routing information from each other and from an authoritative route server.

For multimedia, the best performance would be achieved if a fixed path (static route) could be allocated, because along this path, guarantees can be met and no or little jitter is experienced. The problem with this extension is that the IP protocol would lose the ability to bypass link-layer failures, which is a fundamental property of the Internet architecture, and should be retained for integrated or differentiated services. Further, in the case of a static route, if no resource reservation would be performed along the fixed path, the flexibility of changing a route (in the case of congestion) on a packet basis would be lost, which would decrease the performance of the best effort service.

An effective routing, which would take into account multiple QoS parameters, is desirable, and leads to complex algorithms that are still subject to research (see Chapter 2 on Quality of Service for brief overview on QoS routing).

Further requirements on IP routing come from the data multicast because in the traditional IP there is no group dependency possible neither in local nor in wide area networks. We will discuss this issue in the following subsections of this chapter.

### 6.2.1.4    Interconnectivity Between Internet Protocol and Underlying Networks

The Internet family of protocols is one of today's most widespread protocol stacks in computer networking. There is a strong interest in transporting the IP datagrams, which may carry multimedia traffic, over different networks, for example, Ethernet, ATM B-ISDN, MPLS, or IEEE 802.11 wireless networks. Hence, the mapping between the Internet protocol and the underlying layers is of importance. Another important function in this task is the *binding* of IP addresses to lower-level network addresses.

For example, in the case of Ethernet LANs, routers need to encapsulate IP packets in a properly addressed Ethernet packet. Ethernet uses 48-bit addressing. The router learns the binding of the IP to the 48-bit LAN address through the *Address Resolution Protocol* (ARP) [Plu82]. This protocol allows a router (or any end host) to broadcast a query containing an IP address, and to receive back the associated LAN address. A related protocol, *Reverse Address Resolution Protocol (RARP)*, can be used to ask which IP address is bound to a given LAN address. This protocol plays an important role during booting and configuration of disk-less end-systems, although it starts to be replaced by the functionally richer protocols such as *Boot Protocol (BOOTP)* [CG85] and *Dynamic Host Configuration Protocol (DHCP)* [Dro97].

Analogously, in the case of ATM LANs, routers need to encapsulate IP packets in properly addressed cells, and vice versa. The corresponding mappings are presented in the ATM specifications for the *Adaptation Layers (AAL)* as well as *LAN Emulation (LANE)* [TEBM95]. *Classical IP over ATM* [Lau94] and *Multiprotocol over ATM (MPOA)* include also set of methods for corresponding mappings between IP and ATM.

### 6.2.2    Internet Protocol Version 6 (IPv6)

The traditional IPv4 protocol started in 1981 and it has been extremely successful. IP has made it possible to handle heterogeneous networks causing dramatic changes in hardware technology and large increase in scale of devices connected to Internet.

However, one of the major reasons why a new version of IP protocol is considered is the limited address space of IPv4. The large increase in scale of IP-based devices, in number and capabilities, implies the requirement for new IP addresses to connect them to the Internet. Second major motivation for changes in IP have arisen from new Internet applications such as audio and video applications. To keep multimedia information flowing through the Internet without disruption, IP needs to define a type of service that can be used for real-time delivery of audio and video. Third motivation is that IPv4 is fully missing security functions and as more and more attacks are being conducted on Internet networks and their devices, new version of secure Internet protocol is necessary.

In 1992, IETF published a "Call for Proposals" for an *Internet Protocol of Next Generation (IPng)*, which led to a set of Requests for Comments (RFCs) and appeared in 1995. IPv6 retains many of the design features that have made IPv4 successful. Hence IPv6 is also connectionless protocol, where each datagram contains a destination address, and each datagram is routed independently. Despite retaining the basic concepts from the current version, IPv6 changes can be categorized as follows: (a) *enhanced addressing and improved routing*, (b) *simplification of IP header format*, (c) *improved support of IP options*, (d) *support of QoS*, (e) *support of security*, and (f) *fragmentation of data*.

### 6.2.2.1    Enhanced Addressing and Improved Routing

IPv6 enhances the size of the IP address to 128 bits from 32 bits and allows significant address space for heterogeneous systems and devices. It also provides the possibility to achieve multi-level address hierarchies and to simplify auto-configuration of addresses. The IPv6 standard explicitly assumes that multiple addresses will be assigned to a single interface and this interface will be then used by specific applications.

In the stateless auto-configuration mode, IPv6 allows to create a *Link-Local Address* from (a) a special fixed prefix and (b) an unambiguous token, e.g., the *MAC-Layer-Address*, without any help of an additional service. On the other hand, in the stateful auto-configuration mode, IPv6 allows to create a *Global Address* by concatenating the token (address) with a variable prefix, forwarded from a router.

IPv6 also defines a set of special addresses that differ dramatically from IPv4 special addresses. In particular, IPv6 does not include a special address for broadcasting on a given network. Instead, each address belongs to one of the three types: (a) *unicast address*, (b) *multicast address* and (c) *anycast address* [Com01].

*Unicast address* corresponds to a single computer and the datagram is sent via shortest path to the destination. *Multicast address* corresponds to a set of computers where the membership changes any time. IPv6 delivers a copy of the datagram to each member of the set. *Anycast address* corresponds to a set of computers that share a common address prefix, for example, reside in a single location. A datagram sent to the address is routed along a shortest path and delivered to exactly one of the computers, for example, the computer closest to the sender. Anycast was originally known as the *cluster addressing* to allow for replication of services. When a user sends a datagram to the anycast address, IPv6 routes the datagram to one of the computers in the cluster. If a user from a different location sends a datagram to the anycast address, IPv6 can choose to route the datagram to a different member of the set, allowing both computers to process requests at the same time. In Figure 6-2 and Figure 6-3, we compare IPv4 versus IPv6 addressing.

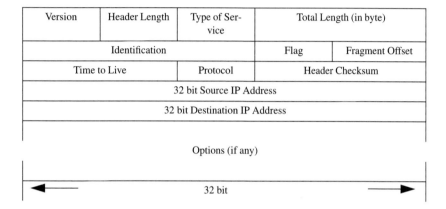

**Figure 6-2**   IPv4 packet header.

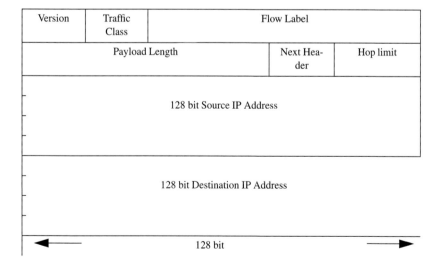

**Figure 6-3**   IPv6 packet header.

### 6.2.2.2    Simplification of IP Header Formats

Although IPv6 addresses are four times longer than IPv4 addresses, the typical IPv6 header is only twice as big as IPv4 header. The reason is that some of the fields in IPv4 header were removed or became optional. This choice had positive impact on the resulting bandwidth utilization as well as average processing of IP headers.

IPv6 datagram format begins with a *base header*, which follows by zero or more extension headers, followed by data. The *base header* includes, besides the information known from IPv4 such as the *payload length, hop limit, source address and destination address*, other fields such as: (1) the *version* field to indicate version 6, (2) the *traffic class* field to specify traffic service class, (3) the field *flow label* for use with new applications that require performance guarantees, and (4) the *next header* field to specify the type of information that follows the current header.

### 6.2.2.3    Improved Support of IP Options

Changes in coding of the IP header allowed an effective forwarding of data, less limited boundaries for the size of the optional parts, and a high flexibility for future enhancements.

IPv6 defines a flexible number of *Next Header Values* which can be used to indicate other optional IP headers or a high-level protocol. This capability allows for extension headers. A receiver uses the next header field in each header to determine what follows. If the value in the field corresponds to a type used for data, the receiver passes the datagram to a software module that handles the data. Some header types have fixed size, so the IPv6 can parse the header and interpret the content. However, some extension headers do not have a fixed size. In this case, the header must contain sufficient information to allow IPv6 to determine where the header ends.

### 6.2.2.4    Support of Quality of Service

Although IPv6 does not provide any support for QoS enforcement, the protocol includes a set of attributes, that allow other mechanisms to use them for reservation and differentiated service of packets.

Especially, the concept of *flows* needs to be considered. These flows represent a stream (flow) of data packets between senders and receivers which belong together and need to be managed together.

Special handling of data flows in the intermediate network nodes, such as bridges, routers, gateways, can be set up and controlled through additional management mechanisms or protocol steps (not included in IPv6), as for example, a reservation protocol. The header of each IPv6 packet includes a 24 bit *flow* label, which can be used to associate data unambiguously with a data flow. A router can then use the flow label for classification of the data flow and decide to which services class the flow will be assigned for handling and forwarding.

Together with the concept of data flows, IPv6 also uses the *traffic class* field (also called priority field) in order to help the router to decide the importance of datagram processing. This field information allows multimedia data of interactive application datagrams to use higher priority and provide preferential processing with respect to the data traffic of lower priority.

IPv6 differentiates between *Congestion Controlled Traffic* with priorities 0 to 7 and *Non-Congestion Controlled Traffic* with priorities 8 to 15 as shown in Table 6-1

Applications use these classes according to their special characteristics and requirements. A data source, which sends "*Congestion Controlled*" data, reacts (e.g., through corresponding algorithms inside of the used protocol) to observed network delays by reducing the sending rate.

Although this type of behavior is appropriate for the non-real-time traffic, it might not be appropriate for multimedia data or other real-time traffic. This type of traffic is then called *Non-Congestion-Controlled* traffic.

| | | |
|---|---|---|
| Non-real-time | 0 - | No specific priorities |
| | 1 - | Background traffic (e.g., Messages) |
| | 2 - | Unexpected asynchronous data transfer (e.g. Email) |
| | 3 - | Reserved for future definition |
| | 4 - | Expected interactive block data transfer (e.g., data file transfer) |
| | 5 - | Reserved for future definition |
| | 6 - | Interactive traffic (e.g., remote login und Windows-systems) |
| | 7 - | Control messages (e.g., routing protocol and network management messages) |
| Real-time | 8 - | Non-Congestion-Controlled traffic |
| | | |
| | 15 - | Non-Congestion-Controlled traffic |

**Table 6-1**   Classification of data flows according to priorities.

### 6.2.2.5   Security

IPv6 supports as its basic functionality *Authentication* to ensure *integrity* and *trust* of data. This functionality is mandatory in all IPv6 implementations and triggers a set of additional security-related methods that were implemented until now in the application level. A short description of algorithms for authentication to ensure trust, key generation and distribution, can be found in Volume 3 in the Chapter on Multimedia Security.

### 6.2.2.6    Fragmentation of Data

In contrast to IPv4, the routers, using IPv6, are not allowed to fragment datagrams (i.e., partition the incoming packet into smaller parts). This functionality can be performed only at the sender side. The sender can fragment packets after identification of the maximum packet size (*Maximum Transfer Unit*, MTU) along the packet's end-to-end path.

To find the MTU size, the host must learn the MTU of each network along the path to the destination, and must choose a datagram size to fit the smallest capacity. The minimum MTU along a path from a source to a destination is known as the *path MTU*, and the process of learning the path MTU is known as the *path MTU discovery*. Hence, the host can use an appropriate protocol, such as the *MTU Discovery Protocol*, or the IP protocol finds out through failed sending of a packet and from corresponding error messages sent by the *Internet Control Message Protocol* (ICMP). It means the path MTU discovery is an interactive process, where a host sends a sequence of various-size datagrams to the destination to see if they arrive without error. Once a datagram is small enough to pass through without fragmentation, the host chooses a datagram size equal to the path MTU.

Using a *Fragment-Headers* information, it will be clearly identified to which datagram the packet belongs and to which fragment offset the packet will be attached during the reassembly process. This approach decreases the processing overhead of intermediate network node systems as they do not need to consider any fragmentation at all. Furthermore, this approach also helps in clear classification of packets according to their content, which is very desirable in firewall systems.

For regular packets, the upper bound on the size of a packet is 64 KBytes, however, there is an option to send even larger packets, so called *Jumbogramms*. It is important to consider that these packets due to their size require larger transmission bandwidth and hence can cause some problems to the real-time traffic over a short period of time.

Due to many IPv4 systems and applications, which use the standard IP stack with address size of 32 bits and the standard header structure, the transition from IPv4 to IPv6 will take long time. Therefore, IPv6 specifies transition steps for step-wise migration. The IPv6 data traffic can be *tunneled* between IPv6 networks when passing through IPv4 infrastructure. For test purposes, a virtual *Overlay Network*, called *6Bone*, was specified [DB98]. Also in a IPv6 network, IPv4 system can be uses through mechanisms of address mapping such as usage of IPv6 compatible and IPv4 mapped addresses or *Dual-Stack-Hosts* approach.

## 6.2.3   Multicast Support

The basic functionality of *IP Multicast* is to allow a sender to send datagrams to all members of a *Multicast Group* addressed with a single multicast address. There is not guarantee in delivery of data to all or even to a single member of the group. The support of multicasting in a WAN environment represents considerable technical challenges [WZ00]. Also, we need to take into consideration that based on a multicast address we cannot make a statement about the location of the receiver.

Inside of a LAN environment, we need to gain and manage information which end-systems are interested to receive multicast data. The underlying network technology (e.g., multicast functionality of Ethernet) then delivers the data to the individual end-hosts in an efficient way. On the other hand, in WAN the routers must exchange the local information with other routers in order to determine which systems are interested in a multicast session. This information is then needed to determine which interfaces of the router will be used to forward multicast packets.

### 6.2.3.1 Delivery of IP-Multicast Packets in LAN

Ethernet, as the most used LAN technology, offers a hardware support for sending multicast packets. Multicast packets are identified in the Protocol Header through the *Multicast Bit*. The *Internet Assigned Numbers Authority* (IANA) registered the Ethernet-MAC-Address with starting block 01-00-5E for the usage of IP Multicast as shown in Figure 6-4.

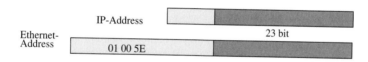

**Figure 6-4** Address mapping for IP Multicast.

To map the IP multicast address to Ethernet multicast address, the mapping procedure places the low-valued 23 bits of the IP-Multicast-Address to the low-valued 23 bits of the Ethernet-Address.

### 6.2.3.2 Internet Group Management Protocol (IGMP)

The *Internet Group Management protocol* (IGMP) [Dee89] was specified in RFC 1112 as its Version 1 and uses the IP packet format with additional IGMP fields, such as the *IGMP-Type* (Host Membership Query, Host Membership Report), *Checksum* and *Group Address* fields (see Figure 6-5).

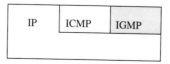

**Figure 6-5** Internet Group Management Protocol.

IGMP is a protocol for managing *Internet multicasting groups*. It is used by conferencing applications to join and leave particular multicast group. The basic service permits a source to send datagrams to all members of a multicast group. There are no guarantees of the delivery to any or all targets in the group.

A multicast router periodically sends queries (*Host Membership Query* messages) with a *Time-to-Live* (TTL) value of 1 (in order not to leave the connected LAN segment) to refresh their knowledge of memberships present on a particular network. If there exist multiple multicast routers on that network segment, one of them will be responsible to respond to the query.

In *IGMPv1*, the query routing is done with the help of routing protocols, used by the routers. However, due to possible deployment of different multicast-routing protocols, various ambiguity problems can occur, hence in *IGMPv2* it was determined, that the router with the lowest IP-Address will be responsible to respond to the query. If this router does not respond to the query due to failures, then a reconfiguration occurs within a specified time-out interval in the presence of other multicast routers.

If no reports are received for a particular group after some number of queries, then the routers assume that the group has no local members, and they do not need to forward remotely originated multicast to the group on the local network. Otherwise, hosts respond to a query by generating reports (*Host Membership Reports*), reporting each host group to which they belong on the network interface from which the query was received.

To avoid an "*implosion*" of concurrent reports there are two possibilities: (1) either a host, rather than sending reports immediately, *delays for a D-second* interval the generation of the report; or (2) a report is sent with an IP destination address equal to the host group address being reported. This causes other members of the same group on the network to overhear the report and only one report per group is presented on the network.

Queries are normally sent infrequently, so as to keep the IGMP overhead on host and routers very low (see Figure 6-6).

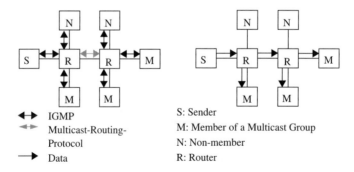

**Figure 6-6**  Data and control flow during multicast transmission.

However, when a multicast router starts up, it may issue several queries to quickly build up its knowledge of local membership. When a host joins a new group, it should immediately transmit a report for that group, rather than wait for a query, in case it is the first member of the group.

The protocol was expanded in *IGMPv2* [Fen97] through an additional query type, the membership query in a *specific multicast group*. Also a query of a specific member is allowed, and the possibility for an explicit request from the end-system to leave the group is considered. In *IGMPv3*, the capability of *Source Filtering* is considered. This feature allows a host, with help of the so called *Inclusion Group-Source Reports* and *Exclusion Group-Source Reports*, to specify its interest or disinterest to receive multicast data from a specific address or from all systems which do not include this address.

In a multimedia scenario, IGMP must loosely cooperate with an appropriate *resource management protocol*, such as RSVP, to provide a resource reservation for a member who wants to join a group during a conference.

In IPv6, no special IGMP protocol exists. These functions will be provided by the enhanced I*nternet Control Message Protocol* (ICMP).

### 6.2.3.3    Multicast Routing

For forwarding of multicast data in WAN and organizing multicast receivers, there exist several routing algorithms (e.g., [Bra93], [Com01], [LPGLA03b]). During our discussion we will assume that a router has input and output ports, called together interfaces. In general, an input can serve simultaneously as an output.

The simplest possibility of multicast routing is *Flooding*. In this case, all multicast packets, which enter the router through an input port, will be sent out through all other output ports (not only output ports which lead towards desired destinations). Flooding ensures that all routers and therefore all potential receivers receive the packets. However, this method is very ineffective because packets are unnecessary using routes and bandwidth in subnetworks, where no receivers reside. Also, this approach provides large overhead on routers due to their information management to avoid loops of packets.

Much more efficient than Flooding is the *Spanning Tree* approach. A Spanning Tree defines a tree as a subset of connections among routers and allows only one path between two points. This approach avoids fully creation of any loops in multicast packet forwarding, hence the router overhead is much less in this approach.

In principle, all multicast data could be considered independent from their senders and group addresses. However, to achieve more efficient approaches, a spanning tree is built for each source. This is performed using the *Reverse Path Broadcasting* approach. In this approach, packets are forwarded only if they arrive at a certain interface that the router considers as part of a shortest path back to the sender. Otherwise, the packet can be dropped.

Neighboring routers exchange messages about information which of their interfaces has the shortest path to the sender. This protocol is called *Distance Vector Protocol*. This approach allows the neighbors to discard forwarding of packets if they recognize that their next neighbor will drop the packet anyway. Furthermore, this approach allows the routers to route packets over their shortest paths.

The disadvantage of Reverse Path Broadcasting approach is that data will be transmitted in parts of networks where no receiver is active. This problem is solved by enhancing the Reverse Path Broadcasting to *Truncated Reverse Path* Broadcasting. This approach forwards packets to a subnet only if a receiver of the multicast group exists there. The knowledge about the receiver state is provided to the router through the above discussed IGMP protocol. This approach decreases the load on the edge networks, but the ultimate decrease in necessary forwarding between routers is achieved by the *Reverse Path Multicasting*.

In *Reverse Path Multicasting*, multicast packets will be transmitted periodically within the whole spanning tree, but if there is a subtree where no interested receiver exists, then the *prune messages* are used to inform routers about these subtrees and avoid useless multicast packet forwarding. These prune messages move in reverse direction towards the source of transmission. To take into account dynamic changes in the network or changes in the topology, the prune messages are periodically dropped after a certain time-out interval. After this period, all multicast packets reach all parts of the network and the IGMP protocol can accept new active receivers to join the tree. If no new active receivers join, then new subtrees are determined which need to be pruned and prune messages are created to inform routers about these subtrees.

Although many multicast routing protocols have been proposed, no Internet-wide multicast routing currently exists. There are other multicast routing protocols such as

- Distance Vector Multicast Routing Protocol (DVMRP) performs local multicast and uses IP-in-IP encapsulation to send multicast datagrams from one site on the Internet to another. It utilizes the Truncated Reverse Path Broadcast approach and in its newer implementations the Truncated Path Multicast approach to support tunneling over unicast connections as well as forwarding of packets over Time-to-Live bounds whose sending diameter is limited.

- *Core-Based Tree Routing (CBT)* deals very well with large size of multicast groups and large size of multicast senders, hence it scales very well. This algorithm selects a *Core* and builds from core routers and non-core routers a backbone used for multicast packet transmission. This backbone is used by all group members and by all sources, hence there are no separate trees per sender only one joined tree used by all.

- *Protocol Independent Multicast (PIM)* uses the same approach as CBT to multicast data. However, the protocol independence emphasizes that although unicast datagrams are used to contact remote destinations when establishing multicast forwarding, PIM does not depend on any particular unicast routing protocol.

- *Multicast extension to the Open Shortest Path First protocol (MOSPF)* is designed for use within an organization and it is built on Open Shortest Path First protocol (OSPF). MOSPF reuses many of the same basic concepts and facilities of OSPF.

### 6.2.3.4  Multicast Transmission in Internet—MBone

Internet supports the transport of multicast data within a *Multicast Backbone*, called *MBone*. Multimedia traffic from video conferencing or video on demand services is often carried by MBone. MBone consists of a set of multicast routers (e.g., UNIX workstations with routing daemon, called *mrouted*, which implements the *DVMRP protocol* [WPD88]) as an overlay network, spanning on top of existing unicast Internet topologies (see Figure 6-7).

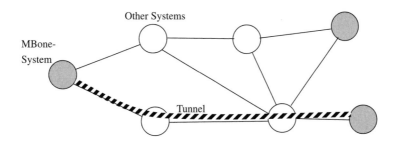

**Figure 6-7**  Multicast transmission in MBone.

In April 1996, MBone includes 2,800 subnetworks in more than 25 countries and it grows steadily. In parts of MBone, other multicast protocols were deployed as well such as the *Multicast Open Shortest Path First (MOSPF)* [Moy94] or *Protocol Independent Multicast (PIM)* [PIM97]. The connections between MBone routers use the same connections as deployed for conventional applications. Between MBone routers, multicast datagrams are tunneled through as IP-in-IP packets (also with the protocol version number 4 in the IP header) and appear to the non-MBone routers as regular unicast traffic.

MBone is gaining experience via transmission of IETF or other conferences. The participants can receive audio and video and passively view the conference activities, or they can actively ask questions and provide contributions to the ongoing discussions. Recently, MBone was used for events such as regular transmissions of lectures, seminars, research events, as well as cultural events such as experimental radio, concerts or television programs. The group communication concepts and mechanisms, used in MBone, will be discussed in more detail in Chapter 7 on Group Communication.

## 6.3 Traditional Transport Protocols and Their Support of Multimedia

Transport protocols serve to support *addressing* of communication end-points within end-systems, *fragmentation* and *reassembly* of data, *flow and congestion control, error control*, as well as *connection establishment* and *closure*.

Transport protocols, to support multimedia transmission, need to have new features and provide the following functions: *timing information, semi-reliability, multicasting, NAK (None-AcKnowledgment)-based error recovery mechanism* and *rate control*. We will concentrate here on examining transport protocols with respect to these characteristics needed for multimedia transport.

In this subsection, we present transport protocols, such as TCP and UDP, which are used in the Internet protocol stack for multimedia transmission, and the following subsections we analyze new emerging transport protocols, such as RTP, and other protocols, which are more suitable for multimedia.

### 6.3.1 Transmission Control Protocol (TCP)

Early implementations of video conferencing applications were implemented on top of the TCP protocol. TCP provides a *reliable*, serial communication path, or virtual circuit, between processes exchanging a full-duplex stream of bytes. Each process is assumed to reside in an Internet host that is identified by an IP address. Each process has a number of logical, full-duplex ports through which it can set up and use full-duplex TCP connections.

Multimedia applications do not always require full-duplex connections for the transport of continuous media. An example is a TV broadcast over LAN, which requires a full-duplex control connection, but often a simplex continuous media connection is sufficient.

During the data transmission over the TCP connection, TCP must achieve *reliable, sequenced delivery* of a stream of bytes by means of an underlying, unreliable IP datagram service. To achieve this, TCP makes use of retransmission on time-outs and positive acknowledgments upon receipt of information. Because retransmission can cause both out-of-order arrival and duplication of data, sequence numbering is crucial. Flow control in TCP makes use of a window technique in which the receiving side of the connection reports to the sending side the sequence numbers it may transmit at any time and those it has received contiguously thus far.

For multimedia, the *positive acknowledgment* causes substantial overhead as all packets are sent with a fixed rate. *Negative acknowledgment* would be a better strategy. Further, TCP is not suitable for real-time video and audio transmission because its retransmission mechanism may cause a violation of deadlines which disrupt the continuity of the continuous media streams. TCP was designed as a transport protocol suitable for non-real-time reliable applications, such as file transfer, where it performs the best. Also the flow control *Slow-Start Algorithm*, which reacts towards network congestion by decreasing the sending rate of transmission and decreasing the network load, represents disadvantages for real-time transmission.

### 6.3.1.1  Techniques to Go Faster

To support multimedia high bandwidth requirements, in the past several techniques were proposed to *speed up the TCP/IP* protocol stack, hence improve the protocol performance and make it more suitable for multimedia traffic [Par94a]. We will present few of those techniques:

- *Better Lookup Techniques*: Looking over the TCP/IP protocol architecture, there exist several cases where a piece of information has to be looked up in a table, e.g. TCP must find the *connection block* for each segment received or IP must find a *route* to be able to send an IP datagram. In worst case, lookup cost can be of $O(log_k n)$, where $n$ is the number of routes or protocol control blocks in the table and $k$ is some base indicating the fraction of the blocks that can be eliminated on average by each comparison. The cost of lookups is large if we consider that other protocol processing costs such as checksum computation on the packet are $O(1)$. Two possible techniques can be used to decrease the lookup cost: (1) use *caches* of frequently used information such as control blocks or routes to avoid general lookups and (2) use *lookup* algorithms with very good average running times such as good *hashing* algorithms.

- *Reducing or Eliminating Checksum Costs*: The checksum presents a similar cost overhead as cost of copying data or lookup cost. The reason is that computing a checksum requires that each byte in the packet be read and added into the sum. One option to optimize a checksum algorithm is to try to do the sum using the host machine's native work size (to optimize memory accesses) and native byte order (to minimize byte swapping costs). Also using RISC processors, which are capable of performing two instructions per clock cycle (e.g., one operation can be loading data from memory or storing data to memory), there is space for two instructions per cycle (if each load or store instructions are running in a separate cycle). This means we could put the instructions for the checksum into those free slots (in one cycle we can run *load data* and *add to the running checksum* instructions, and in the second cycle we can run *add carry* and *store data* instructions). Hence, we eliminate the cost of doing the checksum by including the checksum into the copy loop. Another optimization of checksum processing could be to move checksum to the end of the packet, a practice known as trailing checksums or *trailers*.

- *Prediction*: TCP behavior is highly predictable, and we can optimize the frequent path through the TCP code in both the receiving and sending TCP implementations. For example, we can use *header predictions* for TCP receivers which look for segments that fit the profile of the segment the receiver expects to receive next (e.g., segments that are already established for connections). Similar predictive schemes can be used for optimizing sending. For example, if application writes its data to the socket (connection handle), this connection handle can be designed to map directly to a control block, thus eliminating control block lookup, and the control block can cache the IP route, those eliminating the routing lookup. Also, the sending TCP can keep a *template TCP header*, whose sequence number is incremented as segments are send, and acknowledgment number is updated as segments are received. The sending becomes a copying operation of the template header onto the front of the TCP data.

### 6.3.1.2    Improving TCP towards QoS Guarantees

In the recent years, a lot of effort was made to extend TCP towards increased level of predictability and QoS guarantees in network services [JBB92, Par94a, GJKF97, Wro97, FKSS99]. This effort is especially beneficial to multimedia applications and other Internet applications sensitive to overload conditions.

We will present briefly one possible solution, fully discussed in [FKSS99], using simple extensions in controlled-load service and a couple of modifications in TCP to augment the performance of TCP to support minimum rate guarantees and hence more stable performance for multimedia streaming applications.

The solution consists of two major changes in the protocol stack: (1) a simple extension to *queueing mechanisms* in current routers within the controlled-load service [Wro97] and (2) a modification to the *congestion control* mechanisms within TCP. These modifications allow the network to guarantee a minimal level of end-to-end throughput to different network session.

*Modifications in Controlled-Load Service*: In controlled-load service scheme, each reserved session is associated with a *traffic envelope*, called *Tspec*, which includes a *long term average rate* $r_{av}$, *short term peak rate* $r_p$ and the *maximum size of a burst b* of data generated by the application. *Tspec* also specifies the *maximum and minimum packet size* to be used by the application. Traffic is policed at the source via a *token bucket approach* and packets conforming to the envelope are *marked*. Non-conformant traffic and best effort traffic are injected into the network *unmarked*.

The routers use an *Enhanced Random Early Detection (ERED)* discard mechanism. Both marked and unmarked packets share the same FIFO queue, and ERED performs its operation over this queue. If the queue length exceeds a certain threshold, packets are dropped randomly as it is done in RED gateways [FJ93]. However, ERED relies on a *selective packet discard approach*. The thresholds apply only to unmarked packets, i.e., unmarked packets are dropped randomly when the average queue length exceeds *minimal threshold (min)* and all are dropped when the average queue length exceeds the *maximum threshold (max)*. Marked packets are only dropped if the queue is *full*. The threshold values must be set so that they can approximately ensure that no marked packets are dropped. For example, in a system with $n$ controlled-load sessions with peak rates $r_p{}^i$, $i=1,..,n$, a service rate of $L$, buffer length $B$, and the same duration of burst for all sources, the following equation should hold:

$$\left( \sum_{i=1}^{n} r_p{}^i - L \right) \times \frac{max}{L} < B - max$$

This approach guarantees that, in the ERED gateway, marked packets have a lower drop probability than the unmarked packets. Furthermore, ERED ensures a low loss rate to conformant controlled load traffic. As elastic and tolerant multimedia playback applications can withstand a reasonable amount of queueing delay, this approach helps towards the guarantees on throughput to improve the overall performance.

*Modifications in TCP*: Connections requesting reservation specify *Tspec*, i.e., a peak and a mean rate of service, and the maximum size of a burst. At the source, tokens are generated at the mean service rate and accumulated in a token bucket. The depth of the token bucket is the same as the maximum burst size. TCP segments, belonging to reserved connections, are transmitted as marked datagrams if there are sufficient tokens available in the token bucket at the time of transmission. Otherwise, they are transmitted as unmarked datagrams. TCP segments belonging to best effort connections are sent as unmarked datagrams. Experiments show that if using only modifications in controlled-load service at routers, as discussed above, and utilizing the token bucket for traffic policing, the compliant portions of the bandwidth, received by all reserved connections, are less than their respective service rate. The reason for this problem is the flow and congestion control mechanism because the TCP sessions with reservations exercise their flow and congestion control in the same way as the best effort connections. The tokens are generated at a reserved rate, but if the source does not have enough data or is unable to transmit packets due to flow and congestion control, the token bucket fills up and token loss occurs.

The *windowing mechanism in flow and congestion control* is partly responsible for the token loss because of the following reasons: TCP uses two windows. The receiver maintains and enforces an *advertised window (AWND)* as a measure of its buffering capacity. The sender enforces a *congestion window (CWND)* as a measure of the capacity of the network. The sender is prohibited from sending more than the minimum of AWND and CWND worth of unacknowledged data. When the loss of a segment is detected, TCP reduces the congestion window and initiates a fast recovery or a slow start phase. For fast recovery, the congestion window is cut to half of its original size while in the slow start phase it is set to 1. For connections with reservations, this is an overly conservative behavior since it is insensitive to the connection's reservation. Thus, even when tokens are present, and the sender is eligible to transmit a new segment, it may be throttled by the congestion window.

Another cause for token loss is the presence of *persistent gaps* in the acknowledgement stream. Since TCP uses acknowledgements to trigger transmission, any significant time gap between the receipt of successive acknowledgements causes the token bucket to overflow. There are several ways for these gaps to develop: (1) *Recovery process*, after a loss is detected, uses TCP fast recovery and fast retransmission mechanisms. After detecting a loss (by the receipt of a given number of duplicate acknowledgments), TCP cuts its congestion window in half by halting additional transmissions until one half of the original windows' packets have cleared the network. Freezing the sender for this period of time causes the token bucket to overflow, and it puts a gap in the data stream which results in a gap in the acknowledgement stream during the next round-trip interval; (2) *Normal dynamic* of network traffic can cause gaps; (3) *Congestion* on the forward and/or reverse path as well as *additional queuing delays and jitters*, experienced as new connections come on-line, can also create gaps.

One way to provide solution to the *token loss problem* is to use a *deeper token bucket*. However, the use of large token buckets allows large bursts of marked packets into the network which can result in loss of marked packets, thus defeating the service differentiation mechanism provided by ERED. As with any service differentiation, in order to ensure correct behavior, admission control must be performed. For ERED queues, this means that the *min* and *max* values must be set appropriately. For a given queue size there is some flexibility, i.e., if the load due to controlled-load traffic increases, the *max* and *min* values can be set higher to improve the throughput of best effort traffic. However, the extend of the threshold flexibility is limited due to the admission condition for the aggregated controlled load traffic, discussed above. Note that the admission condition is very pessimistic, hence if one would use empirical and statistical admission control [JDSZ95], the network can operate at a higher utilization and maintain low loss rates for conformant controlled-load traffic.

Since deeper token buckets require larger buffers at routers and less flows can be admitted, it is better to keep the token buckets small. So another solution to approach the token loss problem due to the effects of persistent gaps, is to use *delayed and timed transmission*.

- *Delayed transmission* means that a segment is held back for a random amount of time when there are not enough tokens to transmit it as a marked packet. This approach works well when the reverse path is lightly loaded, but it is not effective in the presence of reverse path congestion.
- *Timed transmission* involves the use of a periodic timer. In this scheme, TCP's acknowledgement-triggered mechanism is modified with a timer-triggered transmission mechanism. The modified mechanism examines the token status not only after each acknowledgement, but also after every timer expires. It means in this mechanism, each reserved connection uses at most one timer, and whenever a periodic timer expires, the connection examines the tokens in the token bucket. If

there are sufficient tokens, and there is room under the advertised window of the receiver, the sender sends the packet as marked, ignoring the value of the congestion window. The timer is then reset to wake up another timer interval later. The use of timers helps prevent sending back-to-back packets, making the resulting traffic stream slightly smoother and more network-friendly. The connection still adheres to the advertised window constraint to avoid overflowing the receiver's buffers. Although the timed transmission mechanism allows the connection to receive its reserved rate, TCP windowing mechanism restricts the controlled-load traffic from competing for the excess bandwidth in the network.

To provide minimal throughput guarantee, *TCP's windowing algorithm* needs to be modified towards the *Rate Adaptive Windowing* as follows: The congestion window *CWND* consists of two parts, a *reserved part* with size *RWND* equal to the product of the reserved rate and the estimated round-trip time, and a *variable part* with size *CWND – RWND* that tries to estimate the residual capacity and share with other active connections. In this modified scheme, only the variable window size is adjusted using the traditional TCP windowing techniques. Specifically, instead of reducing *CWND* by half at the beginning of fast recovery, the sender sets the congestion window to *RWND + (CWND – RWND)/2*. At the beginning of slow start after detection of a lost segment through the retransmission time-out, it sets *CWND* to *RWND+1* instead of 1. In both cases, *SSTHRES* is set to the minimum of *RWND + (CWND-RWND)/2* and *AWND* instead of *CWND/2* and *AWND*. Also, because packets sent under *RWND* should not clock congestion window increases, window increases needed to be scaled by *(CWND – RWND)/CWND*. Note that even with these modifications, the sender must still adhere to the *AWND* restriction, i.e., it is prohibited to send more than the minimum of *AWND* and *CWND* worth of unacknowledged data. Because of this, the size of the receiver's buffer must be at least the size of the reservation window to sustain the reserved rate using TCP.

It is important to note that the modified congestion control algorithm should be deployed only if and only if the network supports minimum rate guarantees through end-to-end signaling, admission control and resource reservation. Without these mechanisms, the use of modified TCP sources may cause collapse in networks.

## 6.3.2  User Datagram Protocol (UDP)

UDP is a simple extension to the Internet network protocol IP that supports multiplexing of datagrams exchanged between pairs of Internet hosts. It offers only *multiplexing* and *checksums*, nothing else. Higher-level protocols using UDP must provide their own retransmission, packetization, reassembly, flow control, congestion avoidance, etc.

In general, UDP is not suitable for continuous media streams because it does not provide the notion of connections, at least at the transport layer; therefore, different service guarantees cannot be provided.

Protocols in higher layers, which use UDP, need to provide their own mechanisms for support of multimedia. A very good example of higher layer protocol using UDP is the *Real-time Transport Protocol (RTP),* based on the *Application-Level Framing* concept [CT90], discussed in the next subsection. Many multimedia applications use this protocol because it provides some degree of real-time transport property, although loss of PDUs may occur. For experimental purposes, UDP above IP can be used as a simple, unreliable connection for medium transport.

Several extensions are proposed to increase the performance of both UDP and TCP protocols so that a larger group of applications (i.e., also multimedia applications) can use them. *Large windows* and *time stamps* are now standards. For example, the above discussed improvements for TCP to support minimum guarantee in throughput could be also considered in RTP or UDP protocols.

## 6.4   New Protocols for Support of Network Quality of Service

With the development and deployment of ARPANET, the ancestor of current Internet, transport of non-real-time data was considered. Especially, robustness and reliability were of importance. The traditional protocols such as TCP/IP were designed towards that goal, and the factor of providing real-time transmission was not considered.

With the increase of multimedia applications importance, such as voice over IP, video conferencing, and with the desire to have network infrastructure that supports real-time and best-effort traffic, changes in the network and its protocols have to be considered.

Newer architectures such as ATM already started to consider service quality issues, and developed and deployed various algorithms to support Quality of Service (QoS) in end-to-end fashion. However, this technology did not achieve its goal of "ATM to the desktops", and stayed only as a technology of the backbones or at the edges of the networks (although even in backbone networks Gigabit Ethernet and Optical Networks are pushing ATM aside). Also, as there are many more IP-based applications, it became of importance to revisit the Internet protocols, modify them or replace some of their algorithms to allow for service quality and differentiation.

In routers, new techniques were introduced to differentiate the handling of packets, such as *Weighted Fair Queueing (WFQ),* the *Random Early Discard* (RED), *congestion avoidance,* or *traffic shaping.* Furthermore, reservation mechanisms were introduced to assist in provision of QoS in networks. These algorithms and concepts are discussed in more detail in the Chapter 2 on QoS.

In the following subsection, we will present *reservation-based protocols,* their requirements, and their capabilities to support network QoS. However, as the usage of these protocols is controversial, we will show also alternative approaches for provision of network QoS.

### 6.4.1 Reservation Concept

If we deal with scarce amount of resources, such as bandwidth, processing capacity or buffer sizes, in order to provide Quality of Service guarantees, we need to use reservation. It means that once the reservation request was admitted, resource will be set aside and reserved for the application's usage during its runtime. This is especially useful if we deal with data streams such as video or audio streams.

In principle, we could consider *reservation management* as one of the tasks for network management, and the reservation could be set manually or by an additional component which serves as a *broker* between the sender and receiver. This entity then needs to be informed about the characteristics of the sender, receiver and Quality of Service requirements to setup the corresponding reservation along the path. This approach is possible, but not used very often.

Reservations are usually triggered through the end-systems and they use *control protocols* along the end-to-end path to distribute their reservation-relevant control information. The processing of a reservation request and the reservation of resources, corresponding to the reservation request, follow on hop-by-hop basis. A router first decides if the reservation request can be admitted and satisfied. In positive case, it stores the information about the flow and its corresponding reservation, and forwards the reservation request to the adjacent router along the path towards the destination.

Current reservation-based protocols can be classified according to the direction and initiation of the reservation request: *sender-oriented* and *receiver-oriented* reservation protocols. In the *sender-oriented* version, the sender initiates the reservation request, and sends the request along the path to its destination(s). As the *reservation request* passes from the sender to the receiver, the routers *admit* and *reserve* the amount of resources demanded by the reservation request. At the receiver side, the reservation request changes into the reservation *allocation message* and the message is sent back to the sender. Along the path from the receiver to the sender the reserved resources are changed from reserved to *allocated* resources. The direction of data transport is from the sender to the receiver. Figure 6-8 shows the sender-oriented reservation.

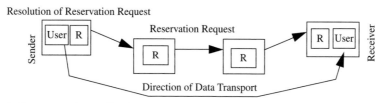

R: Components for specification, management and communication of
   reservation information

**Figure 6-8** Sender-oriented reservation.

In the *receiver-oriented* version, the receiver initiates the reservation request and the request is being processed in the direction from the receiver towards the sender. In this direction the resources are reserved and on way back from the sender to the receiver the resources are allocated. The data transmission is then in the direction from the sender to the receiver. Figure 6-9 shows the receiver-oriented reservation.

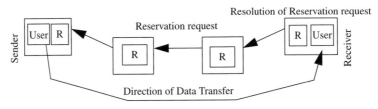

R: Components for specification, management and communication of
   reservation information

**Figure 6-9**   Receiver-oriented reservation.

Reservation protocols can be also classified according to the reservation state, which is maintained at routers along the end-to-end path. The reservation protocol can be a hard state or soft state. The *Hard state* represents a reservation state that is maintained at routers during the whole session of the application, i.e., from the time the connection is setup until the connection is teared down. An example of hard reservation state is the ATM reservation state. The *Soft state* represents a reservation state that is maintained at routers only for a specific period of time and expires after that. This means that after the reservation time-out, the resources are automatically released and can be considered for a new reservation and allocation. Hence if a data flow wants to use this reservation over the duration of its session, this state needs to be periodically refreshed.

### 6.4.2   Early Reservation-based Protocols

#### 6.4.2.1    STream Protocol, Version 2 (ST-II)

ST-II provides a connection-oriented, guaranteed service for data transport based on the stream model [Top90]. The connections between the sender and several receivers are setup as uni-directional connections, although also duplex connections can be setup.

ST-II and its newest version ST-2+ are extensions of the original ST protocol [For79]. The ST-II protocol consists of two components: the *ST Control Message Protocol (SCMP)*, which is a reliable, connectionless transport for the protocol messages and the *ST* protocol itself, which is an unreliable transport for the data.

ST-II provides a resource reservation during the connection setup. The reservation is originated from the source. It sends a SCMP message with a *flow specification*, which describes the stream requirements (QoS) in terms of packet size, data rate, etc. If the destination accepts the call, it returns the final flow specification to the source. To perform processing in the nodes, ST data packets do not carry complete addressing information. They have a *HOP IDentifier (HIP)*, similar to a virtual circuit number, which is negotiated for each hop during the setup phase.

If a receiver accepts the connection setup, it sends back to the source the agreed-upon flow specification. If the requirements of the flow specification cannot be satisfied, data connection will not be setup. The protocol uses a hard state for the reservation information in routers.

ST-II is suitable for multimedia transmission because of its resource reservation along the path between the sender and receiver. However, note that this approach leads also to high overheads at the sender side if the sender needs to setup many connections to receivers as the sender has a central control over all reservation states towards the receivers, i.e., it must know all receivers as well as manage all reservations. The ST-2+ version started to support mixed reservation requirements as provided by the RSVP protocol and since 1998 it is deployed by the company Bay Networks within the Bay Network Routing Services (BayRS) to provide network QoS.

### 6.4.2.2 Real-Time Internet Protocol

In the Tenet scheme, the services of RTIP (*Real-Time Internet Protocol*) are used together with the *sender-oriented reservation protocol*, called RCAP. RTIP provides for connection-oriented, performance-guaranteed, unreliable delivery of packets [VZ91]. It occupies an analogous place in the Tenet protocol stack as the IP in the Internet protocol suite. It communicates with RCAP for resource reservation, therefore it provides guaranteed service [Mah93]. The Tenet protocol suite was designed for real-time communication, with particular emphasis on multimedia transmission.

## 6.4.3 Internet Integrated Services

To provide network QoS in the Internet and to deploy *Internet Integrated Services*, IETF reacted by creating the Working Group (IntServ) which analyzed the requirements and possible solutions to develop a framework architecture and appropriate protocols [Gro00a]. One of the main results of the working group efforts was the *Resource Reservation Protocol (RSVP)* to transport reservation requests [Gro00b] [KSS01]. We will discuss this protocol in more detail in Chapter 6.4.4. This protocol allows the exchange of network QoS parameters, needed for QoS-aware network services such as the *guaranteed service*, providing guaranteed QoS, and *controlled-load service*, providing controlled load and statistical QoS [JNK99]. Other services were discussed in IntServ working group, but were not further explored.

The specification of the *guaranteed service* requires that the end-to-end delay be enforced according to the specified QoS requirement, if the data flow behaves according to its specified and contracted traffic shape. The average behavior is described according to the *Token-Bucket Model*. This service is suitable for data transport with hard real-time requirements (e.g., for audio transmission).

The specification of the *controlled-load service* requires that the network elements behave as in the best-effort situation, but under lightly loaded conditions and without any congestion. This means that this service will require similar QoS parameters to the guaranteed service (we have described the QoS parameters as *Tspec* in the above discussion on TCP improvements), and it is expected that the service aims towards satisfying the average values of QoS parameters in lightly loaded networks. However, in heavily loaded networks errors can occur. Hence, this service is suitable for adaptive multimedia applications.

### 6.4.4  Resource Reservation Protocol

To implement Integrated Services, we have to provide four components: (1) a *reservation protocol* for connection setup, (2) an algorithm for reservation admission (*admission control*), (3) a possibility to classify data traffic (*packet classifier*), and (4) a *packet scheduler* which processes packets accordingly, e.g., orders the packet according to weights or earliest deadline [YD99] (see Figure 6-10).

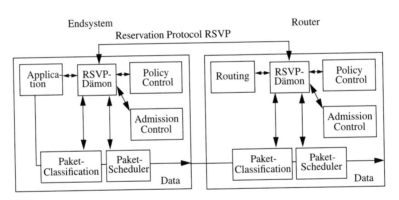

**Figure 6-10**  Components and inter-relations of Internet Integrated Services (RSVP-based solutions).

The *Resource Reservation Protocol (RSVP)* was specified by the IETF [Gro00b]. The protocol design considers the following goals:

- The protocol should satisfy *heterogeneous requirements* with respect to various receivers
- It should allow a *flexible control* how reservations can be shared within a multicast tree.
- It should allow *basic operations* such as join or removal of individual or several senders and receivers to and from existing set.

- It should be *robust* and it should *scale* if used for large multicast groups.
- It should allow for *advanced reservation* of resources and satisfy special requirements.

RSVP is a protocol which sends reservation messages between network nodes and these nodes maintain soft states about the admitted reservations. RSVP does not include any transport functions for data, hence in contrast to ST-II it needs a network transport protocol like IP to achieve transport of its reservation messages between routers. Furthermore, RSVP does not have any impact on routing of packets in the network, it uses the underlying routing algorithms of IP and it follows any route changes which occur due to router failure. RSVP exchanges periodically reservation-relevant *PATH* and *RESV* messages along the end-to-end path which is also used by the actual data flow.

### 6.4.4.1    Basic Principles of RSVP

RSVP provides reservations for data flows, which can be identified through the address information and optionally through the port information in the packet header, as well as through special flow labels in IPv6 headers. During the transmission, data packets are assigned to the packet classifier which then decides according to the corresponding reservation how the packet will be forwarded. According to the *traffic specification, Tspec*, the characteristics of the data flow will be determined. A description of the required quality of service is given through the *request specification,* called *RSpec*, and it describes the desired flow behavior. The sender ensures that the generated data flow is sent and behaves according to the *Tspec* specification. In case of a successful reservation, the data flow expects treatment from routers according to the *Rspec* specification.

RSVP is a *receiver-oriented* and *uni-directional reservation* protocol, i.e., the reservation request will be initiated at the receiver and sent towards the senders. To inform the receivers about the data characteristics, hence to give the receivers information for their reservation request, the sender sends the corresponding information via *PATH messages* to all potential receivers.

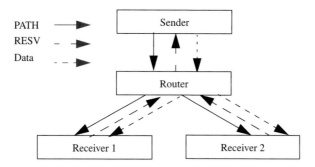

**Figure 6-11**   Control and data flow of RSVP.

A receiver system, which is interested in the described data flow, generates a *RESV message* (with "*FlowSpec*", which includes the desired Quality of Service parameter and *Filter specification*). It sends the RESV message along the same path to the sender, as the PATH message was sent (see Figure 6-11). The usage of the same path for RESV, PATH message and the data transfer is important in RSVP because the IP routing actually does not guarantee that paths from sender to receiver and from receiver to sender are the same. However, only through the usage of the same path in both directions we can guarantee the reservation requirements.

RSVP messages are sent as IP datagrams and they create a *soft state* for a per-flow reservation in intermediate routers. The soft state needs to be periodically refreshed by repeated reservation requests. If a reservation is not refreshed within a given interval, the reservation ceases to exist. Even though RSVP uses soft state only, there is a need to further reduce the RSVP refresh overhead [BGS$^+$00].

### 6.4.4.2    Mixing of Reservation under Various Filter Specifications

In RSVP, each receiver decides the size of reservation according to the data characteristics and its requirements. This feature is a positive attribute of the receiver-oriented protocol and it allows to support heterogeneous receivers. Hence, RSVP provides a possibility of different reservations coming from independent receivers.

The protocol describes three reservation modi in the current specification. The reservation modi are classified according to their filter specification. A detailed description of the filters is given in the Chapter 2 on QoS.

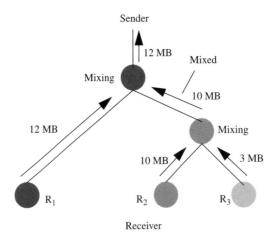

**Figure 6-12**    Mixing of resource requirements.

Mixing of requirements (see example in Figure 6-12) ensures an efficient resource management without redundant reservations. Through the usage of *Wildcard Filters*, respectively *Shared-Explicit Modus*, it is also possible to cover multiple senders during the reservation request. A single reservation request for each sender would lead to unnecessary over-reservation and over-booking of resources.

Note that a reservation request in RSVP can fail, even if the initiating system was informed about the successful reservation. The reason for this failure comes from the receiver-oriented protocol, which uses a hop-by-hop processing of reservation requests, and the possibilities that requests for data flows can be aggregated. It means that if a second reservation request arrives at a router, and there already exists the same or large soft reservation state for a previous reservation request towards the sender, then the new incoming reservation can be mixed with the first reservation, and the second reservation request is admitted by the router. So the receiver of the second reservation request receives successful reservation response. However, if the first reservation fails somewhere higher in the tree along the path towards the sender, then all receivers that wanted to share (mix) with the first reservation will receive an error message.

### 6.4.4.3    Advanced Reservation

RSVP as well as the reservation mechanisms in ATM allow for *immediate* reservation. However, there are applications such as video conferencing or other transmission applications of audio and video data, which would benefit from an *advanced* reservation as they know their exact starting point of playback and the duration of their play-time.

*Advanced Reservation* of resources separates the reservation negotiation from the resource allocation according to its *reservation contract* [WS97]. However, as the duration of the application runtime can change in the future, the reservation negotiation includes also release of reservations or extending of reservations and their resource allocation.

### 6.4.5    Alternative Reservation Approaches

Although RSVP was designed as a light-weighted reservation protocol and in comparison to ATM signaling protocol the goals were achieved, there are concerns about RSVP. The concerns include the overall applicability of RSVP, especially in scenarios when many heterogeneous receivers are being used.

A set of other approaches was designed such as the sender-oriented reservation approach, called *YESSIR* [PS97], which is based on in-band signaling. YESSIR uses the RTP/RTCP protocol for its packet transmission in connection with the IP *Router-Alert-Option* to initiate flow specific and dynamic reservations. Other approaches such as the *Scalable Resource Reservation Protocol (SRP)* [AFB98] are being discussed. SRP does not work with flows, but with reservation states, which are already available at router interfaces and ready for the learning process of the reservation approach.

### 6.4.6  Internet Differentiated Services

Using a per-flow reservation approach such as RSVP, the routers have to maintain large amount of information for each RSVP-based flow. Examples of the information are time interval to sustain the reservation, flow specification for all receivers, and the assigned interface. Also, the amount of refresh messages to renew the soft state of reservations represents a considerable overhead and load on networks and routers. Therefore, there is a concern that this approach will not scale in the backbone networks, where a very large number of flows need to be processed and forwarded.

A short-term solution and concept to handle large amount of individual flows was developed by the IETF DiffServ Working Group, called *Differentiated Services*. This solution relies on the specific usage of the IPv4-TOS Field (Type of Service). This concept was also created due to the needs to differentiate traffic according to their service classes and their corresponding cost and pricing [BBGS00].

The IPv4 header with its TOS field (see Figure 6-13) allows to indicate a specific type of transmitted data, hence to indicate a certain required service. The field specifies ordering relation and service requirements such as the minimum delay, maximum throughput, maximum reliability, minimum transmission cost, or a processing without any requirements.

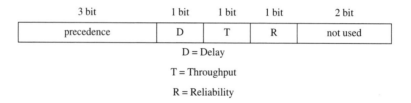

**Figure 6-13**   Structure of the TOS field in the IPv4 header.

The DiffServ Working Group specified various service classes such as the *Premium Service Class*, and the *Assured Service Class*, and mapped them to the bits of the TOS field (note that for these new services the original semantics, as shown in Figure 6-13, is not valid anymore). Inside the backbone, the service class concept allows for efficient recognition and processing of already aggregated data flows. The differentiated processing is achieved through priority mechanisms such as the *Delay Priority*, the *Drop Priority*, and the *Interface-based Priority*.

The marking of packets, to which class they belong, is performed usually through the Internet Service Provider in the so-called *Edge Routers* at the edges of the network. Here, the decision is made what to do with mis-behaved data packets by applying various approaches such as delay treatment, dropping approaches (e.g., RED) or redirection to another lower service class (e.g., best effort class).

Descriptions of the data flow characteristics as well as its QoS requirements are given in the *Service Level Agreements (SLA)*. SLA exists between the end-systems and the service provider as well as between different service providers.

There are considerations to combine RSVP with the DiffServ approach. This integration occurs at the edge routers where IntServ and DiffServ need to coexist. It yields mappings between the IntServ service types and the DiffServ service types. The mappings consider the aggregation of IntServ data flows and provide static SLAs as well as dynamic SLAs.

## 6.5  New Protocols for Transport of Multimedia

### 6.5.1  Early Multimedia Transport Protocols

#### 6.5.1.1  Express Transport Protocol (XTP)

*Xpress Transport Protocol* (XTP) was designed to be an efficient protocol, taking into account the low error ratios and higher speeds of current networks [SDW92]. It is still in the process of augmentation by the XTP Forum to provide a better platform for the incoming variety of applications. XTP integrates transport and network protocol functionalities to have more control over the environment in which it operates. XTP is intended to be useful in a wide variety of environments, from real-time control systems to remote procedure calls in distributed operating systems and distributed databases to bulk data transfer. It defines for this purpose six service types: connection, transaction, unacknowledged data gram, acknowledged datagram, isochronous stream and bulk data.

In XTP, the end-user is represented by a *context* becoming active within an XTP implementation. Two contexts (or several in multicast mode) are joined together to form an *association*. The path between two XTP sites is called a *route*. There are two types of XTP packets: information packets which carry user data, and control packets which are used for protocol management.

For *flow control*, XTP uses sliding window, or rate-based flow control. If window-based control is selected, the window size is negotiated during the connection setup. To advance the flow-control window, XTP uses a *combined mechanism* between a cumulative acknowledgment (e.g., TCP also uses a cumulative acknowledgment mechanism) and a selective acknowledgment, with a run-length encoding.

Data packet *retransmissions* are triggered by the arrival of status reports showing missing data. Status reports are requested and a certain timer controls the duration of the response to the request. After the timer expires and a status report was not received, a new status report is issued, and XTP enters a *synchronizing handshake*, where all further data transmission are halted until the correct status is received. Therefore, XTP will never retransmit a data packet without positive indication that it has not been received.

The error management is different for each of these service types. Therefore, XTP error control is primary a set of building blocks, known as *mechanisms*, from which a variety of *error control policies* can be constructed. Therefore, error control features can be tailored to the needs of the user.

There are some features which meet the requirements for multimedia communication, such as [Mil93]:

- XTP provides a connection-oriented transport and network transmission, hence it gives the benefit to map XTP on ATM networks and to use the possibilities of bandwidth reservation of ATM networks.
- Different transport services are provided: connection-mode, connectionless-mode and transaction-mode. Very important is the fast-connect-establishment for tele-transaction service.
- Flexible error management allows the turning off of the retransmission mechanism, which is useful for multimedia applications.
- XTP has rate-based flow control which allows it to provide a convenient mechanism for throughput and bandwidth reservation when QoS request is issued.

There are some problems with XTP in regard to supporting continuous media transmission:

- XTP was designed to be implemented in VLSI to achieve high performance, because it is too complex. However, most current implementations of XTP are done in software and their performance is too slow for transmission of continuous media streams [SGC94].
- If the round rotation time of the underlying network (e.g., Ethernet) frequently fluctuates, XTP constantly enters the synchronizing handshake which is very undesirable in high-speed networks and for continuous media transmission.
- XTP has a *large header*, which creates an overhead of 44 bytes regardless of mode. For example, if an audio stream, with 160-bytes packet size (or less for compressed audio coding) is being transmitted, the header overhead represents 27% of the body content which is more than just a nuisance.
- Source identification and discrimination are missing in XTP. Source discrimination refers to the necessity to discriminate among several sync and content sources, all arriving through the same network transport association. This feature is important for security and authentication reasons.
- Internetworking with other protocols is not worked out to provide QoS handling and resource reservation.

### 6.5.1.2    Tenet Transport Protocols

The Tenet protocol suite for support of multimedia transmission was developed by the Tenet Group at the University of California at Berkeley. The transport protocols in this protocol stack are the *Real-time Message Transport Protocol (RMTP)* and *Continuous*

*Media Transport Protocol (CMTP)*. They run above the *Real-Time Internet Protocol (RTIP)*.

The RMTP provides connection-oriented, performance-guaranteed, unreliable delivery of messages. This transport layer is quite lightweight. Two features frequently associated with transport layers, connection management and reliable delivery through retransmission, are absent from this protocol. Thus, the main functions of this transport layer are flow control (accomplished by rate control) and the fragmentation and reassembly of messages.

CMTP is designed to support the transport of periodic network traffic with performance guarantees. The RMTP and CMTP provide data and continuous media (periodic network traffic) transmission, but they obey the resource administration done by the *Real-time Channel Administration Protocol (RCAP)* which provides resource reservation, admission and QoS handling. Therefore, together the protocol stack also provides guaranteed services with deterministic and statistical QoS bounds [Gup94, BM91].

### 6.5.1.3   Heidelberg Transport System (HeiTS)

The *Heidelberg Transport System (HeiTS)* is a transport system for multimedia communication. It was developed at the IBM European Networking Center (ENC), Heidelberg. HeiTS provides the raw transport of multimedia over networks. It uses the *Heidelberg Continuous media Realm* (HeiCoRe), which is a real-time environment for handling multimedia data within workstations. The central issue of HeiCoRe and HeiTS together is to provide guaranteed services during multimedia transmission. HeiCoRe includes the *Heidelberg Resource Administration Technique* (HeiRAT), a resource management subsystem that addresses these issues [VHN92].

### 6.5.1.4   METS: A Multimedia Enhanced Transport Service

METS is the multimedia transport service developed at the University of Lancaster [CCH93]. It runs on top of ATM networks. The transport protocol provides an ordered, but non-assured, connection-oriented communication service and features resource allocation based on the user's QoS specification. It allows the user to select upcalls for the notification of corrupt and lost data at the receiver, and also allows the user to re-negotiate QoS levels. The protocol incorporates buffer sharing, rate regulation, scheduling, and basic flow monitoring modules to provide different services, such as guaranteed services with deterministic QoS, statistical QoS bounds and best effort services.

## 6.5.2   Real-time Transport Protocol (RTP)

Real-time flows have a common requirement that distinguishes them from traditional Internet services: (1) *Sequencing*, where packets must be re-ordered in real-time at the receiver if they arrive out of order, (2) *Intra-media synchronization,* (3) *Inter-media synchronization* if a number of different media are being used in a session, (4) *Payload identification*, and (5) *Frame identification* as audio and video are sent in logical units called frames. These services are provided by a transport protocol, and in Internet, the *Real-time Transport Protocol* (RTP) is used.

RTP, shown in Figure 6-14, is an end-to-end protocol, developed by Henning Schulzrinne [SCFJ96, SR02]. It provides network transport functions suitable for applications transmitting real-time data, such as audio, video or simulation data over multicast or unicast network services. It is based on the *Application Level Framing concept* [CT90]. RTP uses an already existing transport protocol, the UDP protocol, i.e., without cooperation with other protocols for real-time transmission, it cannot guarantee any support for multimedia.

RTP has two components, *RTP* itself and the *Real-time Control Protocol* (RTCP). Transport protocols for real-time media are not new, however, RTP provides new functionalities beyond resequencing and loss detection: RTP is *multicast-friendly*, *media independent*, and it provides *mixers* and *translators*, *QoS feedback*, *loose session control* as well as *encryption*.

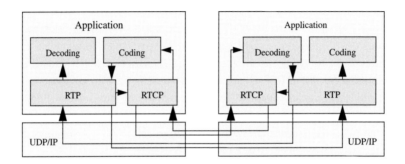

**Figure 6-14**   Relation between RTP and RTCP as an example of Application Level Framing concept for multimedia applications.

### 6.5.2.1   RTP Protocol Specification

RTP is used in conjunction with the *User Datagram Protocol (UDP)*, but can make use of any packet-based lower-layer protocol such as ST-II, IPX (from Company Novell) or over Native ATM using ATM Adaptation Layer (AAL5). When a host wishes to send a media packet, it takes the media, formats it for packetization, adds any media-specific packet headers, prefix the RTP header and places it in a lower layer payload. It is then sent into the network, either to a multicast group or unicast to another participant.

The RTP header, shown in Figure 6-15, is 12 bytes long. The field '1' indicates the *protocol version*. If field '2' is set, the payload is padded to ensure proper alignment *for encryption*, and the field '3' signals the presence of a *header extension* between the fixed header and the payload.

Users within multicast group are distinguished by a random 32-bit *synchronization source SSRT* identifier,. Having an application-layer identifier allows to easily distinguish streams coming from the same translator or mixed and associated receiver reports with sources. If two users choose the same identifier, they redraw their SSRCs.

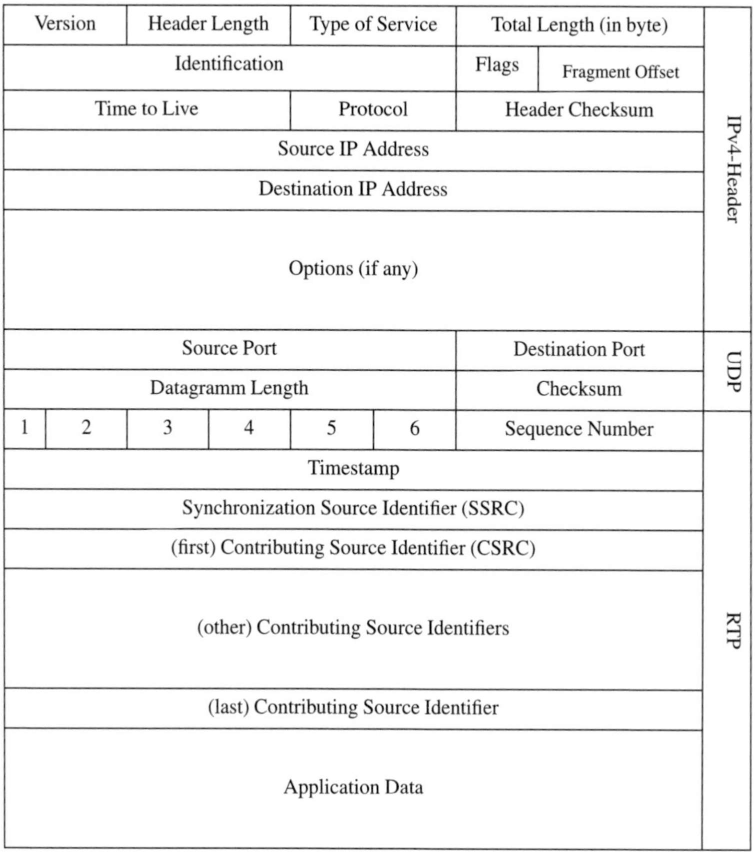

| Version | Header Length | Type of Service | Total Length (in byte) | |
|---------|---------------|-----------------|------------------------|---|
| Identification | | | Flags | Fragment Offset |
| Time to Live | | Protocol | Header Checksum | |
| Source IP Address | | | | |
| Destination IP Address | | | | |
| Options (if any) | | | | |

Figure 6-15   Structure of RTP packets, transmitted over IPv4/UDP.

RTP allows mixing functionality, where a mixer combines media streams from several sources, e.g., a conference bridge might mix the audio of all active participants. The *Contributing SSRC (CSRC) list,* whose length is indicated by the *CSRC length field* (field '4'), lists all the SSRC that contributed content to the packet. For example, in an audio conference, it would be the list of all active speakers.

RTP supports the notion of media-dependent framing to assist in the reconstruction and playout. The *marker* (field '5' in the RTP header) bit provides information for this purpose. For example, in case of audio stream, the first packet in a voice talkspurt can be scheduled for playout independently of those in the previous talkspurt. The marker bit is used to indicate the first packet in a talkspurt. In case of video stream, a video frame is rendered only when its last packet has arrived. The marker bit is used to indicate the last packet in a video frame.

The field '6' is the *payload type* and it identifies the media encoding formats used in the packet. These payload formats describe the syntax and semantics of the RTP payload. The particular semantics is communicated in the payload type indicator bits and these bits are mapped to actual codecs and formats via a binding to names, registered with the Internet Assigned Numbers Authority (IANA), and conveyed out of band. Any number of bindings can be conveyed out of band which allows a RTP source to change the coding formats mid-stream without explicit signaling. It means that if the encoding changes during the transmission, the sender can immediately indicate it in the payload type and no separate negotiation is needed. RTP media payload formats have been defined for H.263, H.261, JPEG, and MPEG video coders. Other audio and video encoders are supported with simpler payload formats. RTP payload formats can be also used for some generic services such as the redundant audio coding, or the parity and Reed Solomon like forward error correction mechanisms.

*Sequence number* increments sequentially from one packet to the next, and is used to detect losses and restore packet order.

The *timestamp,* incremented with the media sampling frequency, indicates when the media frame was generated.

RTP protocol is a flexible protocol, it can be implemented with very little additional effort, and it can be adjusted to various individual applications. With the help of *Profiles,* it is possible to use parts of the header for special groups description. This means that media specific information, e.g., a set of possible formats, such as coding descriptions or description how formats should be put together, can be stored in a audio/video profile.

### 6.5.2.2    Real-time Control Protocol (RTCP)

RTCP accompanies RTP protocol. Media senders and receivers send periodically RTCP packets to the same multicast group, but to different ports as RTP packets. Each RTCP packet, as shown in Figure 6-16, contains: (1) *Sender Report*, that is generated by a user who is also sending media. This report describes the amount of data sent so far, as well as it correlates the RTP sampling timestamp and absolute time to allow for synchronization between different media; (2) *Receiver Report,* that is sent by a RTP session participant, receiving media. Each report contains one block per RTP source in the group, that describes the instantaneous and cumulative loss rate and jitter from that source; the block also indicates the last timestamp and delay since receiving a sender report, allowing sources to estimate their distances from sinks; (3) *Source Descriptor* (SDES) packets, that are used for session control. They contain *CNAME (Canonical Name)*, a globally unique identifier, which is used for resolving conflicts in the SSRC value and associate different media streams generated by the same user. These packets also allow for user identification through its name, phone and email, hence, they provide a simple form of session control.

Since the sender reports, receiver reports and SDES packets contain continuously changing information, it is necessary to send these packets periodically. If the RTP sessions send RTP packets with a fixed period, the bandwidth used in the multicast group will grow linearly with the group size, which is undesirable. Instead, each session member counts the number of other sessions members it hears from via RTCP packets, and the period between RTCP packets from each user is the determined to scale linearly with the number of group members. This approach ensures that the bandwidth used for RTCP reports remains fixed independent of group size.

The feedback information of the reports can be also used by the senders to adjust its sending behavior. The generation of these information can be initiated by monitoring applications at the receiver, which are not part of the media transmission protocol, but only observe the overall behavior. The observation of the reports can be also used to determine the group set.

### 6.5.2.3    Support of Heterogeneity

To support the requirements of heterogeneous participants and transmission paths, RTP deploys *translators* and *mixers*. These components are active members of the internal network infrastructure and they can be used to change the characteristics of transmitted data in order to satisfy the heterogeneous requirements. It means they can use media scaling, filtering, adjustments of transmission rates, modification of data formats or aggregation of several data flows into a joined flow.

A mixer and a translator are differentiated through the header fields *Synchronization Source Identifier (SSRC) and Contributing Source Identifier (CSRC)*. A SSRC is assigned to each source of multimedia data and uses its own range of timestamps and sequence numbers. SSRC is unambiguously selected during a session. If a source sends more data flows, each flow is assigned its own SSRC.

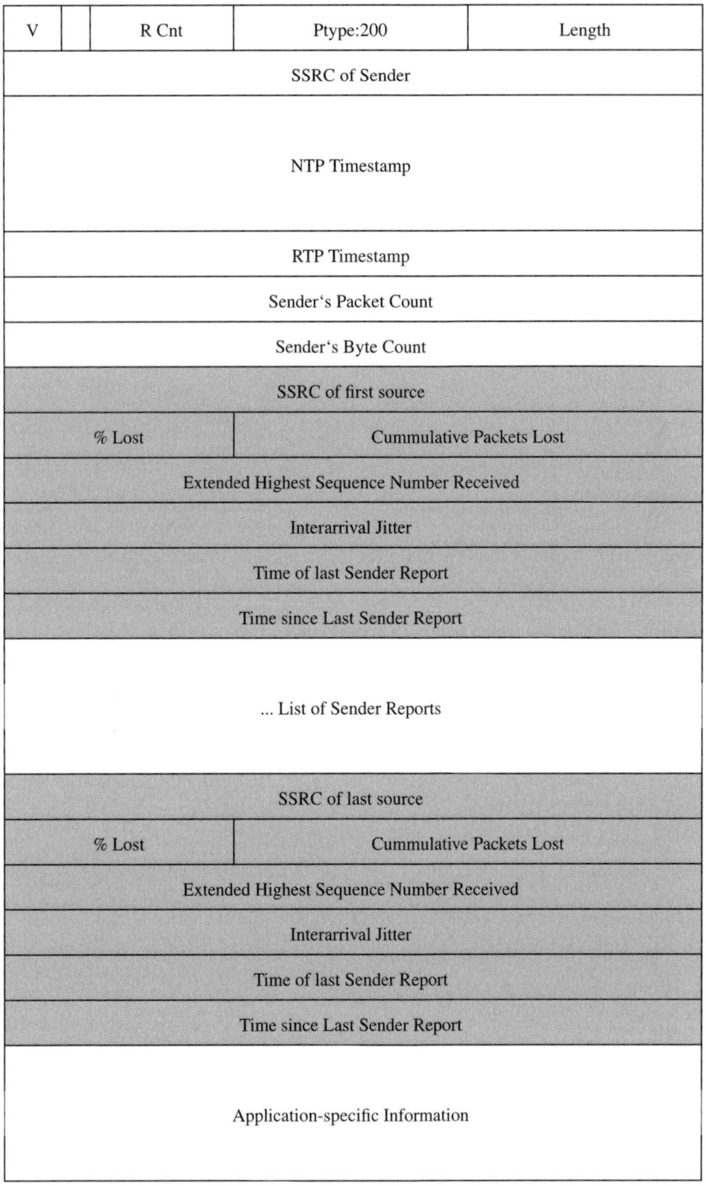

| V |  | R Cnt | Ptype:200 | Length |
|---|---|---|---|---|

| SSRC of Sender |
|---|

| NTP Timestamp |
|---|

| RTP Timestamp |
|---|

| Sender's Packet Count |
|---|

| Sender's Byte Count |
|---|

| SSRC of first source |
|---|

| % Lost | Cummulative Packets Lost |
|---|---|

| Extended Highest Sequence Number Received |
|---|

| Interarrival Jitter |
|---|

| Time of last Sender Report |
|---|

| Time since Last Sender Report |
|---|

| ... List of Sender Reports |
|---|

| SSRC of last source |
|---|

| % Lost | Cummulative Packets Lost |
|---|---|

| Extended Highest Sequence Number Received |
|---|

| Interarrival Jitter |
|---|

| Time of last Sender Report |
|---|

| Time since Last Sender Report |
|---|

| Application-specific Information |
|---|

**Figure 6-16**   Structure of a RTCP Sender Report.

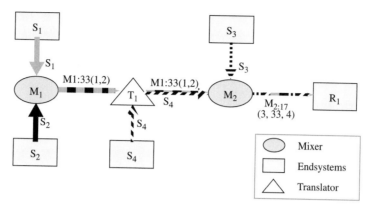

**Figure 6-17** Differences between mixers and translators in RTP.

Through the *Mixers* (see Figure 6-17), multiple data flows are mixed (aggregated) together and the mixed flow is assigned its own new SSRC. Mixers can be used, for example, for mixing of audio data, The sources, which contribute to a mixed flow, are enlisted through the CSRC list, as shown in Figure 6-15, in the RTP header. The number of sources is shown in the *Content Source Count* field (field '4' in Figure 6-15).

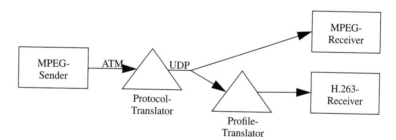

**Figure 6-18** Usage of RTP translators in a heterogeneous environment.

The data flows, which go through *Translators*, keep their own SSRC. However, the data flow will be changed in terms of its format or data rate or other changes performed on that flow, as shown in the Figure 6-18 example.

### 6.5.2.4 Other Aspects of RTP

To keep packet delays minimal, multimedia data are usually transmitted in relatively small packets. Therefore, the header size overhead can be quite substantial. To decrease the size of RTP headers, *RTP-Header-Compression* [CBE97] was specified and applied. This approach identifies data in the header which are not used in each packet, or they change in a deterministic way. These data will be transmitted in a less redundant fashion.

RTCP control information are sent in periodic time intervals to all participants of the session, hence the protocol can be used by the routers to maintain a *Soft State*. For transmission control, RTP uses an *adaptive mechanism,* which depends on the number of participants in a RTP session, and it ensures that (a) the *volume of control data* does not increase substantially, and (b) RTCP packets are not sent to all active systems at the *same time*. A soft state of a participant will be releases if the participant sends a BYE RTCP control message or the participant's soft state was not refreshed over a specified time interval.

There are efforts to use RTP and RTCP, due to their inband signaling, for reservation purposes. The reason is that existing protocols such as RSVP are rather complex. Hence, RTCP messages could be used to tell routers along the path to reserve sufficient resources [PS98]. To determine the amount of bandwidth for the reservation, RTCP sender reports can be used as they are, i.e., by observing the difference between two subsequent sender reports byte counts, or by inserting an additional field to specify the desired grade of service. RTCP messages carrying reservation are then marked for special handling by a router alert option. The receiver reports back whether the reservation was completely or only partially successful. The advantage of this reservation approach is that there are already many RTP-based applications, hence they could gain reservation capabilities without deploying an additional external reservation protocol.

### 6.5.3  Handling of Heterogeneous Requirements in Multicast Scenarios

During a RTP session, data, describing the quality of receivers, are sent back from receivers to the senders. This type of behavior is a typical communication scenario and can be solved at different communication layers. Using the information from various receivers, the sender learns the different heterogeneous requirements and actual receiver qualities, and can react adequately. The sender can then use methods such as scaling, discussed in Chapter 2 on QoS, to react.

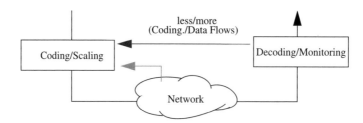

**Figure 6-19**  Application of feedback loops.

*Feedback loops*, which help to deal with heterogeneous requirements between two parties, are known and used approaches. The question is how to deal with heterogeneous requirements in a multicast scenario with receivers of various coding formats or different data rates. This can be the case when network connections to individual receivers are of different bandwidth or the processing capabilities of receivers differ. In this case, the sender cannot adapt to individual receivers (e.g., via feedback loops per receiver), but other solutions are needed.

### 6.5.3.1 Filter

One possible solution, to satisfy individual heterogeneous receivers, is to use *Filter Mechanisms* within communication systems. In one or multiple network nodes, using filters, the size of forwarded data or the coding format can be changed.

Filters are a general concept, and can be applied in each part of the network. This means that each network node (e.g., routers) need to have components which are parameterized and can filter through the data according to the data classification.

Although filtering is a generic approach, some problems might occur such as the processing overhead during filtering. Due to the filter processing, end-to-end delays may occur and they can lead to violation of end-to-end QoS guarantees. Another problem can be security. Due to router security, it is often undesirable to upload user programs for specific filters. However, if uploading of filters is prohibited, this will limit the possibility to rely on a set of predefined and pre-installed parameterized filters. On the other hand, many transport systems (e.g., ATM network layer) do not have the capabilities or necessary computing power to upload new filter components.

To avoid these problems or partially to provide a solution, the networks can provide the filtering functionality on special nodes. Approaches of *active networks*, which can provide active mechanisms to upload new functional components in a secure and functionally correct manner, might be considered.

### 6.5.3.2 Layered Transmission

Another approach to handle heterogeneous requirements in multicast scenarios is to use *hierarchical coding*, such as applying layered compression algorithms, with *layered transport mechanisms*. In this approach a signal is encoded into a number of layers that can be incrementally combined to provide progressive refinement. By dropping layers at choke points in the network, i.e., selectively forwarding only the number of layers that any given link can manage, heterogeneity is managed by locally degrading quality of the transmitted signal. It means the sender partitions the sending data into layers and the receivers receive only corresponding layers according to their communication and computing resource availability. The merits of layered transmission have been studied, e.g., in [RSS02].

For example, if we consider a video frame, one can decompose the video frame into several resolution layers. The highest resolution will have a large number of bits per pixel, where the lowest resolution will have only few (e.g., 1 bit per pixel). These individual resolution layers can be transmitted to individual receivers according to their bandwidth. Appropriate decomposition algorithms can guarantee an intelligent utilization of bandwidth. Another example of video decomposition can be found in MPEG coding. MPEG coding decomposes the video stream into I, P, or B quality frames. Sending different quality frames represents different layers (I frames represent one layer, P frames represent second layer and B frames represent a third layer). Depending on bandwidth availability, the sender can send to receivers only all I frames as the lowest quality flow, or I and P frames as the second quality flow (combining layer one and layer two), or all I, P, and B frames as the highest quality flow (combining all three layers). At the receivers, the information is composed together from the individual layers that arrive, and according to the computing capacity, corresponding data will be shown. Data which cannot be used will be dropped.

A practical implementation of the above approach exists within the *Receiver-driven Layered Multicast (RLM)*, which was refined through application of additional error detection and error correction mechanisms [MJV96].

RLM works within the existing IP model and requires no new machinery in the network. It assume (a) only *best effort, multipoint packet delivery* without any guarantees for packet ordering and minimum bandwidth, (b) the delivery efficiency of *IP multicast*, and (c) *group-oriented communication*, where senders do not need to know that receivers exist and receivers can dynamically join and leave the communication group in an efficient and timely manner. These three assumptions are sufficient to support any number of receivers in RLM.

In RML, the receivers start to receive the basic information and after that they activate step-wise the receipt of additional data (layers). They register either for all layers sent to the multicast group, or they observe packet losses, caused by network congestion. In this case they remove some less important layers (e.g., B frames in MPEG), and register only receipt of layers they can receive without any problems.

Through this approach, the receivers search actively for the optimal degree of reception and simultaneously they behave cooperatively with respect to other users in order to avoid network congestion.

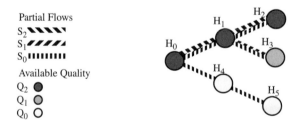

**Figure 6-20** Adaptation to hierarchical requirements through hierarchical coding and transmission.

Figure 6-20 shows the RLM scheme. We assume that the source is transmitting three layers of video to receivers, and we consider three partial streams ($S_0$, $S_1$, $S_2$). Because the path between $H_0$ and $H_2$ has the highest capacity, $H_2$ can successfully subscribe to all three layers and receive all three streams $S_0$, $S_1$, $S_2$, hence the highest quality $Q_2$ signal. $H_3$ has a lower bandwidth availability, hence it can subscribe only to two layers and can achieve the quality $Q_1$. The $H_5$ receiver has the lowest bandwidth, hence it can subscribe only to one layer, and receive the stream $S_0$ and quality $Q_0$.

Due to the *Prunning Mechanisms* in IP multicast forwarding, only partial flows, for which there is an interest in Internet, will be transmitted. This leads to an efficient approach. Furthermore, this approach can be intergrated with reservation protocols such as RSVP.

One possible disadvantage comes from the fact that different delays can occur for the individual partial streams and this may lead to synchronization problems. The research of these issues is becoming clear as the multimedia streaming is starting to use MPEG-4 coding which yields a large number of possible partial flows.

### 6.5.4   Reliable Multicast Transmission

With IP multicast, there exists an efficient and scalable possibility to transmit information to all potential receivers simultaneously. However, IP multicast does not provide any guarantee in delivery of messages. This might be sufficient for some applications such as audio and video conferencing, or some additional mechanisms for error correction can be applied such as Forward Error Correction or interpolation of missing or damaged data.

However, in multimedia area, there exist also applications which require high reliability in data delivery to all receivers. Examples of such applications are software distribution to a larger group of receivers (*Datacast*), distribution of stock market data to all receivers, or tele-medicine.

In unicast scenarios, there exist various mechanisms for error detection and error correction such as various acknowledgment schemes and retransmission schemes. For example, TCP provides a reliable transport of data using positive acknowledgements, sliding windows technique, and retransmission mechanism. However, these mechanisms are not scalable if considering large number of receivers. With no modification to the present schemes, the multicast application can end up with a large number of acknowledgements sent back to the sender as well as redundant effort for new data transmission along the common transport path. This can then lead to large load overheads on the network and additional lost packets.

Depending on (a) real-time requirements, (b) number of senders, (c) number of receivers, (d) acceptable transmission delays for packets, (e) accepted network environment (LAN, WAN symmetric or asymmetric paths), (f) specific requirements coming from applications, various designs and implementations for *reliable multicast* exist.

Usually, these approaches use redundant data transmission mechanisms such as *Forward Error Correction*, *Negative Acknowledgment* mechanisms, *Selective Retransmission*, and *Hierarchical methods*. In hierarchical methods, data is partitioned into layers, and intermediate network nodes are selected which will (a) *cache* the most important layers in case of needed retransmission and (b) *receive, aggregate* acknowledgement, and *forward* the new aggregated acknowledgement. Furthermore, solutions based on organizing receivers into clusters are proposed as well [LPGLA03a].

IETF did not yet determined any specific standard for reliable multicast. However, there exist several solutions such as the *Reliable Multicast Protocol* (RMP) [WKM94], the *Reliable Multicast Transport Protocol* (RMTP) [LP96], the *Reliable Adaptive Multicast Protocol* (RAMP), *Loss Colelction RTP* (LC_RTP) [ZJGS00], and others.

## 6.6   Closing Remarks

Driving multimedia application are having great impact on broadband Internet access and the overall network design to satisfy the dynamics of streaming media. Especially, the deployment of Internet access technologies like xDSL and cable modem is enabling streaming media applications. This chapter identified and characterized some of the networking and transport protocol issues faced by media streaming.

It is clear that the characteristics of media streaming media are often application, media and transport protocol specific. For example, interactive streaming multimedia applications such as video conferencing and IP telephony require low latency and delay jitter bounds. Non-interactive streaming multimedia applications do not require strict latency bounds and can alleviate delay jitter by using receiver-side buffers to smooth media playback. Hence, all of these streaming applications need not only a common network and transport support such as *multicast* to efficiently distribute media to a group of receivers, but also *adaptive schemes* to adjust against network congestion in a differentiated manner, and satisfy the diverse quality requirements of multimedia applications. A lot of research is directed towards solving these problems. Several solutions already provide results in this direction (e.g., [LHJea02], [KW02b], [HOV02], [TC01], [LLZ03]).

As we have seen in this chapter, many network and transport algorithms need to be extended, modified or newly developed because the perceived loss in quality that occurs within different packet loss and data rates is very media-specific and highly non-linear [MP02]. Recent research results provide some answers (e.g., [KR03], [WMS02], [BHea02], [AS02].

The media specific and non-linear quality loss complicates the design of any adaptation scheme within the Internet protocol stack. For example, *TCP-style congestion control and avoidance* (i.e., slow start and multiplicative decrease) is often not appropriate for continuos media applications because large and sudden changes in data rate result extremely in poor perceived media quality. Thus, alternative mechanisms and protocols have been proposed, such as the TCP-Friendly Rate Control (TFRC) protocol [FHPW00] [ZGSS03]. Furthermore, the interaction between streaming media and network queue management policies such as RED, which were designed specifically for TCP-like congestion control, is complicated and not well understood (e.g., [CC00]).

The media specific and non-linear quality loss presents also challenges for *multicast,* especially how to efficiently distribute media to a group of heterogeneous receivers. Dealing with heterogeneous connectivity to receivers defeats *source-controlled adaptation* strategies because no transmission rate is appropriate for all receivers. Further, performance feedback information in multicast environments is probabilistic at best because explicit feedback from receivers will not scale as group membership grows.

Besides multicast, large range of problems are explored and several solutions exist in *broadcasting and patching* of video streams to provide for Internet streaming video delivery (e.g., [ea03], [GKT02]).

More recently a lot attention has been given given to multimedia transport over wireless networks. Intensive research is going on in understanding TCP for different types of traffic in wireless multi-hop networks (e.g., [GTB99], [DB01], [FGML02]), in bandwidth management (e.g., [SCN03]), in energy-efficient network protocols (e.g., [KB02]), in pricing to achieve optimal resource allocation (e.g., [QM03]) and in many other open problems.

In summary, dealing with all these aspects of streaming media at the network and transport level is a formidable challenge. The issues raised by high bandwidth multimedia streams center and must be solved by considering effective *network resource utilization*, *adaptation schemes* to adjust to congestion, as well as *end-to-end strategies*, employed to cope with varying network conditions.

# Group Communication

Computer supported cooperative work (CSCW) means that multiple activities among several users involve concurrency of activities, distribution across several workstations or host systems, and complex data and document management tasks. Emerging systems use multimedia technologies to enhance functionality and user-friendliness for such cooperative work. This chapter deals with the aspects of cooperative office systems, building on the discussion of communication system services in Chapter 6. We begin with a general description of a framework architecture for computer supported cooperative work, including a detailed representation of the multicast segment in the Internet called MBone, the protocols used, and selected MBone applications.

## 7.1  Computer Supported Cooperative Work (CSCW)

A widely available infrastructure of networked computers with the capability of processing audio and video streams allows cooperative work among a number of users, overcoming both space and time distances. The integration of multimedia components into end systems and networks creates a work environment for users to participate in cooperative work at their computers.

Currently, there is a wide range of applications for *Computer Supported Cooperative Work* (*CSCW*), including electronic mail, news groups, screen sharing among several applications, e.g., *ShowMe* of SunSoft, or *kibitz*, an application based on Tcl/Expert, text-based conference systems, e.g., *Internet Relay Chat* (*IRC*), or forums in CompuServe or America Online, teleconference or conference room applications, e.g., *VideoWindow* of Bellcore, *DOLPHIN* [SGHH94]), *Well* [Rou02b], and video conference systems, e.g., the MBone applications *nv* and *vat*. In addition, a large number of systems has been implemented that group some of the components of a full CSCW system, presenting them in a uniform user interface. These include the older products *Rapport* of AT&T and *MERMAID* of NEC. More recent developments, such as *Cooperative Document Repository (CDR)* [TBR98] integrate the aspects of cooperative document management and processing by use of modern technologies for multimedia communication, allowing users easy access to the technologies and tools used.

This section describes a framework architecture for cooperative computing and studies general aspects of this field, explaining the underlying concepts by use of examples for various systems and tools.

### 7.1.1   Dimensions of CSCW

The literature normally classifies computer supported cooperative work in a two-dimensional scheme, as shown in Table 7-1, where classification along the area borders is partly flexible. For example, an application for joint software authoring could be used by authors working in the same or different locations. The use of stored video conferences at different times is another conceivable example.

| Place/Time | Same Time | Different Time |
|---|---|---|
| Same location | Joint ("face-to-face") work using shared applications | Use of jointly used cooperation planning, and decision tools |
| Different location | Video conferences, distributed cooperative document editing or software development | Electronic mail, newsgroups |

**Table 7-1**   Classification of CSCW applications.

Note that a parameter called *type of control* could be an additional perspective [WSM+91].

#### 7.1.1.1   The Time Dimension

When considering cooperative work with regard to the *time* dimension, then two different modes for synchronous and asynchronous cooperation can be identified. The asynchronous mode includes all forms where the cooperation is independent of time and does not necessarily occur at the same time, while synchronous cooperation occurs concurrently.

## 7.1.1.2    User Groups

The *user group* parameter describes whether a single user is cooperating with another user, or whether the cooperation refers to a group of more than two participants. We can classify these groups as follows [St}94]:

- *A group can be static or dynamic during its existence.* A group is *static* if its members are determined in advance and if the membership does not change during one specific activity. In contrast, a group is *dynamic* if its members change during a specific cooperative activity, i.e., when participants can join or leave the group at any given time.

- During their cooperation, individual users within the group can assume different *roles*, for example, they can be a member of the group (if listed in a description of the group), as participants of a group activity (if they are successful in joining such a group), or as initiator or coordinator of a session, as manager of a token used to control a session, or as observer.

- Groups can be formed by members, having *homogeneous* or *heterogeneous* properties and requirements with regard to their inclusion into the cooperative environment.

## 7.1.1.3    Control

The control of an active cooperative session can be either *centralized* or *distributed*. In a centralized control, there is a coordinator executing central control functions, and who serves as central contact for the individual participants with regard to requirements, inquiries, or reports, or who assigns activities and gives instructions to users. In contrast, each participant in a distributed control environment conducts activities under their own account and control. Under a distributed control, the group cooperation is organized by distributed control protocols to ensure consistent work.

Other parameters that can be used to organize the type of cooperation include the *local distribution* (locality) and the degree of *explicit awareness of the cooperation* in a cooperative system (collaboration awareness).

The cooperation can take place either at a *common location* (e.g., when all group members are locally present in an office or conference room) or between remote users at *different locations* who cooperate by means of a communication system. This form, which is also called *telecooperation*, will be described in detail below. In this context, we will use the following definition: Telecooperation designates the media-supported division of jobs among individual owners of tasks, organizational units, and organizations distributed across several locations.

Depending on the characteristics of the cooperation component, we distinguish systems, where the users cooperate in a *transparent* way (collaboration-transparent) and those where they work in explicit *awareness* (collaboration-aware).

Applications for *transparent* cooperation can be created, for example, by expanding existing applications (e.g., word processing or spreadsheet programs) to cooperation components, which may have been used independently by a single user. This means that some modern document processing systems offer transparent cooperation, because editors provided for single users can be expanded for joint and concurrent document editing among several users.

In contrast, software developed especially for conference and collaboration applications, such as a video conference system, belong to the collaboration-aware system class.

The systems studied here can be further classified into computer-augmented collaborative systems, which emphasize the aspect of cooperation, and collaboration-augmented computing systems, which concentrate on the aspect of computer-supported processing [MR94]. *Computer-supported* cooperation emphasizes the support of a social activity, such as a discussion or decision processes by use of computers and networks. In contrast, *collaboration-augmented* computing concentrates more on the application idea, i.e., the availability of applications, meeting the requirements of several concurrent users.

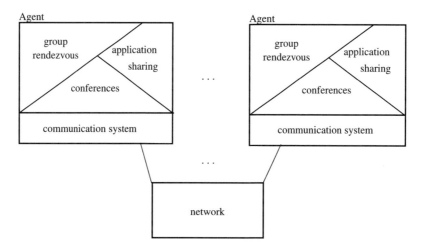

**Figure 7-1**   Cooperation of group communication agents.

## 7.2   Architecture

Group communication includes the synchronous or asynchronous communication of several users under central or distributed control (see Figure 7-1). An architectural model for this communication comprises a support model, a system model, and an interface model [WSM+91].

The support model includes group communication agents, which communicate over a network (see Figure 7-1). These agents include individual components, each dedicated to special aspects:

**The Rendezvous Component** describes processes allowing the organization of a meeting of the participating communication parts (group rendezvous). In this connection, both static and dynamic information about the potential or current participants as well as specific information about current or future sessions has to be managed and exchanged.

**The Cooperation Component** describes techniques allowing the concurrent replication of information among a large number of participants. This creates so-called *shared applications*. Within these shared applications, remote participants can point to special aspects of a piece of information (tele-pointing), or modify a piece of information so that other participants can share the resulting modification (e.g., in distributed document editing).

**The Conference Component** offers services allowing several participants to communication by use of multiple media streams. At the same time, the component also supports group management.

## 7.2.1 Establishing Communication Relationships (Group Rendezvous)

Methods for the establishment of communication relationships can be used to set up sessions among several group members and offer static and dynamic information about groups as well as current and future sessions. These can be prepared by appropriate applications, e.g., grouped by the type of activities and represented to the user as an overview.

With regard to the group rendezvous, we distinguish between synchronous and asynchronous approaches.

### 7.2.1.1 Synchronous Methods

Synchronous methods use *directory services* and explicit invitations. Directory services (e.g., X.500) allow access to special conference information, stored in an appropriate knowledge base. This information includes, for example, the name of the conference, registered participants, authorized users, or the names and special functions of participants. Examples for conference systems using the directory method for group rendezvous are:

- The MBone tools for session directories, *sd* and *sdr*; these tools will be described in a section dedicated to the MBone system.
- The *Nameserver Query* of the Touring Machine of Bellcore, where a name server serves as a central storage and query engine for both static and dynamic information, such as the number of authorized users, registered clients, and active sessions

[Lab93]. A client can request information about all sessions it is interested in, in which it could participate, or about participants in a specific session.

- *Directory Service* of MONET. This system offers directory and registration services over a directory server. The server can access a list of various resources, such as users, computers, and applications within the network. A registration service allows the registration of participants and user groups for conferences [SRB+92].

In the method with explicit invitations, the invitations are sent to potential conference participants either point-to-point or multicast. In this connection, there is an inherent problem that the initiator of a conference has to know how and where he or she can reach other users.

One example for the establishment of communication relationships by means of explicit invitations is *mmcc*, a so-called *Session Orchestration Tool* developed by ISI (USC Information Science Institute) [SW94a]. Another example is the *MMusic* protocol suite used in MBone, which offers this possibility by using the *Session Initiation Protocol* (*SIP*).

### 7.2.1.2    Asynchronous Methods

Asynchronous methods can be implemented by use of electronic mail or news groups as well as by presentation in the World Wide Web (WWW) [IET94]. Borenstein proposes e-mail as a common platform for the participants of a group. This should be embedded in synchronous conference applications [Bor92].

The e-mail-based mechanism sends the information required for the establishment of a session of several participants in the data part of a message. This scheme builds both on the addressing of participants and on the mailing of required information on the existing and proven e-mail infrastructure.

## 7.3    Joint Use of Applications

The joint use of applications, or *application sharing*, is considered a central and mandatory feature for the support of cooperative work.

Application sharing means that the resulting changes effected on a distributed object (e.g., a piece of text) is distributed to all participants, so that it is transparent for all participants as objects are edited by one user within a distributed application (e.g., an editor). Strictly speaking, application sharing distributes only the outputs and multiplexes the inputs (window sharing / screen sharing). Distributed objects are displayed in so-called *shared windows* [HTM92].

Application sharing is normally implemented in "collaboration-transparent systems", but it can also be realized in the "collaboration-aware mode" in special applications. An example for a software toolkit supporting the development of distributed applications is the *Rendenz-Vous System* (language and architecture) developed by

Bellcore [HBP+93]. Jointly used applications can also be used as a supporting component in teleconferences for joint document editing or for cooperative software engineering projects.

An important aspect of joint use of applications is the common control. One of the central architecture decisions during the development of such applications is to establish whether these applications should be *centralized* or implemented by *replication* [OMS+92, SW94a].

**Centralized Architecture**   In a centralized architecture, only one single instance of the jointly used application is executed on exactly one of the participating systems. The inputs from all participants are returned to this application, and the outputs are, in turn, distributed back to all participating systems. Figure 7-2 shows an example for a centralized architecture.

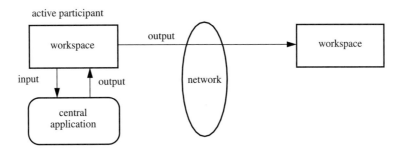

**Figure 7-2**   Centralized architecture.

A major benefit of the centralized approach is the easy management of the resulting state, because only one single instance of the shared object can be modified immediately at a given time. The drawback is its high network traffic, because the outputs of the application have to be distributed permanently to all participants. If this distribution is complete and not incremental, then the data stream resulting from graphical outputs can be enormous. For this reason, such applications require a network with appropriate bandwidth.

**Replication Architecture**   In a replication architecture, one instance of the application is executed on each of the participating systems. Inputs are transmitted to all participating computers, where they are processed and edited locally. Figure 7-3 shows an example for a replication architecture.

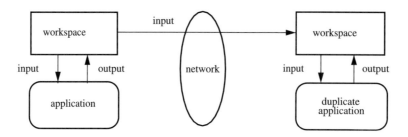

**Figure 7-3**   Replication architecture.

The replication approach offers the following benefits:

- Less network traffic, because only inputs, which are normally less voluminous, have to be transmitted between the systems.
- Shorter response times, resulting from the fact that processing or editing is done locally, and the outputs can be displayed directly.

However, the replication architecture has also certain drawbacks. One major drawback is the necessity to provide a uniform execution environment on all participating systems and a more complex management to ensure consistency, which will be discussed below.

An important and major problem in the implementation of distributed applications consists in a replication architecture in the maintenance of consistency *across the entire system* for the jointly manipulated objects. There is a large number of mechanisms that can be used to ensure data consistency within a set of group members. Examples are central locking mechanisms, floor passing mechanisms, and dependency detection. At this point, we will describe the floor passing method, because this type of control is the most important for group communication.

The abstraction of a *floor* is used to ensure consistency of distributed data objects (e.g., multimedia documents), or applications used jointly by several users. Only one member of the group, namely the one who currently owns the floor, called the *floor holder*, has the right to manipulate distributed objects within the shared workspace. Consequently, the floor holder can run operations, such as opening or closing a workspace, or loading documents into a workspace. The floor holder is the only user who can create input events for the shared application, i.e., modify data, which will then be available to all users.

One possible architecture for multiple applications to access shared data is shown in Figure 7-4.

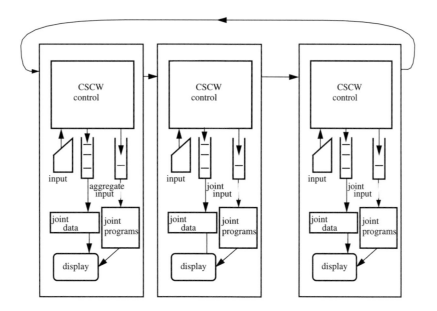

**Figure 7-4**    Architecture for the manipulation of shared data.

More specifically, a control component exists on each of the participating systems and distributes the inputs received there by an input device (e.g., keyboard, mouse). The control component checks whether the system is currently used by the set of floor holders. If this is the case, then the inputs are accepted locally and processed, and then passed on to the other systems. If the local system is not a floor holder, then the local inputs are rejected by the control component. However, the control component accepts input events transmitted by other participating systems.

A replication architecture is used in various CSCW applications, for example in *MERMAID* (Multimedia Environment for Remote Multiple Attendee Interactive Decision-making) of NEC [OMS+92], or in the broadband-ISDN-based group telework system by Hitachi [HTM92]. In addition, there are development libraries (toolkits or frameworks), which greatly facilitate the development of interactive CSCQ applications, e.g., *COAST* [SKSH96], or *GroupKit* [RG96].

## 7.3.1  Conferences

Conferences support collaborative work by making use of computers. This form of activity is also called *synchronous telecooperation*. It essentially requires a service that distributes the media streams used to all participants with the goal to supply as true a simulation as possible of an immediate simultaneous communication from face to face. Audio and video are the media used in a teleconference system (e.g., [KW02a]) with the purposes described below.

### 7.3.1.1    Video Representation

Video is used in technical discussions to represent the participating persons either directly or by pointing to their participation symbol used in the session (e.g., in the form of a picture or animation) as well as graphics, which are part of the presentation. Gestures and mimics are information carriers; their transmission creates a more natural way of direct communication and is therefore considered a very important feature. Workstations, PCs, or video boards can be used for display.

For conferences with more than three or four participants, the space required to display the concurrent representation of all members can quickly turn into a big problem, in particular when additional applications, such as shared editors or drawing boards, are used. For this reason, mechanisms are required to allow easy manipulation of the representation of each participant, i.e., to zoom in or out or bring active activities into the foreground.

This situation has also led to considerations that conference rooms, equipped accordingly with large video walls, with several high-resolution display units, e.g., *VideoWindow* of Bellcore [FKRR93], would be required for special applications even if all workplace computers were equipped with appropriate video hardware. Systems that support conference rooms with video walls attempt to support the entire wealth of human communication. They allow, for example, the transmission of brief meetings in public areas (e.g., *Cruiser* of Bellcore), seminars with variable group membership, floor discussions (e.g., *MediaSpace* of Xerox PARC), court hearings or educational events, open up a large number of participants, and help reduce traveling time and cost.

### 7.3.1.2    Audio Playback

Audio plays a very important role in the description and explanation of the information visually represented in a conference. Often, audio itself is more important than video. For this reason, a high-quality audio transmission with a full-duplex communication means and echo suppression is desirable. If space information (stereo) can be transmitted in addition, or if the active speaker can be allocated to the pertaining image information, then the usability can be further improved.

Conference applications require a very low delay in the underlying network as well as a high available bandwidth for the media transmission that can be highly data intensive, to ensure acceptable interactivity between the users. In addition, they require a service for the distribution of messages along with the transmission of both data and control information to all participants (*distributed messaging*).

### 7.3.2  Conference Control

Conference services control a conference (i.e., a series of distributed information, such as the name of the conference, the start time, the number of participants, rules to be observed, and other information). The conference control mechanism assumes various functions:

- Conference control includes the *establishment* of a conference, during which the participants have to coordinate and agree to a common state, e.g., who should assume the role of a moderator, access rights and modalities (floor control), and encoding rules for the media used. Conference systems can support the registration of participants, the access control and the negotiation of described parameters during the establishment phase of a conference, but they should be flexible, allowing participants to join later, or leave individual partial transmission (e.g., of media streams), or to leave the entire conference. This flexibility depends on the control model used.
- Mechanisms to add new participants or remove participants leaving the conference are required.
- Conference control should also allow to *exit* a conference.

The mechanisms for conference control use the *session management* functions described in Section 7.4 and cooperate with these functions.

The state information pertaining to a conference can operate either on a central machine (central control), which runs a *central* application in the form of a stored instance, or it can be stored in a *distributed* environment. The control model is determined by the location where this state information is stored, i.e., the control model itself can also be either centralized or distributed.

### 7.3.2.1 Centralized Conference Control

Centralized conference control means that the conference is set up at one central location. An initiator opens the conference by selecting and explicitly inviting an initial group of participants. This means that the initiator needs to know the addresses of all conference participants. Information on the current state of a conference is polled from a central directory server. First, the clients have to inform this directory server about their locations and other details.

In the second step, each invited client responds to the invitation, informing the initiator who exactly will participate in the conference. Subsequently, the participants negotiate the rules for the conference. This step also involves negotiations about the allocation and release of resources. During the negotiation phase, the common conference state is distributed to all participants by use of a protocol for reliable message transmission. The entire set of information concerning the conference is then stored on a central system.

This static control, which is realized by the explicit exchange of status information, guarantees consistency for each participant and is well suitable for smaller conferences. The guaranteed consistency is the main advantage of the centralized control approach. Its drawback is that, when a new participant who was not on the initial invitation list wants to join the conference, all participants will have to be informed about this event by explicitly exchange information about a forthcoming change in the session state, which can cause considerable delays. In addition, when the connection to a participant is interrupted, it is rather difficult to reestablish the consistent session state.

### 7.3.2.2 Distributed Conference Control

Distributed conference control is based on a distributed conference state. This state is achieved as follows: The initiator of the conference selects one or several multicast addresses for the transmission of information to the participants, and opens the conference. Conference participants can join by responding to the receipt of special multicast data. The announcement information (multicast address, port) required for this purpose is previously sent or made available to the participants by use of the group rendezvous protocols described above.

Each participating system transmits its own participation status to the other conference participants. However, there is no centrally managed knowledge about the group members and no guarantee that all participants will have the same uniform view of the current overall state. Subsequently, this loose control is realized by the periodic retransmission of state information, using an insecure service (e.g., the IP multicast service does not guarantee the sender neither the delivery to the intended receivers, nor that data may not have been corrupted). This phase is needed to eventually achieve a consistent view for all participants, even if this is not guaranteed.

This loose control is well suited for large conferences. For example, it is used in so-called *lightweight sessions* [JMF93] like those used for conferences in MBone.

Some of the benefits of the distributed conference control are its error tolerance and the possibility to scale to a large number of participants. If, during a conference, a network connection goes down and comes back later, then it is easier to reestablish a common conference state, because there are no strict consistency requirements.

However, if a large number of users participate in the conference, which is basically well supported by the technology, then it should be noted that the sending times and the intervals for exchange of state information are adapted to both the size and extent of the conference. Otherwise, there would be a risk of message flooding. The major drawback of the distributed conference control approach is that it does not guarantee that all participants will have the same view and idea of the current state of the conference.

Considering the large number of different types of cooperation, it is rather difficult to devise a general and generic protocol for conference control matching all kinds of requirements. Appropriate proposals have been made, for example with the *Conference Control Channel Protocol* (*CCCP*) [HW94].

A good idea is seen in the development of common underlying control functions and to allow their combination according to specific requirements [Sch94]. In addition, so-called state-agreement protocols can be used to coordinate a common state, which is also called *ephemeral teleconferencing state* [SW94b]. This state is short-lived (ephemeral), because it persists and is valid only for the duration of a conference.

Agreement protocols for distributed conference control include special rules or *policies* to control the state of a session. [SW94b] defines three aspects for these policies:

- The first aspect called *initiator-of-policies* identifies the participants who may initiate certain modification operations.
- The second aspect called *voting policies* describes policies for the decision on a modification of the state initiated by a participant. A change to the common state is based on voting rules.
- The third aspect is a set of *consistency policies* and concerns policies to ensure consistency. To achieve and maintain consistency, several things in view of a common state have to be defined and established, including the type of agreement on a common state, the functions for floor and access control, the negotiation of the media used and their encoding, the directory services for conferences, or the services used to invite or find participants.

## 7.4   Session Management

*Session management* is an important component of the multimedia communication architecture, forming the very part that separates the control functions required during the transport from the actual data transport. This issue is subject to intensive research work and proposals. We will discuss the aspects of the underlying architecture in detail in the following subsection.

### 7.4.1   Architecture

A session management architecture is built around a special instance or *session manager*, which separates control aspects from the transport aspects [SC92]. By creating a reusable session manager, which is implemented separately by the user interface, additional cost for implementation of the functionality in multiple conference-oriented applications can be avoided. Figure 7-5 shows one possible session control architecture. Its components (session manager, media agents, shared workspace agent) are described below.

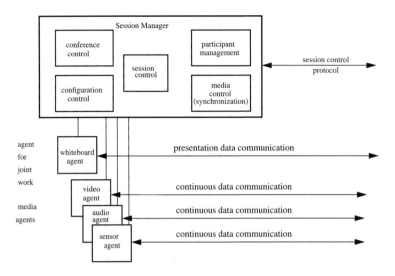

**Figure 7-5**    Example of a session control architecture.

### 7.4.1.1    Session Manager

Session managers assume local and remote functions. Local functions include:

- The tasks involved in membership control management, such as authentication of participants, or manage appropriately coordinated user interface.
- Monitoring shared workspaces, e.g., by use of floor control.
- The coordination tasks involved in the media control management, such as the communication between the media agents, which are each responsible for a medium, or the synchronization of the media involved.
- The tasks involved in configuration management, in the exchange of quality-of-service (QoS) parameters, or in the selection of appropriate services to ensure the expected or negotiated quality of service.
- Tasks involved in conference control management, such as establishment, modification, or termination of a conference.

Remote functions include the communication with other session managers to exchange status information, which may include floor information and configuration information. It is important to note that different conference systems embed the conference and activity control either in the application layer, e.g., the *Group-Teleworking System* of Hitachi, or in the session layer, e.g., the *Touring Machine* of Bellcore.

### 7.4.1.2    Media Agents

Media agents are independent from the session manager and responsible for decisions concerning one specific medium. This modularity allows the replacement of an agent depending on the given application environment. Each agent runs its own control operations, e.g., start and stop a transmission, set to mute and reactivate, or change the encoding method and the quality it allows for a given medium.

### 7.4.1.3    Shared Workspace Agent

The shared workspace agent transmits shared objects (e.g., the coordinates of a telepointer, graphical elements, or text elements) between the shared applications.

## 7.4.2    Session Control

Each session is described by its session state. The state information (name of the session, start, valid policies) is either *private* (e.g., local resources), or *shared* by all participants.

Session management includes two steps for state processing, i.e., the establishment and the modification of a session. During the establishment of a session, a session manager negotiates the logical state of its own session, agrees on a state, and finally establishes the state. In coordination and by appropriate negotiation with other session managers, binding policies, e.g., tariffing, are defined. A session can then be published by using a group rendezvous mechanism. This allows other participants to find the session and joint it. The session manager negotiates and specifies the transport topology for the transport system.

Depending on the functionality required by an application and on the services made available by the session control, various control mechanisms are embedded in the session management. The following subsections describe the most important control mechanisms.

### 7.4.2.1    Activity and Access Control

An activity and access control mechanism is required within the shared workspaces to ensure and coordinate fair access to the workspaces. Each system takes decisions as to what degree of simultaneity and granularity should be controlled with regard to accessing the resources.

In the simplest form, the applications use a mechanism for explicit activity passing supported by a token, e.g., *gavel passing* [SW94a], or *chalk passing* [Sch94]. Explicit floor passing means that only exactly one participant owns the floor or activity at a given time. Upon request, the access right is passed on to another participant. To obtain the access right, a participant has to become explicitly active and announce the desired change of token assignment.

In many applications, activity control is not only used under a purely technical aspect to maintain consistency, but also for a realistic mapping of social behavior. For example, a social protocol defines who within a real-time audio conference, where formal data consistency does not have a meaningful correspondence, can or must ask for the right to speak, how this should be done, and by what rules this right will eventually be granted or passed on. This is typical particularly in scenarios with a relatively formal flow or progress (e.g., use of the microphone at a speaker's desk). To create an environment similar to a relaxed formless meeting, it is often better not to use an explicit activity control mechanism. However, this requires some discipline from the participants.

For real-time transmission of video data, an access control mechanism is partly used to control and limit the resulting bandwidth.

### 7.4.2.2    Conference Control

A conference control mechanism is used in conference applications. One possible variant was described in an earlier section in our discussion of a centralized approach with static control versus the distributed approach with loose control.

### 7.4.2.3    Media Control

Media control includes particularly functions to synchronize media streams, which will be described in detail in Chapter 8.

### 7.4.2.4    Configuration Control

Configuration control includes tasks to control the quality supported by the media encoding method used, to negotiate the quality-of-service parameters, to ensure the availability of system resources and other components, and other aspects, so that a session can be made available according to the user requirements. Issues regarding the quality of service and the related management of resources are discussed in the context of general quality-of-service issues in Chapter 2. This control can include services, such as the initial media quality, or further negotiations about the media quality during a session.

### 7.4.2.5    Membership Control

Membership control can include services to invite users to a session, register participants, or change the membership during a session.

To distribute common information pertaining to the session control between the session managers, reliable notification services or insecure services with a periodic refresh option can be used.

The goal is here to offer a distributed notification mechanism with various degrees of achievable reliability. For example, cyclically repeated refresh information may not require any reliability at all. In contrast, it may be absolutely necessary that a specific message is delivered to all participants in a conference or meeting based on floor passing. For different conference participants, the reliable delivery of a message may be very critical [HW94].

A suitable communication mechanism has to be chosen under this aspect. Alternatives are introduced in connection with the introduction of the Internet transport protocols, or with the proposals for implementation of a reliable multicast mechanism in Chapter 5 and Chapter 6.

## 7.5 Internet Protocols and their Use in MBone

The *Real-time Transport Protocol* (*RTP*) in combination with an option based on the approach of "application level framing" (ALF) for the transport of multimedia data was described in Chapter 6. In addition to the pure media transport, the implementation of applications has to solve a number of additional tasks, e.g., establishment and control of multimedia sessions. The IETF working group *MMusic* (*Multiparty MUltimedia Session Control*) was formed to develop and describe suitable protocols and mechanisms for use within video conferences over the Internet. Based on the universality of the relevant approaches, several of the protocols developed, which mainly belong to the application layer, become more and more important also for other application areas, e.g., modern IP telephony.

### 7.5.1 Protocols

#### 7.5.1.1 The Session Description Protocol (SDP)

The *Session Description Protocol* (*SDP*) [HJ98] offers a way to announce conferences and their parameters. It is not responsible for the negotiation of multicast addresses, nor for the encoding method applied on the media streams of a specific session; but it describes

- the name and purpose of a session;
- the period or periods in which a session is active;
- the media streams used during a session (audio, video, text, transport protocol, and encoding used); and
- information how to receive the media streams (addresses, ports, formats).

This information is represented in ASCII in the following form:

```
<type of information> = <value>
```

Table 7-2 shows an example of an SDP session description.

| o | = | shuttle 3100022588 3100022882IN IP4 128.102.84.134 |
|---|---|---|
| s | = | NASA - Television |
| i | = | Test for University of Mississippi. This session is provided as a service to the MBone community |
| p | = | NASA ARC Digital Video Lab (415) 604-6145 |
| e | = | NASA ARC Digital Video Lab <mallard@mail.arc.nasa.gov> |
| t | = | 3100021200 3102440400 |
| m | = | audio 18476 RTP/AVP5 |
| c | = | IN IP4 224.2.145.142/127 |
| m | = | video 51796 RTP/AVP 31 |
| c | = | IN IP4 224.2.3.34 |
| o | - | owner/creator and session identifier |
| s | - | session name |
| i | - | session information |
| p | - | phone number |
| e | - | email address |
| t | - | time the session is alive |
| m | - | media name and transport address |
| c | - | connection information |

**Table 7-2**   Example of an SDP session description.

The transport of SDP information is not limited to a specific mechanism or protocol. The session description can be the contents of an e-mail (using MIME, the Multimedia Internet Mail Extension Format), or reside on an HTTP server, or it can be distributed actively by means of one of the protocols described in the following subsections.

### 7.5.1.2   The Session Announcement Protocol (SAP)

While SDP does not make any assumptions how the session description is sent to potential participants or made available for polling from a server, the *Session Announcement Protocol (SAP)* [Han98] specifies how the session description is transmitted via multicast to a multicast address permanently assigned to the protocol (e.g., 224.2.127.254) and to a corresponding port (e.g., 9875) to announce sessions.

A SAP package is composed of a header that contains the name and address of the announcing sender, the type of message, a unique message identifier, and the actual session description in the payload part. A modified announcement in a SAP package with the same identifier and the instruction for modification or deletion can be used to make subsequent changes, or to cancel a session. To verify the authenticity of the announcing party and to allow confidentiality or integrity of an announcement, the protocol also supports the use of public or private cryptographic methods.

### 7.5.1.3    The Session Initiation Protocol (SIP)

The *Session Initiation Protocol* (*SIP*) [HSSR98] is a text-based client/server protocol used to establish connections to one or several participants. Its operation is basically similar to the signaling of a telephone call in the conventional telephone network.

The initiator of the connection contacts the intended communication partner with his or her connection wish. This user responds, informing the initiator that he or she will either accept, or forward, or reject the connection request. Communication partners contacted by this procedure can be program users, but it is also conceivable that, as a response to a SIP invitation, a program starts automatically, e.g., a recording program used to record MBone data streams. Once the connection is up, the protocol can be used during the active connection for further signaling, e.g., to explicitly announce a change to the type of data transport, with regard to the encoding type, and the addresses used. Finally, the protocol also allows to break down the connection.

In cooperation with suitable directory services, e.g., X.500 [Org88] or LDAP [WHK98], the SIP protocol also supports the search for specific users. To find a specific user, SIP does not necessarily need to know the IP address of that user's current location, because SIP uses the much more comfortable symbolic addressing.

Aspects of mobility of communication partners are handled by the proxy or redirection mode of the protocol. While the former is used to forward the communication to a "caller" immediately, the latter mode sends a piece of information to the caller, so that the caller can contact the called party at a convenient time.

SIP can be used for communication among several partners both in a multicast environment and by use of so-called *multipoint control units* (*MCUs*) in a sufficiently meshed unicast environment.

In addition to its original field of application for the establishment of MBone sessions, the SIP protocol gains increasingly significance in a number of other scenarios. [SR97] proposes the use of SIP for signaling and control of IP telephony applications. For this purpose, it has also been proposed to expand the protocol and integrate ways for confidential generation of cryptographic keys, which can be used subsequently by the communication partners to communicate over a confidential connection.

### 7.5.1.4    The Real-Time Streaming Protocol (RTSP)

While there is a simple and suitable solution for the transport of text, files, or single images from a server over the HTTP protocol, this protocol is not fully capable of meeting the requirements of continuous multimedia data. For example, a user may want to download a video-on-demand movie completely to his or her system before he or she will begin playing it. A much better method would be to be able to start, stop and manipulate the playback.

The *Real-Time Streaming Protocol* (*RTSP*) was developed with the support of such functions in mind. It allows the description of offered contents and transmission parameters, supports the negotiation and specification of the transmission channel and the transport method, and the control of several media streams belonging to one transmission, and it addresses licensing issues. Very precise timestamps can be used for digital editing operations (e.g., movie cutting).

RTSP is similar to the HTTP protocol in several mechanisms, such as redirection options, possible use of proxies, possible use of security-relevant mechanisms (transport layer security, basic authentication, digest authentication). And RTSP cooperates closely with HTTP, e.g., a media stream can be referenced from an HTML page by use of an RTSP-URL address. Figure 7-6 shows how HTTP and RTSP cooperate.

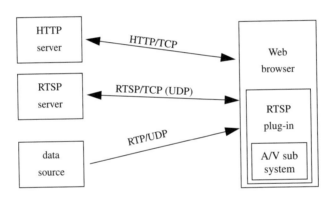

**Figure 7-6**   Illustrating the cooperation of HTTP and RTSP.

RTSP operates independently of the underlying transport protocol, so that it can be used both over UDP and TCP. The protocol uses a stateful server and introduces a series of new methods, and can also enhance them by additional parameters. Media data can be embedded directly into the control data stream.

The power of the basic command set corresponds to the current implementations of media servers, offering functions to establish and terminate data streams, or start or stop a playback or recording process, and it can also be expanded for special requirements. While it was mainly designed for the control of RTP-based multimedia applications, RTSP is also suitable for other applications. For example, IBM introduced an RTSP-based control interface for communication with a high-performance chess computer.

## 7.5.1.5    The Simple Conference Control Protocol (SCCP)

The *Simple Conference Control Protocol (SCCP)* was designed to ensure a common state, the so-called *conference context*, for all conference participants and to let them manipulate this state. The primary functions of SCCP are the management of the set of conference participants and the media streams used during a conference.

The implementation of floor control, which can be implemented by use of a token, plays a central role. The protocol lets you also select and specify participants who will assume a special management function. SCCP is text-based and uses operations like JOIN, ACCEPT, and LEAVE for the establishment and control of the group, as well as TOKEN-WANT, TOKEN-GIVE, and TOKEN-RELEASE to manage the token, which can assume either the FREE, EXCLUSIVE, or SHARED state.

## 7.5.1.6    The Real-Time Traffic Flow Measurement Protocol (RTFM)

It is desirable to dispose of a set of generic measurement tools to monitor the behavior of networks, but also to control the achieved quality of service, and to generate billing information. A recent effort led to the development of the *Real-Time Traffic Flow Measurement (RTFM)* protocol, which can act as a uniform basis for these purposes. It is expected that RTFM will be highly significant for specific billing and tariffing for the use of connections (replacing the current flat-rate model) and the available quality of service.

## 7.5.2  MBone Applications

Chapter 6 discussed protocols used for the transmission of multimedia and control data. In this chapter, we began with an introduction of the basic concepts for collaborative computing. The following sections give a selective overview of applications for the presentation of media contents and cooperative work based on the MBone system.

The applications we will describe, which can be classified as shown in Figure 7-7, were initially developed to run on UNIX systems. Meanwhile, however, some have been ported to other platforms, including personal computers under Microsoft Windows, and Macintosh computers as well as a number of adaptations to various hardware for recording and playback of audio and video data.

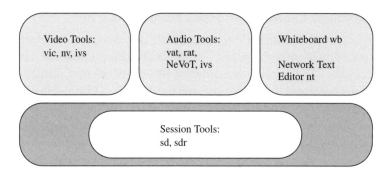

**Figure 7-7**   Classification of MBone applications.

MBone applications use *session tools* to announce transmissions, or obtain information about transmissions. Depending on the intended use and the type of network connection available to potential receivers, the presentation of media data streams can be implemented by audio and video applications. While these applications ensure an important and direct reference between the participants within their cooperative work, it would also be meaningful to use appropriate display programs or common editors for the presentation of prepared sheets or share editing document editing.

### 7.5.2.1   Session Directory Applications

Although transmissions can be started ad-hoc and information required for participation can be passed on by electronic mail or directly in the basic MBone system, the use of *session directory* applications offer additional features that are particularly useful for groups where the number of members is not known in advance.

The session directory program called *sdr* is part of the SAP protocol and used to announce sessions, and to generate and send SDP descriptions. This means that it serves both for a general announcement of sessions and for personal invitation of individual users or user groups.

In the case of an announcement sent by multicast, the range of visibility can be limited to the specific multicast package by setting the *time-to-live* (*TTL*) field to an appropriate value. In general, the transmission of a specific media stream should be announced with the same range of visibility used subsequently to send the media data themselves. This means that local sessions are announced only locally, and the receiver of an announcement should then have an option to participate in the session. The user who initiates a session selects a multicast address and a port for the session, using the information he or she knows about other sessions to avoid collisions. The interval between repeated attempts to send an announcement depends on the total number of announcements visible to the program to limit the total network traffic generated by these announcements.

By becoming itself a member of the multicast group using SAP, the program receives session information sent by other users and stores this information in a *cache*. Caching based on appropriate aging and removal of announcements received and which cannot be refreshed in time ensures both quick availability of information after another program start and removes old announcements, unless they have been explicitly removed, or if the program was not active at the time when old announcements were removed. Figure 7-8 shows an overview of announced MBone sessions in the sdr session directory.

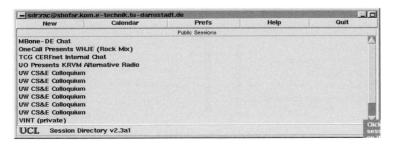

**Figure 7-8**   Overview of announced MBone sessions in the sdr session directory.

For the required continuous transmission of announcements and their continuous receipt, it is also possible to implement expansions using a so-called *daemon* or *proxy* receiver mode. A graphical user interface displays current announcements for the user. The user can gain an overview on current or forthcoming sessions easily from this user interface, and select a session from the list to get more detailed information to eventually decide whether he or she wants to click a description of contained media to start a user-defined display application. Figure 7-9 shows a sample screen with detailed information about an MBone session selected by the user.

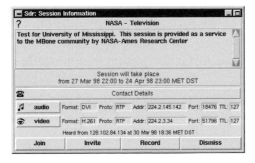

**Figure 7-9**   Detailed information about an MBone session; the user can select and start a session in a display program from this screen.

### 7.5.2.2    Audio Applications

There is a large number of audio applications, such as *vat* (audio tool), *rat* (Reliable Audio Tool), or *NeVoT* (Network Voice Terminal), just to name a few, which support a shared subset of audio encoding methods that allow them to interoperate within an application scenario and communicate with heterogeneous receivers. As a representative example for this type of applications, Figure 7-10 shows the user interface of rat (Reliable Audio Tool).

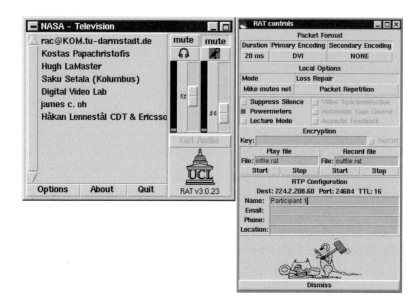

**Figure 7-10**    The rat (Reliable Audio Tool) user interface.

In addition to the basic functionality used for the transmission of audio data, these applications offer additional services, such as the display of participating and active senders, the recording and playback processes of audio files, or the encryption of the data stream. Switching between input and output devices, automatic volume control, and display synchronization to a video stream transmitted in parallel allow easy and efficient work.

While a loss, flaw, or delay of video information is normally tolerated by most users, this is not the case for audio information. For this reason, one of the main objects in the design, implementation, and use of audio applications is to minimize failures or interruptions in the audio stream. To achieve this goal, audio applications use receive buffers with variable size, error correction mechanisms, such as redundant audio data that are transmitted in addition, or the interpolation of missing samples with network jitter, to compensate timing deviations between the encoder at the sender and the playback device at the receiver, or network failures.

### 7.5.2.3    Video Applications

Software programs like *vic*, *nv*, or *ivs* can be used to record and play video data. Apart from functions to control the encoding method and the frame rate, the size of the transmitted or represented images and their parameters, such as hue and contrast, these tools also offer additional functions. For example, *vic* is a program allowing speaker synchronization to the audio data received in the corresponding *vat* program. The window currently assigned to the active speaker can be brought to the foreground automatically. Interruptions in the transmitted image information are clearly more acceptable than interruptions in the audio transmission. An appropriate cooperative behavior of the applications can help compensate this situation when delays in the network are observed. Figure 7-11 shows an example of an MBone live transmission.

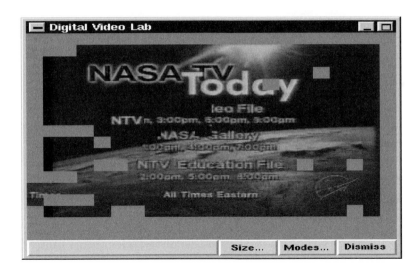

**Figure 7-11**   MBone live transmission of a space shuttle mission.

### 7.5.2.4    Recording MBone Sessions

It is desirable in many application cases to use a feature to record or replay multimedia sessions. For example, to record a lecture transmitted via MBone, to transport or distribute the copy in a suitable way, and to subsequently replay the recorded media at another location at any time and as often as needed. MBone-VCR [Hol97] can be used for this purpose.

The application was originally developed as a monolithic program, but was later enhanced to *MBone VCR-on-Demand*. This modern and recent version of the MBone application should run on a central server, based on appropriately performing systems with appropriate storage, and distributed onto a client for control of the server. Figure 7-12 shows the user interface of MBone VCR-on-Demand.

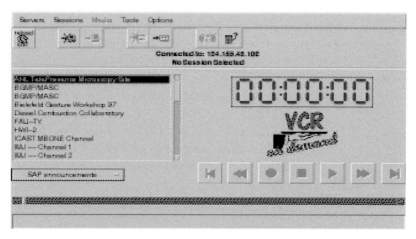

**Figure 7-12**   The user interface of MBone VCR-on-Demand.

Clients can be implemented either as independent programs, or as Java applets, and allow easy control of the server by using the R*emote DataPump Control Protocol* (*RDCP*), which is a subset of the functionality of the Real-Time Streaming Protocol (RTSP). More specifically, the VCR uses the RTP format to store data; the RTP format is additionally used to transmit data. This means that the capability for automatic description, synchronization, and separation of the subsets of streams or their subsequent editing are maintained.

### 7.5.2.5   Displaying Graphics, Text, and Distributed Document Editing

Collaborative work in projects in particular, but also the presentation of images in general, e.g., accompanying a lecture, are suitable applications for appropriate display or editing tools. While video transmission allows to observe an impression of the reaction of the participants, their mimics and gestures, this is less suitable for the display of graphics and text due to the partly bad readability, and obviously inefficient for static contents, e.g., on spreadsheets. To display documents, programs like *Whiteboard* (*wb*) can be used instead. Such a program allows the display of PostScript data and their distributed further editing by use of tools to create graphical primitives, but also free-style drawings. The result of such a job created by collaborative work is visible to all participants, and can be stored for later use. Figure 7-13 shows a distributed display and editing of documents in wb.

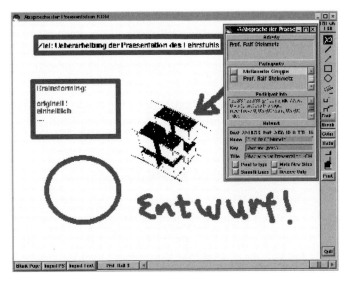

**Figure 7-13**   Distributed display and editing of a document in wb.

The *nte* network text editor is especially suitable for text editing. It can be used for shared document editing, and marking and moving of text blocks. In addition, it represents the participating users and the originators of changes are visible to all participants. Figure 7-14 shows an example of shared document editing in *nte*.

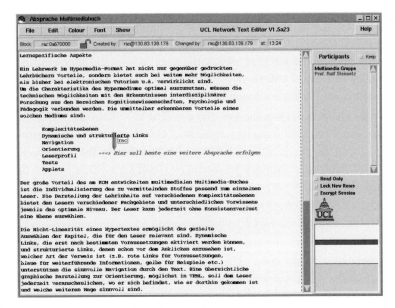

**Figure 7-14**   Shared document editing in nte.

For some of the applications described here, which were initially designed for use with a best-effort transport method to transmit multimedia data, there are expansions, which have been developed in an attempt to achieve a higher transmission quality by means of reservation or the use of particularities of the underlying transmission technology (e.g., ATM).

The use of the applications described here is not always intuitive, but it can be very efficient for the intended work processes. Most of these applications are subject to further development and improvement.

### 7.5.3  Cooperation of Protocols in an MBone Session

Within the scope of a typical MBone session, the user can reproduce the function and interplay of a number of mechanisms described in the two previous sections.

For example, a session normally begins by starting a session directory program, e.g., *sdr*. To activate the receipt of SAP packages sent via multicast, including session descriptions encoded in the SDP format, the program becomes a member of the multicast group used by the SAP protocol. Unless already done by other receivers in the network, the program will inform the multicast-capable router about this fact by use of particular packages for routing control in the Internet (IGMP packages).

The router, in turn, cooperates with other multicast routers and uses a multicast routing protocol to ensure that the relevant packages are fed into the subnetwork, to which the user is connected. For this purpose, the MBone system can also run over a Unicast connection and the additional use of an appropriate tunnel.

Incoming SDP descriptions are represented so that the user can start a suitable display program. For these display programs, to activate the receipt of the media data, there is an analogous approach that allows the user to joint another multicast group. If the transmission is effected within layered multicast, then it would also be meaningful to gradually add partial streams, depending on the requirements of the receiver.

Media data arrive in RTP packages and can first be synchronized, if they belong to several media streams with relating contents, based on the timestamps, and then decoded and output. If the encoding method changes during the course of a transmission, then this can be seen directly from the *payload type identifier* of the RTP data stream and handled appropriately.

The realization of feedback mechanisms is possible by use of *receiver reports* and *sender reports* transmitted via RTCP, which are created by the senders.

Finally, to ensure and improve the quality of service available to the receiver, appropriate mechanisms are used. These mechanisms can be activated explicitly by cooperation of sender and receiver, using a reservation protocol, e.g., RSVP. This protocol has to be supported by the applications or by the respective components running on the end systems.

Equally, there is also an option for the user to first make transparent use of mechanisms based on an in-band signaling method or on the differentiated services approach, the latter being controlled by the network operator.

When the MBone application is terminated, then the reservations maintained by soft state in the transport system are released, and the applications inform the router in their network that they are about to leave the corresponding multicast group. The router can detect this also when there are no more responses to group membership queries. Next, the forwarding of multicast data to the subnetwork and eventually also in parts of the spanning tree built during multicast routing, which is under the control of the router, is deactivated as soon as the router detects that there are no more receivers.

## 7.6  Closing Remarks

Multimedia conferencing, group communication, and other collaborative systems have made considerable progress in terms of development and proof-of-concept deployment of concepts, protocols, and data management algorithms as discussed above and shown in many recent research results (e.g., [For02]). Furthermore, we are observing commercial products that allow point-to-point or one-to-few communication such as the Poly-Com systems, or Net-Meeting system from Microsoft. Experimental video conferenceing systems for larger group communication, such as the Access Grid, have been explored by the National Laboratories, such as Argonne National Laboratory, and Academic Centers such as the NCSA at University of Illinois, Urbana-Champaign.

However, the reliability, quality and scalability of group communication systems as well as their easy installation, management and use at the user interfaces need further work and future research. First results can be found in the most recent multimedia conferences and journals (e.g., [Rou02a]), but future investigations and large scale experiments are necessary.

# Synchronization

**M**any multimedia products are local systems that do not support any communication of audio and video data and do not accept inputs in the form of audio and motion picture signals from distributed sources. Normally, these systems support only few and simple relationships between selected media. When making a choice between various concepts and subsequent implementation of prototype or product developments, particular attention should be paid to the capability of such a system to integrate into existing hardware and software environments. This chapter studies and discusses the issues of synchronization and both known and new concepts, including their implementation capabilities. It should be noted that emphasis is placed on the field of *live synchronization*, and that both the definition and evaluation of synchronization relationships, mainly in the form of stored information, is not one of the issues we will study here in depth (for a discussion of the so-called synthetic synchronization, see also Section 8.5).

## 8.1  Defining "Synchronization"

From the definition of the term *multimedia system* (see Volume 1 Chapter 2) we can derive that there is a reference—a synchronization—between the information encoded in various media. This reference has to be derived, because it is a prerequisite for integrated processing, storage, representation, communication, generation, and manipulation of multimedia information. The Merriam-Webster Dictionary defines the term *synchronization* as follows:

*Synchronization = the act or result of synchronizing; the state of being synchronous.*

*Synchronize = to happen at the same time; to represent or arrange (events) to indicate coincidence or coexistence; to make synchronous in operation; to make (motion picture sound) exactly simultaneous with the action.*

Synchronization creates a relationship between independent objects (pieces of information, media, processes, data streams, LDUs). Synchronization between media objects includes relationships between time-dependent and time-independent objects. An example for synchronization of continuous media from everyday life is the synchronization of visual and acoustic information in television broadcasting. A multimedia system has to produce a similar synchronization for audio and motion picture information. An example for temporal relationships of time-dependent and time-independent media is a slide show. The representation of the slides is synchronized to the commented audio stream. To implement a slide show in a multimedia system, we have to synchronize the playback of pictures to the relevant sections of the audio stream.

In multimedia systems, there are the three relationships between two or more objects that occur most frequently; we will explain them below. Figure 8-1 represents a schematic view of these relationships.

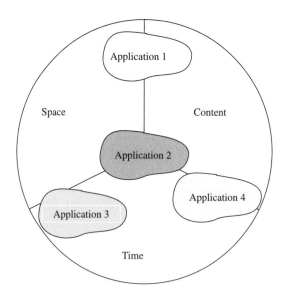

**Figure 8-1**   Relationships between data units.

**Content Relationships**  These relationships define a connection between various media objects or data. For example, a content relationship in a document could exist between the data in a table and a relevant picture. The data is represented in various ways (table or picture), or various aspects of an interrelated fact are presented. In such a desirable form of integrated documents, the *input data*, the links, and the type of presentation are defined or edited. All actual *output data* resulting from the representation of linked input data (in this example the table and a picture) cannot be directly changed or edited. If input data is changed, then this can have various effects on the output data in different places of the document. Techniques to maintain consistency are known from database systems and could be transferred to the range of different media in multimedia systems. In general, an implementation of content relationships origins from common data structures. The presentation can be in various media, but it always expresses a consistent fact.

**Spatial Relationships**  These relationships are normally called *layout relationships*; they define the space for the representation of a media object from an output device of a multimedia presentation at a specific point in time. In two-dimensional output devices (e.g., monitor or paper), the layout defines the two-dimensional area to be used.

These relationships are important for the presentation on paper and monitor. They determine the layout in the user interface: The objects are arranged in a two-dimensional space to each other. Here, purely spatial information is significant. In desktop publishing documents, this is usually expressed in frames. A *frame* is inserted and contents are assigned to the frame. Such frames can also be used to insert motion pictures. Windows systems use several windows for this purpose. A window can offer the reader additional degrees of freedom by use of operations like "zoom in", "zoom out", or "move". Holographic experiments and three-dimensional projections onto surfaces allow also an arrangement on a third dimension (the depth), which Windows systems show only in a rudimentary overlapping. Descriptive attributes include *cascade* and *tile*. Note that spatial references can exist even in the presentation of audio, when using the stereo effect [LCP90]. In a workstation conference, several participants can be acoustically arranged. To produce a direct reference to single images or motion pictures of the other persons, the video windows are represented in the same spatial arrangement on the monitor. This technique has a positive effect on the acceptance of an application, i.e., the users can follow a discussion in a more natural way. Without acoustic placement, the speaker can be identified only by recognizing his or her voice, by the contents, or by his or her lip movements.

**Temporal Relationships**  These relationships define time relationships between media objects. They are important whenever there are time-dependent media objects.

A temporal relationship like "play back at the same time" is significant, particularly when viewing time-specific media. For example, the playback of motion pictures and sound should be correlated in terms of time. The temporal reference between objects represents synchronization in the true sense of the word. Descriptive attributes include *concurrent*, *independent*, or *consecutive*.

The synchronization relationships across several spaces have been considered in standard specifications, e.g., in MHEG und HyTime [Org92] [ MHE93]. All three relationship types are normally important for an integrative multimedia system. As shown in Figure 8-1, various applications can use one or several of these relationship types. We will focus on the temporal reference (synchronization) and describe it in detail in this chapter, because this aspect is particularly significant for the integration of time-dependent media.

**Note**   Content and spatial relationships are well known from desktop publishing and application systems integrating databases, spreadsheets with graphical tools, and word processors. The key aspects in multimedia systems are the temporal relationships resulting from the integration of time-dependent media objects. For this reason, the remainder of this chapter will deal exclusively with temporal relationships.

### 8.1.1   Intra- and Inter-object Synchronization

We distinguish between temporal relationships between single components of a time-dependent media object and temporal relationships between various media objects. This classification will help us understand the mechanisms required to support the two very different relationship types.

- *Intra-object synchronization*: Intra-object synchronization refers to the temporal relationships between various presentation units within one time-dependent media object. One good example is the time ratio of single frames of a video sequence. In a video with a refresh rate of 25 frames per second, each frame has to be shown for at least 40 ms. Figure 8-2 shows this situation by using a video sequence as an example. The sequence shows a bouncing ball.

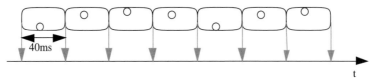

**Figure 8-2**   Video sequence showing a bouncing ball.

- *Inter-object synchronization*: Inter-object synchronization refers to the time relationships between different media objects. Figure 8-3 shows an example for a time relationship in a multimedia synchronization of an audiovisual sequence, following a series of pictures and an animation, which is commented by an audiovisual sequence.

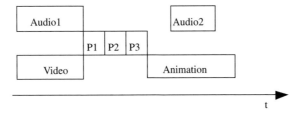

**Figure 8-3** Inter-object synchronization of images, one animation, and audiovisual sequences.

## 8.1.2 Time-dependent Presentation Units

### 8.1.2.1 Logical Data Units (LDUs)

Time-dependent media normally consists of a sequence of information units called *logical data units* (*LDUs*). The LDUs of a media object often consist of several granularities. For example, a symphony (see Figure 8-4) can be composed of several movements. Each of these movements is an independent part of the composition. It exists, in turn, of a sequence of notes for various instruments. In a digital system, each note represents a sequence of audio samples. In the case of PCM-encoded uncompressed CD quality, a sampling rate of 44,100 Hz on two channels and a 16-bit resolution per channel are used. These values are grouped into blocks with a length of 1/75 s each.

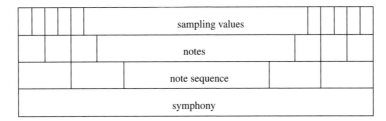

**Figure 8-4** LDU hierarchy.

The *granularity* depends on the application. You can consider the entire symphony, i.e., the movements, the notes, the samples, or the samples grouped into blocks, as LDUs. Which LDUs are selected depends on the operations applied on the media object. For simple operations like "playback", the entire symphony or the movements are meaningful LDUs. When applying instrument-based playback events, the notes represent the smallest description units of a suitable granularity. In digital signal processing, the operations are based on samples or blocks.

Another example is an uncompressed video object, divided into scenes and frames. The frames can be divided into areas with a size of 16 × 16 pixels. Each pixel, in turn, consists of luminance and chrominance values. All these units are examples of LDUs.

In a video sequence encoded in MPEG format [ISO93], redundancies within consecutive frames can be used to reduce the volume of the digital data required to represent the image contents (inter-frame compression). In this case, a sequence of inter-frame compressed images can be thought of as an LDU.

The granularity implies a hierarchical division of media objects. Often, there are two types of hierarchies: The first hierarchy is a *content* hierarchy, based on the contents of the media objects. In our symphony example, this would be the hierarchy of the symphony, the movements, and the notes. The second hierarchy can be thought of as an *encoding* hierarchy, based on the data encoding of the media object. In our symphony example, this could be a media object representing a movement and divided into blocks and samples. The samples represent the lowest level of the encoding hierarchy.

In addition, we can classify LDUs in closed and open LDUs. *Closed LDUs* have a foreseeable duration. Examples for closed LDUs are LDUs representing parts of stored media, e.g., audio or video, or stored media objects with a fixed duration. In contrast, the duration of *open LDUs* is not known until its presentation is executed. Open LDUs normally represent inputs from a live source, e.g., a camera or a microphone, or media objects including some user interaction.

### 8.1.2.2    Classification of Logical Data Units

For digital video, we would normally select the single frames as LDUs. For example, in a video with 30 images per second, each LDU is a closed LDU with a duration of 1/30 s (see Figure 8-5).

**Figure 8-5**   Video LDUs.

When the elementary physical units are too small to be meaningful for processing, then LDUs that group the blocks purposefully into units of fixed duration are often selected. A typical example would be an audio stream. For an audio stream, the duration of the elementary physical units would be very small, so LDUs with blocks of 512 samples each are formed. The example shown in Figure 8-6 encodes each sample with one byte, so that each block consists of 512 bytes.

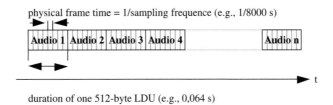

Figure 8-6   Audio LDUs.

Recorded media have normally a natural LDU basic length. In computer-generated media objects, the duration of LDUs can be selected by the user. An example for such a user-defined LDU duration would be the frames of an animation sequence. For an animation sequence with a length of 2 s, we can generate 30 to 60 images, depending on the required representation quality. Consequently, the LDU duration depends on the selected frame rate (see Figure 8-7).

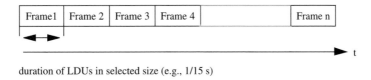

Figure 8-7   User defined LDU duration.

When the duration of the LDUs varies, then the resulting data streams are more complex. One example would be the recording of events in a graphical user interface, involving some user interaction. In this example, an LDU would be an event that lasts until the the next event begins. The duration of the LDUs depends on the user interaction and varies accordingly (see Figure 8-8).

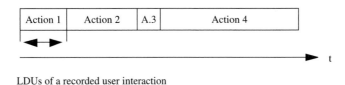

Figure 8-8   LDUs with variable duration.

Open LDUs with indefinite duration exist when an LDU does not have an inherent duration. An example for an open LDU (i.e., an LDU without inherent duration) would be a user interaction, where the time when the user will interact is not known in advance (see Figure 8-9).

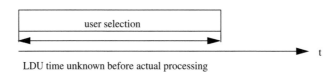

**Figure 8-9**   Open LDU representing a user interaction.

Timers can be thought of as streams consisting of empty LDUs with a fixed duration (see Figure 8-10).

**Figure 8-10**   The LDUs of a timer.

Table 8-1 gives an overview on the LDU types discussed above.

|  | **LDU duration defined while recording** | **LDU duration defined by user** |
| --- | --- | --- |
| Fixed LDU duration | audio, video | animation, timer |
| Variable, unknown LDU duration | recorded interaction | user interaction |

**Table 8-1**   LDU types.

### 8.1.2.3   Other Examples

The following three examples show LDU-based synchronization types.

1. Lip synchronization requires a close interleaving of audio and video streams. The synchronization can be defined by a maximum skew between two media streams (see Figure 8-11).

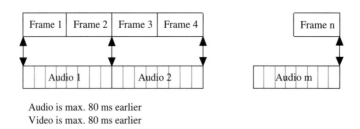

**Figure 8-11**   The LDU type for lip synchronization.

2. In a slide show including some audio comment, a temporal relationship of the slide changes to the audio comments is required (see Figure 8-12).

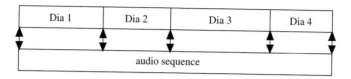

**Figure 8-12**  The LDU type for a slide show.

The next example shown in Figure 8-13 will be used frequently in this text to explain synchronization-specific methods.

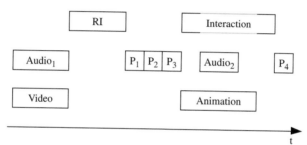

**Figure 8-13**  Synchronization example.

3. A lip-synchronized audiovisual sequence (*Audio₁* and *Video*) precedes the play-back of a user interaction (*RI*), followed by a slide sequence ($P_1$ to $P_3$) and an animation (*Animation*), which is partly commented by an audio sequence (*Audio₂*). At the beginning of the presentation of the animation, the user is asked a multiple-choice question. Once the user has chosen his or her answers, the last picture ($P_4$) is shown.

## 8.2  Particularities of Synchronization in Multimedia Systems

### 8.2.1  Overview

This section deals with the particularities of temporal relationships between time-independent and time-dependent information units in the context of multimedia systems, which do not occur in conventional data processing systems.

Such temporal references have formerly (i.e., in non-multimedia systems) been known mostly from the field of dedicated audio and video combination. Sound and motion pictures in television broadcasting are represented synchronously by television receivers. To achieve this synchronous presentation, appropriate signals are transmitted concurrently by use of a multiplexing method. A delay in the transmission always affects both channels (video and audio) at the same time, but the synchronization is maintained. No particular measures are required to maintain this synchronization. This chapter does not discuss synchronization in the context of image or line synchronization, i.e., not in connection with the detection of the beginning or end of an LDU (television technology uses very sophisticated methods for this type of synchronization). When attempting to expand synchronization to time-independent media, and when the LDUs, which should be put in relationship, represent independent units, then we cannot store all combinations required for the presentation in an *interleaved* way in advance.

Another aspect relates to the communication of these data streams over computer networks, where various media can use different connections with different *quality-of-service (QoS)* characteristics.

Currently, there have been only few or dedicated concepts and prototypes for integrated workstation computers capable of processing several independent, continuous and discrete media concurrently, and then transmitting these different media types over computer networks. These efforts are motivated by the objective to integrate multimedia systems.

This means that the definition of synchronization relationships and their implementation in the context of audio, video, and different discrete media in a networked workstation environment is important and the main issues of this book.

### 8.2.1.1    Hard Synchronization Requirements

The primary receiver of continuous media (audio and video) are humans. This statement means that we can derive several of the required characteristics alone from the actual source and the sink, namely humans: The required time horizons that have to be observed in a synchronization are not as rigid as they are stated in the actual synchronization specification, where processes and the related information flows are synchronized exactly.

When studying the mechanisms of synchronization between multimedia LDUs, then this means that an exact time reference is established between two information units. The eventual processing speed (e.g., during a process change) and the actual concurrency (e.g., required by *multiprogramming*) will always produce minor time differences. These time differences do not exist on the conceptional level.

### 8.2.1.2    Soft Synchronization Requirements

The hard synchronization requirements described above do not occur in continuous information:

- As our first example, we will look at the *synchronization of audio and video* data. The requirement of interest during the presentation is described by the term *lip synchronization*. It means that the time limits when a human perceives audio and video as being synchronous have to be determined. Empirical studies have shown that there are interesting differences between the output of audio before or after the video data [SE93]. Many people do not find it disturbing when audio data are output up to 80 ms after the video data, which means that this delay between audio and video is still perceived as being lip synchronous. If the same audio information is played back before the video data, then a delay of 80 ms is still considered tolerable. However, a closer look at this acceptance shows that "audio behind video" is tolerated better than the opposite. This phenomenon of time asymmetry could be explained as follows, where the explanation was derived from different propagation speeds of sound and light waves: Humans are used to optically perceive events occurring at a far distance and perceiving the pertaining sound event with some delay. These phenomena will be described in more detail in Section 8.2.2.

Experience has shown that the optical stimulus and the acoustic phenomenon are closely related. Experiences from everyday life involving high speeds (e.g., driving a car) confront us often with this phenomenon. In contrast to visual impressions, which are perceived before the corresponding sound, sound is almost never perceived by the human before the pertaining optical information.

- An example for the *synchronization of video and text* is a movie with subtitles. The descriptive text is normally shown in a separate window displayed alongside the bottom border of the video window. In this case, too, there is no hard time requirement. We could even work with more flexible limits. Often, all that is required is to display the subtitles for a sufficiently long period. A fluctuation of, say, 50 ms would not have the least significance in this example. The tolerable delays depend primarily on the duration of the motion picture scene, which is dubbed by a text synchronization. Moreover, the amount of text to be represented is relevant, with an indicative value being in the range of approx. 250 ms.

- One application for the *synchronization of voice, or music and a picture or text* could be a multimedia music dictionary. Such a dictionary would show pictures of composers or verbose descriptions of their work, set in relation with the corresponding music. Here too, there are no hard time limits, so that an indicative value of 250 ms appears to be a good assumption for a maximum delay.

However, if we attempt to synchronize notes with the corresponding sound, we will have to meet more exact requirements [BBNS02]. In fact, it is important to see the corresponding note when hearing the piece of sound (e.g., by highlighting the note). This delay should not exceed 5 ms in critical cases. Note that this type of application currently runs locally on *one* computer.

- Another data stream to be synchronized, particularly in conference applications, is generated by the *mouse pointer*. When pointing to an element, the corresponding verbose description should ideally appear at the same time. Otherwise, a time delay between the pointer and the comments could lead to misunderstandings. Maximum delay values for this type of application are considered to be 750 ms for the audio output before the pointer and 500 ms for the pointer output before the audio [SE93]. These phenomena will be discussed in more detail in Section 8.2.3.

These are examples for *soft time requirements*, which were first proposed [Ste90] for the specification of tolerable time intervals as an addition to the actual synchronization issue.

Processes were thought to be either *synchronized* or *unsynchronized*. This absolute Yes/No classification totally neglects the existence of soft time requirements. Now, a synchronization can be "excellent", "good", "bad", or "unacceptable". In this respect, we can work with a *synchronization quality*. Whatever is supposed to be *synchronized* depends on media and content. Conditions have to be formulated for tolerable time intervals in the desired optimum. Depending on these conditions, we can then execute a set of application-defined operations.

The following considerations are based on a comparison between the properties of known synchronization mechanisms in the field of inter-process communication and inter-process synchronization and the properties of synchronization required for multimedia [AS83, HH89]. The approach to this analysis and the results with regard to the underlying properties of the mechanisms used in inter-process communication and inter-process synchronization will be discussed in the further course of this chapter.

In this study, it was found that the two areas have many similarities. However, there are some properties of synchronization specific to multimedia systems, which have are not known in the field of inter-process communication and inter-process synchronization, and they are not even necessary. In addition to the above introduction of tolerance intervals, another difference relating to the blocking of processes or data streams was identified.

*Blocking* can be used to make processes wait for each other. In addition, a data stream composed of discrete LDUs can also be *stopped*. The situation is totally different with audio and motion picture sequences, where the following issues arise:

• What does the blocking of a motion picture stream mean for the connected output device?
• Should or can the last picture be displayed?
• Should part of a voice or music clip be allowed to repeat?
• How long may a gap like the one shown in Figure 8-14 persist?

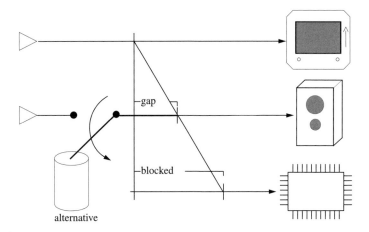

**Figure 8-14** The gap problem: conditional blocking.

This situation has become known as the *gap problem* [R.S89, Ste90]. Current systems solve the gap problem in motion pictures simply by having the output device switch between dark and white, or by displaying the last motion picture as a single picture. A better and application-oriented solution should take the time factor into account. This means that it is very important whether or not such a gap is in the range of milliseconds or even seconds or minutes. Only the application concerned (and not the system) can define the optimal solution. For this reason, a synchronization method should offer alternatives, depending on the expected blocking time.

This concept of alternative operations is shown in Figure 8-14. This example shows how, in the case of a gap between audio and delayed video, the process switches to an alternative presentation after a predefined threshold. When the gap is shorter, then the audio presentation can be stopped till the gap is closed. When the preset threshold value is exceeded, the blocking mechanism triggers, which means that other single pictures, picture sequences, or audio signals can be output, or existing media are simply repeated to close the gap. This blocking method, or the blocking of audio and video streams, is called *restricted blocking*.

### 8.2.1.3 Resampling

The restricted blocking mechanism uses the repeated presentation of the last few samples or an alternative presentation to achieve resynchronization. Another alternative is based on the *resampling* of streams. The basic idea behind resampling is to accelerate or slow down some streams for the purpose of synchronization. We distinguish between online and offline resampling.

*Offline resampling* is used after the recording of media streams, e.g., a concert recorded by means of a multi-channel recording device and a video camera. These devices are not connected. When the recording device and the camera, just like many real-world devices, do not dispose of very precise quartz clocks, then the playback duration of the audio and video sequences stored according to the chosen sampling rate can differ. However, it is possible to adapt the presentation to the same theoretical playback duration before it is executed.

*Online resampling* is applied when, during the runtime of the presentation, a gap occurs between some media streams. In this case, the following resampling methods can be used:

- Redefine the output rate;
- duplicate samples;
- interpolate samples;
- skip samples; and
- recalculate the entire sequence.

How humans perceive a resampled presentation depends strongly on the medium. Resampling of video sequences can be achieved by inserting or deleting individual frames in or from the stream, respectively.

In contrast, audio streams are more complex. A hearer would certainly perceive duplicated or missing audio blocks as very disturbing. And changing the refresh rate is not an appropriate solution either, because this could be easily be perceived in the playback, particularly in music playback, due to a change in the audio frequency. The same applies to a simple interpolation of samples. Although there are algorithms that can be used to achieve a time stretch in the audio sequence, without causing a change in frequency, they do not support real-time requirements, so that they can be applied exclusively to offline resampling.

The following section introduces some more detailed research results with regard to lip and pointer synchronization in the field of inter-object synchronization to better explain the importance of perception aspects from the user's perspective with regard to the presentation accuracy. Subsequently, we will give a summary of other synchronization methods.

### 8.2.2  Requirements to Lip Synchronization

Lip synchronization refers to the time relationship between an audio stream and a video stream in the particular case of the human voice. The time difference or offset between interrelated audio and video LDUs is called *skew*. Perfectly synchronized (*in-sync*) streams have no skew (i.e., a skew of 0 ms). Experiments conducted at the IBM European Networking Center [SE93] measured whether or not a skew is perceived as unsynchronized (*out-of-sync*). The test persons who participated in these experiments stated frequently that "something was wrong with the synchronization", but that they did not feel it impaired the quality of the presentation. For this reason, additional work involved the evaluation of the tolerance shown by the test persons, by interviewing them whether or not unsynchronized data meant a deterioration of the presentation's quality.

Expert discussion forums on the audio and video subject observed in various studies that a large skew (up to 240 ms) could be tolerated. The comparability and the general use of these values were in doubt, because the conditions under which they were produced cannot be compared. In some studies, a "head view" in front of a one-color background on a high-resolution professional monitor was used, while other experiments used a "body view" in a video window with a resolution of $240 \times 256$ pixels.

To achieve a good skew tolerance level in the experiment described below, a speaker was selected in an environment similar to television news, i.e., in a head-and-shoulder setting (see Figure 8-15). In this orientation, the viewer is not distracted by background information and can concentrate on the gestures and eye and lip movements of the speaker.

**Figure 8-15**   Left: head view; center: shoulder view; right: body view.

The study was conducted in an environment similar to those of television news broadcasting. For this purpose, the presentation was recorded and subsequently played back. Professional editing equipment was used to insert artificial skews at intervals of 40 ms, e.g., at -120 ms, -80 ms, -40 ms, 0 ms, +40 ms, +80 ms, +120 ms. A 40-ms incrementation was chosen for the following reasons:

1. Due to the difficulty of human perception to distinguish lip synchronization skew in a higher resolution.
2. Due to the capability of the multimedia software and hardware used to refresh motion picture every 33 or 40 ms.

Figure 8-16 shows an overview of the results. The vertical axis designates the relative number of test candidates who discovered a synchronization error, regardless of whether or not they were able to detect that audio came before or after the video. Originally, it was assumed that the three curves, representing the different views, would be very different. We can see in Figure 8-16 that this was not the case.

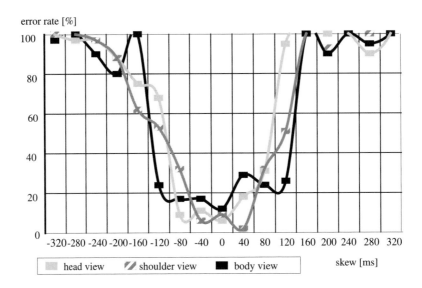

**Figure 8-16**  Perception of synchronization errors with regard to the three different views; left area: negative skew, video before audio; right area: positive skew, video after audio.

A careful analysis should supply explanations about the asymmetry, a few periodic waves, and minor differences between the results gained from the different body views.

### 8.2.2.1    Alternative Explanations of the Curves

The area on the left side of the central axis designates negative skew values; video runs ahead of audio. The right-hand side shows the area where audio runs ahead of video.

We all experience the situation in our daily lives when we perceive lip movements a little earlier before we hear the sound. This is due to the higher speed of light, compared to the speed of sound, and explains the steeper rise of the curves on the right side in the graph.

The curve of the "body view" is wider than that of the "head view", because the former has a slight skew. The curve of the "head view" is also more asymmetric than that of the "body view". This can be ascribed to the fact that it is more difficult to detect an error the further a listener is away from the speaker. When the skew is higher, the curves show periodic small waves, particularly where audio runs ahead of video. Some test persons had obvious difficulties to detect the synchronization errors, even when the skew values were very high. A careful analysis of this phenomenon is difficult due to the small sampling (approx. 100 persons). One plausible explanation could be the following: In the relative minimum values, the voice signal was closely correlated to the lip movement, which is quasi periodic. Errors could be easily detected at the beginning and end of pauses, or when the speaker changed tone (e.g., to make a point), while it was more difficult to detect errors in the middle of a sentence. Also, humans tend to concentrate more on the beginning of a talk until the contents of a sentence have come across. A follow-up experiment to study these minimum values using video clips without pauses and without intonation changes caused problems in identifying synchronization errors.

Figure 8-17 shows areas that will be described below, which were found to be on a disturbing level (see Figure 8-18).

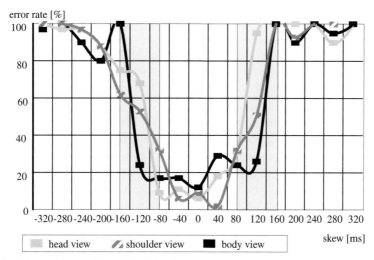

**Figure 8-17**   Perception of synchronization errors.

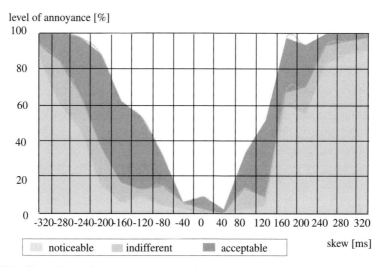

**Figure 8-18**   Skew level found to be annoying.

The "in-sync" region extends from -80 ms (audio behind video) to +80 ms (audio before video). In this zone, most test candidates did not notice the synchronization error. Very few stated that they felt disturbed by an error. In addition, some test persons mentioned even that the perfectly synchronized clip was "out of sync". Obviously, lip synchronization errors within these limits can be tolerated.

The "out-of-sync" areas were observed at a skew with values larger than +/-160 ms. Almost every test candidate discovered this error and was accordingly annoyed. Data transmitted with such a skew are generally unacceptable. In addition, it distracted the viewers/listeners from the actual contents as they became more busy with the "out-of-sync" effect itself.

In the "transient" area, the error was detected by many test persons, but not experienced as a nuisance. One interesting effect was observed in this connection: video before audio is better tolerated than the opposite. This effect became more significant as the speaker close-up was incremented.

There seems to be a plausible explanation for this asymmetry. In a conversation between two people at a distance of 20 m from each other, the visual impression will always be 60 ms ahead of the acoustic impression due to the higher speed of light, compared to the speed of sound. The test persons are merely better used to this situation versus the opposite case.

### 8.2.3   Requirements to Pointer Synchronization

In a computer-supported cooperative work environment (CSCW), both cameras and microphones are normally connected to the users' workstations. The experiment described below observed the test persons while viewing a business report that included accompanying pictures. All participants had a desktop computer with a window displaying these pictures at their disposal. A common pointer was used to conduct the discussion. This pointer was used by the speakers to describe individual graphical elements relevant in the ongoing discussion. This means that the experiment made obvious use of a synchronization of audio to the remotely controlled telepointer. More specifically, two experiments were conducted:

- The first experiment dealt with a few technical details to explain a sailboat, while the pointer pointed to the current area of discussion (see Figure 8-19). The shorter the explanation, the more important became the synchronization. For this purpose, a person who spoke very quickly and used short words was chosen as the speaker.

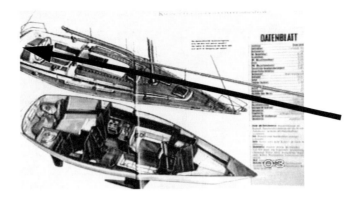

**Figure 8-19**   Experiment for pointer synchronization based on a technical drawing.

- A second experiment was conducted to explain a traveling route on a map (see Figure 8-20). In this experiment, the pointer movement was continuous.

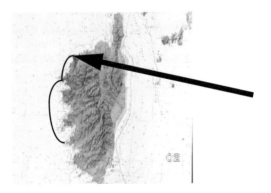

**Figure 8-20**   Experiment for pointer synchronization based on a map.

With regard to the human perception, the pointer synchronization differs strongly from the lip synchronization, because it is very difficult to detect "out-of-sync" errors when there are no errors. While the skews should be in a range between 40 ms and 160 ms for lip synchronization errors, they are in the range from 250 ms and 1500 ms for pointer synchronization errors. Figure 8-21 shows a few results from the pointer experiment.

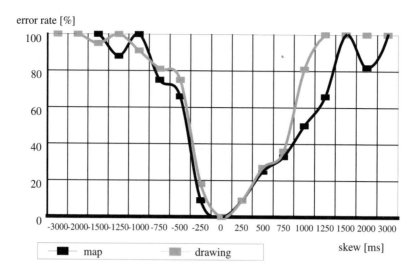

**Figure 8-21**    Perception of pointer synchronization errors.

### 8.2.3.1    Evaluation of the Pointer Synchronization Experiment

Although both the lip synchronization and the pointer synchronization experiment used the same evaluation criteria, the "in-sync" area in the pointer synchronization varies by 750 ms (*audio before pointer*) to 500 ms (*pointer before audio*). This range allows a clear definition of the "out-of-sync" behavior, regardless of the contents actually viewed.

The "out-of-sync" area includes a skew outside an interval from -1000 ms to +1250 ms. Beyond these limits, the candidates started mentioning that the skew made the attempted synchronization worthless, and that they had been distracted. This observation was less significant when the speaker talked more slowly, or moved the pointer more slowly. From the user's view, this is not acceptable. Obviously, it is meaningless to point to an area on a technical drawing while a speaker talks about something else.

In the "transient" area, many candidates observed the "out-of-sync" effect, but they did not find it annoying. This differs obviously from the lip synchronization experiment, where the viewers responded more sensitively with regard to perceiving synchronization errors, which they doubtlessly found very annoying.

Figure 8-22 shows the number of test persons who perceived an annoying pointer synchronization error, and those who responded indifferently. Note that, although the candidates noticed an error when there were many skew values, they did not finding it annoying in view of the wide "in-sync" areas and the "transient" areas.

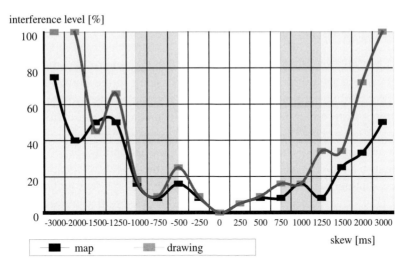

**Figure 8-22**   Level of skew perceived as annoying pointer synchronization errors.

## 8.2.4   Elementary Media Synchronization

Both the lip synchronization and the pointer synchronization were studied in detail due to inconsistent results from other available sources. The following section gives an overview on the findings gained from other synchronization experiments.

Since the advent of digital audio, the so-called *jitter* has been studied as a parameter tolerable by hardware. Dannenberg offers a few references and results in [Ble78]. Based on this work, the maximum tolerable jitter for high-quality 16-bit audio is 200 ns in one sampling period, which corresponds to an error in the least significant bit (LSB) of a full 20-kHz signal at maximum frequency. [Sto72] describes a few perception experiments with a recommended maximum tolerable jitter of 5 ns to 10 ns. Other perception experiments were studied in [Lic51] and [Woo51]. The maximum distance between short clicks, which were perceived as an interrelated sound, is 2 ms [RM80].

The requirements to the combination of audio and video are normally less rigid and similar to those for lip synchronization. For example, the multimedia presentation of a dance course could show the dancing steps as an animated sequence in connection with the accompanying music. By utilizing the interactive options, individual sequences could be shown over and over again. Note that the synchronization of music and animation is particularly important in this example. Experience has shown that a skew of +/- 80 ms meets the viewers' expectations. One issue subject to dispute is the correlation of a loud event and its visual representation, e.g., simulation of a frontal crash of two cars. In such a situation, we would have to deal with the same requirements as for lip synchronization, i.e., a skew of +/-80 ms.

Any two audio tracks could be closely or loosely coupled. The effect of the coupled audio streams will normally depend on their contents.

- A *stereo signal* includes information about the location of the sound source and is closely interleaved with it. The correct processing in the human brain is possible only provided that the phases of the acoustic signal are transmitted correctly. This requires a skew smaller than the distance between two consecutive samples, i.e., approx. 20 ms. [DS93b] reports that the perceivable phase shift of an audio channel is around 17 ms. This value origins from a headphone experiment. Considering that a delay in one channel will move the apparent location of the sound source, Dannenberg suggests a maximum skew of +/-11 ms between stereo channels. This value was also derived from the knowledge that a skew of exactly one sample with a sampling rate of 44 kHz can be heard.

- Loosely coupled *audio channels* represent a speaker and background music or similar background. In such scenarios, we normally find a maximum admissible skew of 500 ms. In the test playback of a dialogue, where the audio data of the participants originated from different sources, an acceptable skew of 120 ms was observed.

A detailed analysis leads to time constraints similar to those in pointer synchronization. In addition to the requirement to maintain a maximum skew of 5 ms in the synchronization of notes to the corresponding sound (see Section 8.2.1), we also have to deal with a maximum of 2 ms when playing back two nominally concurrent notes [Cly85] [RM80] [Ste87].

The *synchronized presentation of audio and a piece of text*, which is normally called *audio comment*, is used as part of an acoustic encyclopedia, to mentioned one application. For a case study the reader is referred to [CC02a]. At times, the audio sequence outputs additional information about a highlighted piece of text. A music dictionary could describe antique instruments and play them at the same time. An example of a closer union would be the playback of a historical speech, e.g., a speech held by J. F. Kennedy, with a simultaneous translation into German or French. The relevant text could be displayed in a separate window, and it is closely coupled to the acoustic signal. The same would apply to a foreign language course, where an acoustically played word could be visually highlighted at the same time. And *Karaoke* systems are a good example for a required audio and text synchronization.

The skew required for this type of media synchronization can be derived from the time it takes to speak a short word. This duration is approx. 500 ms, so that a skew of 240 ms would appear tolerable.

Video and text, or video and pictures can be synchronized in either of the following two ways:

- In the *overlay mode*, text often represents an additional description to a displayed motion picture sequence. For example, a video showing a pool game could use an additional picture to follow the exact path of the ball after the last stroke. The simultaneous presentation of the video with the overlaid picture is important for correct human perception of these synchronized data. The same applies to a piece of text shown together with video pictures. Instead of always showing subtitles in the bottom display area, it is also conceivable to place the text near the corresponding item of discussion. This would mean additional production cost for subtitle editing, so that it may not be of general significance for commercial movies, but it could be useful for educational applications. In an overlay project, the text has to be synchronized with the video to ensure that it will be used in the correct place. The exact skew value can be derived from the minimum time required. One single word should appear on the screen for a specific time to ensure that the viewer can perceive it correctly. It is assumed that 1 s is an appropriate value. If the media producer wants to utilize the flash effect, then such a word should appear on the screen for at least 500 ms. For this reason, 240 ms are considered absolutely sufficient, regardless of the video contents.

- The second mode is the so-called *non-overlay mode*, where the skew is less critical. Consider architectural drawings of medieval buildings shown together with a video about these buildings, then the pictures could show the floor plan, while the video could represent the architecture of the same buildings in a separate window. The human perception of even simple images would take at least 1 s. This value can be verified in an experiment with a slide show. During the successive projection of uncorrelated images, it takes the viewer an interval of about 1 s between the image change to recognize at least a few essential visual pieces of information in the slides. A synchronization with a skew of 500 ms (half of the 1-s value just mentioned) would be sufficient for this type of application.

To better explain this mode, we will use the pool game example again. Consider a video that shows two pool balls bouncing, while the image showing the "route" of one of the balls is represented by an animated sequence. Instead of a sequence of static images, the ball is visualized by animation, drawing the route of the balls as they bounce across the table. In this example, each "out-of-sync" effect can be perceived immediately. In order for humans to perceive the ball as a motion picture, the ball has to be visible in several consecutive images at slightly shifted positions. A satisfactory result can be achieved if the ball moves to a different position by a distance corresponding to its diameter in each of the three consecutive frames. A lower rate could cause a continuity problem, which can often be observed when watching a tennis match on television. As each frame takes approx. 40 ms and three consecutive images are required, a skew of 120 ms appears to be acceptable. This very close synchronization is appropriate in the example used here. Other examples for a combination of video and animation are movies with computer-generated characters, e.g., "Jurassic Park".

Multimedia systems also include real-time processing of control data. Tele-surgery is a good example for the representation of graphical information based on measurements from syringes or similar medical instruments. However, note that no general time requirements can be stated for this type of applications, because the skew depends mainly on the application itself. Table 8-2 shows a summary of the requirements to the synchronization quality of two linked media objects.

| Media Objects | | Mode, Application | QoS |
|---|---|---|---|
| Video | Anima-tion | Correlated | +/- 120 ms |
| | Audio | Lip synchronization | +/-80 ms |
| | Image | Overlay | +/- 240 ms |
| | | Non-overlay | +/- 500 ms |
| | Text | Overlay | +/- 240 ms |
| | | Non-overlay | +/- 500 ms |
| Audio | Anima-tion | Events-correlated | +/-80 ms |
| | Audio | Closely coupled (stereo) | +/-11 μs |
| | | Loosely coupled (e.g., dialog mode among several participants) | +/- 120 ms |
| | | Loosely coupled (e.g., background music) | +/- 500 ms |
| | Image | Closely coupled (e.g., music with notes) | +/-5 ms |
| | | Loosely coupled (e.g., slide show) | +/- 500 ms |
| | Text | Audio comment | +/- 240 ms |
| | Pointer | Audio in relation to the displayed object | -500 ms +750 ms |

**Table 8-2**    Service quality requirements for the synchronization of two media objects.

## 8.2.5  Analysis of Existing Synchronization Mechanisms

This section includes a short presentation of the results from a comparison of the synchronization of multimedia LDUs with the well-known mechanisms for inter-process communication and inter-process synchronization. We will concentrate on the methods used in this analysis.

One of the first steps involves the identification of concrete applications and system configurations. Currently, multimedia aspects by the definition used in this book, in combination with the communication between several computers have been used seldom. This initial step also collects the requirements. For example, it was determined to what extent interrelated voice and motion pictures can be apart in terms of time before it is found annoying. [Syn88] describes an upper limit of 150 ms, but more recent values verified on the basis of this work suggest 80 ms (see also Section 8.2.2).

The next step attempts to use existing synchronization mechanisms. One of the first questions to be solved is whether or not existing mechanisms would meet all requirements of this new environment. If the answer is positive, then we need to verify whether or not the interesting applications and system configurations will live up to these requirements.

Considering that the analysis of existing concepts did not supply a satisfactory solution, the next step involved an extraction of the properties of existing mechanisms, and then comparing them with the multimedia requirements. For example, one property was the blocking or non-blocking of processes. The properties known from the literature were complete within the scope of this analysis (see Table 8-3). A detailed description of all characteristics with regard to multimedia systems is found in [Ste90]. We will discuss the behavior of processes when waiting for a synchronization event as a representative example.

In some mechanisms for inter-process communication and inter-process synchronization, processes can be blocked while waiting for a synchronization event. In this case, the executing process will be stopped until the corresponding synchronization event occurs. In a communication relationship, both the sending and the receiving process can be blocked, while other mechanisms do not block processes. In one method, all processes continue computing until the amount of available resources left is insufficient. In this context, resources could be storage space used for message exchange. Subsequently, any reset operation as may be necessary will be executed; there is no blocking at the time of synchronization. Yet another method blocks the simulation processes at the synchronization time, if the synchronization condition is not met.

The approach described in this section to determine required synchronization properties led to the discovery of the gap problem (see Section 8.2.1) and to the specification of tolerable time intervals.

| Property | Characteristics | | | |
|---|---|---|---|---|
| Number of participating, interacting processes | always two | one with many, many with one | | many with many |
| Behavior of a process while waiting for a synchronization event | blocking | non-blocking | conditional blocking *(multimedia-specific)* | |
| Addressing of the process | direct | | indirect | |
| Influence of external processes on an existing synchronization | possible | | impossible | |
| Combination of elementary synchronization relationships | impossible | at receiver end | at sender end | at both, receiver and sender ends |
| Sequence of combined synchronization events | pre-defined | can be defined with priorities | can be defined with conditions | can be defined with priorities and conditions |
| Symmetry relationship with regard to the behavior of a process while waiting for a synchronization event | symmetric, multi-sided synchronization, if all block | | asymmetric, one-sided synchronization | |
| Symmetry relationship when adressing processes | symmetric | | asymmetric | |
| Symmetry relationship with regard to the combination of elementary synchronization relationships | symmetric | | asymmetric | |
| Specification of time conditions | impossible | as a real-time condition | with time constraints *(multimedia-specific)* | |
| Type of contents of communicating information | data types (without pointers) | including pointers | including procedures | including procedures |
| Time when type of communicating information becomes known | during specification (translation) | | at runtime | |

**Table 8-3**   Basic synchronization and communication properties.

## 8.3    Requirements to the Presentation

The correct transmission of multimedia data at the user interface requires ynchroniza-tion. It is impossible to state an objective measure for the synchronization from the view of the subjective human perception. As the human perception differs from one person to another, only heuristic criteria can be defined as to whether or not a presentation stream is correct.

Requirements to the presentation include the accuracy with regard to the presenta-tion of LDUs for intra-object synchronization, and the accuracy with regard to the par-allelism of the presentation of media objects for inter-object synchronization. In intra-object synchronization, we should attempt to avoid jitter or variance in an two consecutive LDUs.

## 8.4    Reference Elements for Synchronization

The previous sections studied temporal relationships between reference elements, with-out discussing these elements themselves. The *reference elements* discussed so far were LDUs, media, processes, and data streams; they were collectively called *objects*.

## 8.5    Synchronization Types

The following applications will be discussed:

1. Two persons talk about a novel work piece or instrument and its instructions for use (text and pictures), each of the two sitting at their computers, which are con-nected. One of the two people has an option to use a camera to transmit a picture of the person itself or an initial production pattern via video. When the person is displayed, then there should be lip synchronism between the audio and the video data streams. When a person uses a pointer pointing to a picture or piece of text on the screen, then this should be time-coupled with the audio data stream. This means that the exact temporal reference between the pointer and the audio is very important (e.g., when the person says "At this point, you will see...", then the pointer should point to the correct place).

2. A student sits at his or her computer studying an educational system that shows a fictitious trip into the world of the Mayas (Surrogate Travel) [Pre90]. This exam-ple is a particularly sophisticated form of a system designed by Intel in coopera-tion with the Bank Street College of Education, New York. Using a joystick, the student moves across a jungle, exploring old ruins of the Mayas. He or she can study details of interest more closely. The video is accompanied by jungle sounds. The user can observe the flora and fauna and activate a video museum any time to obtain further information about details. Such a system could form the basis of a comprehensive educational system with a structure of the lessions, pick up at spe-cific points after interruptions and use controls for the learning success. The goal

of this application is primarily to compose information from individual elements, where certain rules have to be observed.

When analyzing the two examples more closely, we can see two types of synchronization, as described in [LG90], which will be explained in the following subsections.

### 8.5.1   Live Synchronization—Overview

The most important requirement in the first example is to present information to the respective partner in the temporal relationship in which is was created. For example, when one person points to a part of the instrument or the text, accompanied by a spoken explanation, then the pointing action should be presented simultaneously with the audio information. Relationships between media should be played back in the form in which they were created. For this reason, this type is also called *live synchronization*. Another example would be a video conference, where voice and motion pictures should be displayed in the sequence of their creation (i.e., in an exact temporal reference). In a live synchronization, the information is normally created quasi at the time when they are presented.

### 8.5.2   Synthetic Synchronization—Overview

In the second example, independent information units are put in a suitable relationship during the presentation. This means that emphasis is placed on the synchronization of stored information. This is often the case in retrieval systems. Individual information units are composed synthetically, so that this type is called *synthetic synchronization* [LG90]. Note that such individual information units can be components of more than one application. In addition, they may be stored on several computers. This type requires a suitable model to describe and manipulate synchronization conditions, using operators like `parallel`, `sequential`, or `independent` [LG90, PGKK88]. Appropriate specification methods can be developed within the scope of information architectures or system interfaces [Nic90]. For example, CD-ROMs and suitable compression methods are such systems, and they are readily available.

    From the synchronization perspective, some applications like video conferencing, which involves the editing of a multimedia document, are very demanding. This document could also contain various audio and video parts. In this case, both synthetic synchronization and live synchronization could occur individually or jointly.

### 8.5.3   Variants of Live Synchronization

The previous examples demonstrated that live synchronization normally occurs in conversation services. When considering an interaction model between sources and sinks, then the functionality of a volatile input occurs always at the sources, while the representation occurs at the corresponding data sinks. A common temporal context between two or more information flows at the sources and sinks will help to better explain how temporal references among LDUs is achieved.

Consider the use of a model. A source in this model represents an acoustic sensor for audio and an optical sensor for video. The sink is also a converter of the respective medium. A *connection* is the data path between one or several sources and one or several sinks, and can represent an exclusive local communication. For this reason, it does not necessarily have to connect source(s) and sink(s) residing on different computer systems (see Figure 8-23).

source              sink                          source / sink

**Figure 8-23**  Live synchronization over direct connection.

### 8.5.3.1    Live Synchronization with Spatial Skew

This first type of live synchronization characterizes the transmission of information with a *spatial skew* between the source and the sink (see Figure 8-24). The signals created at the source should be played back at the sink as true to nature as possible. The only way for the sink to influence this data flow is to initiate an adaptation between source and sink. Such an adaptation can refer to several aspect, e.g., the resolution of images or the refresh rate. If, for a video conference, the source requires a video image to have a resolution of only $128 \times 128$ pixels and 15 pictures per second, then the sender could set the encoding accordingly. This helps save bandwidth in the data transmission. Note that there is no actual control of the data flow. The data are represented in the rate used to record the information in the system.

source                                                                           sink

**Figure 8-24**  Live synchronization with spatial skew.

### 8.5.3.2    Live Synchronization with Temporal Decoupling

A second type of live synchronization is achieved by *temporal decoupling* between source(s) and sink(s) (see Figure 8-25). More specifically, the system stores the data input at the sources and outputs them at a later point in time. One application example for this live synchronization type would be if we record a transmission and reproduce it later at a remote location. When recording, the temporal references between the set of data streams have to be included. In this first phase, the data input represents the source and the storage represents the sink. A subsequent reproduction interprets this information and ensures live synchronization between the data streams. In the second phase, the playback of the stored information represents the source, while the actual presentation represents the sink.

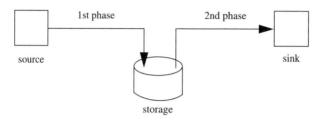

**Figure 8-25**   Live synchronization with temporal decoupling.

In contrast to the first example, this approach includes some minor interaction between the sink and the source (i.e., the stored information). In fact, the speed can vary between the display of a single image, the slow-motion, and the quick-motion in both directions (forward and backward). This interaction is controlled by the application at the sink. Also, this approach allows optional access. The goal of live synchronization is always concentrated on the correct temporal playback of the interrelated information flows. The temporal references are fixed in advance, i.e., determined by how they were recorded.

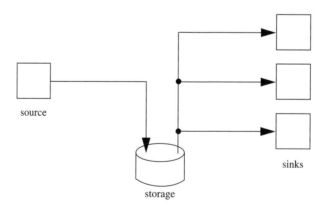

**Figure 8-26**   Three sinks connected over a multicast connection.

If we generalize the communication structure of live synchronization from a point-to-point relationship to a relationship between one source and multiple sinks, then an interaction would always affect all sinks. Consider a highly compressed scene of a soccer game stored on hard disk and a multicast connection connecting 3 sinks (see Figure 8-26). If one of these sinks activates a slow-motion event, then the other sinks would see the same.

When information from multiple sources is played back at one sink, then we would first have to explicitly request a live synchronization, because the data streams are combined only at the sink, i.e., at the location and time of presentation. Another requirement would be to play back the information in the way it was created at these sources in terms of temporal relationship. This means that a temporal reference has to be made through local distribution. An interaction between the sink and the set of sources will then be similar to a spatial skew.

In Summary, we can see that the primary requirement, i.e., live synchronization, in any variant is as good a true playback of LDU relationships, which were created with temporal and/or spatial skews. The degree of a possible interaction between sink and source is a secondary characteristic. This means that, in the simplest case, the sink could just represent all data streams and LDU relationships created at the source. If there is an option for additional interaction, such as starting and stopping, slow motion and quick motion, etc., then this has to be taken into account during the synchronization.

### 8.5.4 Synthetic Synchronization

In contrast to live synchronization, the main goal in synthetic synchronization is not the true playback of LDU relationships, but instead its flexible handling.

1. Temporal relationships between LDUs are specified during the *definition phase*. The following example shows this process for the creation of a multimedia message. In this example, four voice-encoded messages were recorded; the messages describe each a single element of an engine. This engine turns once by 360 degrees in an existing motion picture sequence. A software tool is used to produce the relationships between the video sequence images and the audio information. Finally, a short letter is added to the message, before it is sent.

2. Previously defined synchronization relationships are evaluated and implemented during the *presentation phase*. In our example, the multimedia message was received and is ready to be represented. For this purpose, the user could read the cover letter and then start the motion picture information. When the user displays one of the described views, the video stream is stopped and the audio segment starts playing. This happens implicitly by evaluating a previously defined LDU relationship.

When taking a closer look at the definition phase, we notice the difference between explicit and implicit definition. The *explicit synchronization* is defined by the creator of the relationship (see the above example, or the definition with the independent, `sequential`, and `parallel` operators in Figure 8-27). An *implicit definition* is done directly by the multimedia system. This process was described in connection with live synchronization, so that it will not be repeated here.

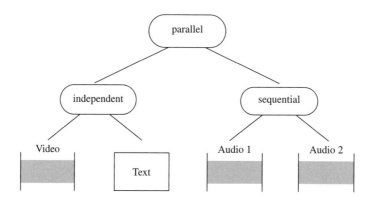

**Figure 8-27**   Synthetic synchronization; example of a definition.

One important characteristic refers to the time when the live synchronization is defined. Normally, this is done when the information is created, but it could also be done during the presentation.

We will now consider an example where a travel agency maintains timetable information on a computer. When a request is made, the system outputs a piece of text and some voice information. In this example, the system does not use all options for complete collection of information; instead, the process is defined when the multimedia information is created. The final synchronization relationships are created automatically during the presentation phase.

### 8.5.4.1   Defining a Synthetic Synchronization

A synthetic synchronization can be defined in many different ways. All the methods available to define a synthetic synchronization relate directly to existing information technologies (e.g., database or office automation systems):

- Databases can be used to express relationships through relations. A *relation* can be thought of as a temporal link, which is interpreted accordingly by a multimedia database system. A query language can then be used to embed such a synthetic synchronization. This specification could also be written by use of time-specific Petri networks (see Section 8.9.3), which are translated into a relational schema [Lit91].
- Hypertext documents use *links* to create relationships between the information units they manage. Such a link could also include the required temporal relationships in hypermedia documents.

- Dedicated multimedia editors normally allow the definition of this type of relationships. [BHL91] introduces such a tool with regard to synchronization. Existing products include languages and other methods to define synthetic synchronization [Moo90].

In the simplest case, a previously defined sequence, based on synthetic synchronization, with the given relationships can be played back during the presentation phase. These relationships are fixed and can not be changed, or should not be changed. Note that this does not violate the user's option to *navigate* through multimedia information. However, existing temporal references should not be changed.

In a more complex environment, it is possible to define an independent synthetic synchronization during the presentation time. In this case, the information and its temporal reference to other information units can be changed by the reader interactively.

Neither of these two options offer the desired solution. We want to be able to both predefine a fixed synthetic synchronization and to change it during the presentation.

The two previous sections emphasized the set of characteristics of the two synchronization types. Live synchronization is *merely* the natural playback of various information relationships that existed in advance and/or remotely. The important point is here that the implementation should be hidden from the user. This aspect could be considered as part of the synthetic synchronization. More specifically, the multimedia system creates the relationships during the definition phase itself and presents them later without any interaction options worth mentioning. In synthetic synchronization, the requirement for a flexible definition method is important, in addition to the representation.

## 8.6 System Components Involved in Synchronization

In this section, we will first deal with live synchronization. We can assume that multimedia applications will always use multiple media. Therefore, these applications normally use one or both synchronization types. However, the use of temporal relationships occurs on very different levels. The actual requirements arise at the user interface, where all references between the media have to be represented correctly. For this reason, we may assume that these references do not have to be evaluated at any other point of the system. The same applies to the presentation of synthetic synchronization. The definition of synchronization relationships has to be embedded in the information architectures and the corresponding tools.

One of the prerequisites for successful live synchronization is that ideal system components, such as storage media with capacities in the gigabyte range, guaranteed real-time behavior, high data transfer rates for motion pictures, and fast optional access, are available, particularly for the presentation. Real system components limit their storage capacity for continuous media and have a very limited data transfer rate with regard to video. For this reason, various parts of computer systems are involved in the synchronization process:

- For example, if we were to create an audiovisual tutorial in acceptable quality we would have to expect very high storage cost, even when using a high compression rate, i.e., at least approx. 650 Mbps per hour. Optical storage devices offer the benefit for playback at much less cost, compared to other random-access storage media. However, random positioning of the laser takes about 120 ms (due to the change in the speed of revolution and positioning of the laser over the corresponding block). For this reason, previously random-stored data streams cannot be combined on CDs for playback. To achieve temporal synchronization, the information has to be stored in an interleaved way. This requirement may have to be taken into account when a live synchronization is created.

- Other hardware components are only indirectly relevant for synchronization. Each component should offer a guaranteed data transfer rate, ideally with constant end-to-end delay. The requirements in this respect are similar to real-time requirements [SH91], having an effect on bus systems and storage components.

- Multimedia database systems can be used to maintain and manage these data volumes [Mey91]. Live synchronization can be defined by use of relations and as an integral part of query languages. These relationships have to be interpreted correctly when synchronized data are reproduced.

- The operating system is responsible for the management of audio and video devices used for input and output, and ensures that the required resources are available for processing. This type of resource management includes the reservation and actual management (*scheduling*) with an efficient internal data flow, adapted to the multimedia requirements. Synchronization requirements have to be communicated to the operating system, so that appropriate actions can be taken. For example, if a piece of text is to appear concurrently with the display of a specific single image in a specific window, then the operating system can call the function selected by the user while it processs the image. Naturally, an appropriate interface has to be available to define such requirements.

For data transmission between multiple computers, the connecting networks and protocols have to be appropriately designed. If we transfer data streams from multiple media over different transport connections, then the following aspects should be taken into account: Individual protocol data units (PDUs) should ideally be transmitted over the same path between a source and one or several sinks; otherwise excessive jitter with increased storage requirement and increased end-to-end delay would result. All protocol data units of the connections relating to the live synchronization would have to meet this requirement. If the live synchronization flows over different connections, then it is very difficult to ensure suitable QoS parameters. Current protocols do not well support a live synchronization between several connections.

This brief excursion into the functions required in different components of a computer system lets assume that neither of the two synchronization types can be fully implemented today. However, if we are ready to make compromises with regard to the maximum requirements of live synchronization and synthetic synchronization (e.g., only selected applications should use this functionality), then current implementations are indeed possible.

The following section describes various possibilities to define relationships between LDUs, which have been implemented in the prototypes mentioned earlier.

## 8.7  A Reference Model for Multimedia Synchronization

A *reference model* helps to understand the large number of requirements to multimedia synchronization. Such a model is useful to identify the structure of runtime mechanisms and the interfaces between runtime mechanisms, and to compare system solutions for multimedia synchronization systems.

We will first discuss existing classification methods, and then present a four-layer model, which can be used to classify multimedia synchronization systems. Considering that many multimedia synchronization mechanisms work in a network environment, we will also discuss special synchronization tasks in a distributed environment, and how they relate to the reference model.

### 8.7.1  Existing Classification Methods

An extensive classification method was introduced by Little and Ghafoor [LG90]. This method distinguishes between a physical level, a system level, and a human level, but does not include a detailed description of classification criteria. Other classification methods distinguish between intra-stream (fine-grained) synchronization and inter-stream (coarse-grained) synchronization, or between live and synthetic synchronization [LG90, SM92b].

The model proposed by Gibbs, Breiteneder and Tschichritzis [GBT93] maps a synchronized media object to a non-interpreted byte stream. In this model, the multimedia objects consist of derived media objects, composed of rearranged media sequences, e.g., scenes from a complete video. The components of these media sequences are themselves components of a non-interpreted byte stream.

Ehley, Furth and Ilyas [EFI94] classify inter-media synchronization technologies that can be used to control *jitter* (delay variation) between media streams, depending on the type and location of the synchronization control. They distinguish between distributed control based on protocols and distributed control based either on servers or on nodes without server structure. For local synchronization control, the authors classify the control on various levels, using local servers.

These classification methods seem to be orthogonal. Each method deals only with a few specific aspects. These methods do not meet the requirements we identified above for a synchronization reference model. A better method called *three-layer classification method* was proposed by Meyer, Effelsberg and Steinmetz [MES93]. The three layers are:

- The media layer for intra-stream synchronization of continuous media.
- The stream layer for inter-stream synchronization of media streams.
- The object layer for presentation, including the presentation of continuous media objects and the specification layer to process complex multi-stream multimedia applications.

Typical objects and operations are identified on each layer. In addition, the application has access on each of these layers, either directly or indirectly over a higher layer. This method meets the requirements identified for a reference model, so that we will discuss this model in more detail below.

Figure 8-28 shows a four-layer synchronization reference model. Each layer implements synchronization mechanisms supplied by a suitable interface. These interfaces can be used to specify and/or implement temporal relationships. Each interface defines services, i.e., it offers the user options to define his or her requirements. An interface can also be used either directly by the application or by the next higher layer to implement an interface. Higher layers implement a programming capability to a higher abstraction level and QoS abstractions.

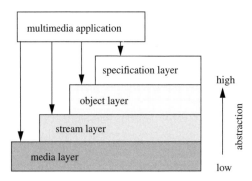

**Figure 8-28**   A four-layer reference model.

## 8.7.2   The Synchronization Reference Model

This section describes the typical objects and operations for each layer in the four-layer synchronization model shown in Figure 8-28. The semantics for objects and operations are the main criteria to ensure that they can be assigned to one of the layers.

Detailed programming examples that can be derived from a real interface are supplied by an interface, a prototype, or a standard. They demonstrate how these methods support a subsequent synchronization process. The scenario of the programming examples given here is to display subtitles during the playback of a digital movie, where these subtitles have to appear at predefined times.

### 8.7.2.1 Media Layer

On the *media layer*, an application handles one single continuous media stream as an LDU sequence. The abstraction offered by this layer is a device-independent interface with operations like read (device-handle, LDU) and write (device-handle, LDU). Systems like the *Audio Device System* of Sun [TP91] offering such types of interfaces have been available since the beginning of the nineties.

To build a continuous media stream that uses the abstractions supplied by the media layer, an application runs one process for each stream in the form shown in the following example:

```
window = open("Videodevice"); \\ Create a video output window
movie = open("File"); \\ Open the video file
while (not eof(movie)) { \\ Loop
  read(movie, &ldu); \\ Read LDU
  if (ldu.time == 20) \\ Start the presentation
    print("Subtitle 1"); \\ of the synchronized subtitles
  else if (ldu.time == 26)
    print("Subtitle 2");
  write(window, ldu);}\\ Present LDU
close(window);\\
Close window close(movie); \\ Close file
```

The process continues reading and writing LDUs as long as there are data available. The synchronous retrieval of a subtitle is controlled by the timestamps contained in the LDUs. An LDU will be retrieved if its timestamp has a specific value.

The application that uses this layer is responsible for resynchronization. For this purpose, it can use mechanisms for flow control between one generating and one consuming device. When several streams run in parallel, then the common use of resources may impair their real-time requirements. Normally, a resource reservation and management system is used to maintain the intra-stream synchronization [VHN92]. The operating system ensures the correct temporal handling of the relevant processes in real-time [MSS92]. In older systems, we also have to take the network components into account [AHS90, Fer91]. In the special case of lip synchronization, inter-stream synchronization could be implemented in a relatively easy way, i.e., by interleaving the simultaneous audio and video frames in the same LDU, e.g., in the form of an MPEG data stream. Note that the application continues displaying discrete media objects and user interventions.

Implementations of the media layer can be either in a simple form, or allow access to interleaved media streams.

### 8.7.2.2    Stream Layer

The *stream layer* deals with continuous media streams and media stream groups. A group presents all streams in parallel by using mechanisms for inter-stream synchronization. The abstraction supplied by the stream layer is called *streams with time parameters*. The quality of service relates to parameters for inter-stream synchronization within a stream and inter-stream synchronization between the streams of the group.

Continuous media in the stream layer are referred to as a *data flow*, which is subject to implicit temporal constraints: individual LDUs are not visible. Streams are processed in a real-time environment (RTE), where each process is limited by well-defined time specifications [Her92]. On the other side, the applications using the stream layer service run in a non real-time environment (NRTE), where the processes of events are controlled by the time management of the operating system.

Typical operations an application could call to control streams and groups within the NRTE include `start (stream)`, `stop (stream)`, `create_group (list_of_streams)`, `start (group)`, and `stop (group)`. The interaction with discrete media objects and user interventions is implemented by appending events to the continuous media streams, e.g., `setcuepoint (stream/group, at, event)`. Such an event is sent to the application whenever the stream reaches a previously specified point during the playback phase. In this layer, the application is also responsible for each discrete media object and the processing of user interventions. This leads to various application interfaces for continuous and discrete media, and user interventions.

The following example shows the use of the stream layer over a string command interface supplied by the MMPM:

```
open digitalvideo alias ex \\ Create video descriptor
load ex video.avs \\ Assign file to video descriptor
setcuepoint ex at 20 return 1 \\ Define event 1 for subtitle 1
setcuepoint ex at 26 return 2 \\ Define event 2 for subtitle 2
setcuepoint ex on \\ Activate
cuepoint events play ex\\ Start playing

switch read event() { \\ Event handling
  case 1: display("Subtitle 1") \\ If event 1 show subtitle 1
  case 2: display("Subtitle 2") \\ If event 2 show subtitle 2
}
```

The skip/pause algorithm introduced in [AH91] provides a detailed discussion how such a behavior can be implemented. The so-called *Orchestration Service* (see Section 8.10.5) [CGCH92] and the synchronization mechanism in ACME [AH91] (see Section 8.10.7) support stream-layer abstractions for distributed multimedia systems.

The stream-layer abstraction was derived from an abstraction normally supplied by the integration of analogous media in a computer system. The *Muse* and *Pygmalion* systems, which are part of the *Athena* project developed by MIT [HSA89], or the *DiME* system [SM92b] transport continuous media over separate channels through the computer. The connected devices can be controlled by sending commands over the RS-232C interface to start and stop media streams. In such systems, the live synchronization between multiple continuous media streams is implemented directly by dedicated process units. Stream-layer implementations can be distinguished by their support of distribution with regard to the guarantees they offer, and with regard to the type of streams they support (analogous and/or digital).

An application that uses the stream layer is responsible for starting, stopping, and grouping streams and for the definition of the quality of service required for temporal parameters supported by the stream layer. In addition, it has to organize the synchronization with other discrete media objects.

### 8.7.2.3 Object Layer

The *object layer* deals with all kinds of media and hides the differences between discrete and continuous media from the user.

The abstraction given by an application is that of a complete and synchronized presentation. This layer accepts a synchronization specification as its input and is responsible for the correct *scheduling* (time plan) of the entire presentation. In this respect, the abstractions are similar to those of the object model, which is discussed in [Ste90].

The object layer assumes the task of closing the gap between the runtime requirements of a synchronized presentation and the requirements of stream-oriented services. The object layer offers functions to calculate and execute complete presentation sequence schedules, including the presentation of non-continuous media objects. In addition, the object layer initiates preparatory actions required to achieve a correctly synchronized presentation. The object layer does not deal with inter-stream and intra-stream synchronization; it uses the services of the stream layer for this purpose.

One example for the integration of this layer is the MHEG specification. The objective of the MHEG standards is to encode multimedia and hypermedia information objects for presentation. We will give a simplified example how the scenario described above can be encoded in MHEG. Our example below uses a simple notation to demonstrate the basics of this reference model.

```
Composite { \\ Composite object
start-up link \\ How to start the
\\ presentation
```

```
viewer start-up viewer-list \\ Virtual views on
Viewer1: reference to Component1\\ component objects
Viewer2: reference to Component2
Viewer3: reference to Component3
Component1  \\ Component objects
reference to content "movie.avs" \\ of the composite
Component2
reference to content "Subtitle1"
Component3
reference to content "Subtitle2"
Link1       \\ Temporal relations
"when timestone status of Viewer1
becomes 20 then start Viewer2"
Link2 "when timestone status of Viewer1
becomes 26 then start Viewer3"
}
```

One possible implementation of the object layer is the MHEG runtime system called *MHEG Engine*. This engine evaluates the status of the objects and executes operations (actions), e.g., to prepare, start, stop, or destroy objects. For continuous media objects, the start operation can be mapped to the initiation of a media stream in the stream layer. For a discrete media object, this requires that the object is available. Preparatory times are required, e.g., to allow the stream layer to build a stream connection, or to prepare for the presentation in case of discrete media objects, e.g., to adapt the colors of an object to the colors supported by the output device. Such a preparation is started by the `prepare` action.

Implementations of the object layer can be divided with regard to the distribution options and the presentation of the calculated schedules. More specifically, we distinguish whether the implementation calculates a schedule and, if it does, whether the schedule is calculated before the presentation or at runtime. With regard to the distribution, implementations can be local, or distributed within a server structure, or fully distributed without any constraints. The application that uses the object layer is responsible for delivering a synchronization specification.

### 8.7.2.4    Specification Layer

The *specification layer* is an "open" layer, which means that it does not provide for an explicit interface. This layer includes applications and tools that can be used to generate synchronization specifications. Such tools include editors for synchronization and multimedia document and authoring systems, and tools used to convert specifications into an object-layer format. For example, such a conversion tool could be a formatting program for multimedia documents, creating a specification, similar to those proposed by [Mar91].

An example for synchronization editors is the synchronization editor included in the *MODE* system (see Section 8.10.4) [BHLM92], which can be used to specify the synchronization example given in Figure 8-13. A graphical interface lets the user select video and text objects, which should be used to display a video preview, to select the matching times when the subtitles should be displayed, to specify the temporal relationships, and to store the synchronization specification.

In addition, the specification layer is responsible for the mapping of the QoS requirements of the user interface to the QoS offered to interface the object layer.

The methods used to specify synchronization can be grouped into the following main categories:

- *Interval-based specifications*, which allow the specification of temporal relationships between the time intervals of the presentation of media objects.
- *Axis-based specifications*, which set the presentation results in relation to the axes, which are used jointly by the presentation objects.
- *Control-flow-based specifications*, where the presentation flow is synchronized at specific synchronization points.
- *Events-based specifications*, where the events of the presentation of media are stated to trigger presentation actions.

### 8.7.3 Synchronization in a Distributed Environment

The synchronization in a *distributed* environment is generally more complex than in a local environment. This is mainly due to the distributed storage of the synchronization information and different storage locations of the media objects embedded in the presentation. The communication between a storage medium and the presentation unit introduces additional delays and jitter. Often, there is also a problem with the communication patterns of different participants.

#### 8.7.3.1 Transporting the Synchronization Specification

The presentation component at the sink needs a synchronization specification at the time when an object is to be represented, which means that the synchronization specification has to be transferred to the sink. We distinguish between three main approaches for the transmission of synchronization requirements to the sink:

- *Transmission of the entire synchronization information before a presentation is started*. This approach is used frequently for synthetic synchronization. Normally, the application at the sink accesses the specification or a reference to the specification at the object-layer interface. The implementation of this approach is simple. With multiple sources, it allows easy handling of the media objects. The drawback of this approach is the delay caused by the transport of the synchronization specification before the presentation, particularly if the specification is stored in another location. The synchronization specification is transmitted by a component that resides in the object layer or in a higher layer.

• *Use of an additional synchronization channel.* This approach is shown in Figure 8-29; it is meaningful only if there is one single source. The approach is preferred for live synchronization, where synchronization information are not known in advance. This method does not introduce any additional delays. The drawback of this approach is that an additional communication channel is required, and this channel could introduce errors due to delays or a loss of synchronization specification units. This approach often neglects that the information for a given object has to be decoded in the synchronization channel, before that object can be presented, so that data communication over this channel has to maintain a certain temporal behavior. In addition, there may be problems when synchronized media objects originating from multiple sources have to be handled. The synchronization channel has to be managed by the object layer and eventually be supported by the stream layer, if streams are defined.

**Figure 8-29**   Use of a separate synchronization channel.

• *Multiplexing data streams.* The main benefit of multiplexing data streams over a communication channel (see Figure 8-30) is that the synchronization information can be transmitted together with the media units, so that no additional synchronization channel is needed. In addition, this approach does not introduce any additional delay. A major problem with this approach is that it can be difficult to select an optimum quality of service meeting the needs of all media involved. The synchronization information can also cause problems when the multiplexed media streams originate from several sources, which means that the stream layer is also involved. The use of multiplexed data streams can be implied by encoding standards, e.g., MPEG. MPEG defines an image stream, combining video, audio, and the related synchronization information. For this reason, this type of image stream can be thought of as one single medium in the stream layer. This type of stream can also be used for the synchronization to other media.

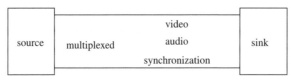

**Figure 8-30**   Multiplexed data streams, including both payload and synchronization information.

Sometimes it is possible to synchronize media objects by combining objects into one new object. This approach can be used to reduce communication resources, as shown in Figure 8-31. In this example, one animation and two bitmaps, which should overlay a video sequence, are mixed at the source to form a new video object, reducing the bandwidth requirements.

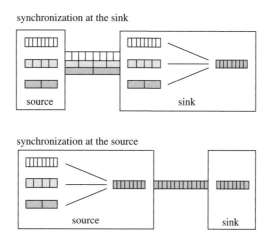

**Figure 8-31**   Arrangement of synchronization operations.

The combination of objects, including discrete media objects, has to be supported by the object layer, while the stream layer has to support the connection of media streams and the mixing of audio channels.

### 8.7.3.2   Clock Synchronization

The synchronization accuracy between the clocks of the source and the sinks is important, particularly in distributed systems. The temporal relationships have to be known in many synchronization schemes. This knowledge forms the basis for a global synchronization scheme using timers and schemes, so that operations on distributed units can be coordinated in terms of time. This ensures timely transmission and the coordination of operations so that they will not be executed too early, which would cause a buffer overflow.

This problem is particularly critical when different sources have to be synchronized (see Figure 8-32). When a synchronized audio/video presentation should start at time $T_{av}$ at the sink, then the audio transmission at source $A$ has to begin at time $T_a = T_{va} - N_{la} - O_a$, where $N_{la}$ is the known network delay, $O_a$ is the clock offset at the source, and $A$ is the clock offset at the sink. At a source, $B$, the transmission begins at time $T_v = T_{av} - N_{lv} - O_v$.

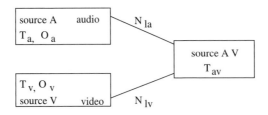

**Figure 8-32**  Synchronizing clocks in a distributed environment.

The offsets $O_a$ and $O_v$ are unknown. The resulting problem of timely transmission to the sink can be solved, if the maximum possible values of $O_a$ and $O_v$ are known. It is possible to allocate buffer capacities at the sink and to start the audio and video transmission in advance to ensure that the required media units will be available in time. The required buffer capacities at the sink depend on the possible matching (under the assumption that the buffer capacities are limited), so that it is important to limit the maximum offset. This can be achieved by using a clock synchronization protocol, e.g., the *Network Time Protocol* [Mil91]. This type of protocol allows to synchronize clocks with an accuracy in the range of 10 ms. When using radio time signals, which are also used by radio clocks, then the accuracies are below a range of milliseconds [Mil93]. This accuracy is considered appropriate for global timer synchronization of for distributed operation schedules.

The correct temporal transmission of the LDUs of a stream is a task assumed by the stream layer, which has to process the clock offset, while the object layer is responsible for timely transmission of discrete media objects.

### 8.7.3.3    Multiple Communication Relationships

Figure 8-33 shows a few communication patterns. Patterns with multiple sinks require the use of multicast and broadcast mechanisms at runtime to reduce the demand of resources (particularly network resources). In addition, inefficient multiple executions of the same operations in different sinks should be avoided. The stream layer is responsible for stream multicasting, while the object layer is responsible for efficient scheduling of the execution of the operations in each of the alternative communication patterns.

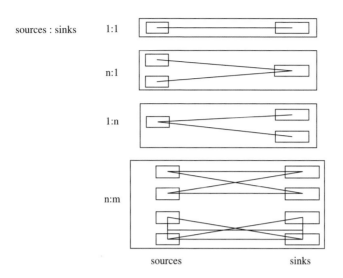

sources : sinks   1:1

n:1

1:n

n:m

sources                    sinks

**Figure 8-33**  Multiple communication relationships.

### 8.7.3.4   Multi-step Synchronization

Synchronization in a distributed environment is normally a process that involves *several steps*. During all these process steps, the synchronization has to be maintained such that the sink can perform the final synchronization. The process steps are as follows:

- Synchronization during the acquisition of an object, e.g., during the digitization of video frames.
- Synchronization of the information call, e.g., synchronized access to frames of a stored video.
- Synchronization during the transmission of the LDUs to the network, e.g., transmission of the frames of a video to the transport service of the interface.
- Synchronization during the transport, e.g., when using isochronous protocols.
- Synchronization of a sink, e.g., synchronized transmission to output devices.
- Synchronization within the output devices.

### 8.7.3.5   Manipulating a Presentation

The support of functions to manipulate objects, e.g., pause, fast forward, and fast reverse, at different presentation speeds, with direct access, and stop and replay options is difficult in a distributed environment. The information required for this support has to be distributed over the entire environment. Objects that have been prepared for the presentation in advance have to be deleted. Network connections may have changed, so that they have to be reestablished. For these reasons, it is difficult to avoid delays in the execution of these manipulation functions.

### 8.7.3.6    Consequences for Synchronization in a Distributed Environment

To achieve synchronization in a distributed environment, many decisions have to be made, including the selection of the transport type for the synchronization specification. At runtime, decisions have to be made about the location of the synchronization operations, which manage the clock offsets and handle the multicast and broadcast mechanisms. In particular, a coherent scheduling of the steps involved in the synchronization process and for the required object operations, e.g., compression, have to be worked out. In addition, some operations for the manipulation of a presentation require additional new scheduling at runtime.

In general, the execution of synchronized distributed presentations is a complex planning problem. The plan resulting from such a calculation is normally called *schedule* (time plan).

## 8.7.4   Characteristics of the Synchronization Reference Model

| Layer | Interface Abstraction | Tasks |
|---|---|---|
| Specification | The tools supporting the tasks in this layer have no higher interface. | Iditing<br>Formating<br>Mapping user-oriented QoS to the WoS abstraction in the object layer |
| Object | Synchronization specification<br>Objects hiding the types of integrated media<br>Media-oriented QoS (with regard to the acceptable skew and jitter) | Plan and coordinate presentation schedules<br>Initiate the presentation of continuous media objects in the stream layer<br>Initiate the presentation of discrete media objects<br>Initiate the preparatory presentation actions |
| Stream | Arrange streams and stream groups<br>Supply guarantees for intra-stream synchronization<br>Supply guarantees for inter-stream synchronization | Reserve resources and schedule LDU processing |
| Media | Provide device-independent access to LDUs<br>Supply guarantees for single LDU processing | File and device access |

**Table 8-4**    Overview on the layers of the synchronization reference model.

The reference model used for synchronization allows to structure and classify synchronization systems. The identification of the interfaces and layers allows a combination of existing solutions to form complete systems. Table 8-4 gives an overview of the interface abstractions and the tasks in all layers of this reference model. The classification of mechanisms and methods by each layer is summarized in Table 8-5.

| Layer | Classification Mechanism or Method |
|---|---|
| Specification | Method for synchronization specification: Interval-based specification Axis-based specification Control-flow-based specification Events-based specification |
| | Tool type: Text tool box Graphical tool box Converter |
| Object | Distribution type: Local Distributed, with servers Distributed, without servers |
| | Schedule calculation type: No calculation Calculation at compile time Calculation at runtime |
| Stream | Distribution type: Local Distributed |
| | Type of QoS guarantees: No QoS guarantees QoS guarantees by resource reservation |
| Media | Accessible data type: Single-medium data Interleaved, complex data |

**Table 8-5**   Classification of mechanisms and methods in the layers.

## 8.8   Sychronization Specification

The synchronization specification of a multimedia object describes all temporal dependencies of the embedded objects. It is generated by means of tools offered in the specification layer and used at the interface to the object layer. The synchronization defines the entire presentation, so that it represents a central task in multimedia systems. The following list describes and evaluates the requirements to the synchronization specification and specification methods.

A synchronization specification should consist of the following components:

- Intra-object specification for the media objects embedded in the presentation.
- Description of the QoS parameters for intra-object synchronization.
- Specification of the inter-object synchronization for media objects embedded in the presentation.
- Description of the QoS parameters for inter-object synchronization.

The synchronization specification is part of the description of a multimedia object. In addition, it can describe the form to be used to represent a media object. For example, a piece of text could be written in the form of characters on the screen or generated as audio sequence. A specification can allow either of these two options or a choice of presentation forms at runtime.

For live synchronization, the temporal relationships are defined implicitly during the recording phase. The QoS requirements of each of the media involved are determined at the beginning of the recording phase.

If synthetic synchronization is applied, then the specification has to be explicitly created. The literature describes various methods that can be used to describe a synthetic synchronization process. Some of these methods will be introduced in the next section.

### 8.8.1   Quality of Service in the Context of Synchronization

The required quality of Service (QoS) depends on the media and application used.

#### 8.8.1.1    QoS for a Media Object

The QoS specification for a media object includes the quality with regard to individual LDUs of a continuous media object and the accuracy required to meet the temporal relationships between the LDUs of that continuous media object.

Table 8-6 shows a few QoS parameters for a media object. The white fields contain qualities that are independent of temporal relationships. The light gray boxes include time-dependent qualities under a limited influence by the presentation system, because the quality depends on a set of choices during the recording process. Normally, the presentation system indicates merely quality losses. The dark gray boxes show the time qualities potentially under the full control of the presentation environment.

| Media | Image (e.g., bitmap) | Video | Audio |
|---|---|---|---|
| QoS | Color (chrominance, luminance) | Color (chrominance, luminance) | Linear or logarithmic sampling |
| | Resolution | Resolution | Sample size |
| | | Frame rate | Sampling rate |
| | | Jitter | Jitter |
| | | Error rate | Error rate |

**Table 8-6**   Some QoS parameters for the presentation of a media object.

### 8.8.1.2   QoS for Two Linked Media Objects

Synchronization requirements can be expressed by a quality-of-service specification. A QoS parameter can define the acceptable skew within the media data involved, in particular, it can define all possible synchronization limits. When audio and video components of a movie are stored as separate entries in a database, then lip synchronization may be an option to be considered, depending on the results mentioned in Section 8.2.2. In this connection, we will introduce the terms *presentation-level synchronization* and *production-level synchronization*:

• *Production-level synchronization* refers to the quality of service to be guaranteed prior to presenting the data at the user interface. It typically includes the recording of synchronized data for later playback. The stored data should be recorded "in sync", i.e., without skew. This applies particularly to situations where a file was stored in interleaved format. On the receiver side, the audiovisual information received is "in sync" with regard to the defined lip synchronization constraints. If we assume that the data are transmitted with a skew of +80 ms,and that audio and video LDUs are transmitted as one single multiplexed stream over the same transport connection, then this stream is represented "in sync". When the data are stored on hard disk and presented simultaneously at a local workstation and at a remote viewer site, then the QoS has to be specified for the correct transmission, i.e., between -160 ms and 0 ms. When the current skew is unknown, then this constraint could be applied twice at the remote viewer's workstation, so that the data would not be "in sync". In general, data intended for later processing or editing should correspond to the quality of the production level, i.e., they should not have skews.

• The presentation requirements discussed in Section 8.3 determine the *presentation-level synchronization*. This synchronization defines requirements for the user interface. It considers no further processing of the synchronized data. Presentation-level synchronization concentrates on the human perception of the synchronization. As shown in the previous section, recording of the current skew as part of control information facilitates the calculation of the required QoS requirement for the synchronization. This means that the QoS requirement of the synchronization is expressed by the admissible skew. The QoS values shown in Table 8-2 refer to the synchronization on the presentation level. Most values are results from comprehensive experiments and practical experience, while others originate from the referenced literature source. They serve as a general guideline for any QoS specification. In experiments for lip and pointer synchronization, it was found that many factors can influence these results. Nevertheless, these values can be generously used, depending on the actual contents.

### 8.8.1.3    QoS for Multiple Linked Media Objects

So far, we have studied media synchronization as a relationship between two different media or different data streams. This is the canonic basis for all types of media synchronization. In practice, however, we often have more than two linked data streams. A highly developed multimedia application scenario includes simultaneous handling of several sessions. As an example, consider a video conference where one window shows a speaker, accompanied by an audio broadcast from a pair of connected loudspeakers.

Video and audio data are put in relation to each other on the basis of the lip synchronization requirements, while Audio and telepointers are put in relation by pointer synchronization. We can then simply combine media synchronization by linking video data with a telepointer. In this example, we define the following skew values:

```
max skew (video ahead_of audio) = 80 ms
max skew (audio ahead_of video) = 80 ms
max skew (audio ahead_of pointer) = 740 ms
max skew (pointer ahead_of audio) = 500 ms
```

The above definition of skew values produces the following derived skew:

```
skew (video ahead_of pointer) =< 820 ms
skew (pointer ahead_of video) =< 580 ms
```

In general, this requirement can be derived easily from an accumulation of the canonic skew, like in the above example. The information collected by grouping the media involved is important both for the user and for the multimedia system, which has provide the service according to these values.

Sometimes, there are too many specifications for a synchronization skew, e.g., a language course including audio data in English and Spanish, and a patching video sequence. The language course could be structured so that video and audio should be lip-synchronized (+/-80 ms), regardless of the language. In addition, the phrases or sentences should be synchronized to ensure that the user can switch between the two languages (in this case, we would select a value of 400 ms). Of course, lip synchronization demands higher requirements than the synchronization between the languages, so that we would write the following skew specification (see Figure 8-34):

```
1. max skew (video ahead_of audio_english) = 80 ms
2. max skew (audio_english ahead_of video) = 80 ms
3. max skew (video ahead_of audio_spanish) = 80 ms
4. max skew (audio_spanish ahead_of video) = 80 ms
5. max skew (audio_english ahead_of audio_spanish) = 400 ms
6. max skew (audio_spanish ahead_of audio_english) = 400 ms
```

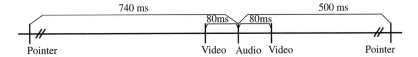

**Figure 8-34**   Example specifying skew values.

This specification consists of one set of linked requirements, which have to be fully met, so that we have to find the largest common denominator. For an arbitrary canonic form, we could calculate the derived skew values as follows:

```
1+2+3+4:
max skew (audio_english ahead_of audio_spanish) = 160 ms
max skew (audio_spanish ahead_of audio_english) = 160 ms

1+2+5+6:
max skew (video ahead_of audio_spanish) = 480 ms
max skew (audio_spanish ahead_of video) = 480 ms

3+4+5+6:
max skew (video ahead_of audio_english) = 480 ms
max skew (audio_english ahead_of video) = 480 ms
```

In the second step, we select the most rigid requirements:

```
1. max skew (video ahead_of audio_english) = 80 ms
2. max skew (audio_english ahead_of video) = 80 ms
3. max skew (video ahead_of audio_spanish) = 80 ms
4. max skew (audio_spanish ahead_of video) = 80 ms
5. max skew (audio_english ahead_of audio_spanish) = 160 ms
6. max skew (audio_spanish ahead_of audio_english) = 160 ms
```

In the next step, we can select an arbitrary set of synchronization requirements from the above derived calculations:

```
max skew (video ahead_of audio_english) = 80 ms
max skew (audio_english ahead_of video) = 80 ms
max skew (audio_english ahead_of audio_spanish) = 160 ms
max skew (audio_spanish ahead_of audio_english) = 160 ms
```

In summary, the procedures described above allow us to solve two related problems:

- When the application demands a set of linked synchronization requirements to be met by a multimedia system, then we can find the requirements that are subject to the largest constraints.
- When a set of individual synchronization requirements from different data streams is to be met, then we can calculate the required relationships between each pair of streams.

Both tasks appear in complex systems, when the QoS requirements have to be estimated, calculated, or negotiated. The next section will deal with these issues.

## 8.9   Specification Methods for Multimedia Synchronization

Complex specifications for multiple object synchronizations, including user interaction, require highly developed specification methods. The following requirements should be met by such a specification method:

- The method should support object consistency and maintenance of synchronization specifications. Media objects should be managed as logical units in the specification.
- The method should supply an abstraction of the contents of each media object. This abstraction should facilitate the specification of temporal relationships, referring to a part of the media object, but continue handling the media object as a logical unit.
- The method should allow easy description of all types of synchronization relationships.
- The method should support the integration of continuous and discrete media objects.
- The method should support the definition of QoS requirements, preferably expressed directly in the method. In addition, the method should support hierarchical synchronization levels to facilitate the processing of large and complex synchronization scenarios.

The following section evaluates specification methods based on the above criteria.

### 8.9.1   Interval-based Specification

An *interval-based synchronization specification* considers the duration of the presentation of an object as an interval. Two time intervals can be synchronized in 13 different types, [All83, Ham72], where some of these types can be inverted. Figure 8-35 shows a section of seven non-inverted rates, according to [LG90]. A simple method for synchronization specification of two media objects is able to use these seven types.

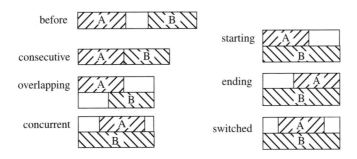

**Figure 8-35**   Types of temporal relationships between two objects.

An improved interval-based model [WR94] is based on interval relations. More specifically, it identifies 29 interval relations, which are defined as disjoint relations of the base interval relations. To facilitate the synchronization specification, ten operators are defined, which can then be used to edit these interval relations. These operations are shown in Figure 8-36. The duration of a presentation, *A* or *B*, a delay, $d_i$, and a subgroup of +0, are not known in advance, because the duration of a presentation or a delay that may occur, are not predictable either. In addition, the operations `before  end-of`, `delayed`, `start in`, `end in`, `cross`, and `overlaps d`$_i$ must not be 0.

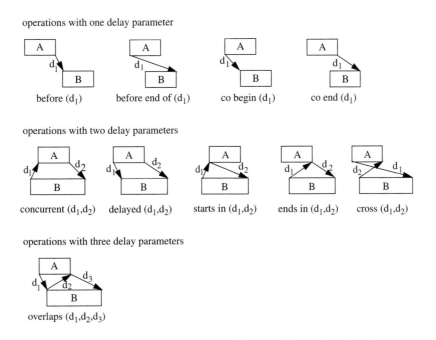

**Figure 8-36**   Operations used in the improved interval-based method.

This model can be used to specify a slide show with the slides $slide_i$ $(1 \leq i \leq 1)$ and an audio object `audio` as follows:

```
Slide1 co begin(0) Audio
Slidei before(0) Slidei+1 . one piece missing here.
```

The lip synchronization between an audio object `audio` and a video object `video` can be specified as follows:

```
Audio while(0,0) Video.
```

The application example shown in Figure 8-13 can be specified as follows:

```
Audio1 while(0,0) Video
Audio1 before(0) Recorded Interaction
Recorded Interaction before(0) B1
P1 before(0) P2
P2 before(0) P3
P3 before(0) Interaction
P3 before(0) Animation
Animation while(2,5) Audio2
Interaction before(0) P4.
```

This model allows us to define the duration of continuous and discrete media objects. This duration is used in the example to specify the presentation duration for the objects $slide_1$ through $slide_3$. The duration of the user intervention is unknown, so that we can specify a duration of +0.

One major advantage of this model is that it deals with LDUs of unknown duration in an easy way, supporting user interaction. For example, we could specify additional indeterminate temporal relationships simply by defining intervals for periods and delays. The disjoint relation of operators can be used to specify non-parallel presentations. In summary, this is a very flexible model, allowing the specification of presentations with many runtime presentation variants.

Note that the model does not include skew specifications. Although temporal relationships between media objects can be specified directly, it does not allow the specification of temporal relationships between subunits of objects. Such relationships have to be defined indirectly in the skew specification, like in the example with the `while` operations for audio and animation, or by decomposing the objects. The flexibility of specified presentations can lead to inconsistencies at runtime. For example, a non-parallel relation is defined for two video objects, *A* and *B*. At runtime, *A* could execute, while *B* could be linked to the end of a user intervention by a `before(0)` relation. Video *B* should start as soon as this user intervention ends. The problem is that it cannot start due to the non-parallel relation. To solve such problems, we have to define how to deal with such inconsistencies in the model; alternatively, we let them be detected and their specifications rejected before runtime. It is easy to define hierarchies. The evaluation of the improved interval-based method is summarized in Table 8-7.

| Benefits | Drawbacks |
|---|---|
| Logical objects can be maintained. | The specification is complex. |
| Good abstraction of media contents. | The skew QoS has to be specified separately. |
| Easy integration of discrete objects. | Allows direct specification of temporal relationships between media objects, but not for subunits of media objects. |
| Easy integration of interactive objects. | Resolution of unknown relations at runtime can cause inconsistencies. |
| Supports the specification of unknown temporal relations. | |

**Table 8-7**   Evaluation of the improved interval-based method.

## 8.9.2   Axis-based Synchronization

*Axis-based synchronization* means that presentation events, such as start and end of a presentation, are mapped to axes, which are common to all objects of a presentation.

### 8.9.2.1   Synchronization Based on a Global Timer

To implement a synchronization based on a global timer, all individual media objects are bound to an axis, representing an abstraction of the real world. This specification method is used in [HSA89], to name one example. This method describes the synchronization by linking all objects. They are mapped independently on a time axis. This means that the removal of one object does not influence the synchronization of the other objects.

With some modifications, this type of specification can also be used in the model of [TGD91]. For this purpose, we could use a *world time* accessible to all objects. Each object can then map this world time to its local time, moving along its local time axis. If the difference between the world time and the local time exceeds a specified threshold value, then the local time has to be resynchronized to the world time. Such a time axis mechanism is also used in [DM92].

Synchronizing objects along a time axis facilitates also a very good abstraction of the internal structure of a single media object and integrates multimedia objects. The definition of the beginning of a subtitle presentation in relation to a scene in a video stream does not require any knowledge about the pertaining video frames. However, the synchronization can be defined only for fixed times, so that problems will arise when objects include LDUs with unknown duration.

In addition, a synchronization based on a global timer may not be sufficient to synchronize relationships between multiple presentation streams. Depending on the coherence of these presentation streams, the synchronization based on a common time axis could be either *too strong* or *too weak*. One solution to this problem is to define an additional QoS requirement for each pair of media streams. The use of global timers requires the media streams to be able to synchronize themselves to the global timer. This could be difficult for audio streams due to resampling problems. For this reason, many designs use the audio stream itself as a global timer. Note that this could still cause problems when several audio streams have to be synchronized.

Figure 8-37 shows the specification for our application example from Figure 8-13. We can see that there is no intuitive way to deal with the unknown duration of a user interaction. Table 8-8 summarizes the evaluation of the time axis method.

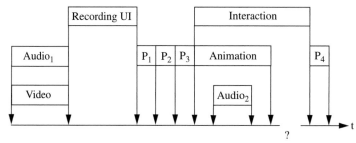

**Figure 8-37**   Example for a time axis specification.

| **Benefits** | **Drawbacks** |
|---|---|
| Easy to understand. | Objects with unknown duration cannot be integrated; expansions to this model are required. |
| Supports easy implementation of hierarchies. | The QoS skew has to be defined indirectly by a common time axis or additional QoS specification. |
| Easy integration of discrete objects. | |
| Easy handling of objects thanks to mutual independence. | |
| Good abstraction of media contents. | |

**Table 8-8**   Evaluating the synchronization based on timers.

## 8.9.2.2    Synchronization Based on Virtual Axes

*Virtual time axes* like those used in the *Athena* project [HSA89] or in the *HyTime* standard [Org92] are a generalization of the time axis approach. We can use this specification method to specify coordinated systems with user-defined measurement units. A synchronization specification is executed along these axes. In addition, it is possible to use several virtual axes to create a virtual coordination space. As an example, consider a music description with notes, as shown in Figure 8-38. The sound frequency is defined by the position on the notes line. Both the sequence and the duration are defined by the axis labeled with the time measurement unit.

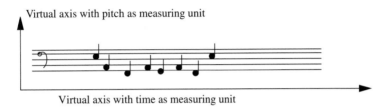

**Figure 8-38**   Musical notes as an example for a virtual axis synchronization.

These virtual axes are mapped to real axes at runtime. In the example shown in Figure 8-38, the pitch axis is mapped to the audio frequency, and the time axis is mapped to a timer. If we want to implement the application example from Figure 8-13 by using this approach, we would specify a time axis and an interaction axis (see Figure 8-39), where the latter should use interaction events as its measurement unit. Table 8-9 summarizes the evaluation of the virtual axis method.

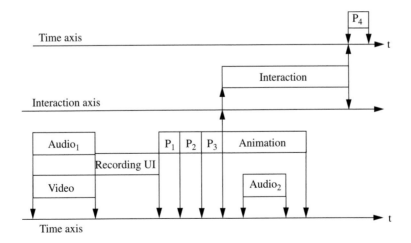

**Figure 8-39**   Example for a virtual time axis specification.

| Benefits | Drawbacks |
|---|---|
| Easy to understand. | Specification can become complicated when several axes are involved. |
| Supports easy implementation of hierarchies. | The skew QoS has to be defined indirectly by additional QoS specifications. |
| The specification can often be created with the possible problem dimension in mind. | The mapping of axes at runtime can become complex and time-consuming. |
| Easy handling of objects thanks to mutual independence. | |
| Good abstraction of media contents. | |

**Table 8-9**   Evaluation of the synchronization specification using virtual axes.

### 8.9.3   Control-flow-based Specification

Specifications based on the *control flow* synchronize the flow of coinciding presentation processes at predefined points within the presentation.

#### 8.9.3.1   Basic Hierarchical Specification

*Hierarchical synchronization descriptions* [Gro89, SS90] are based on two main synchronization operations: the *serial synchronization* and the *parallel synchronization* of actions (see Figure 8-40). In a hierarchical synchronization specification, multimedia objects are viewed as a tree with nodes representing the serial or parallel presentation of branching subtrees.

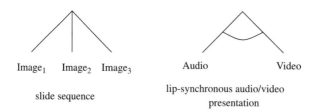

**Figure 8-40**   Serial and parallel presentations.

An action can be either *atomic* or *bound*. An atomic action treats the presentation of one single media object, user input, or delay. A bound action is a combination of synchronization operators and atomic actions.

The introduction of a delay as a possible action [LG90] enables us to model additional synchronization behavior, e.g., delays in serial presentations, or delayed presentations of objects in a parallel synchronization.

Hierarchical structures are easy to handle and commonly used. Restrictions of the hierarchical structure result from the fact that each action can be synchronized either at its beginning or at its end. This means, for example, that the presentation of subtitles in parts of a video stream requires that the video stream needs to be decomposed into several consecutive components. Figure 8-41 shows this situation with the synchronization specification for the animation and audio blocks from our example introduced in Section 8.1.2. The animation has to be decomposed into several parts, i.e., `Animation₁`, `Animation₂`, and `Animation₃`, to ensure that it will be synchronized correctly to the audio block.

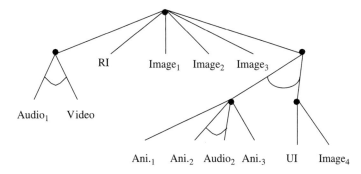

**Figure 8-41** Example for a hierarchical specification (RI = recorded interaction, Aud = Audio, Ani = Animation, UI = user interaction).

Accordingly, a synchronized multimedia object used as a component in another synchronization can no longer be handled as an abstract unit, when we have to synchronize between the beginning and the end of a presentation. This means that hierarchical structures do not support an adequate abstraction for the internal structure of a multimedia object. In addition, some synchronization conditions cannot be represented in hierarchical structures.

The three objects shown in Figure 8-42 are presented in parallel, where each pair of objects is synchronized to each other, but independently of a third object. To specify this synchronization, we have to add more synchronization points. Table 8-10 summarizes the evaluation of the basic hierarchical method.

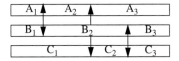

**Figure 8-42**  Example for a synchronization that cannot be described.

| Benefits | Drawbacks |
|---|---|
| Easy to understand. | Presentation points have to be added for discrete media objects. |
| Intuitive support of hierarchies. | The skew QoS has to be described separately. |
| Esy integration of interactive objects. | Media objects have to be decomposed into several components for synchronization. |
| | No appropriate abstraction for contents of the media objects. |
| | Some synchronization scenarios cannot be described. |

**Table 8-10**  Evaluation of the basic hierarchical specification.

### 8.9.3.2    Reference Points

In *synchronization over reference points* [Ste90, BHLM92], continuous single media objects are handled as sequences of closed LDUs. The start and stop times for the presentation of a media object, introduced in addition to the start times for the subunits of continuous media objects, are called *reference points*. The synchronization between media objects is specified by connecting the reference points defined for these media objects. A set of connected reference points is called *synchronization point*. The presentation of the subunits that belong to the same synchronization point has to be started or stopped when the synchronization point is reached. This approach specifies temporal relationships between objects without making explicit reference to time.

Similar to the synchronization based on a time axis, this description allows us to synchronize objects at an arbitrary time. In addition, this method lets us easily integrate presentations of objects with unknown duration. Another benefit is that the use of this type of specification is very intuitive.

One drawback of the synchronization with reference points is that it requires mechanisms to discover inconsistencies. In addition, this synchronization does not allow the specification of delays in a multimedia presentation. To solve this problem, Steinmetz [Ste90] proposes a *time specification* that can be used to specify explicit time-based delays. Another solution to this problem is to use timers. The specification based on a global timer can be thought of as a subgroup of the synchronization with reference points. More specifically, a timer like the one shown in Figure 8-10 can be used globally, where all objects will then synchronize exclusively to this timer.

In a synchronization specification with reference points, the coherence between data streams can be described by an appropriate set of synchronization points between two given data streams. A tight lip synchronization with a maximum skew of +/-80 ms can be implemented by setting a specific synchronization point, e.g., for the second frame of a video (see Figure 8-43). If no lip synchronization is required, then it may be sufficient to define a set of synchronization points every ten frames in the video. This means that this specification method integrates the specification of the skew QoS.

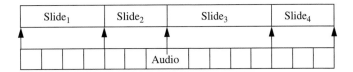

**Figure 8-43**   Example of a slide show with an audio sequence, using the reference point model.

Figure 8-44 shows an example of the synchronized integration of continuous and discrete media objects. The start and stop of a slide show are initiated when the matching LDUs in the audio presentation are reached.

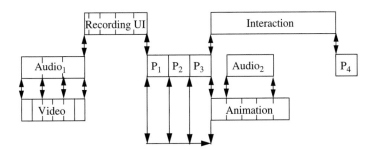

**Figure 8-44**   Example of a specification with reference points, integrating both continuous and discrete media and open and closed LDUs.

The application example shown in Figure 8-41 can be fully specified by the synchronization model with reference points. In the synchronization method with reference points, hierarchies can be created by treating a set of synchronized objects as one single object, where the beginning of the first object and the end of the last object serve as reference points. Virtual reference points can be specified for this presentation and mapped to the reference points within the hierarchy. However, the semantics of this mapping can become complex when objects with unknown duration have to be integrated into the hierarchy. Table 8-11 summarizes the evaluation of this reference point method.

| Benefits | Drawbacks |
|---|---|
| Easy integration of interactive objects. | Difficult to handle. |
| Expands easily to new events. | Complex specification. |
| Flexible, because each event can be specified. | Difficult to maintain. |
|  | Integration of continuous objects requires additional timers. |
|  | Skew QoS has to be described separately. |
|  | Use of hierarchies is difficult. |

**Table 8-11**     Evaluation of the specification by reference points.

### 8.9.3.3     Time-specific Petri Networks

Another type of specification is based on *Petri networks* [Gun92, LG91], which expands the time specifications at various points. A time-specific Petri network is based on the following rules:

- A transition fires when there is a non-blocking token in all input places.
- When a transition fires, the token is removed from all input points and placed to the output lines.
- Once a token was placed to a new place, it is blocked for as long as it remains in this place.

For example, a slide show could be specified by allocating the corresponding duration to points (see Figure 8-45).

**Figure 8-45**     Example of a slide show in Petri network specification.

For continuous media objects, each point in the Petri network represents one LDU. Lip synchronization can be modeled by using transitions to connect the appropriate LDUs (see Figure 8-46).

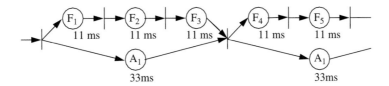

**Figure 8-46**   Lip synchronization in Petri network specification.

It is also possible to combine a set of related LDUs at one point, as long as there is no inter-object synchronization between these LDUs and other LDUs. A hierarchy can be built by subnetworks allocated to one point. The duration of the longest path in this subnetwork is then allocated to that point (Figure 8-47).

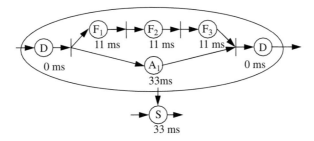

**Figure 8-47**   A Petri network hierarchy, including the synchronization of $A_1$ and $F_1$ through $F_3$.

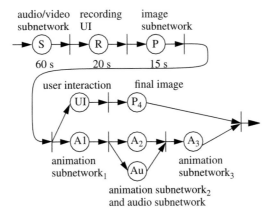

**Figure 8-48**   Application example from Figure 8-13 in Petri network specification.

Our application example from Figure 8-13 could be modeled as shown in Figure 8-48. Note that this figure does not show the subnetworks, because they can be created by simply using the techniques described above.

Time-specific Petri networks support any type of synchronization specification. However, its main drawbacks are that the specification is rather complex and the abstraction of the contents of media objects is insufficient, because the media objects have to be decomposed into subobjects, similar to the hierarchical specification. Table 8-12 summarizes the evaluation of time-specific Petri networks.

| Benefits | Drawbacks |
|---|---|
| Allows the creation of hierarchies. | Difficult to handle. |
| Easy integration of discrete objects. | Complex specification. |
| Easy integration of interactive objects. | Media objects have to be decomposed. |
| Integrated skew QoS. | No appropriate abstraction for the contents of media objects. |

**Table 8-12**    Evaluation of the synchronization specification by use of Petri networks.

### 8.9.4   Events-based Synchronization

In an *events-based synchronization*, presentation actions are initiated by synchronization events, similar to *HyTime* (see Section 8.10.2) and *HyperODA* [App89]. Typical presentation actions are:

- Start a presentation.
- Stop a presentation.
- Prepare a presentation.

The events initiated by presentation actions can be external (e.g., generated by a timer) or internal with regard to the presentation, in which case events are triggered when a continuous media object reaches the specific LDU. Table 8-13 shows an events-based synchronization for parts of our application example.

| Event / Action | Start | Audio$_1$.stop | Timer$_1$.ready | ... |
|---|---|---|---|---|
| Audio$_1$ | start | | | |
| Video | start | | | |
| Image$_1$ | | start | | |
| Timer$_1$ | | start(3) | stop | |
| Image$_2$ | | | start | |
| ... | | | | |

**Table 8-13**    Example for an events-based specification.

This type of specification expands easily to new synchronization types. Its main drawback is that it is difficult to handle in realistic scenarios. The user may easily get confused by the type of state transitions defined in the synchronization specification, so that both the creation and the maintenance are difficult. Table 8-14 summarizes the evaluation of the events-based method.

| Benefits | Drawbacks |
|---|---|
| Expands easily to new events. | Difficult to handle. |
| Flexible, because each event can be specified. | Complex specification. |
| Easy integration of interactive objects. | Difficult to maintain. |
| | Integration of continuous objects requires additional timers. |
| | Use of hierarchies is difficult. |
| | Skew QoS has to be described separately. |

**Table 8-14**    Evaluation of the events-based specification.

## 8.9.5   Scripts

A *script* in this context is a textual description of a synchronization scenario [IBM90, TGD91]. The elements of a script are activities and subscripts. Scripts often grow into complete programming languages implementing time operations. Scripts can relate to or make use of various specification methods. A typical example is a script based on a fundamental hierarchical method, supporting three main operations: the serial presentation, the parallel presentation, and the repeated presentation of media objects.

The following example shows a script for our application example from Figure 8-13, where >> designates a serial presentation, \& designates a parallel presentation, and n designates a presentation that is repeated *n* times [TGD91].

```
activity DigAudio Audio("video.au");
activity SMP  Video("video.smp");
activity XRecorder Recorder("window.rec");
activity Picture  Picture1("picture1.jpeg");
activity Picture Picture2("picture2.jpeg");
activity Picture  Picture3("picture3.jpeg");
activity Picture Picture4("picture4.jpeg");
activity StartInteraction  Selection;
activity DigAudio AniAudio("animation.au");
activity RTAnima  Animation("animation.ani");
script Picture_sequence 3Pictures= Picture1.Duration(5) >>
Picture2.Duration(5) >>
Picture3.Duration(5);
script Lipsynch AV = Audio & Video;
script AniComment AA = Animation & AniAudio.Translate(2);
script Multimedia Application_example {
AV >>
Record. UI >>
3Pictures >>
( (Selection >> Picture4) & AA )
```

Scripts offer many options, because they represent a complete programming environment. One drawback is that these methods are procedural rather than declarative, while the declarative approach appears to be easier to understand for non-expert users. Table 8-15 summarizes the evaluation of the script method.

| Benefits | Drawbacks |
|---|---|
| Good support of hierarchies. | Difficult to handle. |
| Logical objects can be maintained. | Complex specification. |
| Easy integration of interactive objects. | Implicit use of common timers. |
| Easy integration of discrete objects. | Skew QoS has to be described separately. |
| Expands easily to new synchronization constructs. | |
| Programmable, offering high flexibility. | |

**Table 8-15**   Evaluation of the synchronization specification by use of scripts.

### 8.9.6 Summary of Synchronization Specification Methods

The specification methods for multimedia synchronization described in this section offer various specification options and differ mainly with regard to their easiness of use. Many of these methods merely present different "views" of the same problem. The set of different specification options limits the portability between specifications in different methods of a common subgroup.

The choice of an appropriate specification method depends on the application and the existing environment. The temporal behavior of multimedia objects is only one part of a presentation, its contents being the major aspect to be kept in mind. The chosen method has to integrate well into the selected environment. There is no "best" or "worst" solution for all cases. For simple presentations without user interaction, the methods based on a global timer appear to be suitable. For complex structures with interaction options, the reference point model seems to be a suitable method.

In many cases, the user will not specify the synchronization directly by using a specification method. Instead, many users will use a graphical authoring system that produces the specifications based on various methods automatically. Experience has shown that the user interface is typically built on one of these specification methods, so that the benefits and drawbacks of a method reflect on the user interface. In addition, many authoring systems allow the author to leave the environment of the highly developed graphical representation to specify a complex synchronization directly on the lowest level of the synchronization specification. This could be the textual level, supplied by the underlying method.

## 8.10 Case Studies

This section described some interesting approaches to multimedia synchronization and classifies each case based on the reference model introduced above. In particular, we will study the synchronization aspects within standardized multimedia synchronization exchange and the pertaining runtime environments as well as multimedia systems that include the layers of the synchronization model discussed in the previous section.

### 8.10.1 Synchronization in MHEG

The most abstract layer in *MHEG* offers a virtual coordination system that can be used to specify the layout and the relationships of contents objects in space and time, according to the specification method based on virtual axes. The highest layer uses a time axis with infinite length, measured in *generic time units* (*GTUs*). The MHEG runtime environment has to map these GTUs to *physical time units* (*PTUs*). If no mapping is specified, then a GTU is used as a default value and mapped to 1 ms. The spatial axes (X for length, Y for width, and Z for height) are used in the highest layer. Each axis has a limited length at an interval of [-32768, +32767]. The units used here are called *generic space units* (*GSUs*). In addition, the *MHEG engine* has to map the virtual to the real coordinate space.

Contents objects are represented based on the exchange of action objects, which are sent to an object. Examples of actions are preparations to put the object into a presentable state, the start of a presentation, or the end of a presentation. Action objects can be combined into an *action list*. Parallel action lists are executed in parallel. Each list consists of a delay, followed by a delayed sequential action, which is processed serially by the MHEG engine (see Figure 8-49).

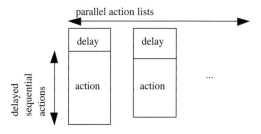

**Figure 8-49**   Example of an action list in MHEG.

References can be used to synchronize presentations based on events. Reference conditions can be linked to an event. If the conditions linked to a reference are met, then the reference is triggered, and actions assigned to this reference are executed. This can be thought of as a form of event-based synchronization.

### 8.10.1.1   The MHEG Engine

The MHEG engine was developed at the European Networking Center of IBM in Heidelberg, Germany [Gra94]. The architecture of the MHEG engine, which is an implementation of the object layer, is shown in Figure 8-50.

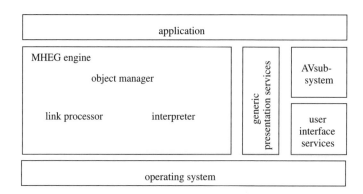

**Figure 8-50**   Architecture of the MHEG engine.

The so-called *generic presentation services* offered by the engine supply abstractions of the presentation modules, used to present contents objects.

The *audio/video subsystem* is an implementation of the stream layer. This component is responsible for the presentation of continuous media streams, e.g., audio and video streams.

The *user interface services* support the presentation of discrete media, e.g., text and images, and process user interventions, e.g., buttons and forms.

The MHEG engine accepts MHEG objects from the application. The *object manager* handles these objects in a runtime environment. The *interpreter* processes action objects and events. It is responsible for the initiation of the preparation and presentation of objects. The *link processor* monitors the status of objects and triggers references, if the condition of a reference is met.

A runtime system uses events to communicate with the presentation services. The *user inter interface services* process the events belonging to user actions. The *audio/ video subsystem* represents status events of the presentation streams, e.g., the end of the presentation of a stream, or reference point within a stream is reached.

### 8.10.1.2 MHEG in the Context of the Reference Model

MHEG is a standardized exchange format used in the object layer. The synchronization is based on the virtual axes and the events-based methods. The MHEG engine represents the runtime environment of the object layer. The object layer implementation of the engine is based on media servers (see Chapter 4). The audio/video subsystem represents the stream layer. Figure 8-51 shows the relationship between MHEG and the synchronization reference model.

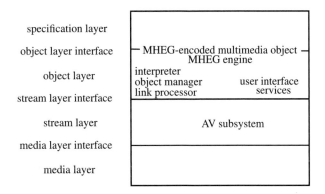

**Figure 8-51** Classification of MHEG within the reference model.

When considering distributed environments, we can identify a drawback of the MHEG processing model: the time between the preparation and the representation of actions is encoded as an MHEG object, while the duration depends on the runtime environment, so that it has to be calculated completely by the MHEG engine.

## 8.10.2 HyTime

*HyTime (Hypermedia/Time-based Structuring Language)* is an international standard specified in ISO/IEC 10744 [Org92] for the structured representation of hypermedia information. HyTime is an application that uses the *Standardized General Markup Language (SGML)* [Smi89] (see Volume 3).

SGML was designed for the exchange of documents, where the document structure plays an important role. In contrast, the layout has only local significance. The logical structure is defined by markup commands embedded in the text. These markup commands organize the text in SGML elements. For each SGML document, there is a *data type definition (DTD)*, which declares the element types of a document and the attributes of each element. It also specifies how the instances relate hierarchically. A typical application of SGML is desktop publishing, where an author is responsible for the contents and structure of a document, while the publisher is responsible for the layout. SGML does not limit the contents of a document, so that elements can be of text or image types, or other multimedia data types.

HyTime specifies how markups and DTDs can be used to describe the structure of hyperlink and time-based multimedia documents. However, it does not specify the format or encoding of elements. Instead, it uses frames that can be used to define the relationships between these elements.

HyTime supports addresses required to identify specific pieces of information within an element, to create references between components of these elements, and for temporal and spatial specifications to describe the relationships between media objects.

The HiTime standard defines the semantics of architectural forms, representing the declaration templates of SGML elements, including their attributes. A designer of HyTime applications creates a HyTime DTD that uses the architectural forms the designers needs for the HyTime document. A HyTime DTD uses a special HyTime attribute to associate each element type with an architectural form. The following attributes are available for architectural forms:

- The *base module* specifies the architectural forms included in a document. A *measurement module* is used to add dimensions and to measure and count documents. Media objects within a document can be arranged on these dimensions.
- The *location address module* provides the tools to address specific points within a document. This module supports three addressing modes:
  - A *name space addressing scheme* to address a name that identifies an information component.
  - A *coordinate location scheme* to address an interval of a coordinated space

by reference, if measurement within the coordinated space is possible, e.g., the address of a component within an audio sequence.

- A *semantic location scheme* to address components by use of application-specific constructs.

- The *scheduling module* puts media objects into so-called *finite coordinate spaces* (*FCSs*). These spaces are collections of application-defined axes. A measurement module is required to address measurements along these axes. HyTime does not know the dimensions of its media objects. Events are used for the presentation of media objects. An *event* is an encapsulated media object, including the layout specification, which is bound to an FCS. Events can be set within the FCS either absolute or relative to other events.

- The *hyperlink module* is used to build reference links between media objects. Endpoints can be defined by use of local addresses, by measurements, or by the scheduling method.

- The *rendition module* specifies how the events of a source FCS, which typically supplies a higher-level presentation description, can be transformed into a target FCS to be used for a specific presentation. Presentation-specific modifications, e.g., a change to the color reproduction, projecting the dimensions from the source to the target FCSs, or scaling of the presentation, are executed during the mapping process.

### 8.10.2.1   The HyTime Engine

The HyTime engine is used to read the output from an SGML parser, to recognize the architectural forms, and to execute HyTime-specific and application-independent processes. Typical tasks of the HyTime engine include the resolution of hyperlinks, addressing of objects, analysis of measurements and schedules, and the transformation of schedules and dimensions. The resulting information is then passed on to the HyTime application.

*HyOctane* is a HyTime engine developed at the university of Massachusetts at Lowell [BRRK94]; it has the following architecture: An SGML parser reads the data type definition used for a document and for HyTime document instances. The parser stores the markups and contents of document objects and the application DTD in the SGML layer of a database. Then the HyTime engine fetches information stored in the SGML layer of the database. It identifies the architectural forms, resolves the addresses maintained by the location addressing module, assumes the function of the scheduling module, and executes the mapping specified in a service module. The engine stores the information about the elements of a document, which represent the instances of architectural forms in the HyTime layer of the database. The application layer of the database stores the objects and their attributes as they were defined in the DTD. An application presenter fetches the information required for the presentation of database contents from the database, including references between objects and presentation coordinates used for the presentation.

### 8.10.2.2    HyTime in the Context of the Reference Model

HyTime can be used in many applications. Instead of standardizing the contents formats, the encoding, the document types, or specific SGML-DTDs, it provides a framework for the addressing of contents in hypermedia documents and the definition of references, the adaptation and the synchronization. In the context of the reference model for synchronization, a HyTime document together with its DTDs can be used as input for the object layer. For synchronization, it uses the method based on virtual axes. Pre-processing related to SGML and HyTime is executed by the HyTime engine in the object layer. The application presenter supplies the other object layers and the functionality of the stream layer. Figure 8-52 shows how HyTime relates to the synchronization reference model.

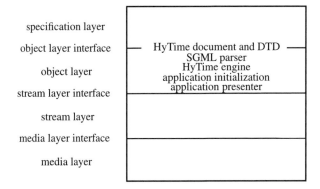

specification layer

object layer interface

object layer

stream layer interface

stream layer

media layer interface

media layer

HyTime document and DTD
SGML parser
HyTime engine
application initialization
application presenter

**Figure 8-52**    HyTime in the context of the reference model.

Other classification options include the use of a database as an interface to the object layer, or the use of databases to generate an MHEG specification. In the latter case, the HyTime engine can be thought of as part of a format conversion tool.

## 8.10.3 The Firefly System

The *Firefly* system approach proposed by Buchanan and Zellweger [BZ93a, BZ93b] was designed to generate consistent presentation schedules for interactive multimedia documents that include the media objects with either a behavior known in advance (e.g., audio and video), or with unknown behavior (e.g., user interactions). The generation algorithm consists of two phases. In the first phase (prior to running the presentation), highly developed temporal specifications are used for a document to calculate a presentation schedule, where objects with unknown duration are widely ignored. In the second phase (during the presentation), the scheduling is completed by identifying and including objects with unknown duration.

The specification of these temporal side conditions distinguishes between a specification of media levels, which describe the temporal behavior of individual media objects, and a specification of document levels, which describe the temporal behavior of a complete multimedia document, in particular the temporal relationships between individual media objects. To specify the media level, media items supplying a reference to a media object and to describe the temporal behavior of that media object are used. A media item includes the following:

- *Events* representing time points during the presentation of a media object. They are similar to a reference point.
- *Durations* specifying the amount of time between two consecutive events in a media object. A duration is represented by three values: `minDuration`, `optDuration`, and `maxDuration`. The duration is fixed if these three values are identical. If they specify an interval, then the presentation can be adapted. No values are assigned if a duration is unknown.
- *Costs*, which can be used as a measurement unit for the declining degree of quality when a presentation is stretched towards the maximum duration, or shrunk towards the minimum duration.

A specification of document levels includes the following:

- *Media items*, which are embedded in the presentation.
- *Temporal side conditions* used to describe explicit temporal relationships between events in one or several schedulers. Temporal side conditions are grouped into those with temporal equality, which describe a fixed temporal relationship between two events (e.g., same time, one event 10 s before the other), and those with temporal inequality, which describe a temporal relationship without a specific time (e.g., one event before the other, or one event at least 10 s and at most 20 s before the other).
- *Operations*, which are related to an event and do not include any alternating presentation-specific operations (e.g., increasing the volume of an audio presentation), and operations that change over time (e.g., increasing the playback speed of a video).
- *Duration and cost*, which can be described according to the media layer. These values are used on the document level to describe the behavior of different instances of one single media item within a document.
- *Unpredictable event control* used to activate and deactivate unpredictable events.

In addition, the system offers options to specify graphical representations and to support the development of temporal specifications. The method used for synchronization specification combines the reference point synchronization (see Section 8.9.3) with the interval-based synchronization (see Section 8.9.1).

The representation scheduler resides in the object layer and is composed of two parts: a *compile-time scheduler* and a *run-time scheduler*. The compile-time scheduler creates a main schedule that controls the predictable parts of a document, and auxiliary schedules which control the parts of a document that depend on unpredictable events. This scheduling is an example for the calculation of an offline schedule in the object layer. The algorithm involves the following steps:

- The first step determines duration values and costs for each media item. For this purpose, the specifications of the media and document levels for a media item are linked and time-altering operations are included in the calculation of duration values.

- The second step determines aggregate components. More specifically, a union-find algorithm is used to identify the linked components of a document. Two events reside in the same aggregate component if they are linked by either a predictable duration or a temporal side condition. An aggregate component is *predictable* if no unpredictable events exist that would trigger the events of that component; otherwise is is *unpredictable*.

- The third step assigns instance times to events, i.e., the time with regard to the start time of a component is calculated for each event of an aggregate component. For this purpose, a simplex algorithm is applied, which uses the duration values and the temporal side conditions, with the main objective to minimize cost.

- The fourth step generates *commands*, i.e., previous results are used to generate execution commands. A command includes the time when it should be executed, the media item to be executed, and an aggregate event that lists unpredictable events which have to be activated or deactivated. All commands for predictable components are integrated in the main schedule, while a separate auxiliary schedule is built for each unpredictable component. To improve the performance of a continuous medium, objects are handled on the basis of fixed duration units, and not with each single event within the media item. This means that it only concerns the start objects of the complete set of media and events referring to other media objects. It is assumed that such a stream will be executed separately as specified by the presentation schedule.

The run-time scheduler is an example for the calculation of an online schedule within the object layer. It controls the document clock and the execution schedule, and processes unpredictable events. Once the compile-time scheduler has calculated the schedules, the run-time schedules copies the main schedules to the runtime scheduler and starts the document clock. When the time set for a specific command expires, that command is executed. When an activated unpredictable event that triggers an unpredictable component is found, then the run-time scheduler links the relevant schedules in the run-time schedule by taking the current document time as the start time for the first command within the schedule. The run-time scheduler marks the instances in the run-time schedule to be able to distinguish the commands for various instances of an unpredictable schedule, because unpredictable components could be called more than once.

### 8.10.3.1 Firefly in the Context of the Reference Model

The Firefly system offers a complete synchronization support, with an editor in the specification layer. The temporal relationships based on the reference point and the interval-based specification methods are used on the object-layer interface. The scheduler supports offline- and online calculations of presentation schedules in the object layer. Schedules for streams are initiated in the object layer and executed in the stream layer. Figure 8-53 shows the Firefly system in the context of the synchronization reference model.

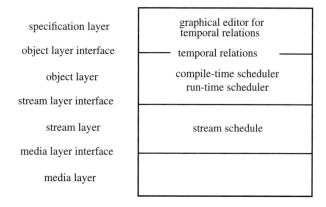

**Figure 8-53**   The Firefly system in the context of the reference model.

The system offers well-organized scheduling and the integration of values for unpredictable events. It does not currently support media preparation times, or presentation restrictions for situations where the local resources are insufficient, or the network introduces delays.

### 8.10.4 The MODE System

The *MODE (Multimedia Objects in a Distributed Environment)* system [Bla93] was developed at the University of Karlsruhe, Germany. It is based on an intuitive approach for network-transparent synchronization specification and for scheduling in heterogeneous, distributed systems. The core of MODE is a distributed multimedia presentation service that shares a tailored multimedia object model, synchronization specifications, and QoS requirements with a given application. In addition, MODE uses the knowledge about networks and workstations jointly with a given runtime environment. This distributed service uses all information available for synchronization scheduling, when an application requests the presentation of a composite multimedia object. MODE refers to the cost model and the QoS requirements of the application, which means that it adapts the quality of service to the available resources. The MODE system includes the following synchronization-specific components:

- The *synchronization editor* in the specification layer creates synchronization and layout specifications for multimedia presentations.

- The *server manager* in the object layer coordinates the execution of the presentation service calls. This includes the coordination of presentation units (presentation objects) from basic information units (information objects), and the transport of objects within a distributed environment.

- The *local synchronizer* accepts presentation objects locally and initiates their local presentation according to the synchronization specification.

- The *optimizer*, which is part of the MODE server manager, schedules distributed synchronization, selects presentation qualities and presentation forms, which depend on the requirements of the user, the network, and the system capabilities of the workstation.

### 8.10.4.1   The Synchronization Model

The MODE system uses a synchronization model based on the synchronization by reference points [BHLM92]. This model can be expanded to handle time intervals, objects with unpredictable duration, and conditions that may arise from the underlying heterogeneous, distributed environment.

A synchronization specification, which was created in the synchronization editor and uses the synchronizer, is stored in textual form. The syntax of this specification is defined by the context-free grammar of the language used to describe the synchronization. This ensures that a synchronization specification can be used independently of MODE components in its implementation language and environment.

MODE distinguishes between *dynamic* and *static* base objects. A presentation of dynamic basic objects is composed of a sequence of presentation objects, corresponding to an LDU stream. The index of each presentation object is called a *reference point*. The presentation of a static basis object, which can also be an interactive or discrete media object, has only two reference points: the beginning and the end of a presentation. The description of a reference point together with the pertaining basic object is called *ynchronization element* or *BasicObjectReferencePoint*. Two or more synchronization elements can be combined at one synchronization point. A complete inter-object synchronization is defined by creating a list of all synchronization points.

The presentation quality can be specified for each basic object. It is described by a set of attributes, including attribute names, preferred values, and the value range for all possible values of an attribute.

### 8.10.4.2   The Local Synchronizer

The local synchronizer runs synchronized presentations according to the synchronization model introduced above. This includes intra-object and inter-object synchronization. For intra-object synchronization, a presentation thread is created, which processes the presentation of a dynamic basic objects. Threads with different priorities can be used to implement priorities for basic objects. All presentations of static basic objects are handled by one single thread.

For synchronization, MODE uses a signaling mechanism. Each presentation thread that reaches a synchronization point sends a signal to all other presentation threads linked to that synchronization point. When these threads receive such a signal, other presentation threads can run acceleration activities, if necessary. Once all signals have been sent, the presentation thread waits for signals to arrive from the other participating threads of the synchronization point; in the meantime, it waits in a loop.

### 8.10.4.3   Scheduling and Running a Distributed Presentation

The optimizer is activated before a presentation can begin. The optimizer uses a heuristic search algorithm that considers the special conditions of a distributed environment, such as multiple steps of a synchronization within a distributed environment, several communication patterns, or buffer requirements and connections. For this purpose, it uses information about the network, e.g., available bandwidth, service quality, available resources in the workstation, and information about processing requirements for media objects. This information is maintained in the environment and in application media descriptions for use by the optimizer [Bla92].

The scheduling result defines the achievable quality for each presentation attribute, corresponding to the requirements for the user, the network, and the workstation resources. The result of this scheduling process is a MODE flow graph [Bla91], describing the nodes and times when specific operations have to be executed. The flow graph is distributed to the embedded nodes and processed by the distributed MODE server manager at runtime.

### 8.10.4.4   Exceptions in a Distributed Environment

The correct and timely execution of a schedule depends on the underlying environment, when workstations and the network make temporal guarantees for the execution of operations. MODE supports several guarantee levels. When the underlying distributed environment is unable to provide full guarantees, then MODE considers potential error conditions. To throw an exception during the presentation time, MODE defines three types of actions:

1. A *wait action* can be used when the presentation of a dynamic basic object has reached a synchronization point and is waiting longer than the time defined for this synchronization point. Possible wait actions include the continuation of a presentation from the object presented last (*freezing* the video), stopping, or pausing a synchronization point.
2. When the presentation of a dynamic basic object has reached a synchronization point and waits for other objects to reach this point, then acceleration actions can be used as an alternative to the wait action. They move the delayed dynamic basic objects to this synchronization point. Possible actions include a temporary increase of the presentation speed, or skipping all objects of the presentation to the synchronization point.
3. An object can be skipped and the next object presented when a presentation object does not arrive in time.

Priorities for basic objects can be used to reflect their sensitivity to delays in the presentation. For example, audio objects normally have a higher priority than video objects, because a user will perceive the jitter in the audio stream rather than in a video stream. Higher-priority presentation objects are preferred versus lower-priority objects, both in the presentation and in the synchronization.

### 8.10.4.5   MODE in the Context of the Reference Model

MODE is a comprehensive synchronization system, especially designed to support synchronization in a distributed environment. MODE offers a synchronization tool in the specification layer. The output of this tool is used as an interface format, similar to the reference point synchronization, between the specification and the object layer. The optimizer is part of the object layer and handles an offline calculation of the presentation schedule before the presentation can begin. The MODE server manager and the synchronizer are also part of the object layer. The threads they generate to handle dynamic media objects are part of the stream layer. Figure 8-54 shows how the MODE system relates to the synchronization reference model.

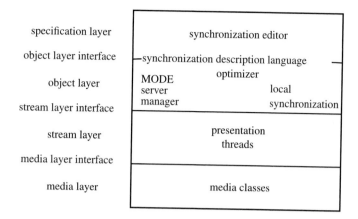

specification layer        synchronization editor

object layer interface     synchronization description language

object layer               MODE          optimizer
                           server                      local
                           manager                     synchronization

stream layer interface

stream layer               presentation
                           threads

media layer interface

media layer                media classes

**Figure 8-54**   The MODE system in the context of the reference model.

## 8.10.5 Multimedia Tele-Orchestra

The Multimedia Communication Research Laboratory (MCRLab), headed by Professor Nicolas D. Georganas, at the University of Ottawa, Canada, developed a multimedia system called *Multimedia-Tele-Orchestra*. This system consists of a highly developed specification scheme, the *time flow graph* (*TFG*) [LKG94], and a synchronization implementation in a distributed environment [KG89]. In contrast to many other specification methods, a TFG assumes that special temporal knowledge can often be relative, i.e., it cannot be described by exact time parameters. The authors call this a *fuzzy scenario*. In addition, the duration of presentations can be imprecise and unknown in advance. For this reason, neither the exact times nor the duration is required to specify a synchronization in this system.

The term *interval* serves as a basis for the TFG. [LKG94] shows that all temporal relationships between intervals can be represented by TFGs. This leads to a partly sequential sequence used by the actual synchronization processing at the presentation time. With regard to the synchronization reference model, a TFG is an interval-based method in the specification layer; it also includes the interface between this layer and the object layer.

The *synchronization controller for multimedia communication* (*SCMC*) [KG89] was developed on the basis of the TFG concept for distributed multimedia synchronization schemes. One of the important properties of this scheme is that data may origin from various sources at various locations. SCMC is designed to run over ATM networks. Nevertheless, the same algorithms can be used for other multimedia-enabling networks, e.g., Ethernet 10Base-T, 100Base-T, and IsoEthernet, or Gigabit Ethernet (see Chapter 5).

The Tele-Orchestra approach uses a second component, the *Temporal Presentation Controller* (*TPC*), that handles the calculation of schedules with earliest possible times for the presentation of objects on a remote computer. The result of the TPC, i.e., the corresponding schedule, is passed on to the SCMC, which actually processes the control data to meet the synchronization specification. With regard to the synchronization reference model, SCMC uses individual LDUs, which means that it does not rely on a stream. SCMC offers users the option to produce a synchronization between individual data streams, which means that SCMC belongs both to the media and the stream layer. Temporal side conditions defined by TFG are mapped by TPC to SCMC primitives. TPC continues calculating local schedules, while SCMC groups all local schedules into an implementation of the required synchronization, which means that TPC belongs to the object layer.

### 8.10.5.1   Tele-Orchestra in the Context of the Reference Model

Tele-Orchestra covers the aspects of all layers of the reference model. The distribution is known and handled in the specification and stream layers. [LLKG93] discusses performance analysis results of this synchronization scheme. Figure 8-55 shows how the Tele-Orchestra system relates to the synchronization reference model.

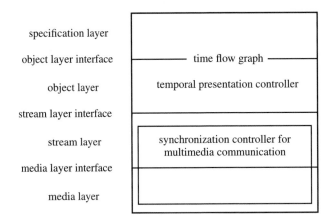

**Figure 8-55**   The Tele-Orchestra system in the context of the synchronization reference model.

### 8.10.6 Little's Framework

The main motivation for the development of a multimedia information system developed at the University of Boston [Lit93] was to integrate the support of the retrieval and transmission of multimedia data. This system consists of methods for synchronization specification, data representation, temporal access controls, and runtime inter-media synchronization. In particular, it offers mechanisms to prevent delays caused by media object storage, communication, and calculation. The system offers other mechanisms for scalability and controlled quality constraints of multimedia services.

The synchronization specification is based on the method using Petri networks (see Section 8.9.3) and the method using global timers (see Section 8.9.2). The specification itself is mapped to a so-called *Temporal Interval Base* (*TIB*) modeling approach. The temporal relationships of this model include a start time, the duration of its presentation, and the end time for each data element. The relative position is defined by the differences between the start times of presentations.

Static and dynamic presentation scheduling is calculated on the basis of this specification. An example for a simple scheduling algorithm in an environment with limited resources is the *Static Playout Schedule Computation Algorithm* [Lit92, LG92]. This algorithm assumes that the data elements of a presentation are stored in a remote database. The data have to be transmitted over a packet-switched network with limited capacity to the output workstation. In a first step, the synchronization specification is used to calculate the time for the beginning of a presentation ($p_i$) for each data unit. This can be done easily by using the presentation duration ($m_i$). When the start points of a presentation are used, then it is necessary to calculate the times when the data units are accessed ($q_i$), because a time ($T_i$) is required to transport them (see Figure 8-56).

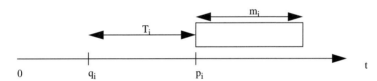

**Figure 8-56**   Static scheduling.

Let us assume that $D_p$ is the constant propagation speed of the data, $D_l$, the delay in proportion to the package size (mean packet size / channel capacity), and $D_v$ is the variable delay depending on the network load, then $T_i$ is defined as $T_i = D_p + D_i + D_l$. For this calculation, the following conditions have to be met:

```
p_i ≤ q_i + T_i (The data units have to be available at the correct time.)
q_{i-1} ≥ q_i - T_{i-1} + D_p (The data should be accessed after completion of
the previous data transmission.)
```

The following algorithm is used to calculate $q_i$:

```
q[m] = p[m] - T[m] // Start with the last data unit.
for i = 0 to m-2
    if q[m-i] < p[m-i-1] - Dp // Collision
       q[m-i-1] = q[m-1] - T[m-i-1] + Dp // Resolve collision
    else q[m-i-1] = p[m-i-1] - T[m-i-1] // No collision
end.
```

Note that static scheduling does not consider any dynamic changes in the environment, nor changing user commands (e.g., presentation speed), so that the dynamic scheduling concept introduced in this system is also called *Limited A Priori* (*LAP*) scheduling. Based on this concept, scheduling and resource reservation are valid only for a brief time. If a multimedia presentation is decomposed into components with similar use of resources, then a schedule and a static resource reservation are calculated. Subsequently, the session scheduler presents the components.

Skew control mechanisms are used to support inter-stream synchronization. They reject and duplicate data units when the queue representing the stream processes exceeds or falls short of specific threshold values.

The definitions of the specification layer are time-oriented and based on Petri networks, but they are mapped to a TIB specification in the interface format of the object layer, which is similar to an interval-based synchronization. Offline and online scheduling belong to the object layer. An additional skew control is available in the stream layer.

### 8.10.6.1    Little's Framework in the Context of the Reference Model

Little's Framework is a well-defined approach, combining all layers involved. The concept concentrates on the retrieval of multimedia objects from one single server, taking only a limited set of parameters into account, namely those relevant for a distribution. Figure 8-57 shows how Little's Framework relates to the synchronization reference model.

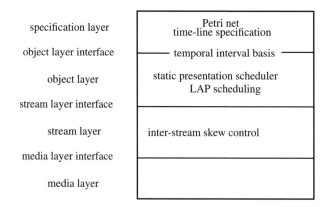

**Figure 8-57**   Little's Framework in the context of the synchronization reference model.

### 8.10.7  ACME

*ACME* (*Abstractions for Continuous MEdia*) [AH91] is an input/output server for continuous data streams within the stream layer. It controls several physical devices. Users can define logical devices as abstractions of physical devices. A transmission path is established to transmit streams from input to output devices. This connection can be a real network link. A stream consists of LDUs, carrying a timestamp.

A so-called *logical time system* (*LTS*) synchronize the input and output to and from logical devices. The LTS has a clock assigned to a specific device, which is normally one that reacts most sensitively to delays, or which is operated over a designated connection.

When a connection blocks, then the input device of the connection is also blocked and has to continue buffering data units. The output device is "starved", because it does not receive the expected number of LDUs. When the maximum skew between the LDU timestamps and the LTS clock is reached, then the blockage is resolved by skipping some LDUs or stopping the LTS. The LTS will be started again, if the timestamp of the logical data approximates the LTS clock, and if an additional data volume was received for the start phase of the resynchronization (see Figure 8-58 and Figure 8-59).

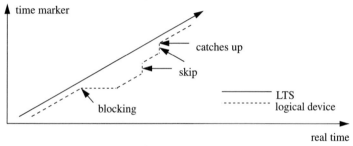

**Figure 8-58**   Resynchronization in ACME.

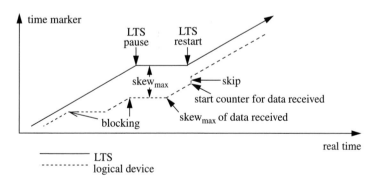

**Figure 8-59**   Resynchronization in ACME (cont'd).

ACME offers a programming interface and supports media streams exclusively in the stream layer.

## 8.10.8 Other Synchronization-specific Systems

Many of the multimedia expansions currently available for operating systems, e.g., *QuickTime* of Apple [DM92], the *multimedia extensions* of Microsoft [Mic91], and the *Multimedia Presentation Manager/2* of IBM [IBM92] include synchronization mechanisms referring to the stream layer of the local environment. Networked systems, such as the IBM *Ultimedia Server*, include additional synchronization mechanisms for a distributed environment.

The *Orchestration Service* [CGCH92] is a stream-oriented interface for synchronized playback of continuous media in a distributed environment. Nicolai [Nic90], Little [LG91], Escobar [EDP92], Shepherd [SS90], Ramanathan [RR93], and Anderson proposed technologies for jitter control of media streams in the stream layer. [EFI94] includes an evaluation and classification of these approaches. Stefani, Harzad and Horn [SHH92] proposed the use of the synchronous *ESTEREL* programming language to write code for multimedia synchronization in the object layer.

The University of Geneva, Switzerland, [TGD91] developed an object-oriented system featuring a global timer-based synchronization specification. A global timer is available to all objects at runtime. Each object maps this time to its own local time, which it uses for its intra-object synchronization. When the skew between the local time and the world time of the global timer exceeds a maximum value, then a resynchronization to the world time is done.

Bulterman's *Framework* [Bul93] deals with the problems of sharing network resources, synchronizing data from different sources, and representing data on different hosts in a distributed environment. The components of Framework can manage the resources for all active application within a distributed environment. The required information is supplied by a specification of the application resource and by synchronization requirements.

The *Tactus System* [DNN+93] includes a server for media synchronization at the sink, and an interface tool that also supports the calculation and control of streams and their transmission to the presentation server. The scheduling is calculated in advance to avoid delays at runtime.

The use of traditional events-based user interface servers can cause synchronization errors caused by a delay between a request of a presentation sent to the server and the current presentation performance of that server. Temporal relationships of a presentation are often lost. One proposal to prevent this problem is to expand the Windows server to the delays of a presentation pending the arrival of an event, which is defined by the client. This allows to reintroduce temporal relationships between presentations on the server.

*HyperODA* [App89] is a standardization effort to define a document exchange format for multimedia. HyperODA actually expands the *Open Document Architecture* (*ODA*) [BB91]. The expansion of ODA to a multimedia and hypermedia document architecture requires new content architectures, e.g., for audio and video, and the definition of a model for the temporal and spatial layout. Intra-object synchronization is implemented by the events-based synchronization method.

## 8.11 Summary and Discussion

Modern integrated multimedia systems should include several aspects with regard to synchronization. Unfortunately, the same term is used by many authors to describe different issues. This chapter defined synchronization-specific conditions and classified the layers in multimedia systems based on a synchronization reference model.

Intra-object synchronization was defined as the synchronization of LDUs of media objects. Inter-object synchronization involves the synchronization between media objects.

In live synchronization, the synchronization results directly from the temporal relationships created during the recording of objects. In synthetic synchronization, the temporal relationship between media objects are explicitly represented.

We discussed various methods for synchronization specifications developed in recent years. The improved interval-based specification defines relationships between presentation intervals. The axis-based method specifies the synchronization by mapping media objects to one or several axes. The basic hierarchical method uses parallel or serial operations to define relations between media objects. The approach based on reference points allows a specification by defining the relationships between media objects. Petri networks can be used to model the presentation flow by using points with values for the duration and by allocating the beginning of presentation operations to fire transitions. The events-based method links presentation operations to events. Scripts are a programming-oriented approach using synchronization operations. All these methods offer different specification options. Conversions or mappings of specifications between these methods are possible, but generally limited to a common subgroup of specification options. Normally, the user uses a graphical editor to specify the synchronization. The basic specification methods reflect normally in the abstraction of the user interface. Editors allow also direct access to these specification methods.

The quality of service (QoS) required for the temporal relationships of the presentation at the output device is derived from the user's perception of a presentation. Experiments have shown that a skew of more than +/- 80 ms between an audio stream and a video stream are found annoying when the presentation involves lip synchronization. We also introduced other QoS requirements and a method to combine QoS requirements.

Subsequently, we defined a synchronization reference model that can be used to classify the synchronization devices and interfaces in layers, and to identify and classify media synchronization approaches. In this model, the specification layer consists of tools that can be used to create and convert synchronization specifications. The object layer accepts the synchronization specification as input on its service interface. It plans and organizes the presentation. In addition, it initiates the presentation of discrete media objects and user interactions. For the presentation of continuous media, it uses the services of the stream layer. The stream layer supports abstractions of streams at its interface. It deals with intra-object synchronization and the synchronization of continuous media streams. The media layer hides the access to multimedia devices at its interface.

For a distributed environment, additional challenges have to be dealt with, especially with regard to the distribution of the media objects and their synchronization specification, the required communication and delays in the distributed environment, and multi-user communication. In a distributed environment, synchronization is a multi-step process and a challenging planning task.

Finally, we discussed some of the well-known systems and classified them in the context of the synchronization reference model. The case studies described in this context allowed us to compare the options offered by the different approaches, and to evaluate the usability of the model.

The expansive development and fast proliferation of multimedia applications require the execution of presentations on heterogeneous platforms. The success of exchange standards for multimedia depends on the availability of runtime environments for these formats. Which standard will prevail in the future remains to be seen. Naturally, the availability of a standard format will also help support authoring systems.

The growing availability of multimedia teleservices requires an open distributed environment that requires, in turn, an open stream mechanism and open object layer services. Initial efforts in the field of open streams in a heterogeneous environment have been made by the Interactive Multimedia Association, an effort driven by the industry for open multimedia services. Further work is needed for the development of open object layer services.

# Bibliography

[AA93]      G. J. Armitage and K. M. Adams. Using the Common LAN to Introduce ATM Connectivity. In *Proceedings of 18th Conference on Local Computer Networks*, pages 34–43, Minneapolis, Minnesota, September 1993.

[Abb84]     C. Abbott. Efficient Editing of Digital Sound on Disc. *Journal of Audio Engineering*, 32(6):394–402, 1984.

[Abd99]     T. Abdelzaher. *QoS Adaptation in Real-Time Systems*. PhD thesis, University of Michigan, Ann Arbor, August 1999.

[ACVS02]    G. Ahn, A. Campbell, A. Veres, and L. Sun. Swan: Service differentiation in stateless wireless ad hoc networks. In *IEEE INFOCOM*, New York, NY, June 2002.

[AFB98]     W. Almesberger, T. Ferrari, and J. Y. Le Boudec. SRP: a scalable resource reservation protocol for the internet. Technical Report Tech. Rep. SSC/ 1998/009, EPFL, Lausanne, Switzerland, March 1998.

[AH91]      D.P. Anderson and G. Homsy. A Continuous Media I/O Server and its Synchronization Mechanism. *IEEE Computer*, 24(10):51–57, October 1991.

[AHS90]     D. P. Anderson, R. G. Herrtwich, and C. Schaefer. A Resource Reservation Protocol for Guaranteed Performance Communication in the Internet. Technical Report 90/006, International Computer Science Institute, Berkeley, CA, February 1990.

[All83]      J. F. Allen. Maintaining Knowledge about Temporal Intervals. *Communications of the ACM*, 26(11):832–843, November 1983.

[And93]      D. P. Anderson. Meta-scheduling for distributed continuous media. *ACM Transaction on Computer Systems*, 11(3), August 1993.

[AOG92]      D. P. Anderson, Y. Osawa, and R. Govindan. A file system for continuous media. *ACM Transaction on Computer Systems*, 10(4):331–337, November 1992.

[App89]      W. Appelt. HyperODA. ISO/IEC/JTC1/SC18/WG3, 1989.

[Arm00]      G. Armitage. *Quality of Service in IP Networks*. Technology Series: MTP (Macmillan Technical Publishing, 2000.

[AS83]       G.B. Andrews and F.B. Schneider. Concepts and Notations for Concurrent Programming. *ACM Computing Surveys*, 15(1):3–43, March 1983.

[As90]       H. van As. Performance Evaluation of the Bandwidth Balancing in the DQDB MAC Protocol. In *Proceedings of 8th Annual EFOC/LAN Conference*, pages 231–239, Munich, Germany, June 1990.

[AS02]       Z. Antoniou and I. Stavrakakis. An efficient deadline-credit-based transport scheme for prerecorded semisoft continuous media applications. *IEEE/ACM Transactions on Networking (ToN)*, 10(5):630–643, 2002.

[ATW+90]     D. P. Anderson, S. Tzou, R. Wahbe, R. Govindan, and M. Andrews. Support for Continuous Media in the DASH System. In *Proceedings of the 10th ICDCS*, Paris, France, May 1990.

[AV98]       J. Altmann and P. Varaiya. Index project: User support for buying qos with regards to user's preferences. In *6th International Workshop on Quality of Service (IWQoS'98)*, Napa, CA, May 1998.

[BA98]       J. Behrens and J.J. Garcia-Luna Aceves. Hierarchical routing using link vectors. In *IEEE INFOCOM'98*, March 1998.

[BB91]       U. Bormann and C. Bormann. Offene Bearbeitung multimedialer Dokumente. *Informatik-Spektrum*, 14:249–260, October 1991.

[BB02]       S. Babachowski and S. Brandt. The best scheduler for integrated processing of best effort and soft real-time processing. In *SPIE/ACM Multimedia Computing and Networking*, San Jose, January 2002.

[BBGS00]     Y. Bernet, Y.S. Blake, D. Grossman, and A. Smith. *An Informal Management Model for DiffServ Routers*. Internet Draft, July 2000.

[BBI93]      S. A. Bly, S. A. Bly, and S. Irwin. Media Space: Bringing People Together in a Video, Audio, and Computing Environment. *Communications of the ACM*, 36(1):28–45, January 1993.

[BBNS02]     P. Bellini, L. Bruno, P. Nesi, and M.B. Spiny. Execution and synchronization of music score pages and real performance audios. In *IEEE International Conference on Multimedia and Expo (ICME)*, pages 125–128, 2002.

[BCS94]      Bob Braden, David Clark, and Scott Shenker. Integrated Services in the Internet Architecture. Internet RFC 1633, June 1994.

[BDH+03]     Bob Briscoe, Vasilios Darlagiannis, Oliver Heckmann, Oliver Huw, Vasilios Siris, Burkhard Stiller, and David Songhurst. A Market Managed Multi-Service Internet. *Computer Communications*, 26(4):405–415, March 2003.

[Bel57]      R.E. Bellman. *Dynamic Programming*. Princeton University Press, Princeton, NJ, 1957.

[Ber01]      Y. Bernet. *Networking Quality of Service and Windows Operating Systems*. Technology Series, New Riders, 2001.

[BG87]       D. Bersekas and R. Gallager. *Data Networks*. Prentice Hall, 1987.

[BGS+00]     L. Berger, D. Gan, G. Swallow, P. Pan, and F. Tommasi. *RSVP Refresh Overhead Reduction Extensions*. Internet Draft, June 2000.

[BGW97]      Michael Baer, Carsten Griwodz, and Lars Wolf. Long-term movie popularity in video-on-demand systems. In *5th ACM International Multimedia Conference*, pages 349–358, Seattle, WA, November 1997.

[BHea02]     A.P. Black, J. Huang, and R. Koster et al. Infopipes: An abstraction for multimedia streaming. *ACM Multimedia Systems Journal*, 8(5):406–419, 2002.

[BHL91]      G. Blakowski, Hübel, and Langrehr. Tools for specifying and executing synchronized multimedia presentations. In *2nd International Workshop on Network and Operating System Support for Digital Audio and Video*, Heidelberg, Nov 1991.

[BHLM92]     P. Binstadt, W. Henhapl, J. Löffler, and U.A. Michelsen. *Informations- und kommunikationstechnische Grundbildung: Konzeptionen — Konkretionen — Gestaltungsvorschläge*. Leuchtturm, Alsbach/Bergstraße, 1992.

[Bie93]      E. W. Biersack. Performance Evaluation of Forward Error Correction in an ATM Environment. *IEEE JSAC*, 11(4):631–640, May 1993.

[Bir95]     Yitzhak Birk. Track pairing: A novel data layout for vod servers with multi-zone recording disks. In *Proceedings of the International Conference on Multimedia Computing and Systems (ICMCS)*, Washington, DC, May 1995.

[Bla91]     G. Blakowski. The MODE-FLOW-GRAPH: A Processing Model for Objects of Distributed Multimedia Applications. In *Proceedings of International Symposium on Communication*, pages 646–649, December 1991.

[Bla92]     G. Blakowski. High Level Services for Distributed Multimedia Applications based on Application Media and Environment Descriptions. *Australian Computer Science Communications*, 14:93–109, January 1992.

[Bla93]     G. Blakowski. *Development and Runtime Support for Distributed Multimedia Applications*. Shaker Verlag, German edition, 1993.

[Ble78]     B. Blesser. Digitization of Audio: A Comprehensive Examination of Theory, Implementation, and Current Practice. *Journal of the Audio Engineering Society*, 26:739–771, October 1978.

[BM91]     A. Banerjea and B. Mah. The Real-Time Channel Administration Protocol. In *2nd International Workshop on Network and Operating System for Digital Audio and Video*, Heidelberg, Germany, November 1991.

[Bor92]     N. S. Borenstein. Computational Mail as Network Infrastructure for Computer-Supported Cooperative Work. In *Proceedings of ACM Conference on Computer-Supported Cooperative Work, CSCW'92*, pages 67–73, Toronto, Canada, October 1992.

[BP00]     A. Bavier and L. Peterson. The power of virtual time for multimedia scheduling. In *10th International Workshop on Network and Operating System Support for Digital Audio and Video (NOSSDAV)*, San Jose, CA, June 2000.

[BPKR97]     M. Buddhikot, G. Parulkar, S.S. Kumar, and P. Veknat Rangan. Design of large scale multimedia-on-demand storage servers and storage hierarchies. In *Handbook of Multimedia Information Management, editors W. Grosky, R. Jain, R. Mehrotra, Prentice Hall*, 1997.

[BPSWL93]  C. C. Bisdikian, B. Patel, F. Schaffa, and M. Willebeek-LeMair. On the Effectiveness of Priorities in Token Ring for Multimedia Traffic. In *Proceedings of 18th Conference on Local Computer Networks*, pages 25–31, Minneapolis, Minnesota, September 1993.

[Bra87]  S. Brand. *The Media Lab, Inventing the Future at MIT*. Viking Penguin, 1987.

[Bra93]  R. Braudes. *Requirements for multicast protocols*, May 1993. Request for Comments (Informational) 1458, Internet Engineering Task Force.

[BRRK94]  J. Budford, L. Rutledge, J. Rutledge, and C. Kestin. HyOctane: A HyTime Engine for a MMIS. *Multimedia Systems*, 1(4):173–185, 1994.

[Bul93]  D.C.A. Bulterman. Specification and Support of Adaptable Networked Multimedia. *Multimedia Systems*, 1(2):68–76, 1993.

[BZ93a]  C. Buchanan and P. T. Zellweger. Automatic Temporal Layout Mechanisms. In *Proceedings of the 1st ACM International Conference on Multimedia*, Anaheim, CA, August 1993.

[BZ93b]  M. C. Buchanan and P. T. Zellweger. Automatically Generating Consistent Schedules for Multimedia Applications. *Multimedia Systems*, 1(2):55–67, 1993.

[BZS97]  D. E. Bakken, J. A. Zinky, and R.D. Schantz. Architectural support for quality of service for corba objects. theory and practive of object systems. Technical report, BBN, Boston, MA, April 1997.

[Cam96]  A. Campbell. *A Quality of Service Architecture*. PhD thesis, Computing Department, Lancaster University, Lancaster, England, 1996.

[Cam97]  A. Campbell. Mobiware: Qos-aware middleware for mobile multimedia communications. In *IFIP 7th International Conference on High Performance Networking*, April 1997.

[CBD+99]  G. Coulson, G. S. Blair, N. Davies, P. Robin, and T. Fitzpatrick. Supporting Mobile Multimedia Applications through Adaptive Middleware. *IEEE Journal on Selected Areas in Communications*, 17(9):1651–1659, September 1999.

[CBE97]  S. Casner, C. Bormann, and M. Engan. *IP header compression over PPP*, Dec 1997. Internet Draft, Internet Engineering Task Force.

[CBM02a]  G. Coulson, S. Baichoo, and O. Moonian. A retrospective on the design of the GOPI middleware platform. *ACM Springer Multimedia Systems*, 8(5):340–352, 2002.

[CBM02b]    G. Coulson, S. Baichoo, and O. Moonian. A retrospective on the design of the gopi middleware platform. *ACM Multimedia Systems Journal*, 8(5):340–352, 2002.

[CC98]      G. Coulson and M.W. Clarke. A distributed object platform infrastructure for multimedia applications. *Computer Communications*, 21(9):802–919, July 1998.

[CC00]      J. Chung and M. Claypool. Demonstration of dynamic class-based queue management. In *8th ACM International Conference on Multimedia*, pages 473–474, 2000.

[CCH93]     A. Campbell, G. Coulson, and D. Hutchison. A Multimedia Enhanced Transport Service in a Quality of Service Architecture. In *Workshop on Network and Operating System Support for Digital Audio and Video '93*, Lancaster, England, November 1993.

[CCH+93]    J. Crowcroft, S. Chuang, S. Hailes, M. Handley, N. Ismail, D. Lewis, and I. Wakeman. Multimedia Application Requirements for Multicast Communications Services. In *Proceedings of INET 93*, San Francisco, CA, August 1993.

[CG85]      W.J. Croft and J. Gilmore. *0951 Bootstrap Protocol*, September 1985. Updated by RFC1395, RFC1497, RFC1532, RFC1542.

[CGCH92]    G. Coulson, F. Garcia, A. Campbell, and D. Hutchison. Orchestration Services for Distributed Multimedia Synchronization. In *Proceedings of the 4th IFIP International Conference on High Performance Networking (HPN)*, Liege, Belgium, December 1992.

[Che02]     M. Chen. Achieving effective floor control with a low-bandwidth gesture-sensitive video conferencing system. In *10th ACM International Conference on Multimedia*, pages 476–483, December 2002.

[Chu99]     H. Chu. *CPU Service Classes: A Soft Real-time Framework for Multimedia Applications*. PhD thesis, University of Illinois at Urbana-Champaign, Department of Computer Science, Urbana, IL, USA, 1999.

[CJRS89]    D. D. Clark, V. Jacobson, J. Romkey, and H. Salwen. An Analysis of TCP Processing Overhead. *IEEE Communications Magazine*, pages 23–29, June 1989.

[CKY93]     M. S. Chen, D. D. Kandlur, and P. S. Yu. Optimization of the Group Sweeping Scheduling (GSS) with Heterogeneous Multimedia Streams. In *Proceedings of the First ACM International Conference on Multimedia*, pages 235–241, Anaheim, CA, 1993.

[CL88]       J. Y. Chung and J. W. S. Liu. Algorithms for Scheduling Periodic Jobs to Minimize Average Error. In *IEEE Real-Time Systems Symposium*, pages 142–151, Huntsville, Alabama, 1988.

[CL89]       J. Y. Chung and J. W. S. Liu. Performance of Algorithms for Scheduling Periodic Jobs to Avoid Timing Faults. In *Proceedings of 22nd Hawaii International Conference on System Sciences*, pages 683–692, Hawaii, 1989.

[CLO02a]    H. Cha, J. Lee, and J. Oh. Constructing a video server with tertiary storage: Practice and experiences. *ACM Multimedia Systems Journal*, 8(5):380–394, 2002.

[CLO02b]    H. Cha, J. Lee, and J. Oh. Constructing a video server with tetiary storage: practice and experience. *ACM Springer Multimedia Systems*, 8(5):380–394, 2002.

[Cly85]      M. Clynes. Secrets of Life in Music: Musicality Realized by Computer. In *Proceedings of the 1984 International Computer Music Conference*, San Francisco, CA, 1985. International Computer Music Association.

[CM01]      G. Coulson and O. Moonian. A Quality of Service Configuration and Concurrency Framework for Object Based Middleware. Concurrency Practice and Experience(to appear), 2001.

[CN97a]     S. Chen and K. Nahrstedt. Distributed QoS Routing. Technical Report UIUCDCS-R-97-2017, University of Illinois at Urbana-Champaign, Urbana, Illinois, July 1997. Technical Report, accepted to International Conference on Local Computer Networks.

[CN97b]     H. Chu and K. Nahrstedt. A soft real time server in UNIX operating system. In *IDMS'97 (European Workshop on Interactive Distributed Multimedia Systems)*, September 1997.

[CN98a]     S. Chen and K. Nahrstedt. Distributed quality-of service routing in high speed networks based on selective probing. In *IEEE Local Computer Networks (LCN)*, October 1998.

[CN98b]     S. Chen and K. Nahrstedt. On finding multi-constrained paths. In *IEEE International Conference on Communications (ICC)*, June 1998.

[CN98c]     S. Chen and K. Nahrstedt. An overview of quality of service routing for next generation high-speed networks: Problems and solutions. *IEEE Network*, December 1998.

[CN99]  H. Chu and K. Nahrstedt. Cpou service classes for multimedia applications. In *IEEE International Conference on Multimedia Computing and Systems (ICMCS'99)*, pages 296–301, Florence, Italy, 1999.

[Com01]  D. E. Comer. *Computer Networks and Internets with Internet Applications*. Prentice Hall, 3rd edition, 2001.

[Cru97]  R. Cruz. SCED+:efficient management of quality of service guarantees. Technical Report 9713, Center for Wireless Communications, UCSD, 1997.

[CS97]  I. Cidon and Y. Shavitt. Multi-path routing combined with resource reservation. In *IEEE INFOCOM*, pages 92–100, Japan, April 1997.

[CSR88]  S. C. Cheng, J. A. Stankovic, and K. Ramamritham. Scheduling Algorithms for Hard Real-Time Systems—A Brief Survey. In J.A. Stankovic and K. Ramamritham, editors, *Hard Real-Time Systems*, pages 150–178, Washington, DC, 1988. IEEE Computer Society Press.

[CSZ92]  D.D. Clark, S. Shenker, and L. Zhang. Supporting Real-Time Applications in an Integrated Services Packet Network: Architecture and Mechanism. In *SIGCOMM'92*, pages 14–22, Baltimore, MD, August 1992.

[CT90]  D. D. Clark and D. L. Tennenhouse. Architectural considerations for a new generation of protocols. *Computer Communications Review*, 20(4):200–208, Sept 1990.

[CT97]  Shenze Chen and Manu Thapar. A novel video layout strategy for near-video-on-demand servers. In *International Conference on Multimedia Computing and Systems (ICMCS)*, pages 37–45, Ottawa, Canada, June 1997.

[CV02]  S. Chandra and A. Vahdat. Application-specific network management for energy-aware streaming of popular multimedia formats. In *USENIX Annual Technical Conference*, Monterey, June 2002.

[CW90]  D. W. Craig and C. M. Woodside. The Rejection Rate for Tasks with Random Arrivals, Deadlines and Preemptive Scheduling. *IEEE Transactions on Software Engineering*, 16(10):1198–1208, October 1990.

[dACDP03]  M. Dias de Amorim, O. Carlos, M.B. Duarte, and G. Pujolle. Distinguishing video quality through differential matrices. *ACM Multimedia Systems Journal*, 9(1):94–103, 2003.

[DB98]     A. Durand and B. Buclin. IPv6 routing issues. Internet Draft, Internet Engineering Task Force, Apr 1998. Work in progress.

[DB01]     T. Dyer and R. Boppana. A comparison of tcp performance over three routing protocols for mobile ad-hoc networks. In *ACM Symposium on Mobile Ad Hoc Networking and Computing (MobiHoc)*, Long Beach, CA, October 2001.

[DBB+93]   A. Danthine, O. Bonaventure, Y. Baguette, G. Leduc, and L. Leonard. QoS Enhancements and the New Transport Services. In *Local Networks Interconnection*, pages 1–22, Raleigh, NC, October 1993. eds.: R.O. Onvural, A.A. Nilsson, Plenum Press, NY (1993).

[Dee89]    S. Deering. Host Extensions for IP Multicasting. RFC 1112, August 1989.

[Der74]    M. L. Dertouzos. *Control Robotics: The Procedural Control of Physical Processing*, volume 74 of *Information Processing*. North Holland Publishing Company, 1974.

[DHH+93]   L. Delgrossi, Ch. Halstrick, D. Hehmann, R. G. Herrtwich, O. Krone, J. Sandvoss, and C. Vogt. Media scaling for audiovisual communication with the heidelberg transport system. Technical Report 43.9305, IBM ENC Heidelberg, Heidelberg, Germany, 1993.

[DHVW93]   Luca Delgrossi, Ralf Guido Herrtwich, Carsten Vogt, and Lars C. Wolf. Reservation Protocols for Internetworks: A Comparison of ST-II and RSVP. In *4rd International Workshop on Network and Operating System Support for Digital Audio and Video, Lancaster (United Kingdom)*, October 1993.

[Dij59]    E. Dijkstra. A Note on Two Problems in Connection with Graphs. *Numerische Mathematik*, 1:269–271, 1959.

[DKS95]    Asit Dan, Martin Kienzle, and Dinkar Sitaram. A dynamic policy of segment replication for load-balancing in video-on-demand servers. *Multimedia Systems*, 3:93–103, 1995.

[DLW93]    B. J. Dempsey, J. Liebeherr, and A. C. Weaver. A New Error Control Scheme for Packetized Voice over High-Speed Local Area Networks. In *Proceedings of 18th Conference on Local Computer Networks*, Minneapolis, Minnesota, September 1993.

[DM92]     D. L. Drucker and M. D. Murie. *QuickTime Handbook*. Hayden, Carmel, CA, 1992.

[DNN+93]   R. D. Dannenberg, T. Neuemdorffer, J. M. Newcomer, D. Rubine, and D. A. Anderson. Tactus: Toolkit-Level Support for Synchronized Interactive Multimedia. *Multimedia Systems*, pages 77–86, 1993.

[DPA91]    R. Govindan D. P. Anderson, Y. Osawa. Real-time disk storage and retrieval of digital audio/video data. Technical Report TR UCB/CSB 91/646, University of California, Berkeley, September 1991.

[Dro97]    R. Droms. *2131 Dynamic Host Configuration Protocol*, March 1997. Status: DRAFT STANDARD.

[DS93a]    Asit Dan and Dinkar Sitaram. Buffer Management Policy for an On-Demand Video Server. RC 19347, IBM Research Division, 1993.

[DS93b]    R. Dannenberg and R. Stern. Experiments Concerning the Allowable Skew of Two Audio Channels Operating in the Stereo Mode. Personal Communication, 1993.

[DS95a]    Asit Dan and Dinkar Sitaram. A Generalized Interval Caching Policy for Mixed Interactive and Long Video Workloads. RC 20206(89404), IBM Research Division, September 1995.

[DS95b]    Asit Dan and Dinkar Sitaram. An Online Video Placement Policy based on Bandwidth to Space Ratio (BSR). In *Proceedings of the 1995 SIGMOD*, pages 376–385, San Jose, California, May 22–25 1995.

[DSS94]    Asit Dan, Dinkar Sitaram, and Perwez Shahabuddin. Dynamic Batching Policies for an On-Demand Video Server. *Multimedia Systems*, 1994.

[DSST94]   Asit Dan, Perwez Shahabuddin, Dinkar Sitaram, and Don Towsley. Channel Allocation under Batching and VCR Control in Video-On-Demand Systems. IBM Research Report, RC 19588, Sept 1994.

[ea89]     R. Levin et al. Operating systems review. *Operating Systems Review*, 23(3), July 1989.

[ea03]     M. K. Bradshaw et al. Periodic broadcast and patching services—implementation, measurement and analysis in internet streaming video testbed. *ACM Multimedia Systems Journal*, 9(1):78–93, 2003.

[EDP92]    J. Escobar, D. Deutsch, and C. Patridge. Flow Synchronization Protocol. In *Proceedings of IEEE Globecom*, pages 1381–1387, 1992. vol. 3.

[EFI94]    L. Ehley, B. Furth, and M. Ilyas. Evaluation of Multimedia Synchronization Techniques. In *Proceedings of the International Conference on Multimedia Computing and Systems*, pages 110–119, Boston, MA, May 1994. IEEE Computer Society Press.

[EGea02]    D. J. Ecklund, V. Goebel, and T. Plagemann et al. Dynamic end-to-end qos management middleware for distributed multimedia systems. *ACM Multimedia Systems Journal*, 8(5):431–442, 2002.

[EGPE02]    D. J. Ecklund, V. Goebel, T. Plagemann, and E. F. Ecklund. Dynamic end-to-end QoS management middleware for distributed multimedia systems. *ACM Springer Multimedia Systems*, 8(5):431–442, 2002.

[FdLS+01]   J. Flinn, A. de Lara, M. Satyanarayanan, D. Wallach, and W. Zwaenepoel. Reducing the energy usage of office applications. In *Middleware 2001*, Heidelberg, Germany, November 2001.

[Fen97]     W. Fenner. *2236 Internet Group Management Protocol, Version 2*, November 1997. Status: PROPOSED STANDARD.

[Fer91]     D. Ferrari. Design and Application of a Delay Jitter Control Scheme for Packet-switching Internetworks. In *Proceedings of 2nd International Workshop on Network and Operating System Support for Digital Audio and Video*, Heidelberg, Germany, November 1991. Also published in Vol. 614 of Lecture Notes in Computer Science, pages 72–83, Springer-Verlag.

[FGML02]    Z. Fu, B. Greenstein, X. Meng, and S. Lu. Desing and implementation of a tcp-friendly transport protocol for ad-hoc wireless networks. In *IEEE International Conference on Network Protocols (ICNP)*, Paris, France, November 2002.

[FHPW00]    Sally Floyd, Mark Handley, Jitendra Padye, and Jörg Widmer. Equation-based congestion control for unicast applicat ions. In *Proceedings of ACM SIGCOMM 2000*, pages 43–56, Stockholm, Sweden, August 2000. ACM.

[Fin91]     G. G. Finn. An Integration of Network Communication with Workstation Architecture. *ACM Computer Communication Review*, 21(5):18–29, October 1991.

[FJ93]      S. Floyd and V. Jacobson. Random early detection gateways for congestion avoidance. *IEEE/ACM Transactions on Networking*, 1:397–413, August 1993.

[FK98]      S. Frolund and J. Koistinen. QML: A language for Quality of Service Specification. HPL-98-10, HP Laboratories, February 1998.

[FKL+99]    I. Foster, C. Kesselman, C. Lee, B. Lindell, K. Nahrstedt, and A. Roy. A Distributed Resource Management Architecture that Supports Advance Reservations and Co-Allocation. IFIP/IEEE IWQoS'99, May 1999.

[FKRR93]  R. S. Fish, R. E. Kraut, R. W. Root, and R. E. Rice. Video as a Technology for Informal Communication. *Communications of the ACM*, 36(1):48–61, January 1993.

[FKSS99]  W. Feng, K. Kandlur, D. Saha, and K. Shin. Understanding and Improving TCP Performance Over Networks with Minimum Rate Guarantees. *IEEE/ACM Transactions on Networking (TON)*, 7(2):173–187, 1999.

[Flo96]  P. Florissi. *QoSME: QoS Management Environment*. PhD thesis, Department of Computer Science, Columbia University, 1996.

[For79]  J. Forgie. ST - A Proposed Internet Strem Protocol. IEN 119, MIT Lincoln Laboratory, September 1979.

[For96]  ATM Forum. *Private Network-Network Interface (PNNI), version 1.0 specifications*. ATM Forum, May 1996.

[For02]  D.J. Foreman. Managing data in distributed multimedia conferencing applications. *IEEE Multimedia*, 9(4):30–37, Oct-Dec 2002.

[Fre82]  S. French. Sequencing and Scheduling: An Introduction to the Mathematics of the Job Shop. Ellis Horwood Limited, Chichester, 1982.

[FV90]  D. Ferrari and D. C. Verma. A Scheme for Real-Time Channel Establishment in Wide-Area Networks. *IEEE JSAC*, 8(3):368–379, April 1990.

[Gar96]  M.W. Garrett. A service architecture for atm: From applications to scheduling. *IEEE Network*, May 1996.

[GBT93]  S. Gibbs, C. Breiteneder, and D. Tsichritzis. Data Modeling of Time-based Media. In *Visual Objects*, pages 1–21, Geneve: Universite de Geneve, Centre Universitaire d'Informatique, June 1993.

[Ger85]  German national standardization body, Berlin–Köln. *Terminology in Computing*, DIN 4300 edition, 1985.

[GGV96]  P. Goyal, X. Guo, and H. Vin. A Hierarchical CPU Scheduler for Multimedia Operating System. In *Second USENIX Symposiun on Operating System Design and Implementation*, October 1996.

[GH94]  D. James Gemmell and Jiawei Han. Multimedia Network File Servers: Multi-Channel Delay Sensitive Data Retrieval. *Multimedia Systems*, 1(6):240–252, 1994.

[GJKF97]    R. Goyal, R. Jain, S. Kalyanaraman, and S. Fahmy. UBR+: Improving performance of TCP over ATM-UBR services. In *IEEE ICC'97*, pages 1042–1048, 1997.

[GK96]    Shahram Ghandeharizadeh and Dongho Kim. On-line Reorganization of Data in Scalable Continuous Media Servers. In *Proceedings of Database and Expert Systems Applications*, pages 751–768, Zurich, Switzerland, 1996.

[GKS95]    Shahram Ghandeharizadeh, Seon Ho Kim, and Cyrus Shahabi. Continuous Display of Video Objects Using Multi-Zone Disks. Technical Report TR 94-592, USC, April 1995.

[GKT02]    L. Gao, J. Kurose, and D. Towsley. Efficient schemes for broadcasting popular videos. *ACM Multimedia Systems Journal*, 8(4):284–294, 2002.

[GLM96]    Leana Golubchik, John C. S. Lui, and Richard R. Muntz. Adaptive Piggybacking: A Novel Technique for Data Sharing in Video-on-Demand Servers. *Multimedia Systems*, 4:140–155, 1996.

[GN02]    X. Gu and K. Nahrstedt. Dynamic QoS-aware Multimedia Service Configuration in Ubiquitous Computing Environment. In *IEEE ICDCS'2002*, Vienna, Austria, 2002.

[GO97]    R. Guerin and A. Orda. QoS-based Routing in Networks with Inaccurate Information: Theory and Algorithms. In *IEEE INFOCOM'97*, April 1997.

[Gol90]    S. Golestani. A Stop-and-Go Queueing Framework for Congestion Management. In *ACM SIGCOMM'90*, pages 8–18, September 1990.

[Gop96]    R. Gopalakrishnan. *Efficient Quality of Service Support Within Endsystems for High-Speed Multimedia Networking*. PhD thesis, Department of Computer Science, Washington University, St. Louis, MI, 1996.

[GP01]    A. Ganz and A. Phonphoem. Robust superpoll with chaining protocol for ieee 82.11 wireless lans in support of multimedia applications. *Wireless Networks*, 7(1):65–73, 2001.

[Gra94]    G. Grassel. Object-oriented Design and Implementation of a MHEG Runtime Environment for the Interactive Presentation of Multimedia Documents in a Distributed Environment. Master's thesis, University of Mannheim, March 1994. Master thesis in German.

[Gro89]     AFNOR Expert Group. *Multimedia Synchronization: Definitions and Model, Input Contribution on Time Variant Aspects and Synchronization in ODA-Extensions.* ISO IE JTC 1/SC 18/WG3, February 1989.

[Gro00a]    IETF Integrated Services Working Group. *Integrated Services Charter*, 2000.

[Gro00b]    IETF RSVP Working Group. *RSVP Charter.* IETF, http://www.ietf.org/html.charters/rsvp-charter.html, 2000.

[GS73]      D. Grossman and H. Silverman. Placement of Records on a Secondary Storage Device to Minimize Access Time. *Journal of the ACM*, 20:429–438, 1973.

[GSYZ02]    K. Ghahremani, C. Shahabi, S-Y. Didi Yao, and R. Zimmermann. Yima: real-time multimedia storage and retrieval. In *10th ACM International Conference on Multimedia (Demonstration Session)*, pages 668–669, juan-les-Pins, France, November 2002.

[GTB99]     M. Gerla, K. Tang, and R. Bagrodia. Tcp performance in wireless multi-hop networks. In *IEEE International Workshop on Mobile Computing Systems and Applications (WMCSA)*, New Orleans, February 1999.

[Gu00]      X. Gu. Visual Quality of Service Programming Environment for Distributed Heterogeneous Systems. Master Thesis, University of Illinois at Urbana-Champaign, December 2000.

[Gun92]     L. Gun. An approximation method for capturing complex traffic behavior in high-speed networks. Technical report, Jan. 1992.

[Gup94]     A. Gupta. Design scheme 2—A Multicast Realtime Protocol Scheme. Talk at the XUNET'94 Meeting, February 1994.

[GVK+02]    D. James Gemmel, H. Vin, D. Kandlur, P. V. Rangan, and L. Rowe. Multimedia Storage Servers: A Tutorial. In K. Jeffray and H. Zhang, editors, *Readings in Multimedia Computing and Networking*, pages 661–670. Morgan Kaufmann, 2002.

[Ham72]     C. Hamblin. Instants and Intervals. In *Proceedings of the 1st Conference of the International Society for the Study of Time*, pages 324–331, 1972.

[Han98]     M. Handley. SAP—Session Announcement Protocol, 1998. Work in Progress.

[HBP+93]    R. D. Hill, T. Brinck, J. F. Patterson, S. L. Rohall, and W. T. Wilner. The Rendezvous Language and Architecture. *Communications of the ACM*, 36(1):62–67, January 1993.

[HDKS01]   Oliver Heckmann, Vasilios Darlagiannis, Martin Karsten, and Ralf Steinmetz. A Price Communication Protocol for a Multi-Service Internet. In *Informatik 2001 — Wirtschaft und Wissenschaft in der Network Economy - Visionen und Wirklichkeit (GI/OCG 2001)*, September 2001.

[Her90]    R. G. Herrtwich. Time Capsules: An Abstraction for Access to Continuous-Media Data. In *IEEE Real-Time Systems Symposium*, pages 11–20, Orlando, Florida, December 1990.

[Her92]    R. G. Herrtwich. An Architecture for Multimedia Data Stream Handling and its Implication for Multimedia Transport Service Interface. In *3rd IEEE Workshop on Future Trends of Distributed Computing Systems*, Taipei, Taiwan, April 1992.

[HH89]     R. G. Herrtwich and G. Hommel. *Kooperation und Konkurrenz*. Springer-Verlag, 1989.

[HH91]     R. Händel and M. Huber. *Integrated Broadband Networks*. Addison-Wesley Publishing Company, Inc., 1991.

[HJ98]     M. Handley and V. Jacobson. *SDP*. ISI/LBNL, April 1998. Request for Comments: 2327.

[HL88]     K. S. Hong and J. Y. T. Leung. On–Line Scheduling of Real-Time of Tasks. In *IEEE Real-Time Systems Symposium*, pages 244–258, Huntsville, Alabama, 1988.

[HL90]     C. Hemrick and L. Lang. Introduction to Switched Multi-Megabit Data Services (SMDS), an Early Broadband Service. In *ISS 90*, Stockholm, Sweden, June 1990.

[HM91]     M. Hayter and D. McAuley. The Desk Area Network. *ACM Operating Systems Review*, 25(4):14–21, October 1991.

[Hol97]    Wieland Holfelder. Interactive Remote Recording and Playback of Multicast Videoconferences. In *IDMS 97 Conference Proceedings*, 1997.

[HOV02]    K.A. Hua, J-H. Oh, and K. Vu. An adaptive video multicast scheme for varying workloads. *ACM Multimedia Systems Journal*, 8(4):258–269, 2002.

[HPG03a]   P. Halvorsen, T. Plagemann, and V. Goebel. Improving the I/O performance of intermediate multimedia storage nodes. *ACM Springer Multimedia Systems*, 9(1):56–67, 2003.

[HPG03b]   P. Halvorsen, T. Plagemann, and V. Goebel. Improving the i/o performance of intermediate multimedia storage nodes. *ACM Multimedia Systems Journal*, 9(1):56–67, 2003.

[HR93]     M. Hamdaoui and P. Ramanathan. Improved Non-Real-Time Communication in FDDI Networks with Real-Time Traffic. In *Proceedings of 18th Conference on Local Computer Networks*, pages 157–166, Minneapolis, Minnesota, September 1993.

[HS89]     D. Haban and K. G. Shin. Application of Real-time Monitoring to Scheduling Tasks with Random Execution Times. In *IEEE-Real-Time Systems Symposium*, pages 172–180, Santa Monica, 1989.

[HSA89]    M. E. Hodges, R. M. Sasnett, and M. S. Ackerman. Athena Muse: A Construction Set for Multimedia Applications. *IEEE Software*, pages 37–43, January 1989.

[HSA01]    C. Hughes, J. Srinivasan, and S. Adve. Saving energy with architectural and frequency adaptations for multimedia applications. In *34th International Symposium on Microarchitecture*, Austin, TX, December 2001.

[HSS02a]   Oliver Heckmann, Jens Schmitt, and Ralf Steinmetz. Multi-Period Resource Allocation at System Edges. In *Proceedings of the 10th International Conference on Telecommunication Systems Modelling and Analysis (ICTSM10) Monterey, USA*, pages 1–25, October 2002.

[HSS02b]   Oliver Heckmann, Jens Schmitt, and Ralf Steinmetz. Robust Bandwidth Allocation Strategies. In *Proceedings of the 10th International Workshop on Quality of Service 2002 (IWQoS'02), Miami, USA*, pages 138–147. IEEE, May 2002. ISBN 0-7803-7426-6.

[HSSR98]   Handley, Schulzrinne, Schooler, and Rosenberg. SIP: Session Initiation Protocol, 1998. MMUSIC WG, Internet Engineering Task Force, Internet Draft, Work in Progress.

[HTM92]    T. Hoshi, Y. Takahashi, and K. Mori. An Integrated Multimedia Desktop Communication and Collaboration Platform for Broadband ISDN: The Broadband ISDN Group Tele-Working System. In *Proceedings of Multimedia'92*, pages 28 –37, April 1992.

[HVWW94]  R. G. Herrtwich, C. Vogt, H. Wittig, and L. Wolf. Resource Management for Distributed Multimedia Systems. Technical Report 43.9403, IBM European Networking Center, IBM Heidelberg, Heidelberg, Germany, 1994.

[HW94]     M. J. Handley and I. Wakeman. CCCP: Conference Control Channel Protocol: A Scalable Base of Building Conference Control Applications. Technical report, Department of Computer Science, University College London, London, England, March 1994.

[IBM90]    Corporation IBM. *Audio Visual Connection User's Guide and Authoring Language Reference*. IBM Corporation, Version 1.05, IBM Form S15f-7134-02 edition, August 1990.

[IBM91]    Corporation IBM. *AIX Version 3.1: RISC System/6000 as a Real-Time System*. IBM International Technical Support Center, Austin, March 1991.

[IBM92]    Corporation IBM. *IBM Multimedia Presentation Manager Programming Reference and Propgramming Guide 1.0*. IBM Corporation, IBM Form: S41G-2919 and S41G-2920 edition, March 1992.

[IET94]    IETF. Minutes of the multipart multimedia session control working group (mmusic). Proceedings of 29th Internet Engineering Task Force, March 1994.

[ISO93]    ISO. Information Technology—Coding of Moving Pictures and Associated Audio for Digital Storage Media up to about 1.5 Mbit/s, 1993. ISO IEC JTC1/SC29.

[JBB92]    V. Jacobson, R. Braden, and D. Borman. TCP extensions for high performance. RFC 1323, May 1992.

[JDSZ95]   S. Jamin, P. Danzig, S. Shenker, and L. Zhang. A measurement-based admission control algorithm for integrated services packet networks. In *SIGCOMM*, pages 2–13, 1995.

[Jef90]    K. Jeffay. Scheduling Sporadic Tasks with Shared Resources in Hard-Real-Time Systems. Technical Report TR90-039, University of North Carolina at Chapel Hill, Department of Computer Science, Chapel Hill, North Carolina, November 1990.

[JMF93]    V. Jacobson, S. McCanne, and S. Floyd. A Conferencing Architecture for Light-Weight Sessions. MICE Seminar Series, University College London, UK, 1993.

[JN01]     J. Jin and K. Nahrstedt. Classification and Comparison of QoS Specification Languages for Distributed Multimedia Applications. Technical report, UIUC, 2001.

[JNK99]     V. Jacobson, K. Nichols, and K.Poduri. *An Expedited Forwarding PHB*. Internet RFC, June 1999.

[JSP91]     K. Jeffay, D.L. Stone, and D.E. Poirier. YARTOS: Kernel Support for Efficient, Predictable Real-Time Systems. In *Proceedings of IFAC, Workshop on Real-Time Programming*, Atlanta, Georgia, May 1991. Pergamon Press.

[JZ02]      K. Jeffay and H-J. Zhang. *Readings in Multimedia Computing and Networking*. Morgan and Kaufmann Publisher, 2002.

[KB02]      E. Krashinsky and H. Balakrishnan. Minimizing energy for wireless web access with bounded slowdown. In *MobiCom*, Atlanta, GA, Sept. 2002.

[KCBN03]    T. Kwon, Y. Choi, Ch. Bisdikian, and M. Naghshineh. Qos provisioning in wireless/mobile multimedia networks using an adaptive framework. *Wireless Networks*, 9(1):51–59, 2003.

[Ken97]     J. Kenney. Intermediate traffic management. CSE Seminar at University of Illinois at Urban-Champaign, November 1997.

[KF98]      C. Kesselman and I. Foster. The Globus Project: A Status Report. In *IPPS/SPDP'98 Heterogeneous Computing Workshop*, pages 4–18, 1998.

[KG89]      A. Karmouch and N. D. Georganas. Multimedia Document Architecture and Database Design for Medical Applications. In *2nd IEEE COMSOC International Multimedia Communications Workshop*, Montebello, Quebec, Canada, April 1989.

[KL91]      C. M. Krishna and Y. H. Lee. Real-Time Systems. *IEEE Computer*, pages 10–11, May 1991.

[KLC97]     J. Kim, Y. Lho, and K. Chung. An Effective Video Block Placement Scheme on VOD Server based on Multi-Zone Recording Disks. In *Proceedings of the International Conference on Multimedia Computing and Systems (ICMCS)97*, pages 29–36, Ottawa, 1997.

[KMR93]     H. Kanakia, P. P. Mishra, and A. Reibman. An Adaptive Congestion Control Scheme for Real-Time Packet Video Transport. In *Proceedings of SIGCOMM '93*, Baltimore, MD, August 1993.

[KN97a]     S. Narayan K. Nahrstedt, H. Chu. Qos-aware Resource Management for Distributed Multimedia Applications. Technical Report UIUCDCS-R-97-2030, CS, UIUC, October 1997. Technical Report, accepted to IOS Journal on High-Speed Networking.

[KN97b]     K. Kim and K. Nahrstedt. QoS Translation and Admission Control for MPEG Video. In *5th IFIP International Workshop on Quality of Service*, May 1997.

[KN98]      S. Narayan K. Nahrstedt, H. Chu. Qos-aware Resource Management for Distributed Multimedia Applications. *accepted to IOS Journal on High-Speed Networking*, 1998. Technical Report, UIUCDCS-R-97-2030, CS Department, UIUC, October 1997.

[Kon00]     F. Kon. *Automatic Configuration of Component-based Distributed Systems*. PhD thesis, Department of Computer Science, UIUC, 2000.

[Kor97]     Jan Korst. Random Duplicated Assignment: An Alternative to Striping in Video Servers. In *Proceedings of the 5th ACM Int'l Multimedia Conference*, pages 219–226, Seattle, Nov. 9-13 1997.

[KPP93]     V. P. Kompella, J. C. Pasquale, and G. C. Polyzos. Multicast Routing for Multimedia Communication. *IEEE/ACM Transactions on Networking*, June 1993.

[KR03]      J-S. Kim and B-H. Roh. An adaptive multiplexing algorithm of delay-sensitive multiple vbr-coded bit streams. *ACM Multimedia Systems Journal*, 9(1):68–77, 2003.

[Kra98]     S. Krakowiak. *Principles of Operating Systems*. MIT Press, Cambridge, 1998.

[KS95]      S. Keshav and H. Saran. Semantics and Implementation of a Native-Mode ATM Protocol Stack. Internal technical memo, AT&T Bell Laboratories, Murray Hill, NJ, January 1995.

[KSS01]     Martin Karsten, Jens Schmitt, and Ralf Steinmetz. Implementation and Evaluation of the KOM RSVP Engine. In *Proceedings of the 20th Annual Joint Conference of the IEEE Computer and Communications Societies (INFOCOM'01), Anchorage, USA*, pages 1290–1299. IEEE, April 2001. ISBN 0-7803-7016-3.

[KVL97]     Rajesh Krishnan, Dinesh Venkatesh, and Thomas D. C. Little. A Failure and Overload Tolerance Mechanism for Continuous Media Servers. In *Proceedings of the ACM MM97 Conference*, pages 131–142, 1997.

[KW02a]     V. Kahmann and L. Wolf. A proxy architecture for collaborative media streaming. *ACM Springer Multimedia Systems*, 8(5):397–405, 2002.

[KW02b]     V. Kahmann and L. Wolf. A proxy architecture for collaborative media streaming. *ACM Multimedia Systems Journal*, 8(5):397–405, 2002.

[KYO96]     J. Kamada, M. Yuhara, and E. Ono. User-level Realtime Scheduler Exploiting Kernel-level Fixed Priority Scheduler. Technical report, Toshiba, Inc., Tokyo, Japan, June 1996.

[Lab93]      Bellcore Information Networking Research Laboratory. The Touring Machine System. *Communications of the ACM*, 36(1):68–77, January 1993.

[Lau94]      M. Laubach. *1577 Classical IP and ARP over ATM*, January 1994. PROPOSED STANDARD.

[LCP90]     S. Lee, S. Chung, and R. Park. A comparative performance study of several global thresholding techniques for segmentation. *Comp. Vision, Graphics and Image Processing*, 52:171–190, 1990.

[LG90]      T.D.C. Little and A. Ghafoor. Synchronization and storage models for multimedia objects. *IEEE J. on Selected Areas in Comm*, 8(3):413–427, 1990.

[LG91]      T. D. C. Little and A. Ghafoor. Spatio-temporal Composition of Distributed Multimedia Objects for Value Added Networks. *IEEE Computer*, 24:42–50, October 1991.

[LG92]      T.D.C. Little and A. Ghafoor. Scheduling of bandwidth constrained multimedia traffic. *Computer Communications*, 15(6):381–387, 1992.

[LG03]      K. Lund and V. Goebel. Adaptive disk scheduling in a multimedia dbms. In *Proceedings of the 11th ACM Multimedia Conference*, pages 65–74, Berkeley (CA), USA, November 2003. ACM.

[LGG+91]   B. Liskow, S. Ghemawat, R. Gruber, P. Johnson, L. Shrira, and M. Williams. Replication in the Harp file system. In *ACM Synposium on Operating System Principles*, pages 226–238, Pacific Grove, 1991.

[LGKP94]   P. M. Chenand E. K. Lee, E. A. Gibson, R. H. Katz, and D. A. Patterson. Raid: High-performance, reliable secondary storage. *ACM Computing Surveys*, 26(2):145–185, June 1994.

[LHJea02]  T. Liu, H-J.Zhang, and W. Qi et al. A systematic rate controller for mpeg-4 fgs video streaming. *ACM Multimedia Systems Journal*, 8(5):369–379, 2002.

[Li00]       B. Li. *Agilos: A Middleware Control Architecture for Application-Aware Quality of Service Adaptations*. PhD thesis, University of Illinois at Urbana-Champaign, 2000.

[Lic51]     J. Licklider. Basic Correlates of the Auditory Stimulus. In S. S. Stevens, editor, *Handbook of Experimental Psychology*. Wiley, 1951.

[Lit91]     T. D. C. Little. *Synchronization for Distributed Multimedia Database Systems*. PhD thesis, Syracuse University, August 1991.

[Lit92]     T. D. C. Little. Protocols for Bandwidth-constrained Multimedia-traffic. In *Proceedings of the 4th IEEE ComSoc International Workshop on Multimedia Communications*, pages 150 –159, April 1992.

[Lit93]     T. D. C. Little. A Framework for Synchronous Delivery of Time-Dependent Multimedia Data. *Multimedia Systems*, 1(2):87–94, 1993.

[LK91]      E. K. Lee and R. H. Katz. Performance consequences of parity placement in disk arrays. In *Proceedings of the 4th International Conference on Architectural Support for Programming Languages and Operating Systems (ASPLOS-IV)*, pages 190–199, New York, 1991.

[LKG94]     L. Li, A. Karmouch, and N. Georganas. Multimedia Teleorchestra with Independent Sources: Part 1 - Temporal Modeling of Collaborative Multimedia Scenarios. *Multimedia Systems*, 1(4):143 – 153, 1994.

[LL73]      C. L. Liu and J. W. Layland. Scheduling Algorithms for Multiprogramming in a Hard Real-Time Environment. *Journal of the ACM*, 20(1):46–61, January 1973.

[LLG98]     Peter W. K. Lie, John C. S. Lui, and Leana Golubchik. Threshold-Based Dynamic Replication in Large-Scale Video-on-Demand Systems. Accepted for RIDE 98, 1998.

[LLKG93]    L. Li, L. Lamont, A. Karmouch, and N. Georganas. A Distributed Synchronization Control Scheme in a Group-oriented Conferencing Systems. In *Proceedings of the 2nd International Conference on Broadband Islands*, Athens, Greece, June 1993.

[LLN87]     J. W. S. Liu, K.-J. Lin, and S. Naturajan. Scheduling Real-Time, Periodic Jobs Using Imprecise Results. In *IEEE Real-Time Systems Symposium*, pages 252–260, San Jose, CA, 1987.

[LLSY91]    J. W. S. Liu, K.-J. Lin, W.-K. Shin, and A. C. Yu. Algorithms for Scheduling Imprecise Computations. *IEEE Computer*, pages 58–68, May 1991.

[LLZ03]     J. Liu, B. Li, and Y-Q. Zhang. Adaptive video multicast over the internet. *IEEE Multimedia*, 10(1):22–33, Jan-Mar 2003.

[LM80]       J. Y. T Leung and M. L. Merrill. A Note on Preemptive Scheduling of Periodic Real-Time Tasks. *Information Processing Letters*, 11(3):115–118, November 1980.

[LMCL01]     H. Luo, P. Medvedev, J. Cheng, and S. Lu. A self coordinating approach to distributed fair queueing in ad hoc wireless networks. In *IEEE INFOCOM*, Anchorage, AK, April 2001.

[LN99]       B. Li and K. Nahrstedt. Dynamic Reconfiguration for Complex Multimedia Applications. In *IEEE International Conference on Multimedia Computing and Systems (ICMCS'99)*, Florence, Italy, June 1999.

[LN00]       K. S. Lui and K. Nahrstedt. Topology Aggregation and Routing in Bandwidth-Delay Sensitive Networks. In *Globecom'00*, San Francisco, CA, December 2000.

[LNH+97]     J. Liu, K. Nahrstedt, D. Hull, S. Chen, and B. Li. EPIQ QoS Characterization. ARPA Report, Quorum Meeting, July 1997, 1997.

[LP96]       John C. Lin and Sanjoy Paul. RMTP: a reliable multicast transport protocol. In *Proceedings of the Conference on Computer Communications (IEEE Infocom)*, San Fransisco, California, Mar 1996.

[LPGLA03a]   B. N. Levine, S. Paul, and J. J. Garcia-Lunes-Aceves. Organizing multicast receivers deterministically by paket-loss correlation. *ACM Springer Multimedia Systems*, 9(1):3–14, 2003.

[LPGLA03b]   B.N. Levine, S. Paul, and JJ. Garcia-Luna-Aceves. Organizing multicast receivers deterministally by packet loss correlation. *ACM Multimedia Systems Journal*, 9(1):3–14, 2003.

[LRM96]      Ch. Lee, R. Rajkumar, and C. Mercer. Experiences with processor reservation and dynamic qos in real-time mach. In *IEEE Multimedia Systems'96*, Hiroshima, Japan, June 1996.

[LS86]       J. P. Lehoczky and L. Sha. Performance of Real-Time Bus Scheduling Algorithms. *ACM Performance Evaluation Review*, 14(1):44–53, May 1986.

[LS93]       P. Lougher and D. Shepherd. The Design of a Storage Service for Continuous Media. *The Computer Journal*, 36(1):32–42, 1993.

[LS01]       J. Lorch and A. Smith. Improving dynamic voltage scaling algorithms with pace. In *ACM SIGMETRICS*, June 2001.

[LSST91]    J. P. Lehoczky, L. Sha, J. K. Strosnider, and H. Tokuda. Fixed Priority
            Scheduling Theory for Hard Real-Time Systems. In *Foundations of Real-
            Time Computing, Scheduling and Resource Management*, pages 1–30.
            Kluwer Academic Publishers, Norwell, 1991.

[LW82]      J. Y. T. Leung and J. Whitehead. On the Complexity of Fixed-Priority
            Scheduling of Periodic Real-Time Tasks. *Performance Evaluation
            (Netherland)*, 2(4):237–350, 1982.

[LXN02a]    B. Li, D. Xu, and K. Nahrstedt. An integrated runtime QoS-aware
            middleware framework for distributed multimedia applications. *ACM
            Springer Multimedia Systems*, 8(5):420–430, 2002.

[LXN02b]    B. Li, D. Xu, and K. Nahrstedt. An integrated runtime qos-aware
            middleware framework for distributed multimedia applications. *ACM
            Multimedia Systems Journal*, 8(5):420–430, 2002.

[Mah93]     B. A. Mah. A Mechanism for the Administration of Real-Time Channels.
            masters thesis, The Tenet Group, University of California at Berkeley and
            International Computer Science Institute, Berkeley, CA, May 1993.

[Mar91]     B.D. Markey. Emerging Hypermedia Standards – Hypermedia Market
            Place Prepares for HyTime and MHEG. In *Proceedings of the USENIX
            Conference about Multimedia - For Now and The Future*, pages 59–74,
            June 1991.

[MB94]      M. Macedonia and D. Brutzman. MBONE, the Multicast Backbone.
            *IEEE Computer*, 27(4):30–36, April 1994.

[Mel94]     L. Melatti. Fast Ethernet: 100 Mbit/s Made Easy. *Data Communications*,
            pages 111–113, November 1994.

[MES93]     Thomas Meyer, Wolfgang Effelsberg, and Ralf Steinmetz. A Taxonomy
            on Multimedia Synchronization. In *4th IEEE Workshop on Future Trends
            of Distributed Computing Systems, Lisboa, Portugal*, pages 97–103,
            September 1993.

[Mey91]     K. Meyer-Wegener. *Multimedia Datenbanken*. B. G. Teubner, Stuttgart,
            1991.

[MHE93]     MHEG. *Information Technology – Coded Representation of Multimedia
            and Hypermedia Information (MHEG), Part 1: Base notation (ASN.1)*.
            Committee draft ISO/IEC CD 13522-1, June 1993. ISO/IEC JTC1/SC29/
            WG12.

[Mic91]     Corporation Microsoft. *Microsoft Windows Multimedia Authoring and Tools Guide*. Microsoft Press, 1991.

[Mil91]     D.L. Mills. Internet Time Synchronization. *IEEE Transactions on Communications*, 38(10):1482–1493, October 1991.

[Mil93]     David M. Mills. Precision Synchronization of Computer Network Clocks. *ACM Computer Communication Review*, 24(2):28–43, April 1993.

[MJV96]     S. McCanne, V. Jacobson, and M. Vetterli. Receiver-driven layered multicast. In *SIGCOMM Symposium on Communications Architectures and Protocols*, pages 117–130, Palo Alto, California, Aug 1996.

[MK93]      S. Mirchandi and R. Khana. *FDDI Technology and Applications*. John Wiley & Sons, Inc., 1993.

[MNOS97]    C. Martin, P. S. Narayanan, B. Ozden, and A. Silberschatz. The Felini Multimedia Storage System. *Journal of Digital Libraries*, 1997.

[MNO+96]    Cliff Martin, P. S. Narayanan, Banu Ozden, Rajeev Rastogi, and Avi Silberschatz. The Fellini Multimedia Storage Server. In *IEEE Multimedia Systems Conference*, pages 117–146, 1996.

[Moo90]     D. J. Moore. Multimedia Presentation Development using the Audio Visual Connection. *IBM Systems Journal*, 29(4):494–508, 1990.

[Moy93]     J. Moy. Multicast Routing Extensions for OSPF. In *Proceedings of INET 93*, San Francisco, CA, August 1993.

[Moy94]     J. Moy. *1584 Multicast Extensions to OSPF*, March 1994. Status: PROPOSED STANDARD.

[Moy97]     J. Moy. *2178 OSPF Version 2*, July 1997. Status: DRAFT STANDARD.

[MP02]      K. Mayer-Patel. Networking and Media Streaming. In K. Jeffray and H. Zhang, editors, *Readings in Multimedia Computing and Networking*. Morgan Kaufmann, 2002.

[MR93]      P. Martini and M. Rumekasten. MAN/WAN Integration – the ATM-to-DQDB Case. In *Proceedings of 18th Conference on Local Computer Networks*, pages 102–109, Minneapolis, Minnesota, September 1993.

[MR94]      M. Mülhäuser and T. Rüdebusch. Context Embedding and Reuse in Cooperative-Software Development. In Jose L. Encarnacao, James D. Foley, and Ralf Guido Herrtwich, editors, *Perspectives of Multimedia Systems*, July 1994. Position Papers of the Dagstuhl Multimedia Seminar.

[MS97]      Q. Ma and P. Steenkiste. Quality of service routing for traffic with performance guarantees. In *Proceedings of 5th IFIP IWQoS'97*, New York, NY, May 1997.

[MSS92]     A. Mauthe, W. Schultz, and R. Steinmetz. Inside the Heidelberg Multimedia Operating System Support: Real-Time Processing of Continuous Media in OS/2. Technical Report 43.9214, IBM European Networking Center, IBM Heidelberg, Germany, 1992.

[MT90]      C. W. Mercer and H. Tokuda. The ARTS Real-Time Object Model. In *IEEE Real-Time System Symposium*, pages 2–10, Lake Buena Vista, Florida, 1990.

[MT94]      C. W. Mercer and S. Savage H. Tokuda. Processor Capacity Reserves: Operating System Support for Multimedia Applications. In *IEEE International Conference on Multimedia Computing and Systems*, May 1994.

[MT02]      M. Mesarina and Y. Turner. Reduced energy decoding of mpeg streams. In *SPIE Multimedia Computing and Networking Conference*, San Jose, January 2002.

[MZ93]      N. Malcolm and W. Zhao. Guaranteeing Synchronous Messages with Arbitrary Deadline Constraints in an FDDI Network. In *Proceedings of 18th Conference on Local Computer Networks*, pages 186–195, Minneapolis, Minnesota, September 1993.

[Nah95]     K. Nahrstedt. *An Architecture for End-to-End Quality of Service Provision and its Experimental Validation*. PhD thesis, CIS Department, University of Pennsylvania, August 1995.

[NBH88]     R. M. Newman, Z. L. Budrikis, and J. L. Hullet. The DQDB MAN. *IEEE Communication Magazine*, 26(4):20–28, April 1988.

[NHK96a]    K. Nahrstedt, A. Hossain, and S. Kang. A Probe-based Algorithm for QoS Specification and Adaptation. In *Proceedings of 4th IFIP Workshop on Quality of Service* , pages 89–100, Paris, France, March 1996.

[NHK96b]    K. Nahrstedt, A. Hossain, and S. Kang. A Probe-based Algorithm for QoS Specification and Adaptation. In *Proceedings of 4th IFIP Workshop on Quality of Service*, pages 89–100, Paris, France, March 1996.

[Nic90]     C. Nicolau. An Architecture for Real-Time Multimedia Communication Systems. *IEEE JSAC*, 8:391–400, April 1990.

[NL97]      J. Nieh and J. Lam. Smart UNIX SVR4 support for Multimedia
            Applications. In *Proceedings of the International Conference on
            Multimedia Computing and Systems*, Ottawa, Canada, 1997.

[NS92]      K. Nahrstedt and J. M. Smith. Integrated Multimedia Architecture for
            High-Speed Networks. In *Proceedings of Multimedia '92*, Monterey, CA,
            April 1992.

[NS95]      K. Nahrstedt and J. M. Smith. The QoS Broker. *IEEE Multimedia*,
            2(1):53–67, Spring 1995.

[NS96]      K. Nahrstedt and J. M. Smith. Design, Implementation and Experiences
            of the OMEGA End-Point Architecture. *IEEE JSAC, Special Issue on
            Distributed Multimedia Systems and Technology*, 14(7):1263–1279,
            September 1996.

[NV92]      R. Nagarajan and C. Vogt. Guaranteed-Performance Transport of
            Multimedia Traffic over the Token Ring. Technical Report 43.9201, IBM
            European Networking Center, IBM Heidelberg, Germany, 1992.

[NWX00]     K. Nahrstedt, D. Wichadakul, and D. Xu. Distributed QoS Compilation
            and Runtime Instantiation. In *IWQoS'2000*, Pittsburgh, PA, June 2000.

[OD89]      J. Ousterhout and F. Douglis. Beating the I/O Bottleneck: A case for Log-
            Structured File Systems. *Operating Systems Review*, 23(1):11–28, 1989.

[OF93]      S. O'Shea and J. Finucane. Reactive DQDB. In *Proceedings of 18th
            Conference on Local Computer Networks*, Minneapolis, Minnesota,
            September 1993.

[OMS+92]    T. Ohmori, K. Maeno, S. Sakata, H. Fukuoka, and K. Watabe. Distributed
            Cooperative Control for Application Sharing Based on Multiparty and
            Multimedia Desktop Conferencing System: MERMAID. In *Proceedings
            of Multimedia '92*, pages 112– 131, April 1992.

[Org88]     International Standardization Organisation. *Information Processing
            Systems—Open Systems Interconnection—The Directory: Overview of
            Concepts, Models and Service*, 1988. ISO/IEC JTC 1/SC21, International
            Standard 9594-1.

[Org92]     International Standard Organization. *Hypermedia/Time-based Document
            Structuring Language (HyTime)*. ISO/IEC, IS10744 edition, 1992.

[OSS03]     Giwon On, Jens Schmitt, and Ralf Steinmetz. Quality of Availability:
            Replica Placement for Widely Distributed Systems. In *IWQoS 2003*,
            pages 325–342, June 2003. Montrey, CA, USA.

[PAA+03]    S. Prabhakar, D. Agrawal, A. E. Abbadi, A. Singh, and T. Smith. Browsing and placement of multi-resolution images on parallel disks. *ACM Springer Multimedia Systems*, 8(6):459–469, 2003.

[PAea03]    S. Prabhakar, D. Agrawal, and A. E. Abbadi et al. Browsing and placement of multi-resolution images on parallel disks. *ACM Multimedia Systems Journal*, 8(6):459–469, 2003.

[Par94a]    C. Partridge. *Gigabit Networking*. Addison Wesley, 1994.

[Par94b]    C. Partridge. *Gigabit Networking*. Addison-Wesley Publishing Company, Inc., 1994.

[PC00]      A. Puri and T. Chen. *Multimedia Systems, Standards, and Networks*. Marcel and Dekker Publisher, 2000.

[Per97]     J. Perl, editor. *Informatik im Sport*. Verlag Karl Hofmann, Schorndorf, 1997.

[PGHA00]    T. Plagemann, V. Goebel, P. Halvorsen, and O. Anshus. Operating system support for multimedia systems. *The Computer Communications Journal, Elsevier*, Vol. 23(No. 3):267–289, February 2000.

[PGK88]     D. A. Patterson, G. Gibson, and R. H. Katz. A Case for Redundant Arrays of Inexpensive Disks (RAID). In *Proceedings of the 1988 ACM Conference on Management of Data (SIGMOD)*, pages 109–116, Chicago, IL, June 1988.

[PGKK88]    J. B. Postel, G. G.Finn, A. R. Katz, and J. K.Reynolds. An experimental multimedia mail system. *ACM Transactions on Office Information Systems*, 6(1):63–81, january 1988.

[PIM97]     *2117 Protocol Independent Multicast-Sparse Mode (PIM-SM): Protocol Specification*, June 1997. Status: EXPERIMENTAL.

[Pla02]     T. Plagemann. Middleware+multimedia=multimedia middleware? *ACM Multimedia Systems Journal*, 8(5):395–396, 2002.

[Plu82]     D.C. Plummer. *0826 Ethernet Address Resolution Protocol: Or converting network protocol addresses to 48.bit Ethernet address for transmission on Ethernet hardware*, Nov-01 1982. Status: STANDARD.

[Pre90]     L. Press. Computer or teleputer? *Communications of the ACM*, 33(9):29–36, September 1990.

[Pry89]     M. de Prycker. Impact of Data Communication on ATM. In *ICC 89*, Boston, MA, June 1989.

[Pry93]     M. de Prycker. *Asynchronous Transfer Mode – Solution for Broadband ISDN*. Ellis Horwood Limited and Market Cross House, 2nd edition, 1993.

[PS97]      P. Pan and H. Schulzrinne. Yessir: A simple reservation mechanism for the internet. Technical Report Technical Report RC 20697, IBM Research, Hawthorne, New York, Sept 1997.

[PS98]      P. P. Pan and H. Schulzrinne. Yessir: A simple reservation mechanism for the internet. In *Proc. International Workshop on Network and Operating System Support for Digital Audio and Video (NOSSDAV)*, Cambridge, England, July 1998.

[PS01]      P. Pillai and K.G. Shin. Real-time dynamic voltage scaling for low-power embedded operating systems. In *18th Symposium on Operating Systems and Principles (SOSP)*, October 2001.

[PSS02]     Krishna Pandit, Jens Schmitt, and Ralf Steinmetz. Aggregation of Heterogeneous Real-Time Flows with Statistical Guarantees. In *Procceedings of 2002 International Symposium on Performance Evaluation of Computer and Telecommunication Systems (SPECTS'02), San Diego, USA*, pages 57–64. SCS, July 2002. ISBN 1-56555-252-0.

[PW72]      E. W. Peterson and E. J. Weldon. *Error-Correcting Codes*. MIT Press, Cambridge, Mass, 2 edition, 1972.

[PZF92]     C. Parris, H. Zhang, and D. Ferrari. A Mechanism for Dynamic Re-routing of Real-Time Services on Packet Networks. Technical report, UC Berkeley, Berkeley, CA, 1992.

[QM03]      Y. Qiu and P. Marbach. Bandwidth allocation in ad hoc networks: A price-based approach. In *IEEE INFOCOM*, San Francisco, April 2003.

[Ran93]     P. V. Rangan. Video Conferencing, File Storage, and Management in Multimedia Computer Systems. *Computer Networks and ISDN Systems*, 25(8):901–919, March 1993.

[RB90]      I. Rubin and J. E. Baker. Media Access Control for High-Speed Local Area and Metropolitan Area Communication Networks. *Proc. of the IEEE*, 78(1), January 1990.

[RB00]      T. Roscoe and G. Bowen. Script-driven Packet Marking for Quality of Service Support in Legacy Applications. In *SPIE Conference on Multimedia Computing and Networking*, San Jose, CA, January 2000.

[RG96]      M. Roseman and S. Greenberg. Building real time groupware with groupkit, a groupware toolkit. *Transactions on Computer Human Interaction (ToCHI)*, 3(1):66–106, March 1996.

[RGKS00]    Utz Roedig, Manuel Goertz, Martin Karsten, and Ralf Steinmetz. RSVP as Firewall Signalling Protocol. Technical Report 6, KOM, December 2000.

[RJ85]      J. W. Reedy and J. R. Jones. Methods of Collision Detection in Fiber Optic CSMA/CD Networks. *IEEE Journal on Selected Areas in Communication*, 3:890–896, November 1985.

[RJMO02]    R. Rajkumar, K. Juvva, A. Molano, and S. Oikawa. Resource kernels: A resource-centric approach to real-time and multimedia systems. In K. Jeffray and H. Zhang, editors, *Readings in Multimedia Computing and Networking*. Morgan Kaufmann, 2002.

[RL95]      Y. Rekhter and T. Li. *1771 A Border Gateway Protocol 4 (BGP-4)*, March 1995. Status: DRAFT STANDARD.

[RM80]      D. Rubinea and P. McAvinney. Programmable Finger-tracking Instrument Controllers. *Computer Music Journal*, 14(1):26–41, Spring 1980.

[Rou02a]    N. Roussel. Experiences in the design of the well, a group communication device for teleconviviality. In *10th ACM International Conference on Multimedia*, pages 146–152, Juan-les-Pins, France, November 2002.

[Rou02b]    N. Roussel. Experiences in the design of the well, a group communication device for teleconviviality. In *Proceedings of the 10th ACM International Conference on Multimedia 2002*, pages 146–152, Juan les Pins, France, 2002.

[RR93]      S. Ramanathan and V. Rangan. Feedback Technique for Intra-media Continuity and Intra-media Synchronization in Distributed Multimedia Systems. *Computer Journal*, 36(1):19–31, 1993.

[R.S89]     R.Steinmetz. Synchronization of multimedia objects. In *5th International Workshop on Telematics*, Denver, CO, USA, September 1989.

[RSS02]     Ivica Rimac, Jens Schmitt, and Ralf Steinmetz. Is Dynamic Multi-Rate Multicast Worthwhile the Effort? In *Proceedings of the 28th EUROMICRO Conference 2002 (Multimedia and Telecommunications Track), Dortmund, Germany*, pages 233–239. IEEE, September 2002. ISBN 0-7695-1787-0.

[RSSS90]    Johannes Rückert, Bernd Schöner, Ralf Steinmetz, and Hermann Schmutz. A Distributed Multimedia Environment for Advanced CSCW Applications. In *IEEE Multimedia '90, Bordeaux, France*, November 1990.

[RT98a]     S.V. Raghavan and S.K. Tripathi. *Networked Multimedia Systems.* Prentice Hall Publisher, 1998.

[RT98b]     S.V. Raghavan and S.T. Tripathi. *Networked Multimedia Systems.* Prentice Hall, Upper Saddle River, New Jersey, 1998.

[RV91]      P. V. Rangan and H. M. Vin. Designing File Systems for Digital Video and Audio. *Operating Systems Review*, 25(2):81–94, October 1991.

[RV93]      P. Venkat Rangan and H. Vin. Designing a Multi-User HDTV Storage Server. *IEEE Journal on Selected Areas in Communications*, 11(1):153–164, January 1993.

[RVG+93]    K.K. Ramakrishnan, L. Vaitzblit, C. Gray, U. Vahalia, D. Ting, P. Tzelnic, S. Glaser, and W. Duso. Operating System Support for Video-On-Demand File Services. In *Workshop on Network and Operating System Support for Digital Audio and Video '93*, Lancaster, England, November 3-5, 1993.

[RW93]      A. L. Narasimha Reddy and Jim Wyllie. Disk scheduling in a multimedia I/O system. In *Proceedings of ACM MM'93*, pages 225–234, Anaheim, CA, August 1993.

[RW94]      A. L. Narasimha Reddy and Jim Wyllie. I/O Issues in a Multimedia System. *COMPUTER*, 27(3):69–74, 1994.

[Sal89]     M. Salmony. *On OSI-Based Transport Systems for Future Applications over High-Speed Networks.* PhD thesis, Lancaster University, 1989.

[SC92]      E. M. Schooler and S. L. Casner. An Architecture for Multimedia Connection Management. In *Proceedings of Multimedia'92*, pages 271–274, April 1992.

[SC95]      K. G. Shin and C. C. Chou. A Distributed Route Selection Scheme for Establishing Real-Time Channel. In *6th IFIP International Conference on High Performance Networking (HPN'95)*, pages 319–329, September 1995.

[SCFJ96]    H. Schulzrinne, S. Casner, R. Friederick, and V. Jacobson. RTP: A Transport Protocol for Real-Time Applications. RFC 1889, January 1996.

[Sch94]   H. Schulzrinne. Conferencing and collaborative computing. In Jose L. Encarnacao, James D. Foley, and Ralf Guido Herrtwich, editors, *Perspectives of Multimedia Systems*, July 1994. Position Papers of the Dagstuhl Multimedia Seminar.

[Sch97]   R. Schulmeister. *Grundlagen hypermedialer Lernsysteme*. Oldenbourg Verlag, München Wien, 1997.

[Sch01]   Jens Burkhard Schmitt. *Heterogeneous Network Quality of Service Systems*. Kluwer Academic Publishers, June 2001. ISBN 0-793-7410-X.

[SCN03]   S. Shah, K. Chen, and K. Nahrstedt. Dynamic bandwdith management for single-hop ad-hoc wireless networks. In *IEEE International Conference on Pervasive Computing and Communications (PerCom)*, Dallas-Fort Worth, TX, March 2003.

[SDS02a]  J. Song, A. Dan, and D. Sitaram. JINSIL: A middleware for presentation of composite multimedia objects in a distributed environment. *ACM Springer Multimedia Systems*, 8(4):295–314, 2002.

[SDS02b]  J. Song, A. Dan, and D. Sitaram. Jinsil: A middleware for presentation of composite multimedia objects in a distributed environment. *ACM Multimedia Systems Journal*, 8(4):295–314, 2002.

[SDW92]   W.T. Strayer, B. Dempsey, and A. Weaver. *XTP: The Xpress Transfer Protocol*. Addison-Wesley Publishing Company, Inc., July 1992.

[SDY93]   Dinkar Sitaram, Asit Dan, and Philip S. Yu. Issues in the Design of Multiserver File Systems to Cope with Load Skew. In *Proceedings of 2nd Int'l Conference on Parallel and Distributed Systems*, pages 214–223, San Diego, CA, January 1993.

[SE93]    R. Steinmetz and C. Engler. Human Perception of Media Synchronization. Technical Report 43.9310, IBM European Networking Center Heidelberg, Heidelberg, Germany, 1993.

[SF92]    R. Steinmetz and Ch. Fritsche. Abstractions for Continuous Media Programming. *Computer Communication*, 15(4), July 1992.

[SG90]    L. Sha and J. B. Goodenough. Real-time Scheduling Theory and ADA. *IEEE Transactions on Computers*, 23(4):53–64, April 1990.

[SGC94]    W.T. Strayer, S. Gray, and R.E. Cline, Jr. An Object-Oriented Implementation of the Xpress Transfer Protocol. In R. Steinmentz (Ed.), editor, *Multimedia: Advanced Teleservices and High-Speed Communication Architectures, 2nd International Workshop, IWACA'94*, pages 387–400, Heidelberg, Germany, September 1994. Lecture Notes in Computer Science, No. 868.

[SGHH94]   N.A. Streitz, J. Geißler, J. M. Haake, and J. Hol. Dolphin: Integrated meeting support across liveboards, local and remote desktop environments. In *Proceedings of the 1994 ACM Conference on Computer Supported Cooperative Work (CSCW '94)*, pages 345–358, Chapel Hill, N.C., October 1994.

[SGRV98]   P. J. Shenoy, P. Goyal, S. S. Rao, and H. M. Vin. Symphony: An integrated multimedia file system. In *In Proceedings of SPIE/ACM Conference on Multimedia Computing and Networking (MMCN 1998)*, pages 124–138, San Jose, CA, Jan 1998.

[SGV02a]   P. Shenoy, P. Goyal, and H. Vin. Architectural considerations for next generation file systems. *ACM Multimedia Systems Journal*, 8(4):270–283, 2002.

[SGV02b]   P. J. Shenoy, P. Goyal, and H. M. Vin. Architectural considerations for next-generation file systems. *ACM Springer Multimedia Systems*, 8(4):270–283, 2002.

[SH91]     Ralf Steinmetz and Ralf Guido Herrtwich. Integrierte verteilte Multimedia-Systeme. *Informatik Spektrum*, 14(5), October 1991.

[Sha99]    N. Sharda. Multimedia networks: fundamentals and future directions. *Communications of the AIS*, 1(2), 1999.

[SHH92]    J.B. Stefani, L. Hazard, and F. Horn. Computational Model for Distributed Multimedia Applications Based on a Synchronous Programming Language. *Computer Communication*, 15:114–128, March 1992.

[SHKS02]   Jens Schmitt, Oliver Heckmann, Martin Karsten, and Ralf Steinmetz. Decoupling Different Time Scales of Network QoS Systems. *Computer Communications (Special Issue on Advances in Performance Evaluation of Computer and Telecommunications Networking)*, 25(11-12):1047–1057, July 2002. ISSN 0140-3664.

[SK00]     D. Schmidt and F. Kuhns. An Overview of the Real-Time CORBA Specification. *IEEE Computer*, 33(6):56–63, June 2000.

[SKG91]     L. Sha, M. H. Klein, and J. B. Goodenough. Rate monotonic analysis for real-time systems. In *Foundations of Real-Time Computing, Scheduling and Resource Management*, pages 129–156. Kluwer Academic Publisher, Norwell, 1991.

[SKSH96]    C. Schuckmann, L. Kirchner, J. Schümmer, and J.M. Haake. Designing object-oriented synchronous groupware with COAST. In M.S. Ackerman, editor, *Proceedings of the ACM 1996 Conference on Computer Supported Cooperative Work (CSCW '96)*, pages 30–38, Boston, Massachusetts, November 1996.

[SM92a]     R. Steinmetz and T. Meyer. Modelling Distributed Multimedia Applications. In *IEEE International Workshop on Advanced Communications and Applications for High-Speed Networks*, München, Germany, March 1992.

[SM92b]     Ralf Steinmetz and Thomas Meyer. Modelling Distributed Multimedia Applications. In *International Workshop on Advanced Communications and Applications for High Speed Networks (IWACA), Munich, Germany*, March 1992.

[Smi89]     J. M. Smith. Standard Generalized Markup Language and Related Standards. *Computer Communication*, 12:80–83, April 1989.

[Spr90]     B. Sprunt. Implementing Sporadic Servers in ADA. Technical report, Carnegie-Mellon University, Pittsburgh, PA, May 1990.

[SR89]      L. Sha and R. Rajkumar. Real-time systems. A Tutorial of the Rate-Monotonic Scheduling Framework with Bus-Related Issues P896.3, Draft 4.0, Futurebus+, 1989.

[SR97]      Schulzrinne and Rosenberg. *SIP Call Control Services*, December 1997. RFC 2251.

[SR02]      H. Schulzrinne and J. Rosenberg. Internet Telephony: architecture and protocols - an IETF perspective. In Kevin Jeffray and Hongjiang Zhang, editors, *Readings in Multimedia Computing and Networking*. Morgan Kaufmann, 2002.

[SRB+92]    K. Srinivas, R. Reddy, A. Babadi, S. Kamana, V. Kumar, and Z. Dai. MONET: A Multi-media System for Conferencing and Application Sharing in Distributed Systems. CERC Technical Report Series CERC-TR-RN-91-009, Concurrent Engineering Research Center, West Virginia University, Morgantown, WV, February 1992.

[SRN+83]    R. V. Schmidt, E. G. Rawson, R. E. Norton, S. B. Jackson, and M. D. Bailey. Fibernet II - A Fiber Optic Ethernet. *IEEE Journal on Selected Areas in Communication*, 1:702–710, November 1983.

[SRV97a]    H. F. Salama, D. S. Reeves, and Y. Viniotis. A Distributed Algorithm for Delay-Constrained Unicast Routing. In *IEEE INFOCOM*, April 1997.

[SRV97b]    H. F. Salama, D. S. Reeves, and Y. Viniotis. Evaluation of Multicast Routing Algorithms for Real-Time Communications on High-Speed Networks. *IEEE Journal on Selected Areas in Communications*, 15(3):332–345, April 1997.

[SS90]      M. Salmony and D. Shepherd. Extending OSI to Support Synchronization Required by Multimedia Applications. *Computer Communication*, 13:399–406, September 1990.

[SSL89]     B. Sprunt, L. Sha, and J. Lehoczky. Aperiodic Task Scheduling for Hard Real-Time Systems. *The Journal of Real-Time Systems*, 1:27–60, 1989.

[St}94]     H. J. Stüttgen. Network evolution and multimedia communication. Technical Report 43.9404, IBM European Networking Center Heidelberg, Heidelberg, Germany, 1994.

[Sta92]     W. Stalling. *ISDN and Broadband ISDN*. Macmillan Publishing Company, 2 edition, 1992.

[Ste87]     M. Stewart. The Feel Factor: Music with Soul. *Electronic Musician*, 3(10):55–66, 1987.

[Ste90]     R. Steinmetz. Analyse von Synchronisationsmechanismen mit Anwendung im Multimedia-Bereich. In *GI ITG Workshop Sprachen und Systeme zur Parallelverarbeitung*, pages 39–47, Arnoldshain, Januar 1990. PARS Mitteilungen Nr.7.

[Ste93]     Ralf Steinmetz. A Networked Multimedia Workbench: The Perspective for TV Video Production. In *Proceedings of Electronic Publishing International '93, Oslo*, June 1993.

[Ste00]     Ralf Steinmetz. *Multimedia-Technologie: Grundlagen, Komponenten und Systeme*. Springer Verlag, October 2000. 3. Auflage (erstmalig mit CD).

[Sto72]     T. Stockham. A/D and D/A Converters: Their Effect on Digital Audio Fidelity. In L. Rabiner and C. Rader, editors, *Digital Signal Processing*, pages 55–66. IEEE Press, New York, 1972.

[SV02]      P. Shenoy and H. Vin. Multimedia Storage Servers. In K. Jeffray and
            H. Zhang, editors, *Chapter 10 in Readings in Multimedia Computing and
            Networking*. Morgan Kaufmann, 2002.

[SW94a]     E. Schooler and A. Weinrib. Multiparty Multimedia Session Control WG.
            Minutes from the 29th IETG, Seattle, WA, posted on rem-conf, March
            1994.

[SW94b]     S. Shenker and A. Weinrib. Managing Shared Ephemeral Tele-
            conferencing State: Policy and Mechanism. ftp site from
            thumper.bellcore.com:pub/abel/agree.ps, March 1994.

[Syn88]     CCETT. Multimedia Synchronization. *CCETT internal note: AFNOR
            adhoc group on AVI standardisation*. CCETT, 1988.

[SZK+98]    R. Schantz, J. Zinky, D. Karr, R. Vanegas, J. Loyall, D. Bakken, and
            K. Anderson. QoS Aspect Languages and Their Runtime Integration.
            *Lecture Notes in Computer Science*, 1511, 1998.

[Tan96]     Andrew S. Tanenbaum. *Computer Networks*, chapter 6.4.6, pages 536–
            539. Prentice Hall, 3rd edition, 1996.

[Tan01]     Andrew S. Tanenbaum. *Modern Operating Systems*. Prentice Hall, 2nd
            edition, 2001.

[TBR92]     D. P. Tranchier, P. E. Boyer, and Y. M. Rowand. Fast Bandwidth
            Allocation in ATM Networks. In *ISS 92*, Yokohama, Japan, October 1992.

[TBR98]     D. A. Tietze, A. Bapat, and R. Reinema. Document-centric groupware for
            distributed governmental agencies. In B. Pernici and C. Thanos, editors,
            *Proceedings of the 10th Conference on Advanced Information Systems
            Engineering (CAiSE '98)*, pages 173–190, Pisa, Italy, June 1998.

[TC01]      A. Tripathi and M. Claypool. Demonstration of improved multimedia
            streaming by using content-aware video scaling. In *9th ACM
            International Conference on Multimedia*, pages 609–610, Ottawa,
            Canada, November 2001.

[TEBM95]    H. L. Truon, W. W. Ellington, J. Y. L. Boudec, and A. X. Meier. LAN
            emulation on an ATM network. *IEEE Communications Magazine*, 1995.

[TF95]      William H. Tetzlaff and Robert Flynn. Elements of Scalable Video
            Servers. In *Proceedings of COMPCON 1995*, pages 239–248, 1995.

[TGD91]     D. Tsichritzis, S. Gibbs, and L. Dami. Active Media. In *Object
            Composition (D. Tsichritzis, ed.)*, pages 115 –132, Universite de Geneve,
            Centre Universitaire d'Informatique, Geneve, June 1991.

[TK91]     A. M. Van Tilborg and G. M. Koob, editors. *Foundations of Real-Time Computing, Scheduling and Resource Management*. Kluwer Academic Publisher, Norwell, 1991.

[TL00]     P. K. C. Tse and C. H. C. Leung. Improving Multimedia Systems Performance Using Constant-Density Recording Disks. *ACM Springer Multimedia Systems*, 8(1):47–56, 2000.

[Top90]    C. Topolocic. Experimental Internet Stream Protocol, Version 2 (ST II). Internet Network Working Group, RFC 1190, October 1990.

[TP91]     R. Terek and J. Pasquale. Experiences with Audio Conferencing Using the X Window System, UNIX and TCP/IP. In *Proceedings of USENIX 91*, pages 405–418, Nashville, TN, June 1991.

[TTCM92]   H. Tokuda, Y. Tobe, S. T. C. Chou, and J. M. F. Moura. Continuous Media Communication with Dynamic QOS Control Using ARTS with an FDDI Network. In *ACM SIGCOMM 92*, pages 88–98, Baltimore, MD, 1992.

[Tur86]    J.S. Turner. New directions in communications (or which way to the information age). *IEEE Communications*, 24(10):8–15, October 1986.

[VBG00]    N. Vaidya, P. Bahl, and S. Gupta. Distributed fair scheduling in a wireless lan. In *ACM MobiCom*, Boston, MA, August 2000.

[Ven98]    V. Venkataramani. A reservation protocol for multimedia resource management system. Technical report, University of Illinois at Urbana-Champaign, Urbana, IL, May 1998. Master Thesis.

[VFJF99]   B. Vandalore, W. Feng, R. Jain, and S. Fahmy. A survey of application layer techniques for adaptive streaming of multimedia. *Special issue on Adaptive Multimedia, Journal of Real-Time Systems, Kluwer Publisher*, April 1999.

[VHN92]    C. Vogt, R. G. Herrtwich, and R. Nagarajan. HeiRAT: The Heidelberg Resource Administration Technique, Design Philosophy and Goals. In *Proceedings of Conference on Communication in Distributed Systems*, München,Germany, 1992. Also published in Informatik Aktuell, Springer-Verlag.

[VL95]     D. Venkatesh and T. D. C. Little. Dynamic Service Aggregation for Efficient Use of Resources in Interactive Video Delivery. In *Proceedings of the 5th NOSSDAV conference*, pages 113–116, Nov. 1995.

[VN97]    N. Venkatasubriamanian and K. Nahrstedt. An integrated metric for video QoS. In *ACM Multimedia Conference*, pages 371–381, Seattle, WA, November 1997.

[VZ91]    D. Verma and H. Zhang. Design documents for RTIP/RMTP. unpublished report, University of California at Berkeley and International Computer Science Institute, Berkeley, CA, May 1991.

[WC87]    C. M. Woodside and D. W. Craig. Local Non-Preemptive Scheduling Policies for Hard Real-Time Distributed Systems. In *IEEE-Real-Time Systems Symposium*, pages 12–17, San Jose, 1987.

[WC96]    Z. Wang and J. Crowcroft. QoS Routing for Supporting Resource Reservation. *IEEE Journal on Selected Areas in Communications*, September 1996.

[WCK03]   H-H. Wu, M. Claypool, and R. Kinicki. Qos and congestion control: A model for mpeg with forward error correction and tcp-friendly bandwidth. In *13th Internationa Workshop on Network and Operating Systems Support for Digital Audio and Video (NOSSDAV)*, pages 122–130, June 2003.

[WD97]    Yuewei Wang and David H. C. Du. Weighted Striping in Multimedia Servers. In *Proceedings of the International Conference on Multimedia Computing and Systems (ICMCS) 97*, pages 102–109, Ottawa, June 3-6 1997.

[WH94]    L. Wolf and R. G. Herrtwich. The System Architecture of the Heidelberg Transport System. *ACM Operating Systems Review*, 28(2), April 1994.

[WHK98]   M. Wahl, T. Howes, and S. Kille. *Lightweight Directory Access Protocol (v3)*, August 1998. Internet Engineering Task Force, MMUSIC WG, Internet Draft.

[Win91]   Microsoft Windows. *Multimedia: Programmer's Workbook*. Microsoft Press, 1991.

[WKM94]   B. Whetten, S. Kaplan, and T. Montgomery. *A high performance totally ordered multicast protocol*, Aug 1994. Research Memorandum.

[WMS02]   M-Y. Wu, S-J. Ma, and W. Shu. Video streaming 2: Scheduled video delivery for scalable on-demand service. In *12th Internationa Workshop on Network and Operating Systems Support for Digital Audio and Video (NOSSDAV)*, pages 167–175, 2002.

[WNGX01]  D. Wichadakul, K. Nahrstedt, X. Gu, and D. Xu. 2KQ+: An Integrated Approach of QoS Compilation and Reconfigurable Component-Based Run-Time Middleware for the Unified QoS Management. In *IFIP Middleware 2001*, pages 373–394, Heidelberg, Germany, November 2001.

[Won83]  C. K. Wong. *Algorithmic Studies in Mass Storage Systems*. Computer Science Press, New York, 1983.

[Woo51]  H. Woodrow. Time Perception. In Stevens S. S, editor, *Handbook of Experimental Psychology*. Wiley, 1951.

[WPD88]  D. Waitzman, C. Patridge, and S. Deering. Distance Vector Multicasting Routing Protocol. FRC 1175, November 1988.

[WR94]  T. Wahl and K. Rothermel. Representing Time in Multimedia Systems. In *Proceedings of International Conference on Multimedia Computing and Systems*, pages 538–543, Boston,MA, May 1994. IEEE Computer Society Press.

[Wro97]  J. Wroclawski. Specification of controlled-load network element service. RFC 2211, September 1997.

[WS97]  Lars Wolf and Ralf Steinmetz. Concepts for Resource Reservation in Advance. *Multimedia Tools and Applications*, 4(3):255–278, May 1997. Special Issue on State of the Art in Multimedia Computing.

[WSM+91]  K. Watabe, S. Sakata, K. Maeno, H. Fukuoka, and T. Ohmori. Distributed Desktop Conferencing System with Multi-user Multimedia Interface. *IEEE JSAC*, 9(4):531–539, May 1991.

[WWDS94]  M. Weiser, B. Welch, A. Demers, and S. Shenker. Scheduling for reduced cpu energy. In *Symposium on Operating Systems Design and Implementation*, November 1994.

[WZ00]  R. Wittman and M. Zitterbart. *Multicast Communication: protocols, Programming and Applications*. Morgan Kaufman, 2000.

[XNW02]  D. Xu, K. Nahrstedt, and D. Wichadakul. MeGaDiP: A Wide Area Media Gateway Discovery Protocol. *Information Science Journal*, 141:37–59, March 2002.

[Xu01]  D. Xu. *A QoS-Aware Framework for Ubiquitous Multimedia Service Provision*. PhD thesis, University of Illinois at Urbana-Champaign, 2001.

[YCK92]    P. S. Yu, M. S. Chen, and D. D. Kandlur. Design and Analysis of a Grouped Sweeping Scheme for Multimedia Storage Management. In *3rd Int'l Workshop on Network and Operating System Support for Digital Audio and Video (NOSSDAV92)*, San Diego, CA, Nov. 1992.

[YD99]     R. Yavatkar and D. Durham. *Inside the Internet's Resource reSerVation Protocol: Foundations for Quality of Service*. Wiley Computer Publishing, 1999.

[YL96]     D. Yau and S.S. Lam. Adaptive Rate-controlled Scheduling for Multimedia Applications. In *ACM Multimedia Conference'96*, Boston, MA, November 1996.

[YN02]     W. Yuan and K. Nahrstedt. Mobile and wireless system integration of dynamic voltage scaling and soft-real-time scheduling for open mobile systems. In *12th International Workshop on Network and Operating Systems Support for Digital Audio and Video (NOSSDAV)*, pages 105–114, Miami, Florida, 2002.

[YN03]     W. Yuan and K. Nahrstedt. Energy-efficient soft real-time cpu scheduling for mobile multimedia systems. In *19th Symposium on Operating Systems and Principles (SOSP)*, NY, October 2003.

[YNK01]    W. Yuan, K. Nahrstedt, and K. Kim. R-EDF: A Reservation-Based EDF Scheduling Algorithm for Multiple Multimedia Task Classes. In *IEEE Real-Time Technology and Applications Symposium (RTAS'2001)*, Taiwan, 2001.

[ZDE+93]   L. Zhang, S. Deering, D. Estrin, S. Shenker, and D. Zappala. RSVP: A new Resource ReSerVation Protocol. *IEEE Computer*, September 1993.

[ZGSS03]   Michael Zink, Carsten Griwodz, Jens Schmitt, and Ralf Steinmetz. Scalable TCP-friendly Video Distribution for Heterogeneous Clients. In *Proceedings of SPIE's Multimedia Computing and Networking Conference 2003 (MMCN'03), Santa Clara, USA*, pages 102–113. SPIE, January 2003. ISBN 0-8194-4819-2.

[ZJGS00]   Michael Zink, Alex Jonas, Carsten Griwodz, and Ralf Steinmetz. LC-RTP (Loss Collection RTP): Reliability for Video Caching in the Internet. In *Proc. of 7th Int'l Conf on Parallel and Distributed Systems (ICPADS): Workshops*, pages 281–286. IEEE, Piscatay Way, NJ, USA, July 2000. ISBN 0-7695-0571-6.

[ZK91]      H. Zhang and S. Keshav. Comparison of Rate-Based Service Disciplines. In *SIGCOMM'91*, pages 113–122, Zürich, Switzerland, September 1991. ACM Press, Computer Communication Review 21(4).

[ZKSS03]    Michael Zink, Oliver Künzel, Jens Schmitt, and Ralf Steinmetz. Subjective Impression of Variations in Layer Encoded Videos. In *Eleventh International Workshop on Quality of Service (IWQoS 2003), Monterey, CA, USA*. Springer Verlag, June 2003.

[ZLSB98]    J. A. Zinky, J. P. Loyall, R. E. Schantz, and D. E. Bakken. Specifying and Measuring Quality of Service in Distributed Object Systems. In *Proceedings of ISORC'98*, Tokyo, Janan, April 1998.

[ZSL+01]    J. Zinky, R. Schantz, J. Loyall, K. Anderson, and J. Megquier. The Quality Objects (QuO) Middleware Framework. Online on Reflective Middleware, http://computer.org/dsonline, 2001.

# Index